Vimy Ridge

Vimy Ridge
A Canadian Reassessment

Edited By
Geoffrey Hayes
Andrew Iarocci
Mike Bechthold

This book has been published with the help of a grant from the Canadian Federation for the Humanities and Social Sciences, through the Aid to Scholarly Publications Programme, using funds provided by the Social Sciences and Humanities Research Council of Canada. We acknowledge the support of the Canada Council for the Arts for our publishing program. We acknowledge the financial support of the Government of Canada through the Book-Publishing Industry Development Program for our publishing activities.

Library and Archives Canada Cataloguing in Publication

Vimy Ridge : a Canadian reassessment / edited by Geoffrey Hayes, Andrew Iarocci, Mike Bechthold.

Includes bibliographical references and index.
ISBN 978-0-88920-508-6

1. Vimy Ridge, Battle of, France, 1917. 2. Canada. Canadian Army. Canadian Corps— History. 3. World War, 1914–1918—Canada. I. Hayes, Geoffrey, 1961– II. Iarocci, Andrew, 1976– III. Bechthold, Michael, 1968–

D545.V5V555 2007   940.4'31   C2007-901176-4

© 2007 Laurier Centre for Military Strategic and Disarmament Studies and Wilfrid Laurier University Press, Waterloo, Ontario, Canada

Cover, photo design, and maps by Mike Bechthold. Text design by Michelle Fowler.

This book is printed on Ancient Forest Friendly paper (100% post-consumer recycled).

Printed in Canada

Contents

Illustrations

Maps

Photographs

Foreword

The battle for Vimy Ridge in April 1917 marked the first occasion during the Great War when all four divisions of the Canadian Corps launched a simultaneous attack upon one front. This is only one of many assertions that have been made about the battle. It has also been said again and again that Vimy was a great strategic victory, the most important Canadian battle of the war and an experience which awakened a sense of Canadian nationalism. These and other claims are carefully examined in this volume. The opening essay in the collection suggests that Vimy Ridge is "regarded in the United Kingdom as a solely Canadian affair" largely because British school children and tourists regularly visit the Canadian Vimy memorial where they receive a Canadian perspective on the battle from Canadian student guides which British school teachers are "ill-equipped to put into wider context or point out the contribution that non-Canadians made to the battle." This book puts the Canadian effort into context. The activities of each of the four Canadian divisions taking part are carefully examined as is the work of the Canadian Engineers, Artillery and Medical Corps. Other chapters are devoted to the German forces who fought at Vimy, as well as the battles that followed the capture of the ridge. There is an essay on the Vimy Ridge poetry that proliferated between 1917 and 1936 which demonstrates "a surprising degree of concordance in terms of theme" by the poets. An essay on the significance of the Vimy memorial, and another on its fate under German occupation during the Second World War greatly enhance our understanding of Canada's Vimy story.

Without doubt the authors collectively present the most comprehensive examination of the Battle of Vimy Ridge which has so far been published. They call for more research to answer new questions that have been raised, and provide grounds for arguing that the Battle of Vimy Ridge is a Canadian epic, if not the greatest, most important or innovative Canadian action during the war.

An epic, the Oxford English Dictionary reminds us, embodies "a nation's conception of its own past or of the events in its history which it finds most worthy of remembrance." But an epic also has undertones which are not universally understood. Historians frequently point out that what happened does not always match what people later say happened. Moreover, those who knew what happened, from personal experience, often never spoke of it. My grandfather's missing right hand was endlessly fascinating when I was a small boy and even a young man. Equally fascinating was his refusal to tell me how he lost that hand at Vimy Ridge in April 1917. Those who knew what happened ninety years ago are all now long gone. But those of us still wishing to know something of what they experienced will be grateful to the authors of this volume. Surely, with the appearance of this book, it will be impossible in the twenty-first century for any reader (even a Canadian Minister of National Defence) to confuse the Battle of Vimy Ridge with the Vichy government in France during the Second World War.

A.M.J. Hyatt
August 2006

Acknowledgements

The editors would like to thank the following people, without whom this project would not have been possible.

Terry Copp is the Director of the Laurier Centre for Military Strategic and Disarmament Studies at Wilfrid Laurier University. Terry's endless curiosity, energy and enthusiasm have inspired countless students of Canadian history. All three editors are lucky to be among them. A very special thanks to Michelle Fowler, who manages the Laurier Centre's daily operations, and whose hard work on this project appears here in countless ways. We also want to thank Brandey Barton, also from the Laurier Centre, whose quiet efficiency has been so much appreciated, and Paul Kelly, who assisted with the book design.

We were especially pleased to have Professor A.M.J. Hyatt agree to write the forward to this work. Again and again the editors found that his writing on Arthur Currie set for us a very high standard of scholarship. In the not too distant past, two of the editors were fortunate to be students of Professor Hyatt, and we only hope that our contribution to understanding Canada's involvement in the First World War may be as enduring as his.

Of course the editors extend many thanks to the authors for their excellent chapters, hard work and patience throughout the project.

From WLU Press, Brian Henderson, Jacqueline Larson and Heather Blain-Yanke showed great enthusiasm for this book. And great patience. We also extend our gratitude to our anonymous readers who commented on the manuscript for the Canadian Federation for the Humanities and Social Sciences.

Photographs were provided by the Canadian Forces Joint Image Centre, the Canadian War Museum, Legion Magazine, the Library and Archives of Canada and Marie-Josée Lafond, a former Vimy guide, and currently the Program Director at the Juno Beach Centre in Normandy.

Mr. Blake Seward and his students at Smiths Falls District Collegiate Institute completed a great deal of research on men who fought and died at Vimy Ridge. Some of their work is found in the appendix. We wish to thank: Rebecca McIlravy, Lauren Quattrocchi, Mac Rutherford, Ally Lowe, Emily Maitland, Kaitlyn McNamara, Charlie Berrigan, Maria Fournier, Rob Reid, Josh Foy, Amy Lett, Robert Porter, Alie McMeekin, Jon Lee and Kayla McMullen for their hard work helping us learn more about the men who fought the Battle of Vimy Ridge.

Among those who contributed to this project in many other ways are: Stephen Badsey, Bertram Frandsen, Richard Goette, Richard Holt, Paul Whitney Lackenbauer, Marc Milner, Mike Ryan, Roger Sarty, James Wood and Barry Ries. Thanks to Dr. David Roger for allowing the reproduction of a photograph from his personal collection.

Those of us who have worked on this project are free to do so in no small part as a consequence of the sacrifices made by the soldiers of the Canadian Corps who fought, died and endured four years of war on the Western Front. This book is dedicated to them.

Introduction

On the morning of Monday, 9 April 1917, troops of the Canadian Corps under General Sir Julian Byng attacked the formidable German defences along Vimy Ridge. The resulting victory was a remarkable achievement, though it came at a cost of 10,602 Canadian casualties, one of the highest casualty rates ever suffered in Canada's history.

In the ninety years since, generations of Canadians have become deeply attached to the symbol of Vimy Ridge. In recent years the editors of this volume have escorted scores of Canadians to the National Vimy Memorial Site near Arras in northern France. For many this visit marks a pilgrimage to an immense open-air cathedral. Walter Allward's sculpture on Hill 145 forms the centerpiece of the park, soaring like an altar above the Douai plain. The monument is striking in its scale and beauty. Around its base are carved 11,285 names, each a Canadian killed in France during the First World War *whose body was never identified*. The park contains several small cemeteries where lie the remains of just a small fraction of the 3,598 Canadians who died there in April 1917. Most of the Vimy dead are found in the many Commonwealth War Cemeteries found nearby, or have no known grave.

After contemplating Allward's memorial, visitors are sometimes surprised to find that this cathedral also contains a vault. The Grange subway is one of thirteen tunnels that were used by the Canadians in the spring of 1917. Today young Canadian guides lead groups down into the damp chalk to offer insights into the lives of the men who prepared for battle here. A small maple leaf carved long ago into the chalk walls is now behind plexiglass, like an icon protected from the hands of the faithful. A casual stroll beyond the tunnel entrance takes one through winding trench lines that overlook deep craters named Grange, Duffield, Winnipeg and Montreal. The German lines are just

1

metres away. Grazing sheep stand vigil in the thickly cratered woods near the road, where a small, worn cairn notes (in English and French) that "This Land is the Free Gift in Perpetuity of the French Nation to the People of Canada." As Jacqueline Hucker reminds us in her chapter, the planners of the Vimy memorial park wanted it to be a symbol of the Canadian nation. Anyone seeking to understand what happened here in the spring of 1917 may have to look elsewhere for answers.

This project comes from a shared belief among a new generation of scholars that there is still more to ask, and much more to learn about the Battle of Vimy Ridge. Like the teams who recently restored Allward's monument, we have started at the foundations to ask basic questions: Why were the Canadians fighting north of Arras in the spring of 1917? How did they achieve the victory at Vimy Ridge? And how did later generations of Canadians come to remember the Battle of Vimy Ridge? These three questions form the blueprint of the studies that follow.

In setting the strategic picture of the operation, our first three contributors work from the basic assumption that the Battle of Vimy Ridge cannot be understood except as part of a wider (and largely unsuccessful) series of Allied offensives through the spring of 1917. These essays introduce important themes that are raised throughout the volume. British historian Gary Sheffield maintains that the Vimy memorial has obscured for the British public as well as scholars the British contribution to Vimy Ridge and the wider Battle of Arras. Paul Dickson reminds us that the preparations for Vimy Ridge coincided with a period of relative stability for the Canadian Corps, due partly to the departure of Sir Sam Hughes, Canada's remarkable minister of Militia and Defence, in November 1916. Dickson also argues that by then the Corps had acquired a 'culture' that allowed leaders to innovate and adapt. Both agree, however, that there was still more to learn. Michael Boire knows the ground of Vimy Ridge well. His survey of the ridge makes the point that the Canadians were indebted to the French and British who fought there before 1917. In many ways, their initiatives and casualties made the Canadian success possible.

The second part of this volume moves closer to the battlefield to explore the preparations and conduct of the battle itself. Mark Osborne Humphries reminds us that the Canadians' efforts to break the German hold on Vimy Ridge drew on Canadian lessons, but also largely on British doctrine and practice. So too, as Pat Brennan reminds us, did the Canadians depend heavily on British staff officers, far more than Canadian historians have generally appreciated. From Tim Cook we see better the intricate level of planning and preparation that went into the artillery battles before and during the infantry's advance. Bill Rawling provides an unprecedented view of the role of the engineers at Vimy Ridge, detailing a battlefield area that resembled some kind of vast industrial enterprise. Finally, Heather Moran describes the process that went into evacuating and treating the many casualties.

It is tempting to conclude that the training, planning and logistical build-up to the battle made the outcome inevitable. But detailed studies of each of the four Canadian divisions suggest otherwise. Indeed, as Andrew Iarocci maintains in his study of Arthur Currie's 1st Division, there was no single experience on Vimy Ridge. Nor was the outcome certain once the battle was joined. David Campbell's view of the 2nd Division, Geoffrey Hayes' study of the 3rd Division and Andrew Godefroy's examination of the 4th Division all highlight different aspects of the operation. But each conveys a similar theme: elaborate planning was one thing; sending thousands of troops across a heavily cratered and (despite the weight and accuracy of the artillery) heavily defended ground was quite another. There was nothing easy about the victory of the Canadian Corps at Vimy Ridge.

The battle was not yet over when commanding officers began to receive letters of congratulations from dignitaries in England and Canada. Andrew Godefroy shows in his study of the Germans at Vimy Ridge that, despite shortcomings in their defence of the ridge, many post-war German unit histories also proclaimed a victory, or at least a draw at Vimy. Given their success elsewhere during the Battle of Arras, this should not be surprising. Indeed, Mike Bechthold finishes our battlefield study by describing the lesser-known battle of the Arleux Loop, fought later in April, where several Canadian battalions lost as many as they had at Vimy Ridge.

This collection is important for the way its contributors view the Battle of Vimy Ridge as both a military and a cultural event. The final section of this work examines how Canadians gave the Battle of Vimy Ridge such an important place in their collective memory. Jonathan Vance argues that it was partly through poetry — some good, but much of it bad — that Canadians understood the symbolism of Vimy Ridge, years before King Edward VIII dedicated Walter Allward's memorial in July 1936. The story of Allward's ambitious vision for Vimy Ridge is told here by Jacqueline Hucker, who has overseen the restoration of the memorial. Finally, Serge Durflinger recounts how the Canadian press kept careful watch on the Vimy memorial during the Second World War. When newspapers reported falsely that the memorial was destroyed during the German advance in the spring of 1940, the memorial came to symbolize for another generation Canadian resolve against German aggression. That resolve was vindicated when the memorial was liberated in the fall of 1944.

This project gave some of us the excuse to go back to the War Diaries, the daily summary of a unit's activities. In this we are grateful to the archivists under Ian Wilson at the Library and Archives of Canada (LAC) who have digitized and placed online nearly all of the war diaries of the Canadian Expeditionary Force. It is a remarkable resource.

War diaries are quirky things, for their quality varies from unit to unit. But in them we found details long forgotten, or simply overlooked. In some materials we were struck by the contrast in tone. A divisional or brigade summary often holds little of the urgency or drama that one finds from the notes of a harried battalion commander or his adjutant on the day of battle.

It was here, too, that we found the men of Vimy Ridge. Although the veterans who fought there are gone now, we can learn more about these men than we ever did before. Another LAC initiative brings online the attestation papers of each person who enlisted for service in the Canadian Expeditionary Force (CEF). When used with their personnel records and with other online resources such as the Veteran's Affairs Virtual Memorial, or the Commonwealth War Graves Commission soldiers' registry, we can find a surprisingly large amount of information about these men.

Blake Seward has long understood the research potential of these resources. An award-winning teacher at Smiths Falls District Collegiate Institute in eastern Ontario, Seward has developed the "Lest We Forget" project so that his classes, and those in other schools, can learn about the men who fought during the First World War. The editors of this project have worked with Blake's classes of 2005-2006 to learn more about the men who were at Vimy Ridge. This collection is much stronger for their contribution.

As of this writing, the Vimy memorial is undergoing a long-overdue restoration that will be completed in April 2007, on the ninetieth anniversary of the battle. We trust that this collection of articles will help a new generation of Canadians appreciate this remarkable event.

The First World War To 1917

In hindsight, each year of the First World War on the Western Front had its own unique character. Michael Boire shows how the autumn of 1914 was characterized by sweeping mobile operations and the gradual onset of stalemate. Both sides soon realized that the war would not be over before Christmas.

A renewed sense of crisis emerged in 1915 as the Allied forces in particular suffered from a chronic deficit of reliable munitions and heavy guns. In another sense, 1915 was cursed with a split personality. On one hand it was a period of build-up and transition to the wartime economy that would support the coming 'Big Push' that was supposed to bring Allied victory. At the same time, Anglo-French forces embarked on a series of costly offensives with hopes of driving the Germans out of France. British commanders usually protested these efforts, but the British Expeditionary Force (BEF) remained the smaller and junior partner throughout the year, and French strategic prerogatives dictated that the Allies attack immediately, with or without material shortages. The French attitude was understandable, since the Germans then occupied some of France's most productive regions, but these early initiatives gained little.

Canada's first contingent arrived in England in October 1914. After training through a rainy winter on Salisbury Plain, the newly formed 1st Division crossed the Channel and entered the front lines near Armentières, along the Franco-Belgian border in March 1915. Within six weeks the Canadians moved up to join V British Corps in the Ypres Salient, an already infamous sector of the Western Front that had witnessed especially heavy fighting during the previous autumn. The Canadians found themselves defending a waterlogged section of ground choked with rotting corpses and debris left from earlier battles. French colonial troops from North Africa were on the left and a British division was on the right. As part of an Allied force the Canadians were about to receive their first taste of sustained action.

On 22 April 1915 the German Fourth Army struck the Ypres salient with chlorine gas, an experimental weapon. Although commanders were initially sceptical of the chlorine's potential, the gas and ensuing infantry assault tore a massive hole in the French sector. The Canadians were spared the worst effects of the gas cloud, but not for long. Two days later the Germans mounted a second attack, this time directly against the Canadian line. By now the exhausted troops had been awake and fighting for nearly 36 hours, and by the end of the day Germans held most of the Canadian positions. The 2nd Brigade remained in its trenches until 25 April, but was soon forced to withdraw. In just a few days of fighting 1st Division lost about one third of its strength, about 6,000 casualties. For the most part, the Canadians performed impressively with the resources at hand, but it was now clear that this was going to be a long and costly war.

Within three weeks the reconstituted 1st Division was back in action, this time on the offensive. While the French Army undertook a major and costly operation against Vimy Ridge and Notre Dame de Lorette in May 1915, the British launched a supporting attack on the La Bassée Front, near the villages of Festubert and Givenchy. The flat, featureless terrain north of the La Bassée Canal favoured the Germans, but the politics of coalition warfare left British commanders with little choice but to cooperate. The 1st Division attacks at Festubert and Givenchy were limited in scope, but cost hundreds of additional casualties. Although artillery support was limited, the Canadians managed to wrestle some difficult objectives from the enemy, most notably a fortified locality known simply as the Orchard.

In September 1915 the 2nd Canadian Division joined the 1st Division in France under a Corps headquarters led by a British officer, Lieutenant-General Edwin Alderson. That same month, General Douglas Haig's First British Army launched its offensive at Loos while the French attacked in Artois. The push was not big enough and the year ended in disappointment, with tens of thousands of Allied casualties and the sacking of the BEF commander, Field Marshal Sir John French.

The year 1916 was marked by a series of grand offensives on a larger scale than ever before. As new British armies were built, Allied war production increased while Germany felt the strangling effects of the British naval blockade. Many hoped that the year would prove decisive, and the French commander-in-chief, General Joseph Joffre, called for a major joint offensive in the Somme River valley. Douglas Haig, now a Field Marshal in command of the BEF, preferred to see British forces in action in Belgian Flanders, closer to the English Channel and British strategic interests. However, Joffre's initiative took priority, especially after French forces were drawn east in February to respond to General Erich von Falkenhayn's surprise offensive against the Verdun salient. Intended to 'bleed the French white,' the French responded with predictable Gallic vigour. Both Germans and French lost heavily at Verdun, creating a fragile stalemate in the west by the summer of 1916.

The new Canadian Corps had played a limited role in the ill-fated Loos offensive in 1915. Not until the spring of 1916 did 2nd Division experience sustained fighting, in a horrific struggle for a series of flooded mine craters near a village named after St. Eloi, the patron saint of metal workers. There were no miracles at St. Eloi. In late March, British forces exploded a series of mines beneath the battlefield and secured a tenuous grip on the craters before handing the sector over to the Canadian Corps. Within days the Germans counterattacked 2nd Division's positions, wresting back much of the area recently taken by the British. With the ground badly torn up and hopelessly flooded, Canadian troops soon lost their bearings. Some battalions were hundreds of metres from their intended positions. A series of Canadian

N

LONDON   W—E   0 10 20 30 40 50
                             kilometres   NETHERLANDS

UNITED
KINGDOM
              Shorncliffe•
                                                 BELGIUM

ENGLISH CHANNEL   •Calais   Poperinge   ❸
                                            Ypres Passchendaele
                                                                  BRUSSELS
Canadian Battles   •Boulogne   Hazebrouck
❶ Vimy Ridge – Apr 1917
❷ Hill 70 – Aug 1917   •Étaples   ❷Hill 70
❸ Passchendaele – Oct-Nov 1917   Lens   Mons
                                            St. Pol•   ❶Vimy   ❼
❹ Amiens – Aug 1918   Valenciennes
❺ Arras – Aug-Sept 1918   Arras ❺
❻ Cambrai – Sept-Oct 1918   Abbeville   ❻Cambrai
❼ Mons – Nov 10-11 1918   Quéant

                                            Albert• Courcelette
      Front Lines   Amiens•
      ——— December 15, 1914   ❹
      ••••• March 20, 1918
      — — July 18, 1918   FRANCE
      ——— November 11, 1918
•Le Havre

The Western Front
1917-1918   PARIS

attacks failed to make any headway through the ravaged morass. With mounting losses, divisional commander Major-General Richard Turner suspended further operations in mid-April 1916. Second Division's baptism of fire at St. Eloi cost 1,400 casualties.

Lieutenant-General Sir Julian Byng replaced General Alderson at the head of the Canadian Corps in late May 1916. At that time, the recently formed 3rd Division was holding trenches near Mount Sorrel in the eastern apex of the Ypres Salient, when the artillery of XIII Württemberg Corps unleashed a barrage so violent that entire companies were obliterated. The divisional commander, Major-General Malcolm Mercer, was killed, while Brigadier-General Victor Williams of the 8th Brigade was captured by German infantry who swarmed into the smashed Canadian trenches. Men of the Princess Patricia's Canadian Light Infantry (PPCLI) managed to hold back the German forces while Major-General Arthur Currie's 1st Division mounted a hasty counterattack the next day. The operation made little headway, but better organized attacks preceded by sophisticated artillery bombardments succeeded in recapturing most of the lost ground by mid-June.

To the south of the Canadians, two British armies were then preparing an offensive along a twenty-four-kilometre front through the Somme River valley, with one French army on their right. Despite a massive build-up, the first day of the offensive, Saturday, 1 July 1916, proved to be one of the most tragic in British military history. On that day, more than 57,000 British troops fell dead, wounded or went missing.

The Somme campaign continued for five more months. Despite horrific losses, Haig regrouped and fought on. Within two weeks British soldiers penetrated the second line of German defences between the Ancre and Somme rivers, while French troops approached Péronne further south. Allied casualties were massive that summer — more than 250,000 by late August — but the Germans sacrificed nearly as many soldiers adhering to a rigid, inelastic defensive doctrine that called for immediate counterattacks every time ground was lost.

The Canadian Corps remained in the Ypres Salient throughout the summer, moving south in September to the Somme front to relieve I Anzac Corps near the village of Pozières. Major-General Currie's 1st Division was first into the line, while 2nd and 3rd Divisions prepared for pending attacks. The Canadians' first major action on the Somme came with the Battle of Flers-Courcelette in mid-September. Here the 2nd Division advanced toward Courcelette along the road from Pozières. With generous artillery support, troops of the 4th and 6th Brigades reached their objectives without great difficulty. Tanks, known originally as landships, were deployed in this operation for the first time, but the six assigned to Canadian forces achieved limited results. Only one reached the objective, while the others broke down, became stuck, or were knocked out by German gunfire.

Later in the month, Canadian efforts focussed on the capture of Thiepval Ridge. The names of German defences in this sector echo through regimental histories and soldiers' memoirs: Zollern Graben, Hessian, Kenora and Regina trenches. Losses were heavy in 1st Division as the Germans modified their defences in October. Having suffered under heavy Allied barrages throughout September, the Germans began dispersing troops across no-man's-land in scattered ditches and craters. Relatively untouched from pre-assault bombardments, these pockets of riflemen and machine gunners were then able to shoot down advancing waves of Canadian infantry.

A second problem confronting all soldiers on the Somme might be described as the 'capture-hold' conundrum. An infantry attack with powerful artillery support was usually able to capture the first or second lines of German trenches, but holding on to gains was difficult in the face of enemy counterattacks. Having advanced to the limits of artillery range, troops were left with little support on their objectives, and in any case the gunners were often unsure of the infantry's precise locations. German reinforcements, meanwhile, were able to approach the crisis area under cover of their own communications trenches and artillery fire. Canadian reinforcements, on the other hand, had to enter the contested zone across a shell-battered and bullet-swept no-man's-land. Too often hard-won gains were abandoned after a few hours of desperate fighting. This was the case for many battalions during the attacks against Regina Trench in October.

The newly formed 4th Canadian Division arrived on the Somme under command of Major-General David Watson that month. It was up to Watson's largely untested battalions to finish the drive toward Regina and Desire trenches. They did so, but at a cost of 4,300 casualties by the end of the campaign in November. The Canadians suffered over 24,000 casualties on the Somme, just a small portion of the nearly half million casualties British and Empire forces endured.

These grim encounters epitomized the exhausting attritional character of warfare on the Western Front. Ground could be captured at great cost, but holding it was an entirely different matter. Careful preparation and massive stockpiling of material were essential for even the most modest of offensive operations, but there was no magic formula for success. For the Canadian Corps, now four divisions strong, 1917 presented the opportunity to examine the lessons of 1915-16 and test new approaches. It was certain, however, that much hard pounding lay ahead in this great war of attrition.

The Allied Plans for 1917

Robert Georges Nivelle began the war as a colonel in command of a French artillery regiment. He was a highly capable gunner, and attracted much favourable attention as commander of French III Corps, which recaptured forts Vaux and Douaumont north of Verdun in 1916. Nivelle's troops succeeded largely through careful assault training and the overwhelming concentration of artillery resources against limited objectives.

Meanwhile, the French people and their leaders had grown tired of General Joseph Joffre's methodical and bloody pounding of the German lines. Joffre, in fact, was slowly destroying the German Army, but his methods were costing France dearly. After two years of war, there seemed no end in sight. In this context of despair, Nivelle promised a quick and relatively bloodless victory. His plan called for a repetition of the tactics of Vaux and Douaumont, but on a much larger scale. In December 1916, Nivelle replaced Joffre as commander-in-chief of the French forces.

The Germans had plans of their own. Sensing that the Allies were on the verge of a major push in early 1917, German forces launched Operation Alberich in February, an extensive withdrawal to prepared positions along what the Allies called the Hindenburg Line. This major readjustment undermined much of Nivelle's plan, but the French commander failed to adjust to the new circumstances. In essence, Nivelle's offensive consisted of a powerful French assault in mid-April against the Chemin des Dames, in the Champagne, against a strongly defended portion of the German line. As a diversion, the BEF was to launch its own attack further north from Arras, about one week in advance of the French. This aspect of the Nivelle offensive came to be known as the Battle of Arras. Vimy Ridge, on the northern flank, formed the Canadian objective in the Battle of Arras.

The First and Third British armies launched the Battle of Arras on 9 April. The results were initially promising. British troops advanced eastward from Arras along the Scarpe River, while on the left flank, the four divisions of the Canadian Corps attacked German positions atop Vimy Ridge, which overlooked the British axis of advance further south. By 12 April the ridge was in Canadian hands and the British had also made impressive gains on the lower ground. Not only were the Anglo-Canadian divisions well supported by artillery, but the German defenders were ill-positioned on forward slopes, leaving them badly exposed to shelling and indirect machine gun fire.

In other respects, however, Vimy and Arras ultimately reinforced what British and Dominion soldiers had already experienced for two years. With careful preparation it was possible to make gains against the enemy's forward lines, but as German reserves moved into the area, the law of diminishing returns quickly took effect. Notwithstanding the capture of Vimy Ridge, it was simply not possible to turn the Arras offensive into a strategic breakthrough.

French troops began their assault (known as the Second Battle of the Aisne) on 16 April in poor weather and with disastrous results. Despite massive artillery support, they made little progress against German forces sheltered on the reverse slopes of the Chemin des Dames. Nivelle, however, refused to call off operations. By early May, French casualties exceeded 100,000 and the French people realized with horror that Nivelle's approach differed little from the attritional offensives of 1915-16. France could ill-aford such attrition by 1917. Junior commanders and ordinary soldiers alike protested further attacks and the French government responded by replacing Nivelle with General Philippe Pétain. This change in command came not a moment too soon. By May, elements of the French Army were in open mutiny, with thousands of soldiers refusing to participate in offensive activity of any sort. Pétain's guiding hand—sensitive to the war's realities, but nonetheless firm—restored order to a broken army before the Germans realized the extent of the French crisis. There was to be no end to the war in 1917.

PART I

The Strategic Background

1

Vimy Ridge and the Battle of Arras
A British Perspective

GARY SHEFFIELD

In early twenty-first century Britain, most of the battles of 1914-18 are forgotten by all but specialist military historians. Vimy Ridge is an exception. In part this reflects the fact that the name, like the Somme or Passchendaele, remains in the British folk memory. It is suggestive that in the 1971 Disney children's film *Bedknobs and Broomsticks*, set on the southern coast of England in 1940 and featuring mainly British actors, a mention of Vimy Ridge (where the father of one of the principal characters had fought) is used early to establish the continuity of the Second World War with British battles of earlier eras.[1] The capture of Vimy Ridge is generally regarded in the UK as a solely Canadian success, where the British and French had previously failed. The symbiotic relationship between the Canadian Corps and the British Expeditionary Force (BEF) of which it formed a part is commonly misunderstood. Forgotten also is the key role played by British units and formations and individual British officers in the 9 April 1917 attack.

That Vimy Ridge lies just off a major highway much used by British tourists has maintained the high visibility of the battle in the United Kingdom. Indeed, the Canadian memorial can be seen from the road. The First World War is a popular topic in British schools and many regularly take parties of children on educational trips to Vimy Ridge, attracted especially by the artificially preserved trenches. There, through tours of the Grange tunnel conducted by Canadian students and views of the impressive Vimy memorial, pupils are exposed to a Canadian perspective. Most British teachers are ill-equipped to put the battle into its wider context or point out the contribution that non-Canadians made to the battle.

The Battle of Arras, of which the Vimy action formed a part, is largely a forgotten battle. This is strange, for the operation that lasted

15

from 9 April to 17 May 1917 was a major offensive that cost 159,000 British and Empire casualties—a daily rate of 4,076 that was higher than for any other major battle. Indeed had Arras continued at the same intensity for 141 days, the length of the Somme offensive in 1916, the losses would have been in the order of 575,000, which would have made it by far the bloodiest British offensive of the war.[2] Moreover, the strategic consequences of Arras were profound and the battle marked an important stage in the operational and tactical "learning curve" of the BEF. On 9 April, for instance, two British divisions, 4th and 9th (Scottish), achieved the longest advance to that time by a British unit under conditions of trench warfare—some 5.5 kilometres. The importance of the Arras campaign belies the lack of attention it has received from historians.

A survey of the literature published in Britain is instructive. The publication of anecdotal histories based on the writings and reminiscences of participants has become something of a boom industry in recent years, yet to the author's knowledge, Jonathan Nicholls's *Cheerful Sacrifice* is the only popular history of Arras that has been published in the UK.[3] In Britain, the phrase "Battle of Arras" is more likely to be associated with the minor British armour/infantry counterattack against advancing German forces on 21 May 1940. Astoundingly, one book on European battlefields edited by a noted military historian included an entry on the 1940 action but ignored the major battle of 1917 altogether.[4] All this contrasts with the publication in Britain of at least five popular histories of Vimy Ridge, in which the Canadians take centre stage, including books by Canadian authors Herbert Fairlie Wood and Pierre Berton.[5]

Scholarly attention to the Battle of Arras is patchy; the only major study of the battle is the relevant volume of the British official history published in 1940.[6] However, there are some short treatments of specific parts of the Arras campaign.[7] British author Jonathan Walker has recently produced an excellent study of the Bullecourt operations on Fifth Army's front and several recent authors have covered the Australian angle of this battle.[8] Surprisingly, neither Tim Travers, nor the team of Robin Prior and Trevor Wilson has covered Arras in any detail in their influential books on command in the BEF.

A common theme is that the capture of Vimy Ridge was somehow decisive, or a turning point in the Great War.[9] It is not easy to see how this claim can be substantiated. The Ridge was certainly an important position and its capture improved the local tactical situation. Vimy Ridge could have been a jumping-off point for a future offensive, but subsequent gains in the days and weeks that immediately followed were modest. For many reasons, the principal Allied efforts for the rest of 1917 took place elsewhere. The real fruits of the capture of Vimy Ridge did not become apparent until almost a year later. The Ridge proved an invaluable defensive position during Operation Mars, the German offensive of 28 March 1918, which took place only seven days after the dramatic German breakthrough south of the Somme. In the Vimy/Arras area, the British VI, XVII and XIII Corps won a highly significant defensive victory. The German attack was stopped dead, derailing Ludendorff's plans, with major consequences for the future development of the German offensive.

It is difficult to avoid the conclusion that if Vimy Ridge had been captured by a British or French formation instead of the Canadian Corps, this action would not enjoy its current celebrity. While the Canadian Corps undoubtedly achieved a fine feat of arms on 9 April 1917, "Vimy Ridge" resonates largely because of its role in the growth of Canadian nationalism. A similar point can be made about Gallipoli if Anzac forces had not been involved. It is likely that a folk memory of the Gallipoli campaign would have survived in the UK, if only because it was an important stage in the career of Winston Churchill and, however misguidedly, the operation is commonly regarded as a great "missed opportunity" to shorten the First World War. There is no doubt that the enduring fascination of Gallipoli is primarily a product of the status it has assumed in the national mythologies of New Zealand and Australia. In the case of both Australia and Canada, a more logical choice of battle to celebrate would be Amiens, 8 August 1918, an action that was genuinely a turning point in the First World War.

Three general points emerge from this preliminary survey. There is a failure to understand the Imperial nature of the force that captured Vimy Ridge; the importance of the Canadian Corps' capture of Vimy Ridge has been exaggerated; and the significance of the wider Battle of Arras has been underrated.

Given freedom of choice, the commander-in-chief of the BEF, Field Marshal Sir Douglas Haig, would not have fought at Arras and Vimy in April-May 1917. When the Somme campaign was halted in November 1916 he fully intended to renew the battle early the next year as a preliminary to shifting his forces to Flanders and launching a major offensive to capture the Belgian coast. This was an operation that was seen as vital if the U-boat menace was to be mastered. Haig's plans were thrown out of gear by the fall from power of Marshal Joseph Joffre in December 1916. Kicked upstairs, Joffre was replaced by General Robert Nivelle. The latter, boasting of new tactics that had indeed produced success on a small scale at Verdun, ditched Joffre's plans and produced a scheme to achieve a decisive breakthough.

Nivelle's objective was the "destruction of enemy main forces on the western front." He envisaged a "prolonged battle" to break the enemy front; the Allies would then defeat the German reserves; and the exploitation phase would follow. The main blow would be launched in Champagne by the French, while British and French forces would attack to pin German divisions in the Arras-Somme area to prevent them from reinforcing Champagne. Specifically, the BEF was to "pierce" the enemy positions, advance to take the Hindenburg Line in the rear in the direction of Valenciennes — Louvain and ultimately to Mons, Tournai and Courtrai. Further to the north, British Second Army was to exploit German weakness in Flanders and push forward.

In practice, the BEF had to relieve French formations to allow Nivelle to build up a strategic reserve and Haig had to abandon his planned operations. On 25 December Haig "agree[d] in principle" to Nivelle's plans but over the next few weeks the precise details were thrashed out. The result was that Haig committed the BEF to the holding offensive, "but not to an indefinite continuation" of the battle; he had no wish to be drawn into a Somme-style attritional struggle. Moreover, if Nivelle's attaque brusquée failed to achieve decisive results, Haig would launch his Flanders offensive. Haig was a loyal ally, but not one who could be pushed around.[10]

Nivelle won over David Lloyd George, British prime minister since December 1916, who harboured deep suspicions of Haig and General Sir William Robertson, the Chief of the Imperial General Staff. At the Calais conference in February 1917 Lloyd George attempted to bounce Haig and Robertson into subordinating the BEF to Nivelle.[11] Although Lloyd George's stated aspiration to achieve unity of command on the Western Front was both sensible and desirable, if his Calais coup had succeeded it would not have brought this about. Simply placing the BEF under the French army would have been an abdication by the Cabinet of British national interests, although in practice Nivelle's freedom of action would have been trammelled by interference from London.

Irrespective of the merits of the proposal, the underhanded way in which Lloyd George sought to bring this about caused lasting damage to his already uneasy relationship with Haig and Robertson. As late as 15 November 1917, senior staff officer Sydney Clive noted that the Nivelle affair was still poisoning Haig's mind against the idea of unity of command.[12] In the event, an uneasy compromise was reached by which Haig was subordinated to Nivelle only for the duration of the forthcoming offensive, with the right of appeal to London. The Calais conference was a serious and surprising blunder coming from such an accomplished politician as Lloyd George. The Battle of Arras was

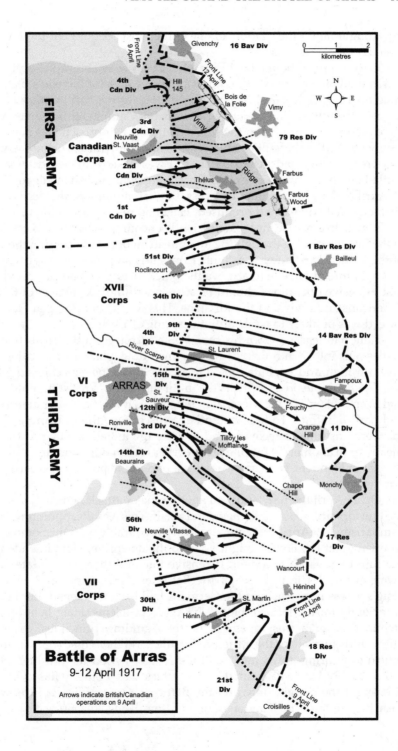

FIRST ARMY

Canadian Corps

4th Cdn Div

Hill 145

Front Line 9 April

Givenchy

16 Bav Div

Front Line 12 April

0   1   2
kilometres

N
W   E
S

Bois de la Folie

Vimy

3rd Cdn Div

Neuville St. Vaast

Vimy

Vimy

79 Res Div

2nd Cdn Div

Thélus

Ridge

Farbus

1st Cdn Div

Farbus Wood

1 Bav Res Div

Bailleul

51st Div

Roclincourt

XVII Corps

34th Div

9th Div

14 Bav Res Div

4th Div

River Scarpe

St. Laurent

VI Corps

ARRAS

15th Div

St. Sauveur

12th Div

Fampoux

Feuchy

Ronville

3rd Div

Orange Hill

11 Div

THIRD ARMY

14th Div

Beaurains

Tilloy les Mofflaines

Chapel Hill

Monchy

56th Div

Neuville Vitasse

17 Res Div

Wancourt

VII Corps

Héninel

30th Div

St. Martin

Front Line 12 April

Hénin

18 Res Div

Battle of Arras
9-12 April 1917

Arrows indicate British/Canadian operations on 9 April

21st Div

Front Line 9 April

Croisilles

thus fought under the shadow of one of the most serious civil-military clashes of the entire war.

In the event, although the BEF landed a very heavy blow on 9 April, it was unable to carry out the more ambitious parts of Nivelle's plan. Haig on 12 April assured Nivelle that in spite of the bad weather his forces were still driving towards Cambrai, but German reinforcements were being brought up and the BEF's methodical approach was being hampered by the difficulties of moving artillery forward. The moment for a breakthrough had passed and the BEF was locked into the attritional battle Haig had wanted to avoid. The Champagne offensive began on 16 April and achieved limited success, but had nothing of the decisive character that Nivelle had promised. Haig had to keep attacking to aid the French. In any case, he was sufficiently encouraged by the successes of the first ten days of the fighting to argue in favour of the continuation of the battle. The context was hints from Paris and London, triggered by the failure of Nivelle to achieve the quick victory he had promised, that offensive operations should be suspended until the arrival of the Americans and revival of the Russians. This was something that Haig judged was unlikely to occur until the spring of 1918.[13]

Haig had learned from his time at Staff College in the 1890s that battles fell into a number of stages, including phases of attrition, breakthrough and exploitation. "Great results are never achieved in war," Haig wrote on 18 April 1917, "until the enemy's resisting power had been broken." In the present circumstances it was "a matter of time and hard fighting." To halt would be to discourage the BEF and give the Germans time to recover "and to seize the initiative either in this theatre or in another."[14] In spite of his earlier reservations and his desire to fight in Flanders, Haig saw Arras as a part of the process of wearing out the enemy.

On 23 April the BEF launched another major attack, which pushed the line forward about a kilometre and a half. This was disappointing in comparison to 9 April, but compared very favourably with the Somme. Knowing that the French might go onto the defensive, Haig intended the BEF to advance to a good defensive line and then consolidate to await events.[15] The final act of the Battle of Arras came on 3 May. Haig's assessment was that the Germans had been weakened, but not sufficiently for a "decisive blow." Nivelle's problems, Haig believed, stemmed from a misjudgement of the "guiding principles" from "time immemorial" of the structured battle "and the remedy now is to return to wearing-down methods for a further period the duration of which cannot yet be calculated."[16] The attack was a bloody fiasco, but it brought the curtain down on the Battle of Arras. Haig could now turn his attention to Flanders. For the time being, the French army was wrecked as an offensive instrument and the BEF would have to shoulder the burden of the Allied offensive.

* * *

An Army Commander held no independent Command, the fronts and flanks of Armies were rigidly tied down, the Army gains were won by hard frontal fighting, almost as mechanical as the movements of a parallel ruler: the art of strategy was almost completely denied to their operations, and these were of necessity methodical rather than brilliant.

The author of these words was Hastings Anderson, who, as a major-general, served as chief of staff to General Sir Henry Horne at First Army in 1917. As Anderson went on to argue, the fact that the Canadian Corps formed "the backbone" of First Army and the "just fame" of the Canadians (and one might add their commanders) "tended to obscure the part played by Lord Horne as an Army Commander."[17] Anderson was correct. While Edmund Allenby, commander of Third Army at Arras, is well known, albeit primarily for his later campaigns in Palestine, Horne remains in obscurity. And yet First Army's role in the battle was by no means negligible.

Horne was a Scot with a background in the Royal Horse Artillery and was something of a protégé of Haig. He commanded XV Corps on the Somme before being promoted to command First Army. Vimy was his first battle as an army commander. Initially reserving his judgment, the successful performance of First Army staff in this operation won Horne's confidence. Haig had issued a warning order for First Army to prepare to assault Vimy Ridge on 17 November 1916 and on 2 January 1917 GHQ issued formal orders. At an early stage Julian Byng, the commander of the Canadian Corps, was informed of the impending offensive. First Army issued a general plan, while the Corps prepared a detailed "scheme of operations."[18] The actual attack of 9 April, the Canadian Corps claimed, "was only the culminating phase of a prolonged and insistent offensive" of raids and artillery during the winter.[19]

Horne and First Army had a supporting but vital role in the Vimy success. They were responsible for "directing, guiding, and combining [the Canadians] with the work of other Corps."[20] This was a role for which Horne was well suited, for he had "a consultative command style, encouraging discussion [and] explaining the overall plan of operations."[21] One example of this came during a conference with his corps commanders on 29 March, when he emphasized the importance (previously stressed by Haig) of coordinating with corps on the flanks when creating a line of resistance. On 15 April, Horne, needing the information for a forthcoming conference of army commanders, asked his corps commanders how quickly they could get ready for a new attack. Perhaps the highest tribute to the role Horne played at Vimy came in a letter written by Byng to his wife on the same day: "Horne has been more than helpful and backed me up in everything."[22]

First Army also played an important role by providing the logistical arrangements that were central to the capture of Vimy Ridge. Horne's concern for the state of roads in the rear area was clear when he took pains to clear up potential confusion about where responsibilities lay between the army and the corps. At the same conference he drew upon his own experience as a gunner to give some important advice on artillery matters, including the apparently mundane matter of care for artillery horses. In fact, given the difficulty of moving guns forward over no-man's-land after the success of 9 April, this point was far from trivial.[23]

The logistical achievements of First Army were considerable. The strength of First Army in April 1917 was approximately 320,000 men and 75,000 horses. On the 5.5 kilometre attack frontage, in a 24-hour period, 7,200 tons of ammunition was expended of the 40,300 tons accumulated in front of railheads. Similarly, 828,000 full-day rations for men and 100,000 for horses had been stockpiled for First Army. Before the attack began, the problem of inadequate roads in the Vimy sector was serious and the Royal Engineers (RE) were clearly proud of their road-building activities during the battle. Over 1.5 kilometres of plank road were constructed between Neuville St. Vaast and Tilleuls in three days, using three RE field companies and an additional labour company. Three thousand men were used during twenty-four hours, working three shifts of six hours each.[24]

The relationship of the Canadian Corps to First Army and the wider BEF was symbiotic in other ways. The heavy artillery support at Vimy consisted of two Canadian and seven British heavy artillery groups. Moreover, the field artillery of three Canadian divisions was supplemented by two British units serving as 4th Canadian Division's artillery and another eight British Royal Field Artillery brigades. Whereas the Canadians and Anzacs concentrated on producing elite "teeth arm" formations, the British did not have that luxury, having to provide everything else needed by a modern army. They also produced, of course, infantry divisions. Moreover, (as will be detailed later in this volume) some key players in the Canadian Corps were British, including Byng and Major Alan Brooke, chief of staff to the Canadian Corps artillery commander, as were a proportion of the fighting troops. British 13th Infantry Brigade, part of 5th Division, was attached to 2nd Canadian Division for the Vimy operation. The Canadian Corps occupied a slightly uncomfortable position both as a proto-national army and a component, albeit an unusual one, of the wider BEF. While it developed its own highly effective style of war fighting, it was never hermetically sealed from the other divisions, whether Imperial or Dominion, on the Western Front.[25]

Over the last twenty years, the image portrayed by such popular writers as Leon Wolff and Alan Clark that the BEF was composed of "lions led by donkeys" has been comprehensively discredited. Instead, from the work of a number of scholars has emerged a nuanced view of the transformation of the BEF from a small, colonially oriented force into a large, sophisticated, technologically advanced and highly effective army. The Battle of Arras marked something of a halfway point in this process. The bloody Somme offensive had been a salutary experience that yielded all manner of lessons on everything from minor tactics to high command. While many had been absorbed and applied while the fighting was in progress, such as the creeping barrage, the winter of 1916-17 allowed a period of more considered reflection. At the end of the battle, the Counter-Battery Staff Office was formed, which gave the BEF "corps-level...centralised staff of artillery personnel dedicated to the suppression of the enemy's batteries through the analysis and tactical application of intelligence."[26] In February 1917 important tactical changes were enshrined in key doctrinal pamphlets. These changes were prompted in part by developments in the French Army: the Canadian Corps was influenced by a visit paid by Arthur Currie to Verdun early in 1917. However, more important were the lessons that had been learned the hard way by British Empire units. Just how effectively these lessons had been learned and applied became clear on 9 April 1917.

Fourteen British and Canadian divisions went over the top on 9 April 1917. The attack frontage was 25,000 yards (22,800 metres), 2,000 yards (1,800 metres) less than on the Somme on 1 July 1916. There were more heavy guns at Arras, 963, or one per twenty-one yards, as opposed to 455, or one per fifty-seven yards and also more ammunition was available. The Arras attack was supported by poison gas, tanks and a massed machine gun barrage. "The task before us is a difficult one," opined the GOC 34th Division in an order to his troops, "but in many respects, especially with regard to the weight of our Artillery Support, it is easier than that allotted to our Division in the early days of July last year when it won for itself a reputation for gallantry and determination second to none in the British Army."[27] This must have been cheering news for veterans of 1 July 1916, when 34th Division had sustained horrendous losses for meagre gains.

Almost everywhere the attack was successful. "Owing to the fact that the whole attack from ZERO until the moment that the 4th Division passed through the 9th Division was carried out exactly to the time table previously arranged," reported the compiler of 26th Brigade's narrative of operations, "there is very little comment on the whole operation."[28] The 28th Brigade complained that the pace of the creeping barrage (100 yards in four minutes) was "too slow for eager men assaulting a trench system that has been treated to thorough Artillery preparation" and that men ran into their own barrage on 9 April and suffered casualties as a result.[29] Conversely, 12th Division, which attacked up Observatory Hill, believed that a creeper that advanced 100 yards in six minutes would have been more realistic. This division's attack fell behind schedule but was still successful, not least because of effective gunnery: "The infantry are loud in the praises of the artillery supporting them."[30] British 13th Brigade, serving under the Canadian Corps on Vimy Ridge, listed four factors in their success on 9 April: "perfect steadiness" of the troops "despite being under a barrage"; "the initiative and dash of Company and Platoon Commanders"; "the intensity and accuracy of the barrage put up by the Canadian [sic] artillery" and "previous practice over the taped course, which all Commanders state was of immense assistance." [31]

In some places there were local setbacks. The 34th Division reported "very feeble resistance" by the enemy and the subsequent capture of objectives on time on all but the left of the left-hand brigade, which imposed delays and casualties. The 34th Division had to complete the capture of its objectives on the following morning.[32] Overall, however, the results were impressive. About 9,000 prisoners were taken. Third Army formations advanced between 2,000 to 6,000 yards; the Canadian Corps captured Vimy Ridge; and VII Corps took some advanced positions of the Hindenburg Line. As Haig wrote to King George V at 1500 hours on 9 April, "Our success is already the largest obtained on this front in *one* day."[33]

The first day of the Arras offensive demonstrated that given careful preparation and staff work, massed artillery and well-trained and motivated infantry, the BEF was capable of capturing strong positions. The second and subsequent days of the battle, however, were to show that while since July 1916 the BEF had learned how to break *into* an enemy position, it had yet to master the art of breaking *out* and fighting a more mobile battle. On 10 and 11 April the advance of the weary troops slowed while German reserves began to reach the battlefield. The British official historian rightly commented that while the gains of 10 April were considerable achievements, they were seen as disappointments given the optimism caused by the success of the previous day.[34] The poor weather limited the aerial reconnaissance that the Royal Flying Corps could carry out, yet on 10 April, according to the biographer of the commander of Third Army, Allenby "was in a state of high excitement, certain that the decisive breakthrough was within his grasp." On the following day he put out an order declaring that "Third Army is now pursuing a defeated enemy and that risks must be freely taken."[35] In fact, by this time the German troops arriving on the Arras battlefield amounted to a fresh force that had to be defeated anew. Allenby's breakthrough did not materialize and the battle bogged down into an attritional struggle.

On 9 April the BEF seized the initiative, but over the next several days was unable to maintain a high operational tempo, or "the rate or rhythm of activity relative to the enemy."[36] A major reason for this was, ironically, that the stupendous bombardment that had made the success of 9 April possible cratered the ground and slowed getting the artillery forward. Given time, engineers and pioneers built roads and tracks which enabled the guns to advance to new positions. But to take time was to slow the tempo of an operation. As a result, British infantry on 11 April were too often committed to battle with insufficient artillery support and came up against uncut wire. The eighteen-pounder guns that should have been used for wire-cutting were still struggling forward to get into range.

This problem was not entirely resolved two weeks later. On 23 April British 5th Division, still serving with the Canadian Corps, launched an attack. Covered by a creeping barrage, the assault troops reached the enemy position without difficulty but then discovered the German wire was poorly cut. "The necessity of filing through gaps in the wire had led to the parties that had penetrated the hostile positions becoming considerably broken up" and the Germans launched counterattacks. "Overwhelmed by weight of numbers" and lacking reinforcements that could not be brought forward, most of the attacking troops were forced to fall back to their own lines. Artillery shortcomings, the failure of wire-cutting, the barrage moving too fast and machine guns not being suppressed were factors directly responsible for the debacle. Denied the long period of preparation available before the beginning of the offensive, this attack and others underlined the limitations of the BEF in semi-open warfare in early 1917.

Quite apart from artillery, there were other areas in which BEF formations struggled to adjust to the changed conditions. The 12th Division attacked at 0345 hours on 3 May, but parties dedicated to the mopping-up role overlooked shell-holes in the dark and failed to clear them out. The result was that German troops were able to assemble in Devil's Trench to the rear of the advanced waves of 12th Division and form a centre of resistance. The "obscurity of the situation" and fear of hitting their own forces prevented an artillery bombardment of Devil's Trench. Divisional commander Major-General A.B. Scott attributed the failure to, in addition to the failure to mop up, "The start in the dark to cover such a depth of ground where objects were not well defined" and the "absolute impossibility during daylight of movement over the open spurs and then the want of any definite information and inability to use supports."[37]

A sober assessment by 34th Division's staff on the operations of 28-29 April encapsulated many of the problems faced by the BEF in the latter stages of the Battle of Arras. The "features" to which they drew attention included:

— The novelty of the operations as compared with those of 9th April for which the troops had been trained and for which time for preparation and reconnaissance had been ample.

— The rapidity in [sic] which plans had to be made, reconnaissances carried out and orders issued.

— The inexperience and lack of training of the greater proportion of the troops — mostly new drafts.

— The weakness of the artillery barrage owing possibly to lack of time for reconnaissance and casualties to materiel and personnel.

— The necessity for time for training in order that a division can "pull its weight" and the necessity for Brigade and Battalion Commanders to anticipate orders and be prepared to move and attack at short notice.[38]

This assessment speaks eloquently of the shortcomings of an army that had learned how to conduct successful set-piece operations, but lacked the skills to fight a mobile or even semi-mobile battle. Over the next eighteen months, the BEF was to acquire those skills. During the Final Hundred Days from August to November 1918, the BEF was able to fight the high tempo, mobile battles that were simply beyond its capability in April 1917. More experienced commanders and staff, greater flexibility in command and control, more artillery, logistic excellence — all of these factors were important.[39] None of them were achieved overnight and Arras, like the Somme before it, was an important point on the learning curve of the BEF.

One particular action during the Arras campaign, the attack on Vimy Ridge, has achieved and retained popular fame largely through the nationality of the troops selected to capture it; the proximity of Vimy to England; and the building of a visitor-(especially pupil-) friendly memorial, complete with artificially preserved trenches. Canadian nationalism has led to an exaggerated sense of the importance of the capture of Vimy Ridge and the British elements of the force that fought in the battle have been airbrushed out of popular memory. This is not to minimize the skill of the troops engaged in the battle, nor its importance to the learning curve of the BEF. However, Vimy cannot be divorced from the wider context of the Battle of Arras, an offensive that had profound strategic consequences and marked an important stage in the tactical and operational development of the BEF. In spite of this, Arras is a campaign that has been neglected by popular memory and historians alike. It deserves a full-scale scholarly reassessment.

Notes

I would like to thank Chris McCarthy for his advice on the Battle of Arras. Crown copyright material in the National Archives appears by permission of HM Stationery Office.

1   This prefigures the repulse of a German amphibious raid by magically animated suits of armour and manikins dressed in uniforms of bygone ages. Possibly Vimy Ridge was chosen because, unlike a battle such as the Somme, it is regarded as a victory.

2   Jonathan Nicholls, *Cheerful Sacrifice: The Battle of Arras 1917* (London: Leo Cooper, 1990), 211.

3   In addition, there are several relevant volumes in the mass-marketed but highly specialized *Battleground Europe* series published by Pen & Sword.

4   David Chandler (ed), *A Traveller's Guide to the Battlefields of Europe*, (Wellingborough: Patrick Stephens, 1989), first published in 1965.

5   Herbert Fairlie Wood, *Vimy!* (London: Corgi, 1972); Pierre Berton, *Vimy* (London: Penguin, 1987); Alexander McKee, *Vimy Ridge* (London: Pan, 1968); Kenneth Macksey, *The Shadow of Vimy Ridge* (London: William Kimber, 1965); Kenneth Macksey, *Vimy Ridge 1914-18* (London: Pan/Ballantine, 1973).

6   Cyril Falls, *History of the Great War: Military Operations, France and Belgium, 1917, Vol. 1; The German Retreat to the Hindenburg Line and the Battle of Arras* (London: Macmillan, 1940). [Official History]

7   See Christopher Page, *Command in the Royal Naval Division: A Military Biography of Brigadier General A M Asquith DSO* (Staplehurst: Spellmount, 1999).

8   Jonathan Walker, *The Blood Tub: General Gough and the Battle of Bullecourt, 1917* (Staplehurst: Spellmount, 1998). For a good Australian example, see Peter Sadler, The Paladin: *A Life of Major-General Sir John Gellibrand*, (Melbourne: Oxford University Press: 2000).

9   An on-line essay posted by a military history enthusiast is wholly typical in this respect: http://www.planetmedalofhonor.com/features/articles/usersubmitted/article0027.shtml. Accessed 21 February 2006.

10   Nivelle's directive, 4 April 1917; Nivelle to Haig, 21 December 1916, War Office [WO] 256/17, Public Record Office [Hereafter PRO] and Haig to Nivelle, 6 January 1917 in Official History, 4-6, 13-15, Appendices 2, 7; John Terraine, *Douglas Haig the Educated Soldier* (London: Hutchinson, 1963), 252.

11   For a recent treatment of this episode, see Andrew Suttie, *Rewriting the First World War: Lloyd George, Politics and Strategy 1914-18* (Basingstoke: Palgrave Macmillan, 2005), 99-119.

12   Clive diary quoted in Gary Sheffield, "Not the Same as Friendship: The British Empire and Coalition Warfare in the Era of the First World War," in Peter Dennis and Jeffrey Grey (eds), *Entangling Alliances: Coalition Warfare in the Twentieth Century* (Canberra: Australian History Military Publications, 2005), 49.

13   Haig diary, 18 April 1917, in G. Sheffield and J. Bourne (eds), *Douglas Haig: War Diaries and letters 1914-1918* (London: Weidenfeld and Nicolson, 2005), 285.

14   Haig to Robertson, O.A.D. 405, 19 Apr 1917, WO 256/17, PRO.

15   David French, "Who Knew What and When? The French Army Mutinies and the British Decision to Launch the Third Battle of Ypres," in L. Freedman, P. Hayes and R. O'Neill (eds), *War, Strategy and International Politics* (Oxford: Clarendon Press, 1992), 141, 144; Report of conference of Haig and Army Commanders, OAD 433, 30 April 1917, WO 256/17, PRO.

16   Haig diary, 1 May 1917, in Sheffield and Bourne, 289.

17   Hastings Anderson, "Lord Horne as an Army Commander," *Journal of the Royal Artillery* vol LVI, no 4 (January 1930), 416-17.

18   Official History, 302-03.

19   "Canadian Corps report on operations..." c. 1917, WO 106/402, PRO.

20   Anderson, 417.

21   Simon Robbins, "Henry Horne," in I.F.W. Beckett and Steven J. Corvi (eds), Haig's Generals (Barnsley: Pen & Sword, 2006), 102.

22   Quoted in Jeffery Williams, *Byng of Vimy* (London: Leo Cooper, 1992), 165.

23   "Report on conference...29 March 1917; "Minutes of conference of Corps commanders...15 Apr. 1917"; "Weekly summary of operations...6/4/17 to 13/4/17," all in WO95/169, PRO.

24   "First Army (Vimy)" statistics; "RE Services (A) Forward Roads"; both in WO95/169, PRO.

25   See G.D. Sheffield, "How even was the learning curve? Reflections on British and Dominion Armies on the Western Front 1916-1918," in Yves Tremblay

(ed) *Canadian Military History since the 17th Century* (Ottawa: Department of National Defence, 2001), 125-31.

26   Albert P. Palazzo, "The British Army's Counter-Battery Staff Office and the Control of the Enemy in World War I," *Journal of Military History* vol 63 (January 1999), 56-57, 73.

27   "Special Order by Major General C.L. Nicholson" 4 April 1917, WO95/2433, PRO.

28   26th Brigade account, 9 April 1917, WO95/1738, PRO.

29   28th Brigade account, 9 April 1917, 1917, WO95/1738, PRO.

30   Report by GOC 12th Div to VI Corps, 20 April 1917, WO95/1824, PRO.

31   13th Brigade report on operations, 18 April 1917, WO95/1514, PRO.

32   "Summary of War Diary 34th Division for April 1917," WO95/2433, PRO.

33   Haig to George V, 9 April 1917, in Sheffield and Bourne, 278.

34   Official History, 253.

35   Lawrence James, *Imperial Warrior: The Life and Times of Field Marshal Viscount Allenby 1861-1936* (London: Weidenfeld and Nicolson, 1993), 101; Official History, 259.

36   John Kiszley, "The British Army and Approaches to Warfare since 1945," in Brian Holden Reid (ed), *Military Power* (London: Cass, 1997), 180.

37   Report by GOC 12th Div to VI Corps, 13 May 1917, WO95/1824, PRO.

38   "Summary of War Diary 34th Division for April 1917," WO95/2433, PRO.

39   Andy Simpson, "British Corps Command on the Western Front, 1914-1918," in Gary Sheffield and Dan Todman (eds), *Command and Control on the Western Front: The British Army's Experience 1914-18* (Staplehurst: Spellmount, 2004), 114.

2

The End of the Beginning
The Canadian Corps in 1917

PAUL DICKSON

If the First World War had ended with a negotiated peace in 1916 or the winter of 1917, the reputation of the Canadian Corps would have been mixed at best. Historians would have pondered the "what ifs?," characterizing the Corps as an overly politicized formation that never fully realized its potential, had expanded too rapidly, had too few senior commanders qualified to lead higher formations and had suffered because Canada's permanent force could not provide the trained staff required to sustain a corps headquarters.

The Canadian Corps that took Vimy Ridge was not the "elite" formation it would become in 1918, but the foundation was firmly in place. The Canadian Corps at Vimy was a work in progress, a formation that had shed the last vestiges of its amateurish politicized beginnings. Its leaders were ready to take advantage of improvements to its reinforcement and training system, new technology and with time, to assess the experiences of the Allied offensive operations on the Western Front. One could argue that the approach to the assault on Vimy Ridge was as much a result of the need to build confidence in the Corps' new direction as it was reflective of a particular operational culture. By 1916, good habits and a good organizational climate were forming. Equally important, by the end of 1916, the Canadian Corps had stability denied most other corps in the British Expeditionary Force (BEF), one paralleled only in the Australian and New Zealand Army Corps. That stability made adaptation to tactical developments quicker and more effective, particularly when the Corps had significant periods of time to consider the lessons of the previous two years. Neither the climate nor the stability came easily. As other studies have demonstrated, the Canadian Corps evolved.[1] Like any evolutionary process, there were winners and losers. The critical element in that evolution was the creation of an organizational climate that fostered and rewarded critical thinking and innovation. By 1917, the officers and men of the Corps who had survived the battles of 1915 and 1916 had more experience. But so did the British, French and German armies on the Western Front. What made the Canadian Corps unique? What kind of army was it?

When the soldiers of the 1st Canadian Division filtered into the trenches on the Western Front in 1915, there was no reason to believe they would be any more or less successful than the soldiers of other national armies. The Canadian Expeditionary Force (CEF) shared many of the problems encountered by other armies on the Western Front as it struggled with the implications of rapid expansion and new technologies that allowed defensive tactics and techniques to stay just ahead of operational developments.

Did the Canadians Corps have better material to work with? The profiles of the Canadian contingents suggest nothing remarkable about the men themselves. The conclusion, still maintained by some historians, that the Canadians had more potential because of their pioneering origins, was a natural consequence of the Canadian Corps' later success.[2] Even General Sir Arthur Currie, who knew better, waxed poetic about the virtues of the Canadian pioneers in the immediate aftermath of the war: "The rugged strength of the Canadian is depicted in his broad shoulders, deep chest and strong, clean-cut limbs...while behind the calm gravity of his mien lies a tenacious and indomitable will." These, he concluded, are the "invaluable gifts of our deep forests and lofty mountains, of our rolling plains and our great waterways, and of the clear light of our Northern skies, gifts which have enabled the Canadian to adapt himself readily and well to the new conditions he found confronting him as a soldier."[3] Stylistic conventions of the period aside, Currie's suggestion that the Canadian Corps' successes stemmed from the pioneering tradition and the results of natural "laws of selection" was still qualified. He concluded that the Canadian soldier was returning to civilian life "still possessing" the qualities that made him an excellent soldier, but in addition "having learned...the value of well-organized, collective effort, backed by discipline and self-restraint."[4] Currie can be forgiven for wanting in the flush of victory to emphasize the contribution of the individual solder; still, even Currie had to acknowledge that the success of the Canadian Corps did not come easily.

The CEF was not far different from the BEF at the beginning of the war. Where they were applied, enlistment standards were similar. Age, height, weight and chest size were the first means of culling the unfit. The minimum dimensions for infantry were a height of 5 feet 3 inches, with a 33.5 inch chest; those in more physically demanding jobs needed to be just 5 feet 7 inches, with a 34.5 inch chest. Single men between eighteen and forty-five were given preference. Eyes and teeth were the next measures, but both proved easy to overcome, more so by July 1915 when standards for height and chest were officially lowered. So unevenly were the medical standards applied that in September 1916 the Militia Department began cracking down on the medical examination requirement. Yet, by 1917, the department had again reduced the standards: 5 feet was the minimum for infantry and 4 feet 11 inches for those in support branches like the medical corps. Enforcement remained a problem. The youngest to enlist in the CEF was ten. The BEF had similar problems maintaining standards. Approximately sixty percent of the volunteers from 1914-15 were deemed medically fit; between 1916-18, with the introduction of conscription, that figure had fallen to approximately thirty-six percent. One study suggests that by 1918 half of the BEF was under nineteen. The maximum age for conscripts had been raised to fifty.[5]

In the early stages of the war, one might argue that the CEF was nothing more than an administrative convenience in the interests of organizing the British Empire war effort. Canadian soldiers were subject to British military law, although paid far better than their British counterparts. Constitutionally, there was no distinction between Canadian and British formations. In terms of ethnic origin, this was true as well. Only thirty percent of the First Contingent sent overseas in the fall of 1914 was born in Canada and even the native born were often only one generation removed from Britain.[6] On the eve of the assault against Vimy Ridge, first generation British immigrants were still in the majority in the Canadian Corps. Prior to the introduction of conscription in October 1917, of 438,806 men enlisted in the CEF, 194,473 (44.3 percent) were Canadian born, 215,769 (49.2 percent) were born in Britain and 26,564 (6 percent) were born in other countries. Even with the introduction of conscription, the Canadian born serving overseas remained in the minority, never rising above forty-seven percent. At a time when seventy-seven percent of Canadians were born in Canada, the majority of the men who fought at Vimy Ridge were drawn from the ten percent of the Canadian population who were British born.[7]

Recruitment figures reveal further divisions. First, despite the image of Canadian troops as rugged pioneers, the numbers suggest an urbanized CEF, with the majority of those enlisting in time to fight at Vimy listing their occupation as manual labourers (65 percent) or clerical workers (18.5 percent). Only 6.5 percent described themselves as farmers or ranchers. Even after conscription, the numbers who listed their occupation as "industrial" was far higher than those who worked the land, the sea or the forests (36.4 percent and 22.4 percent respectively). The occupational profile reflected both the British origins of the enlisted personnel as well as the fact that most were single (79.6 percent). By contrast, about sixty-two percent of officers were single and when based on a snapshot of the senior command, tended to be Canadian born (78.3 percent). This was an army of white-collar and industrial workers, closer to the British model than the Australian. It was also an older army than we usually realize, with 26.3 the average age at enlistment and a significant percentage (28.3 percent) older than that.[8]

The intensely local nature of recruiting produced a wide variation in recruitment rates. As with the British army, the regiment was the main vehicle for recruiting and reinforcement in the Canadian forces. The disparity in volunteerism was a source of dismay to contemporary observers and not just in Quebec, where the militia infrastructure was less extensive. In January 1915, recruiting officers in some rural areas reported that they were having difficulty meeting their quotas. Toronto's *The Globe* asked, "Will the rural regiments allow the city regiments to put them to shame?"[9] For a country that was still half rural, such low levels of rural enlistment were significant. Studies of local responses suggest that the reasons for low recruitment were in part economic, with immigrants less rooted and less well-paid than native born Canadians. This did not change the reality. As the Guelph *Mercury* reasoned, Canadians were "just as brave" as the British, but either failed to recognize the need or were unwilling to accept the drop in wages.[10]

A significant number of those who enlisted in the CEF had some military experience: of over 619,000 total enlistments, 152,865 (24.7 percent) reported previous military experience in their attestation papers, most of it with the militia. Approximately 19,000 (3 percent) were former British regulars. Most of the CEF officer corps was ex-militia. Some had more professional training, or at least as much as Canada could offer. By November 1918, nearly 600 CEF officers were ex-cadets of the Royal Military College, a small percentage of the total, but a figure that included many senior officers, including two of the four divisional commanders.[11] The most significant experience came from two sources: the front lines and the loan of British staff officers. It is hard to exaggerate the contribution of the latter, a point that will be taken up in later chapters.

Any examination of the evolution of the CEF must consider the heavy toll of casualties on the First and Second contingents. Brigadier-General Arthur Currie's 2nd Canadian Infantry Brigade had to be rebuilt after May 1915 when it lost seventy-five percent of its establishment. The Princess Patricia's Canadian Light Infantry [PPCLI] suffered nearly a complete turnover of personnel during the same battle, the casualties including a draft of reinforcements that were fed into battle in early May.[12] There is some evidence, however, to suggest that the attrition rate in the Canadian Corps was lower than in the BEF. The "Old Contemptibles" (members of the pre-war army) of the BEF were practically wiped out in the fall of 1914; similarly, Kitchener's New Armies suffered heavily over the course of the war. One study estimates an attrition rate of ninety-seven percent.[13] Through 1915 and 1916, the Canadians suffered about eighty-seven percent casualties, which might suggest some leavening of experience throughout the Canadian Corps prior to Vimy Ridge.[14]

The CEF enjoyed no special advantages with its equipment. Despite adhering to the principle of standardizing weapons and equipment with the British army, the practice of favouring Canadian manufacturers left the CEF with a variety of equipment, some of it of dubious quality. Equipping the CEF with the Ross rifle, for all its faults, was at first the result of an honest attempt to address the inability of British manufacturers to meet Canadian demand. The Canadians also used kit that proved troublesome as soon as the First Contingent arrived in England: Colt machine guns, MacAdam shield-shovels and even Canadian-made boots, many of which fell apart in the rain of Salisbury Plain, were all criticized and eventually replaced with British issue. The debate over the Ross rifle remained unsettled until Mount Sorrel in June 1916 when it was finally rejected for the British Lee-Enfield.[15]

Certainly the policy and administrative support for the CEF did not hint at the promise of the Canadian Corps. When Sam Hughes, the minister of Militia and Defence ignored a pre-war mobilization plan and issued a call for volunteers, he set a pattern that characterized his approach until his removal in November 1916. Hughes reflected a celebration of the amateur over the professional, of the national over the effective, with the organizing principle being that all decisions ended up in the minister's office. Hughes' CEF had its parallel in the British Secretary of State for War Lord Kitchener's New Armies, which were raised outside the framework of the Territorial Army. In contrast to Hughes, Kitchener seems to have been concerned with the quality of the non-professional soldiers, based on his pre-war experiences, but the results may have been the same. "I prefer men who know nothing to those who have been taught a smattering of the wrong thing," he informed the daughter of British Prime Minister H.H. Asquith, a statement of principle with which Hughes would probably have heartily agreed.[16]

From 1914, Canadian recruitment campaigns were driven by the combination of Hughes' fervent belief in the virtues of the volunteer amateur soldier and Sir Robert Borden's escalation of Canada's commitment to the war. Hughes' recruiting system was appealing, cheap and initially successful. In the first five months of 1915, he invited thirty-five colonels to raise battalions. This initiative was in fact too successful. By mid-1916, the authorities noted that for "administrative and financial reasons" it preferred to send drafts of soldiers overseas. Still, they conceded that "the despatch of complete battalions would gratify the senior ranks and appeal to local sentiment."[17]

Turning recruits into reinforcements proved more problematic. Even with an efficient recruitment organization, a nation of barely eight million was hard-pressed to recruit and sustain a CEF of half a million men. However, this fundamental problem was only made worse by the Canadian organization in the United Kingdom, which scattered responsibility for training and reinforcements among at least six senior military and political representatives, all of whom believed they had some say in promotions, policy and training questions. The Canadian administration in the United Kingdom was completely unsuited to sorting out the mess created in Canada.[18]

What then changed the Canadian Corps? Military culture is a concept with a relatively short life in Canada, but one could argue that the Canadian Corps had an organizational climate in which its leaders played a crucial role in instilling rewards and punishment, imparting values and priorities and defining and measuring progress.[19] An organizational climate addresses how an army learns and creates a doctrine.[20] Paul Johnson argues that measuring the evolution of doctrine involves not just examining the re-release of field manuals, but also changes in training, personnel, promotion and even recruitment policies.[21] His questions suggest the defining features of a military organization's climate and culture: What are that army's collective experiences? What proclivities are rewarded? What are the formative experiences in the careers of its officers? And then, how can all of those things and more be shaped so that they tend to create the appropriate mindset?

It may be sacrilege to suggest that Hughes established one of the key elements of the organizational climate of the Canadian Corps and set it on the path that would ultimately make it so successful, but his decision to throw out the rule book and depend on the volunteer spirit of the militia eventually provided a remarkable return. While the recruitment approach proved problematic and his continued interference eventually led to his political demise, Hughes established a tone that encouraged, or rather demanded, breaking with regular British Army conventions. Casting aside conventions, however, is not the same as being unconventional or innovative. Hughes tried to create a personalized promotion system based on favouritism and nativism. He wanted Canadians in charge and he preferred that they be Canadians he knew. The idiosyncratic nature of that system was evident in 1914 when he organized the First Canadian Contingent at Valcartier. He exercised direct control over all matters of training, administration and senior appointments even as the CEF expanded and went into operations.

The spirit of this approach infused the administration in Britain and the senior formation headquarters. For example, Colonel J.W. Carson, a militia officer from Montreal, headed the First Canadian Contingent's advance party and remained in England as Hughes' "special representative." Carson promoted himself as "an agent of the Minister of Militia." In the summer of 1915, following Second Ypres, Carson attempted to have all Canadian battalion commanders in France promoted to the rank of colonel, "as some slight reward for their magnificent work during the trying times of the last few weeks." Alternatively, they could all be made brevet colonels, a suggestion approved by Hughes. The British quietly but firmly indicated that this was not possible and no promotions were forthcoming, despite Carson's seven letters to Hughes on the matter.[22] Hughes' appointments also created tensions and jealousy between headquarters, a problem that was to plague the CEF until at least 1916.

Intensely local political cronyism and an almost fanatical faith in volunteerism may have had a parallel in the British professional officer corps where a personalized system of rewards and promotion worked, in the view of some, to its detriment.[23] British General Headquarters (GHQ) controlled all promotions down to battalion and some analysts argue that regular Army cronyism and prejudice against the civilian-soldiers hampered the effectiveness of the British Expeditionary Force.[24] This judgment provides a useful basis for comparison with the Canadian experience and the importance of removing political influence through 1916.

The first General Officer Commanding (GOC) of 1st Canadian Division was Lieutenant-General Edwin Alderson, a British officer and not Hughes' choice. Alderson demonstrated a willingness to make his own decisions early on, providing an example for the commanders and staff of the division. He was not always successful, particularly in the absence of practical experience, but his attitude took root and he cultivated it among his own officer corps. Alderson also followed his own instincts, providing, against Kitchener's and Hughes' wishes, wet canteens for the Canadians on Salisbury Plain and insisting that Canadian units change their establishment to meet their own needs, to cite two examples. When, in January 1915, the 1st Division adopted the establishment of the 29th (British) Division, Alderson insisted that a large number of the surplus staff and regimental officers accompany it to France to compensate for the division's inexperience and lack of training. He added, "My experience of active service is that a shortage of officers comes all too soon." Though never adopted in the British Army, additional staff officers permitted closer contact between the divisional commander and his troops and the practice was continued in Canadian formations throughout the war.[25]

Alderson's changes were hardly revolutionary, but they signaled a willingness to do things differently. Perhaps the better evidence for this was his rejection of the shoddy equipment with which the First Contingent was first saddled, a pattern he repeated with his investigation of the Ross rifle, when his willingness to set aside convention came up against Sam Hughes' belief that nationalism trumped everything else.[26]

However, when the 1st Canadian Division entered the line in early 1915, most argue that it was far from prepared for modern warfare and its future direction was not clear. Historian Denis Winter, a fan of both the Canadian Corps and its final commander, Arthur Currie, characterized the formation as a "disorganized rabble" in 1915. Contemporary observers referred to the CEF as the "Comedian Contingent."[27] Lieutenant-General Sir Julian Byng himself was kinder, but no less accurate, when he observed in 1916 that the Canadians lacked discipline. He also commented on the rivalry that existed between units, which, in his view, hindered cooperation. Other observers noted the tensions between the immigrants and native-born, hinting that the former delayed the maturation of the First Contingent.[28]

Second Ypres in April-May 1915 demonstrated that the Canadian soldier, no less than his British counterpart, was willing to sacrifice himself for the greater good. As other studies have suggested, the problems at Second Ypres were overshadowed by the congratulatory tone of the British. The Canadians demonstrated remarkable tenacity in defence, but a significant percentage of their casualties resulted from poorly coordinated massed counterattacks. The division lost nearly half of its fighting strength and even officers like Currie, who then commanded 2nd Infantry Brigade, made questionable decisions.[29]

Equally reflective of the operational skills of the Canadians was the Battle of Festubert in May 1915, an action characterized by the official history as "inconclusive" and "frustrating." The division suffered 2,500 casualties and failed to reach the enemy line after five attempts. An initiative to reorganize an ad hoc headquarters under Alderson collapsed. The staff was too small and too inexperienced, working with formations and units with which they were unfamiliar.[30]

The Canadian response to their introduction to modern warfare in 1915 says much about the direction the Canadian Corps might have taken. The political response was to increase Canada's commitment to 150,000 in June 1915, then to 250,000 in November. The establishment of a second and then a third Canadian division prompted the formation of a corps headquarters on 13 September 1915, with Alderson in command. But it was the consequent debates about command and staff appointments that illustrated this organization's constraints.

Of course, every army experienced difficulties given the rate of expansion demanded by the cost of fighting on the Western Front. The BEF suffered from a severe shortage of experienced officers. The Canadian situation was exacerbated as Hughes did his best to direct the appointments, irrespective of experience in the field. His attempt to secure a brigade command for his son Garnet was one example. Alderson did not want the unproven Garnet at the head of the inexperienced 2nd Canadian Division. Currie, now GOC, 1st Canadian Division, opposed moving the minister's son to command a brigade in his division.[31] The minister won and Garnet Hughes was appointed to lead Currie's 1st Brigade, but the resistance and the delay, as well as Currie's support for a British regular officer, Lieutenant-Colonel L.F. Lipsett as a brigade commander, galled the elder Hughes.

The debate over the balance between national imperatives and experience was most fervent in the question of staffing the new headquarters. Few Canadians were qualified. Only twelve Canadians had passed through British Staff College by 1914, in part because of Hughes' bias against such professional education. British staff officers filled the senior staff positions of the Corps for the first two years of the war. By 1917, a call for increased Canadian staff was tempered by the recognition that appointments should go to the most competent regardless of nationality. As part of this Canadianization of the staff, specially qualified officers were selected for the wartime staff courses at Camberley or attached to formations for staff instruction as understudies. By 1917 the selection process was rigorous and thorough, based on competence and talent.[32]

The importance of the British staff officers and their mentorship of the Canadian staff cannot be overstated. The quality of the staff officers lent by the British was represented by Major Alan Brooke, the future Lord Alanbrooke, Britain's top soldier in the Second World War. Brooke was just one exceptional British staff officer serving with the Canadian Corps whose contribution and abilities would be remembered "with respect and gratitude." Future general Harry Crerar remembered his apprenticeship with Brooke as crucial. "I am quite sure that I could not have carried out my part in arrangements for [Amiens] if it had not been for the professional assistance given me by Brookie…and, in particular, the clear memoranda and notes on artillery planning requirements, at the corps level, for a full-scale and hastily executed surprise attack."[33] Brooke was less enthusiastic about the benefits of Canadianization, but recognized the importance of teaching and mentoring those with limited experience or technical education.[34] As will be argued elsewhere in this volume, the British made a critical contribution to professionalizing the Canadian Corps.

It was the Canadians' willingness to forgo nationalism in the interests of efficiency and effectiveness that marked a new phase in the Corps' maturation. As the Corps expanded in 1915, Canadians like Currie fought Hughes' policy of promoting inexperienced Canadians, noting that it was not a question of "whether a man was Canadian or otherwise, it is one of the best man for the job."[35] This attitude was critical, not least because the British proved willing to provide some of their best men for the senior staff positions. It was a delicate subject as many, including Currie, had benefited from the personalized reward system they now opposed. Paradoxically, one by-product of the elevation of professional measures over national was that some officers after the war viewed the Canadian Corps, an iconic Canadian symbol, as a model of imperial cooperation and promise.[36]

Following Festubert and Givenchy in May and June 1915, the Canadian Corps was not involved in sustained operations until March 1916. But the period was marked by an eagerness to learn and innovate. In November 1915, the 1st Division launched its first large scale trench raid, a controversial practice for which the Canadians gained some fame.[37] Raiding offered one of the few systematic approaches to learning available to the Canadians at the time. Personal inclination also proved important, as Currie demonstrated, embarking on an intense course of personal study.[38]

For the enlisted ranks, NCOs and junior officers, training and learning were stymied by the problem of inadequate reinforcements as the Canadian Corps tried to rebuild its depleted battalions. The problems with the Hughes system were evident as early as April 1915 when the War Office asked the Canadian government to dispatch approximately 6,000 reinforcements every month to meet the division's losses. Hughes responded by trying to copy the success of the British "Pals" battalions, which intensified the local recruiting system. There was some success, but continued local recruitment highlighted the training system's inefficiencies. Morale declined as the new battalions dispatched from Canada were broken up. Recruits who signed up on the promise of fighting with friends and colleagues found themselves scattered throughout the depleted units of the Corps. Surplus officers were a source of discontent and worse, became responsible for training the new recruits in the UK. Hughes responded by making the recruiting, reinforcement and training system even more complex and inefficient. In early 1916, Alderson was informed that only 2,300 of the 25,000 Canadians training in the UK were available as reinforcements. By June 1916, it was estimated that the Corps was short 7,000 men.[39]

The Battle of St. Eloi Craters in March and April 1916 illustrated numerous problems in the CEF, including tension within the headquarters as well as inexperience and inadequate training. Tim Cook has described the St. Eloi battlefield as a "murder hole where the inexperienced men of the 2nd Canadian Division were squandered without proper guidance" from their commanders and staff. The most glaring mistake was the misinterpretation of the intelligence, but the poorly coordinated handovers—notably and at the insistence of the Canadians, the first time an entire Corps replaced another on a wide front—and minimal control also demonstrated the weakness of the staff and command.[40] The battle cost some 1,400 casualties and illustrated the dangers of command appointments where political support and nationality were important criteria for promotion. Following the mistakes of the St. Eloi operation, the debate over responsibility highlighted the struggle between Hughes' nationalist cronyism and the emerging merit-based perspective of the Corps. Alderson was the most prominent casualty, although it could be argued his days were numbered as he ran afoul of Hughes by continuing to examine the reliability of the Ross rifle and because he was British. Alderson's last success was to see off the Ross rifle, but Hughes seems to have settled on Alderson as the main obstacle to his Canadianization efforts. Alderson was kicked upstairs to the empty position of Inspector-General of Canadian Forces in England. As Hughes intended, Alderson resigned several months later as there was nothing for him to do.[41] In a sense, the crisis engendered by St. Eloi represented the struggle to strike the right balance between the Corps' Canadianization, as defined by Hughes and its effectiveness.

Lieutenant-General Sir Julian Byng arrived at the Corps on 28 May 1916. Hughes' biographer suggests that he did not want Byng, preferring a Canadian, probably Major-General Richard Turner of 2nd Canadian Division and a survivor of the St. Eloi debacle.[42] Neither was Byng thrilled to have assumed command of the Canadian Corps. According to Byng's biographer, Byng admired the Canadians for their "fighting qualities and their high morale" but believed that they were undisciplined and inadequately trained. Byng, however, took command of a corps that was almost complete, in structure if not in personality. Alderson had been increasingly preoccupied with what Haig described as "so many administrative and political questions to discuss with the Canadian government" that it would be "nigh impossible" for him to command the Corps in the field. Indeed, Byng recognized that command and control loomed as two significant problems. Cooperation between units was another. Much of this stemmed, in Byng's view, from poorly trained and inadequate officers. Byng was soon embroiled in Hughes' attempts to foist what Byng described as the minister's "politicians and dollar magnates" on the Canadian Corps. The new GOC complained of the political interference and was prepared to resign over the issue. [43]

The Battle of Mount Sorrel in June 1916 proved a turning point for the future of the Canadian Corps. On 2 June 1916, the Germans attacked the Canadian positions near Sanctuary Wood, southeast of Ypres, virtually wiping out two Canadian units, killing Major-General M.S. Mercer, the GOC of 3rd Canadian Division and taking high ground that gave the Germans tactical advantages over the Allied lines. A hastily organized and poorly coordinated counterattack by the Canadians was beaten off with heavy losses. With Ypres threatened, Byng had little choice but to attempt another operation. He decided to mount a limited set-piece counterattack to retake Hills 61 and 62 (Tor Top) and Mount Sorrel, giving the responsibility to Currie's 1st Canadian Division. In the torrential rain and swamp-like conditions, Currie regrouped his strongest battalions into two purpose-built brigades and insisted that the artillery register targets using new aerial reconnaissance while the infantry methodically plan its assault. The operation was a success and was a model for future operations. Perhaps most telling was that Byng allowed Currie, as he had Mercer, the autonomy to make his own appreciations and his own mistakes. Equally important were the innovative artillery plan designed to surprise and confuse the German defenders and Currie's willingness to tailor his plans and units to the task at hand. [44]

A few months later, Canadian participation in the Battle of the Somme demonstrated not so much that the Corps and its formations still had much to learn, but that its senior command's willingness to learn was still limited by external constraints and the need to reconstruct the depleted battalions of the Corps. Currie, the exemplar of the self-taught general, was driven to his pre-Vimy studies both by the successes at Flers-Courcelette and the failure of his 1st Division on the Somme. Regina Trench resisted his efforts three times and was finally captured by the fresh troops of the 4th Division. Total Canadian casualties on the Somme exceeded 24,000. In October 1916, the Canadian Corps, minus the 4th Division, was moved to the quiet sector of Lens-Arras, opposite Vimy Ridge.

Despite the problems at Mount Sorrel and the Somme, the Canadian Corps was about to benefit from a major shift in the political leadership and culture of the Canadian war effort. Concurrent with operations during the spring and summer of 1916, Hughes was quickly expending his political capital. Immediately after Mercer's death at Mount Sorrel, Hughes sent Byng a terse note, "Give Garnet [Hughes] 3rd Division." Instead, Byng gave it to a British regular, Louis Lipsett. Equally telling of Hughes' diminished influence, the Ross rifle was withdrawn from service over the course of 1916.[45]

But it was the reinforcement and training issue and Hughes' refusal to relent on control that eventually brought matters to a breaking point. Byng secured an ally in Haig, who wrote the King that the "jealousy and friction between the several Canadian Divisions" had diminished and there was a "greatly improved atmosphere" as the "recent hardships suffered by that corps…[brought] out the necessity for trained officers instead of ones agreeable to the politicians of Ottawa." Haig concluded, however, that problems continued among the Canadians in the UK.[46] Ottawa was aware of the problem and attempted to marginalize Hughes in an effort to streamline training and reinforcement. Hughes fought back, but an accusatory letter to Sir Robert Borden proved too much and Borden asked for Hughes' resignation. On 31 October, Sir George Perley was appointed "Minister of Overseas Military Forces from Canada in the United Kingdom" and by the end of 1916 the Overseas ministry was firmly established. It did not completely solve the problems of administering the CEF overseas, but for the first time since 1914, all Canadian military control in the UK was concentrated in a single authority. There were still, by one estimate, 250 units in various states of training and organization, but a structure that administered the flow of reinforcements from Canada to France provided a more systematic fourteen-week training syllabus for new arrivals.[47] This was the first step in easing the reinforcement crisis, although it did not end it. According to the official history, by the end of December 1916 there were 7,240 officers and 128,980 other ranks of the CEF in the United Kingdom (as compared with 2,467 officers and 49,379 other ranks a year previously). At the same time strength returns showed 2,526 officers and 105,640 other ranks in France.[48]

The eight months from September 1916 to April 1917 were probably the most important in the Corps' history. Hughes' dismissal in November of 1916 marked the beginning of a new era. Although battles about a fifth and sixth division and an army headquarters were still to be fought, expansion was at an end. A period of relative stability was beginning in which the four divisions and the headquarters could adapt to the tasks at hand. In Lens-Arras, the Canadian Corps had five months to absorb both reinforcements and the lessons of the previous year. This time also allowed the quality of new senior command and staff to emerge during the fall and winter of 1916/17.[49] Freed from some of the political fights that had bedeviled Alderson and very familiar with the Vimy sector, Byng and his staff focused on the job at hand and introduced a new organizational climate that emphasized a willingness to learn, innovate and reward merit.

Arthur Currie's visit in January 1917 to study the French evaluations of their offensive operations at Verdun reflected the caution imbued by the reverses suffered by the Canadians in 1916.[50] Currie implicitly admitted that limited objectives provided the best means of success given the strength of the defence. A set-piece operation allowed for protection of the troops while they captured limited and predetermined objectives. Currie's lessons of Verdun were rooted in an understanding of the particular strengths and weaknesses of the Canadian Corps and in the nature of the German defensive positions, both at Vimy and later. The Canadian Corps' artillery was particularly effective in adapting its role, making changes in its organization and command structure through 1916.[51] Artillery tactics were now defined by the needs of the infantry and technology instead of the tactics conforming to the command structure.

The approach to the operation at Vimy Ridge was also aimed at boosting the confidence of the troops, both in themselves and their commanders. This was a practice used by the French General Henri-Phillip Pétain, who recognized how set-piece attacks with limited objectives helped build morale, especially after the French army's mutinies in the spring of 1917.[52] It is easy to exaggerate the extent of the changes to infantry tactics as the success of the artillery made Vimy Ridge less of a test than it might otherwise have been. And the Canadians were perhaps fortunate that the new German defensive doctrine was imperfectly applied at Vimy Ridge.[53] Still, given his report's emphasis on the training, protection and morale of the infantry, it is hard to escape the conclusion that Currie recognized the need of a clear-cut victory to restore confidence within the Canadian Corps.[54]

Of course, Currie did not make his observations in a vacuum. Contrary to popular perception, there was no shortage of discussion within the British (and French) armies on how to resolve the tactical impasse. British commanders had long understood the importance of adequate preparation, training and small unit tactics. Major-General Ivor Maxse's 18th (Eastern) Division achieved its objectives on 1 July 1916, but failure elsewhere overshadowed this success. The British Army distilled and circulated the tactical lessons of the Somme in official pamphlets SS 143 and SS 144.[55] More important in the long term, it appears that Maxse's ideas were not disseminated nor were there any methods to ensure they would have been instituted had they been.[56] The tactical pamphlets were distributed and doubtless taught in each of the central training schools organized in the five British armies and nineteen corps, but as British divisions were the largest self-contained formations and they circulated frequently among different corps, such lessons were not taught uniformly.[57] Divisional successes like that of the British 4th and 9th (Scottish) Divisions at Vimy, with advances of 5.6 kilometres, were hard to build on as the divisions and staff moved on to new corps.[58] The autonomy afforded army and corps commanders to train their own formations worked in the Canadians' favour, even as it constrained progress in the British army.

The Canadian Corps of April 1917 was a purpose-built machine. Its target was Vimy Ridge and it developed an organization suited to that specific task. But the Canadian Corps was still a work in progress. Many of the developments that made it the elite formation of 1918 were in the future, products of Currie's recognition of its strengths. In late 1917, in the face of looming manpower shortages and cognizant of the operational effectiveness of his divisional structure, Currie insisted that Canadian divisions not be weakened when the British Army reorganized. He also opposed forming a fifth division and an army headquarters for he believed that the Canadian Corps had developed in response to the particular conditions of the Western Front and that it was the best vehicle for effecting and responding to tactical change. Experimentation continued until the end of the war. In May 1918, Currie formed an engineering brigade that, in his view, made one of the most significant contributions to victory, not least by freeing the infantry to focus on their own craft.

Innovation was a defining feature of the Corps' approach to operations and organization; innovators in these areas were rewarded with promotion and a degree of autonomy. Lieutenant-Colonel Andrew McNaughton's appointment as counter battery staff officer before Vimy Ridge was a prime example. In 1919, his protégé, Lieutenant-Colonel Harry Crerar, emphasized the "elasticity of methods and procedure" in McNaughton's headquarters, as experience suggested "that in six months time the changes in the general situation would be so great as to necessitate the whole procedure being revised and thought out afresh." Flexible staff and command arrangements were equally important. Crerar, schooled by Brooke and McNaughton, criticized too lavish an acceptance of doctrine as an end in itself rather than a means to an end.[59] The technological developments of the period also suggest that while the Corps' response was evolutionary it was in the midst of changes that were more dramatic.[60]

When Currie took command of the Canadian Corps in June 1917, it had already begun the process of transforming itself. The successes of the Canadian Corps through 1918 were costly, but it proved capable of sustained and successful operations.[61] Experience alone does not explain the progress of the Corps, for it can retard as well as develop an organization. While the Canadian Corps was still incomplete in April 1917, it had matured and begun to innovate. Perhaps more importantly, it had developed a climate where that innovation was rewarded. The assault against Vimy Ridge was a test of the new climate and a confidence builder. The success proved that the Canadian Corps was on the correct path.

Notes

1   For example, see Shane Schreiber, *Shock Army of the British Empire: The Canadian Corps in the Last 100 Days of the Great War* (St. Catharines: Vanwell, 2004); Ian M. Brown, "Not Glamorous, But Effective: The Canadian Corps and the Set-piece Attack, 1917-1918," The Journal of Military History vol 58 (July 1994), 421-44 and Bill Rawling, Surviving Trench Warfare: Technology and the Canadian Corps, 1914-1918 (Toronto: University of Toronto Press, 1992).
2   See, Pierre Berton, *Vimy* (Toronto: Anchor Canada, 2001).
3   General Sir Arthur Currie, "Introduction," in Colonel George G. Nasmith, *Canada's Sons and Great Britain in the World War* (Toronto: John C. Winston Limited, 1919), iv.
4   Ibid, ix.
5   Statistics drawn from "Appendix: A Statistical Profile of the CEF," Desmond Morton, *When Your Number's Up: The Canadian Soldier in the First World War* (Toronto: Random House, 1993), 277-79, 8-9, 66; Desmond Morton and J.L. Granatstein, *Marching to Armageddon: Canadians and the Great War, 1914-1919* (Toronto: Lester & Orpen Dennys, 1989), 32; David Englander, "Discipline and Morale in the British Army, 1917-1918," in J. Horne (ed), *State, Society, and Mobilization in Europe during the First World War* (Oxford: Oxford University Press, 1998), 125-43; Denis Winter, *Death's Men: Soldiers of the Great War* (London: Penguin, 1979), 30.
6   Barbara M. Wilson (ed), *Ontario and the First World War, 1914-1918* (Toronto: Champlain Society and the University of Toronto Press, 1977), xxi.
7   "Appendix: A Statistical Profile of the CEF," Morton, *When Your Number's Up*, 277-79; Statistics Canada, Historical Statistics of Canada Webpage, 11-516-X1E, Section A: Population and Migration, A297-326, "Country of birth of the other British-born and the foreign-born population, census dates, 1871 to 1971," www.statcan.ca/english/freepub/11-516-XIE/sectiona/sectiona.htm#Population, last accessed, 25 September 2006. The figure for British born includes immigrants from Newfoundland, then a crown colony.

8   Morton, *When Your Number's Up*, 277-79; A.M.J. Hyatt, "Canadian Generals in the First World War and the Popular View of Military Leadership," *Social History* vol 12, no 24 (November 1979), 418-30.

9   Wilson, xxix. For more on the variety of local responses, see Ian Miller, *Our Glory and Our Grief: Torontonians and the Great War* (Toronto: University of Toronto Press, 2002).

10   Cited in Robert Rutherdale, *Hometown Horizons: Local Responses to Canada's Great War* (Vancouver: University of British Columbia Press, 2004), 78-82.

11   G.W.L. Nicholson, *Canadian Expeditionary Force, 1914-1919: The Official History of the Canadian Army in the First World War* (Ottawa: Queen's Printer, 1962), Appendix C, Table 1: Appointments and Enlistments by Months, 1914-1920. Total enlistments for the war are 619,636; Morton, *When Your Number's Up*, 279; Richard Arthur Preston, *Canada's RMC: A History of the Royal Military College* (Toronto: University of Toronto Press, 1969), 220-21.

12   Jeffrey Williams, *First in the Field: Gault of the Patricias* (St. Catharines: Vanwell, 1995), 93-95; A.M.J. Hyatt, *General Sir Arthur Currie: A Military Biography* (Toronto: University of Toronto Press, 1987), 160.

13   Englander, 125-43; Peter Simkins, "The War Experience of a Typical Kitchener Divison: the 18th Division, 1914-1919," in Hugh Cecil and Peter H. Liddle (eds), *Facing Armageddon: The First World War Experience* (London, 1996), 308-09.

14   Hyatt, *Currie*, 160.

15   Rawling, 62-66.

16   Peter Simkins, *Kitchener's Army: The Raising of the New Armies, 1914-16* (Manchester: Manchester University Press, 1988), 40-45.

17   Nicholson, 201.

18   Desmond Morton, *A Peculiar Kind of Politics: Canada's Overseas Ministry in the First World War* (Toronto: University of Toronto Press, 1982), 41-65.

19   Allan D. English, *Understanding Military Culture: A Canadian Perspective* (Kingston: McGill-Queen's University Press, 2005), 5-17.

20   Ibid, 28-41.

21   Paul Johnson, "Doctrine is Not Enough: The Effect of Doctrine on the Behavior of Armies," *Parameters* (Autumn 2000), 30-39.

22   Nicholson, 178-79.

23   Tim Travers, *The Killing Ground: The British Army, the Western Front and the Emergence of Modern Warfare, 1900-1918* (London: Unwin Hyman, 1990), 18-27.

24   Denis Winter, *Haig's Command: A Reassessment* (London: Penguin Books, 1992), 131; Morton, When Your Number's Up, 132-34.

25   Nicholson, 38; Quoted in A.F. Duguid, *The Official History of the Canadian Forces in the Great War, 1914-19, Volume I* (Ottawa: King's Printer, 1938), 140.

26   Duguid, 140-42.

27   Winter, *Haig's Command*, 131; Morton, *When Your Numbers Up*, 31.

28   5 January 1915, 'World War One Diary,' vol 15, D268, H.D.G. Crerar Papers, Library and Archives of Canada [LAC].

29   See Daniel Dancocks, *Sir Arthur Currie: A Biography* (Toronto: Methuen, 1985). See also Tim Travers, "Currie and 1st Canadian Division at Second Ypres, April 1915: Controversy, Criticism and Official History," *Canadian Military History* vol 5, no 2 (Autumn 1996), 7-15.
30   Nicholson, 88-92.
31   Hyatt, Currie, 52.
32   C.P. Stacey, "The Staff Officer: A Footnote to Canadian History," Canadian Defence Quarterly vol 3 (1973/74), 46-47; Stephen Harris, *Canadian Brass: The Making of a Professional Army, 1860-1939* (Toronto: University of Toronto Press, 1988), 127-30.
33   Crerar to Lt-General Sir Otto Lund, 17 October 1952, vol 20, Crerar Papers; 3/A/1, vol 1, 60, Alan Brooke Papers, Liddell Hart Centre for Military Archives [LHCMA].
34   Brooke to Montgomery, 11 July 1944, BLM 1/101, Bernard Law Montgomery Papers, Imperial War Museum [IWM].
35   Hyatt, Currie, 51-52.
36   "The Development of Closer Relations Between the Military Forces of the Empire," 30 January 1926, vol 9, D219, Crerar Papers.
37   Tony Ashworth, *Trench Warfare, 1914-1918: The Live and Let Live System* (London: Pan Books, 2000), 172-75.
38   Hyatt, *Currie*, 59.
39   John Swettenham, *To Seize the Victory: The Canadian Corps in World War I* (Toronto: McGraw-Hill Ryerson, 1965), 128-31.
40   Tim Cook, "The Blind Leading the Blind: The Battle of the St. Eloi Craters," *Canadian Military History* vol 5, no 2 (Autumn 1996), 24-36.
41   Ronald Haycock, *Sam Hughes: The Public Career of a Controversial Canadian, 1885-1916* (Waterloo: Wilfrid Laurier University Press, 1986), 295-99.
42   Ibid, 299-300.
43   Jeffrey Williams, *Byng of Vimy: General and Governor General* (London: Leo Cooper, 1985), 118, 127-30.
44   Hyatt, *Currie*, 57-58; Williams, 120-27; Nicholson, 134-35.
45   Williams, 127.
46   Ibid, 130.
47   Morton, *A Peculiar Kind of Politics*, 100-03.
48   Nicholson, 203.
49   Patrick Brennan and Thomas Leppard, "How the Lessons were Learned: Senior Commanders and the Moulding of the Canadian Corps after the Somme," in Yves Tremblay (ed) *Canadian Military History Since the 17th Century* (Ottawa: Department of National Defence, 2001), 135-46.
50   Arthur Currie, "Notes on French Attacks North-East of Verdun in October and December 1916," January 1917, Currie Papers, Manuscript Group [MG] 30 E100, LAC.
51   G.W.L. Nicholson, *The Gunners of Canada: The History of the Royal Regiment of Canadian Artillery, Volume 1: 1534-1919* (Toronto, McClelland and Stewart, 1967), 242-44.

52 Jonathan M. House, *Towards Combined Arms Warfare: A Survey of Twentieth Century Tactics, Doctrine and Organization* (Fort Leavenworth: United States Army Command and General Staff College, 1984), 24-25.

53 Jack English, "Lessons from the Great War," *Canadian Military Journal* vol 4 (Summer 2003), 55-63.

54 "Notes on French Attacks..."

55 Paddy Griffith, *Battle Tactics of the Western Front: The British Army's Art of Attack, 1916-18* (New Haven: Yale University Press, 1994), 78-79.

56 J.A. English, "Great War 1914-18: The 'Riddle of the Trenches,'" *Canadian Defence Quarterly* vol 15 (Autumn 1985), 44-45.

57 Winter, *Haig's Command*, 146-47; *Death's Men*, 54.

58 Griffith, 74-80.

59 "Organization and Procedure of Counter-Battery Office, Jan 25, 1919," folder 7, file 10, vol 3922, RG 9, LAC.

60 Sheffield, *Forgotten Victory, The First World War: Myths and Realities* (London: Headline, 2002), 117-19.

61 Brown, 421-44.

3

Vimy Ridge
The Battlefield before the Canadians, 1914-1916

MICHAEL BOIRE

The battles fought in the Vimy sector of the Western Front by the French and Germans in 1914 and 1915, then by the British and Germans in 1916, contributed significantly to the Canadian Corps' successful assault. Two long years of ferocious attacks and counterattacks, supported by prolonged bombardments, transformed the terrain of Vimy Ridge. Ironically, these changes created both benefits as well as severe constraints for the Canadians when it came time to seize the Ridge on Easter Monday 1917.

Despite years of planning and preparation, neither the French Plan XVII, nor the German Schlieffen mobilization plans produced the resounding success their creators had predicted. In August 1914, both plans had set the conditions for battles of speed that were reminiscent of the Napoleonic tradition of the nineteenth century. Several key strategic decisions taken in September on both sides of the line launched the French, British and German armies in a succession of vicious engagements from the Aisne, northward across Picardy, through the Arras-Vimy sector, along the Douai Plain, ending finally at Ypres. Understanding how this 'race to the sea' unfolded remains crucial to appreciating the critical role the Vimy sector played for all three Allied armies in four bloody years of fighting.

At the first Battle of the Marne, in early September 1914, three French armies and the British Expeditionary Force stopped two German armies that were descending on Paris from the north. The victory cost the French 250,000 casualties, but it saved the French capital. As the Germans retired northward toward the Aisne, the general-in-chief of the French Army, Joseph Joffre, remained determined to eject the invaders from the occupied departments in eastern and northern France by enveloping their open western flank and making them the victims of their own doctrine of annihilation. Indeed, his intent did not waver until the war of movement ended at Ypres in November. Joffre thought that his enemy was on the run in mid-September, so he tried to retain the initiative by marshalling the combined offensive weight of his battered armies to attack on the left and right of the long front line that separated the combatants. This combination of alternating jabs was intended to so unbalance the Germans that they would not be able to oppose the French envelopment on their western flank. Unfortunately, Joffre's enemy would not cooperate.[1]

After driving the Germans from the Marne back to the Aisne River, Joffre launched his Sixth Army around and behind his opponent's open flank on 17 September. This initial effort failed, but only just, defeated by a quick redeployment of German reserves that were force-marched from General Alexander von Kluck's First Army behind the Aisne River. As the combatants continued to wheel and pivot around the flank, their frequent and bloody engagements pushed the front line northwestward out of the Aisne valley, across the Oise River and into the Picardy Plain where the open and gently rolling countryside encouraged swift maneuvre. The tempo of battle increased dramatically. Undeterred by his first failure to outflank the enemy, Joffre launched a second attempt with General Noel de Castelnau's Second Army, railing it across France from Lorraine to Amiens in record time and launching it against the exposed German right wing between the Oise and the Somme rivers. General Karl von Bulow railed and force-marched his German Second Army from Lorraine and Belgium to parry that threat. Though it was another near-run battle, Castelnau's attack failed to penetrate the lengthening German right wing. But this valiant French effort prevented the Germans' long envelopment from reaching the Channel and encircling Joffre's armies.

As September ended, the race to the sea entered a new phase as the Germans attempted a wide envelopment for a third time. Damaged rail lines had slowed Crown Prince Rupprecht's Sixth Army during its journey across France from the east. With the German infantry and cavalry corps pressing west through the long slopes of the Baupaume Gap into the Douai Plain, Joffre realized that the threat of envelopment still loomed. He was also determined that the French city of Lille must not fall into German hands and that the Belgians had to be helped, if only to keep their army in the fight. Above all, the Germans were to be denied the Channel ports, which provided vital supply arteries for the British forces and Arras, a strategic centre that controlled rail and road access with the Channel ports. To that end, Joffre sent General Louis de Maud'huy to organize the Tenth French Army at Arras.[2]

The mission of this new army would be, at best, to launch a wide envelopment across the Douai Plain into the German rear and, at worst, to limit German gains in France. Joffre remained convinced that the French still had the strength to outflank the German army, but the Tenth Army's General de Maud'huy was less certain. To give direction and energy to this vital new operation, Joffre named one of his trusted protégés, Ferdinand Foch, to oversee operations in northern France.[3]

The battle for Arras began on the evening of 30 September 1914 with a cavalry engagement southeast of the city. As German and French screens fought for the high ground dominating the southern approaches to Arras, the French commanders remained confident that they could still turn the German flank. Maud'huy used the first day of October to move his infantry into strong attack positions south and west of the town astride the roads to Cambrai and Bapaume and in Lens on the Douai Plain north of Arras. As the enemy's screen pushed towards Arras, the French cavalry broke contact and galloped back through the supporting infantry into a reserve position in the fields north of Arras near Vimy Ridge. The IV German Corps appeared from the mist at nightfall to attack the defenders of Arras. Nearly a week of relentless German frontal attacks, supported by heavy artillery, drove the Tenth Army's infantry divisions into a semi-circle around the outer suburbs of Arras. North of the town, the Germans pushed the French from the Douai Plain, up and over Vimy Ridge and onto the plateau to the west. By 9 October, the Battle of Arras was over. Maud'huy's Tenth Army had not turned the open German flank on the Douai Plain. Nor had it held the city of Lens, but it had saved Arras. Despite desperate local counterattacks by the French to retake lost terrain, the front line around Arras began to stabilize. As it happened, neither side had the resources to encircle the other before they reached the English Channel. With the end of the First Battle of Ypres in November, the front extended from the Channel to the Alps.[4]

Still the Vimy sector continued to be the focus of attention for Joffre. Capturing the ridge would permit the Allies to move into the Douai Plain towards Cambrai. This would return maneuvre to the war and create the conditions for the Anglo-French armies to throw the Germans back across the Meuse, cutting the main rail link to Flanders. Combining a thrust at Arras with one in Champagne would permit Joffre's armies to cut off the vast Noyon salient whose apex was just 60 kilometres from Paris. After three weeks of careful preparation, closely supervised by Foch and Joffre himself, on 17 December Maud'huy's Tenth Army launched its attack on Vimy Ridge. The main effort was with General Henri-Philippe Petain's XXXIII Corps, attacking along the Berthonval Ridge to seize Hill 145, where the Canadian memorial stands today. On Petain's northern flank, General Paul Maistre's XXI Corps was to seize Souchez and in the south General Desforges' X Corps was to clear the approaches and northeastern suburbs of Arras. Still short of ammunition for its field artillery and without enough heavy guns to give the attack much destructive power, the attack collapsed in the deep mud churned up by the winter rains.[5] The First Battle of Artois was over. The French Tenth Army lost nearly 30,000 soldiers, killed, wounded, missing and taken prisoner in its first attempt to capture Vimy Ridge.[6]

As 1915 began, the French and the British did not share a common strategic vision. The French wanted a concerted Allied offensive in the spring to push the Germans from France while keeping Russia in the war. In London considerable disagreement began that lasted throughout the conflict as to whether the main effort should be on the Western Front or in a peripheral theatre like the Eastern Mediterranean. Though Joffre wanted to follow the first offensive in the Artois with another soon after, negotiating an Anglo-French campaign in the northeast took up most of the spring of 1915. The February offensive in the Champagne went ahead, but without the corresponding attack in the Artois. The results were disastrous. Without sufficient Allied pressure on the western front, General Erich von Falkenhayn, who had replaced General Helmuth von Moltke as the German chief of the general staff the previous fall, continued to shift divisions to the eastern theatre. As spring became summer, it was clear that all sides had vastly underestimated the impact and costs of total war. The only consolation to be drawn from the butchery of 1914 and early 1915 was that armies were improving their methods for waging war.[7]

In early April 1915, Joffre named General Victor D'Urbal, who had commanded X Corps during the first Artois offensive, to replace Maud'huy in command of Tenth Army. D'Urbal's orders were to break the German line at Vimy Ridge. The Tenth Army had grown considerably by the spring of 1915, having tripled its infantry and nearly doubled its artillery to include a heavy artillery group. The tactical plan concentrated more destructive power on the ridge's German defences, but Joffre insisted on a frontal attack with a continuous rush from the French front line to the final objectives atop the ridge and if possible, into the Douai Plain. The frontages of attacking units were drastically decreased from what they had been during December's attack, when Petain's XXXIII Corps had fought alone on the ridge. For this second Artois offensive, three more infantry corps were squeezed into the ten-kilometre wide Vimy sector. Like Maud'huy before him, D'Urbal assigned Petain's corps the main effort to capture the heights of Vimy.[8]

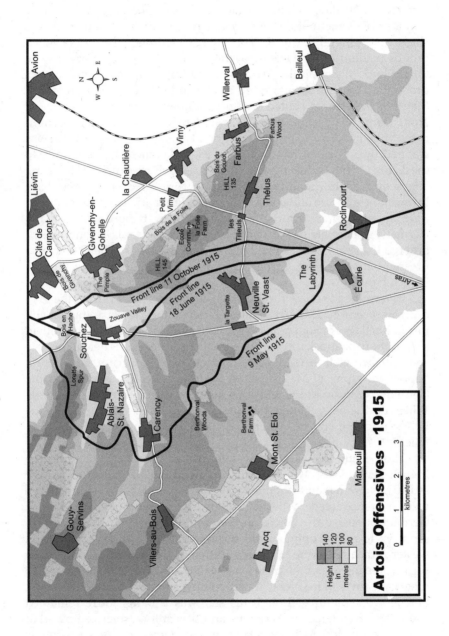

Artois Offensives - 1915

On 9 May 1915, after four days of preparatory bombardment, the Tenth Army attacked. Though none of the corps captured and held their objectives that day, Petain's came the closest. The Legionnaires and tirailleurs (riflemen) of the Moroccan Division attacking alongside the chasseurs alpins (alpine troops) of 77th Division went up Hill 145. Small groups made it to the far side of the ridge, but French reserves were too far back to exploit their success and rapid German counterattacks drove the French from the ridge by the end of the day. In the north, Maistre's XXI Corps stalled when it bumped into solid resistance at Notre Dame de Lorette, while General M. Balfourier's XX Corps fought to the outskirts of the German strongpoint at Neuville St. Vaast, but was stopped by a maze of fortified trenches, nicknamed the Labyrinth, to the south. On the British front to the north, the First Army's supporting attack on Aubers Ridge failed to gain surprise and was beaten back by machine gun fire and concentrated artillery barrages. Persuaded by Joffre to support his efforts on Vimy Ridge by tying down as many Germans as possible in the British area, Field Marshal Sir John French ordered General Douglas Haig to continue the attack. The French also pressed on; by 14 May, Carency and most of the Lorette Spur were in French hands.

Determined to break through the German defences during the 1915 campaign season, D'Urbal planned a new attack to seize the heavily fortified villages of Souchez and Neuville St. Vaast and the Labyrinth in preparation for attacks on the ridge itself. This time, units held in reserve were pushed well forward to be ready to exploit success anywhere it happened. From 20 May onward, D'Urbal's artillery hammered the Germans on Vimy Ridge while his infantry advanced metre by metre. When Foch finally halted the attack on 18 June, Souchez and the Labyrinth were still out of French reach, but Neuville St. Vaast had fallen.[9]

The Second Artois offensives had been bloodbaths, costing the French Tenth Army 103,000 casualties, with the Germans losing over 80,000 men from their front line units.[10] French advances on Vimy Ridge were overshadowed by the enormous achievement of the successful German offensive in Galicia on the eastern front. French politicians, sensitive to public opinion, did not understand that the eastern and western theatres were radically different battlefields. For French society, reeling under the increasing weight of war, Vimy Ridge was no longer merely a place name; it had become a metaphor for frustration, butchery and failure. Though his star was waning, Joffre remained committed to offensive operations and was still mesmerized by what Vimy represented to his strategic vision. However, two enormous failures had shifted his attention to the possibility that attacks on a broad front might rupture a large section of the German front line that could be exploited by reserves.[11]

Having received assurances from Sir John French that the British would launch a supporting attack against Loos, Joffre ordered planning on 12 July 1915 for an autumn offensive that would reduce the Noyon Salient by attacking its shoulders in the Artois and Champagne regions. This time, priority would be given to the Champagne operation, so the Tenth Army would not receive the same support it had in the spring. With fewer soldiers and a limited supply of heavy artillery ammunition, the infantry divisions' assaulting power, as well as their ability to hold a captured objective against German counterattacks, was considerably weakened. Given British assistance on the northern flank, Foch declared his confidence that the Tenth would capture the ridge. Behind closed doors, however, Foch made his operational priorities at Vimy quite clear. The point of the attack on the ridge was not necessarily to capture it. The greater priority lay in supporting the Champagne offensive and in keeping the British in the offensive until it was over. After a spring and summer of difficult inter-Allied negotiations, the British had finally pledged their support to the French autumn offensive. Keeping that support alive became far more important to the French high command than capturing Vimy Ridge. Joffre's dream that Vimy Ridge opened the doorway to a renewed war of movement on the Douai Plain had faded.[12]

Offensives in the Champagne and Artois regions began on 25 September 1915. Just after first light, French infantrymen burst from their trenches along the base of Vimy Ridge beneath an artillery bombardment that had been pounding German positions for a week. With gains being made all along the slopes of the ridge, a torrential downpour thirty minutes into the attack turned the ground into a morass of deep, clinging mud; the assaulting infantry slid, stumbled and fell. Though the Tenth Army's advance stalled, its soldiers' determination did not. The fortress of Souchez fell the next day and after four days of brutal attacks on the slopes of Hill 145, elements of III and XXXIII Corps emerged on the western summit of the ridge. In the north, the British First Army had overwhelmed the enemy at several points at Loos, breaking through the German first line trenches before being halted by strong positions in the second line. Both allies realized that a simultaneous Anglo-French attack would take them onto the Douai Plain. A joint attack was planned for 10 October, but errors in communication and coordination, shortages of infantry reinforcements and artillery ammunition and a strong German counterattack on 8 October disrupted Allied preparations. The French launched their last effort of the autumn offensive on 11 October, the British two days later, but neither advanced the Allied cause. The main effort in the Champagne region also came to a halt in mid-October.[13] This third and final attempt to capture Vimy Ridge cost the French Tenth Army over 50,000 soldiers. The German Army put its losses at 56,000, though the French insist that this number is closer to 125,000.[14]

Joffre's orders to suspend the third Artois offensive did not stop the fighting on Vimy Ridge. Through October and November, both sides raided by night and counterattacked by day. Soaked by the autumn rains and stuck in hip-deep mud, the French fought hard to hang on to their gains on the summit of the ridge. The Germans resisted fiercely, for they realized how precarious their hold was on that key terrain. To be thrown off the ridge was to lose control of the Douai Plain, which would in turn jeopardize the entire German position in northern France. Holding just the summit was not enough to safeguard it; the German defenders had to regain lost ground that dominated its approaches. Between 23 January and 21 February 1916, the Germans attacked along the Vimy front line. Starting at the Labyrinth and running north to the heights overlooking Givenchy, the Germans exploded mines beneath the French trenches and then followed up with local attacks. The French were ejected from over a kilometre of their front line trenches along the summit and northern slopes of the ridge, but their positions remained strong. General D'Urbal ordered the front line regiments of his Tenth Army to regain lost ground where possible, while he speeded counter-mining in sectors where German miners were active. But while these orders were being executed, the Germans were taking the strategic initiative elsewhere.

As Haig assumed command of the BEF in December 1915 and Joffre became commander-in-chief of the French armies, the British and French looked back on the campaign year of 1915 with little satisfaction. French offensives in the Artois and Champagne and their supporting British attacks at Aubers Ridge, Festubert and Loos had produced high casualties and no clear outcome. The Germans were still in France, seemingly stronger than ever. Poison gas had decimated British, Canadian and French troops at Ypres in April. The Russians were reeling in the East as the Italian and Austrian armies were deadlocked along the Isonzo. In the Balkans, the Franco-British expedition was held up at Salonika, unable to assist its Serbian ally. The British invasion at Gallipoli had failed and in Egypt, the Turks still threatened the Suez Canal.

On 14 February 1916, at an inter-Allied meeting to discuss joint operations in 1916, Haig reluctantly agreed to Joffre's request that the British take over the French Tenth Army's sector in the Artois. Just a week later, as the Germans launched their attack on the French at Verdun, Haig began to stretch the First Army southwards from Loos and the Third Army northwards from the suburbs southeast of Arras. Finding the trenches they inherited in a dilapidated condition, thousands of British soldiers dug day and night for several weeks. On the other side of no-man's-land, the Germans followed the British lead and improved their own positions. Both sides then put down their shovels and resumed hostilities.[15]

The British also discovered that the Germans were then winning the war beneath Vimy Ridge. To fight back, ten Royal Engineer tunnelling companies took up the struggle in the spring and summer of 1916. In the Arras and Vimy sector, the British exploded over 100 large mines, causing heavy casualties within the German defences. Concerned that the increasingly successful British mining effort would corrode German morale and make the ridge untenable, the commander of IX Reserve Corps ordered an attack down the ridge's western slopes to seize the British tunnel entrances. On 21 May, the Germans pushed a brigade of the British 47th Division back to the Zouave Valley at the base of the western slopes of the ridge. Though the British immediately prepared a full-scale counterattack to regain their lost positions, Haig cancelled it. With the Somme offensive slated for the following month, he preferred not to waste lives and ammunition on a secondary effort. Meanwhile, the Germans withdrew to a new position halfway up the slope on top of the contested tunnel entrances. Throughout the summer and fall of 1916, both sides sniped, raided and shelled each other mercilessly. Vimy Ridge earned a reputation as the "windy corner of the Western Front."[16]

By the time the Canadian Corps marched from the Somme to relieve IV British Corps at Vimy in October 1916, this ground had been fought over many times, claiming over 300,000 French, British and German casualties. As the Corps began preparing for operations in this area, its staff began to consider the legacy of two years of war in the Vimy sector. What constraints and benefits did the Canadian Corps inherit from the armies that had already fought at Vimy? The first was the poor state of the battlefield's infrastructure. Two years of war had transformed the sector into a lunarscape of craters, shell holes and wreckage. The road and track network had disappeared under the mud and had to be rebuilt, then supplemented with tramways and light railways to assure a steady supply of ammunition forward and an uninterrupted evacuation of casualties rearward. Drinking water was in short supply because the natural wells had long been plugged by mud or collapsed by shellfire. Water for the entire Corps, men and horses, had to be shipped into the Vimy sector. Though the engineers of the First British Army had started to repair all the damage during the summer of 1916, Canadian engineers met all these challenges and more during the winter of 1916-1917.

The second limitation was the asymmetric nature of the Vimy battlefield. The Tenth French Army's battles had moved the front line to the base of Hill 145 on the northern and highest section of the Ridge. In the south, where the slopes were gentler, the maze of trenches in the Labyrinth had blocked all French attacks, keeping the front line well away from the southern end of the ridge. Because the Canadian Corps' objectives were either right on or just beyond the summit, each assaulting division faced a different distance to cross during the assault. In effect, the Corps' plan had to answer the challenge of harmonizing four distinct tactical operations.

The third impediment came from the unintended results of British mining operations conducted under the ridge during the summer of 1916. When the Germans seized the mining tunnels near the summit of Hill 145 during the attack of 21 May, they quickly transformed them into deep dugouts for the infantry. On 9 April 1917, the Germans sheltered there survived the bombardment to wreak havoc among the advancing Canadian battalions. This caused the success of the assault to hang in the balance for most of that day as the brigades of the 4th Division fought their way to the summit of Hill 145.

The long French fight for Vimy Ridge also created benefits for the Canadian Corps. During the three Artois offensives the French had squeezed the Germans into a small yet densely fortified perimeter on Hill 145 and its adjacent defences. Though a deep and well-protected position, it was an ideal target for the heavy artillery because so many defenders had been packed into a reduced area. The reverse could be said of the southern part of the ridge, where the long open spaces between the front line and the Canadian Corps' objectives gave the German defenders the space to construct numerous mutually supporting trench systems.

Finally, the Canadian assault owed a great deal to the French determination to capture the key terrain that dominated the approaches to the ridge. It is difficult to imagine, even with the overwhelming artillery support assigned to the Canadian Corps on Easter Monday 1917, how an assault that included the Notre Dame de Lorette spur, the fortified villages of Souchez and Neuville St. Vaast and the Labyrinth could have succeeded. French blood and bravery were fundamental ingredients of the Canadian success at Vimy Ridge. It was an Allied victory, in the best sense.

Notes

1   Ministère de la Guerre, État-Major de la Armée, Service Historique, *Les Armées Françaises dans la Grande Guerre* (Paris: Imprimerie Nationale, 1933) [hereafter AFGG], Tome I, Vol 4, ii-v; Robert A. Doughty, *Pyrrhic Victory: French Strategy and Operations in the Great War* (Cambridge, Mass: Belknap Press, 2005), 70-72.

2   AFGG, Tome II, Vol 2, 175-79.

3   AFGG, Tome I, Vol 4, iv-v.

4   Robert T. Foley, *German Strategy and the Path to Verdun: Erich von Falkenhayn and the Development of Attrition, 1870-1916* (Cambridge: Cambridge University Press, 2005), 99-101; AFGG, Tome I, Vol 4, 178-92; Doughty, 95-100.

5   Doughty, 128; AFGG, Tome II, Vol 2, 145-48.

6   AFFG, Tome I, 554.

7   Doughty, 136-52.

8   AFGG, Tome II, Vol 2, 158-62; Doughty, 159.

9   Doughty, 165.

10   AFGG Tome III, 100-01.

11   Doughty, 165-68.

12   Ibid, 196.

13   Ibid, 195-01.

14   AFGG Tome III, 540-42.

15   J.E. Edmonds, *Official History of the Great War, Military Operations, France and Belgium, 1916* (London: Macmillan, 1932), 210-16.

16   Ibid, 210-21.

PART II

The Battle for Vimy Ridge, 9-12 April 1917

4

"Old Wine in New Bottles"

A Comparison of British and Canadian
Preparations for the Battle of Arras

MARK OSBORNE HUMPHRIES

By 1917, every army commander understood that careful
preparations were required if there was to be any hope of a successful
offensive on the Western Front. Since the autumn of 1914, generals
on both sides had been exasperated by tactical deadlock. With two
undulating lines of parallel trenches running from the Swiss border
to the Channel Coast, neither side had room to manoeuvre. In April
1915, the Germans had tried a new weapon, asphyxiating gas, to break
the stalemate but to no avail. The British and French launched limited
frontal attacks hoping for a local breakthrough, but again with few
positive results.

In 1916, the armies of the Allies and Central Powers tried to smash
their way through the deadlock using brute force. In February, the
German Army launched a massive attack at Verdun. In front of the
German onslaught, the French fell back, losing several key positions.
For a time, it looked as if the French might break entirely under the
weight of the German advance. In part to take the pressure off the
French, the British responded with their own great offensive in the
Somme river valley.

On 1 July 1916, a sustained week-long barrage of the enemy's
position by nearly 500 heavy guns ended and the British infantry went
over the top. While the gunfire devastated the landscape, the 1.5 million
shells expended proved largely ineffective against an enemy that had
sought cover in deep dugouts. When the barrage ended, the Germans
emerged in time to man their machine guns and rifles and inflict 57,470
British casualties on the first day of the offensive alone.

Over the next four months, the Somme offensive became a battle
of attrition. When the onset of winter ended offensive operations in
November, no clear winner had emerged. While General Douglas

Haig claimed that his battle of attrition was a success, there had been no breakthrough and British generals again began to question their tactics.

At the Somme, the artillery bombardment before the advance was intended to pulverize the German positions. The British then used linear infantry tactics to cross no-man's-land: each assault was divided into waves of horizontal lines of soldiers with bayonets fixed. These waves moved towards the enemy trenches simultaneously across the whole front in the hope that a large portion of the enemy's position could be overrun at the same time. The use of multiple waves and multiple lines was supposed to negate the effect of local setbacks and failures in the belief that the enemy would simply be overwhelmed by the sheer weight of the offensive.

Beginning in the late autumn of 1916, the British and the Canadians, as part of the British Expeditionary Force (BEF), began to re-examine their art of attack. The historiography has generally depicted December 1916 to April 1917 as a watershed in Great War infantry tactics during which outdated ideas gave way to innovation.[1] For example, Paddy Griffith suggests that this period "may be seen as a vital milestone in tactics, marking a changeover from the Victorian era of riflemen in lines to the twentieth-century era of flexible small groups built around a variety of high-firepower weapons."[2] Canadian historians have placed the Canadian Corps and its officers at the forefront of this "tactical revolution."[3] Pierre Berton argued that, "unlike most British senior officers, Byng [the commander of the Canadian Corps] insisted on treating his troops as adults. The old assault machine in which every soldier was an automaton, blindly slogging forward without any clear idea of the battle plan, was about to be scrapped."[4] Likewise, Jeffery Williams suggests that in the winter of 1916-1917, "the assault machine was scrapped [by the Canadians]. Henceforth platoon commanders and their NCOs would be given a chance to use their brains instead of only their courage."[5] What emerges from the historiography is a coming of age narrative in which the soldiers of the young nation of Canada surpass the conservative generals of the old country.

This idea that the Canadian Corps began to come into its own at Vimy Ridge has taken hold in the popular memory and has even been extended to suggest that Canada's national identity was born at Vimy Ridge. This interpretation, while spiritually satisfying, is problematic because it rests on the premise that the paths of the Canadian Corps and the British Army diverged in the months before Vimy Ridge. During the Great War, however, the Canadian Corps was but one part of the BEF. Orders and directives issued from British General Headquarters (GHQ) and British First Army (in which the Canadian Corps served during the winter of 1916-1917) carried as much weight in the Canadian Corps as in other British units.

In order to understand the Canadian preparations for the Battle of Vimy Ridge, we must reassess the experiences of the Canadian Corps and its place in the BEF. Such an examination suggests that Canadian preparations for the battle were not unique. During the tactical debates of the winter of 1916-1917, while Canadian officers presented their own solutions to the riddle of the trenches, GHQ, the final arbiter in the process, ultimately chose not to abandon linear tactics. Canadian and British units thus adopted a similarly linear attack doctrine that formed the basis of British and Canadian training before the Battle of Arras began on 9 April 1917.

The search to solve the riddle of the trenches began in late 1916 when British generals began to examine the methods used by the French at Verdun. While Verdun began as a German advance, it ended with a remarkable series of French counterattacks, led by the French General Robert Nivelle, which recaptured much of the lost ground. Nivelle's tactics relied on a creeping artillery barrage, behind which the infantry attacked in waves of small groups, rather than lines of soldiers. British staff officers were interested in the potential of Nivelle's tactics and accordingly groups of observers were dispatched to report on the "new" French tactics.

On 5 January 1917 the commander of 1st Canadian Division Major-General Arthur Currie, was appointed with other British officers of First Army to visit the French Second Army where it was hoped they would learn from the French experience at Verdun. Upon his return, Currie submitted a report to General Julian Byng on 23 January 1917, titled "Notes on French Attacks North-East of Verdun in October and December, 1916." The report highlighted many of the lessons he felt the Canadian Corps could learn from the French and especially emphasized the importance of an extensive reconnaissance of the battlefield by the attacking infantry and the use of obvious features of the ground as objectives (rather than arbitrary lines on a map). Currie also stressed the importance of training the assaulting infantry for the specific tasks they would have to perform and pointed out that the French paid "special attention...to the best way of tactically employing the latest weapons, namely rifle grenades, automatic rifles, bombs, 37 mm guns, etc."[6]

For Currie, however, the most important lesson was that French tactics were rooted in an elastic doctrine that fostered innovation and initiative on the part of junior officers and non-commissioned officers (NCOs). Currie wrote:

the French do not lay down any rules as to the number of waves in which the attack should be made and, in my mind, rightly so. There are so many factors which govern this; namely the resistance you expect to encounter, the depth of your attack, hostile artillery fire...In the matter of the number of waves, we must guard against becoming hide-bound or pedantic. I have seen it laid down that a certain division always attacks successfully in eight waves, thereby intimating that all attacks should be made in like manner. It is pernicious to lay down such a doctrine.[7]

Currie's Verdun report was an argument against the use of linear tactics and instead suggested that command and control be handed down to the commander of the platoon, a group of about forty soldiers. While today this idea seems self-evident, in 1917 it was somewhat revolutionary. During the war, many British professional soldiers were apprehensive about the fighting potential of the non-professional, citizen-soldiers recruited for the BEF and felt that strict discipline was the only way to use the inexperienced common man on the battlefield.[8] Currie believed that by 1917 many of these junior officers and NCOs, if given the chance, could direct their own portion of an attack more effectively than a company or battalion commander who could not be everywhere on the battlefield at once. Currie wanted to see the platoon become a truly self-reliant unit, capable of deploying a flexible doctrine of the attack.[9]

Currie recognized that many of his ideas had deep roots. He wrote: "it may be pointed out that there is nothing new in this system of training. Before the war we endeavoured to make the platoon a self-reliant and self-sufficient unit of battle...It is necessary for us to revise our own training on the old lines."[10] Indeed, Currie understood that the prewar manuals, which were designed to train professional soldiers, had preached a far more decentralized, elastic doctrine than had been seen in the first two years of the war.[11] He continued: "Therefore, get back to the pre-war self-sufficient, self-reliant platoon; remember that now this self-sufficiency requires a number of weapons instead of the two (the rifle and bayonet) of pre-war days and the need for the efficient co-ordination of all of them."[12] Currie believed that the flexibility of prewar doctrine was lost when the platoon ceased to be a self-reliant unit. He believed that to regain tactical elasticity, the platoon needed to be reorganized.[13]

During the First World War, British and Canadian battalions were divided into four companies of four platoons, each comprising four sections of approximately ten men. Before the war, the soldiers in an infantry battalion carried only the rifle and bayonet. The stalemate on the battlefields of the Great War brought innovations in weaponry, however, and as new weapons like the Lewis gun (an automatic rifle), Stokes mortar, Mills bomb (grenade) and rifle grenade became available, the number of men carrying each of these weapons increased.[14] Before 1917, these specialists were segregated into distinct sections, separate from the platoon and under the direct command of battalion and company commanders; this not only reduced the manpower of the platoon, but it centralized control of fire support in the officer responsible for deploying these specialist sections.[15] In other words, the new weapons were not under control of the often green platoon commander at the sharp end, but under the direction of more senior officers farther to the rear. Even before Currie returned from Verdun, the Canadian Corps' general staff had identified this as a problem.

On 27 December 1916, the Brigadier-General, General Staff (BGGS) of the Canadian Corps, Percy "P. de B." Radcliffe, pointed out that the separation of the specialists from the platoon, "has resulted in reducing the Platoon to a mere skeleton, consisting of 15 or 20 riflemen only, without the complement of other weapons necessary to enable it to develop its full power." Foreshadowing the findings of Currie's report, Radcliffe went on:

> Recent experience has proved that the present organization and training of our infantry have not succeeded in developing the maximum offensive power bestowed by the weapons with which it is now armed. One reason for this failure appears to be the want of combination in the employment of these weapons, viz, the rifle, the bayonet, the Lewis gun, the bomb and the rifle grenade...The Platoon Commander is...in most cases, the only man who can personally influence the local situation. In fact, it is not too much to say that this is the Platoon Commander's war.[16]

Radcliffe wanted to reincorporate the specialists into the platoon and place them under the direct command of the platoon commander. He pointed out that the platoon commander was usually the only one capable of assessing the local situation on the battlefield and it thus made sense to place the most tools at *his* disposal rather than in the hands of a company or battalion commander. This proposed reorganization complemented Currie's recommendations for increased tactical flexibility, and in early January 1917, under Byng's direction, the Canadian Corps began to reorganize the infantry platoon into four specialized sections: one each of riflemen, Lewis gunners, rifle grenadiers and bombers.[17] This not only made the platoon a more self-reliant unit, but it also devolved the command of these weapons to the platoon commander, making him a more important officer on the battlefield.

The British, however, had to consider more than just tactics, for they were then facing a manpower crisis.[18] As Douglas Haig, the commander-in-chief of the British Expeditionary Force confided to his diary in November 1916, "my principle needs were *men*. [emphasis in original] We were still 90,000 below War Establishment [and] 113,000 were required as soon as possible."[19] After the casualties of the Somme there were not enough soldiers to fill the ranks. To compound the problem, the quality of new recruits was questionable. Before the Great War, the British Army had been a small but highly professional regular force. Unlike the French or the Germans, British civilians received no pre-war compulsory military training. Thus, when the "old contemptibles" of the prewar army perished in the battles of 1914, the British had only eager but untrained citizens with which to fill their ranks. Professional British generals were sceptical of the quality of the training that new soldiers received and were wary of delegating control to inexperienced officers and NCOs.[20] Unlike the Canadians, British GHQ thus set out to solve a two-fold problem: how to economize manpower while using tactics that could be easily understood and taught during the limited time available for training.

The British first examined platoon organization, not from a tactical but rather a logistical point of view.[21] A GHQ and First Army subcommittee on manpower summarized the British view: "with existing numbers it was impossible...to keep up 16 fighting platoons in a battalion." The committee discussed various solutions aimed at economizing manpower within the battalion, including reducing the number of companies in a battalion to three, or the number of platoons in a company to three. The committee recommended that control of the specialists be devolved from the purview of the battalion commanders to the platoons, thereby refilling the dwindling ranks with the specialists.[22]

The British reorganization mirrored Radcliffe's suggestions, but for a different purpose that became significant when the British later defined how the new platoon was to fight. Like the Canadians, the British were inspired by the French experience at Verdun. An unnamed general staff officer (GSO) from First Army GHQ, who visited the French Seventh Army in January of 1917, drew different conclusions than Currie. While he agreed that the British could learn much from French battle preparations and training methods, he disagreed as to the tactical lessons that could be drawn from Verdun. For him, it was the standardization of French infantry doctrine and the use of a "normal formation of the attack" that was important. He wrote: "The normal [French] formation of a battalion, company or platoon in the attack on trenches is laid down. These formations need only slight modification to meet varying conditions."[23] Unlike Currie, the British GSO saw standardization as a key ingredient in the French success. He summarized: "the most striking features of the French system of training are: 1) the standardization and continuity of the training carried out at the various centres and depots, 2) the laying down of a definite doctrine as to the conduct of the attack by the smaller units, 3) the general military knowledge and initiative of all ranks."[24] Such a standardized doctrine was attractive to the British because it promised to reduce combat to a series of rules in which citizen-soldiers could be quickly trained. This emphasis on standardization also supported the continued use of linear tactics, a tactical concept that still held much currency within British GHQ.[25]

General Launcelot Kiggell, Haig's chief of staff, was a lifelong, dogmatic supporter of linear tactics. In the course of a discussion on the future of warfare at the general staff conference in 1911, Kiggell "intervened to say that he envisioned a battlefield with lines of infantry pressing forward, bayonets fixed, to close with the enemy."[26] The bayonet epitomized Kiggell's idea of warfare: the strength of the bayonet charge was based on courage and guts and masses of infantry. In many ways, this conceptualization of the battlefield became a self-fulfilling prophesy. Beginning in May 1916, Kiggell authored several tactical bulletins that emphasized these linear tactics. In his directives, Kiggell drove home the point that the key to victory was precision and standardization. It is thus hardly surprising that when the tactics of 1916 failed to achieve significant results, Kiggell set out to modify them within a framework that he had supported for so many years.[27]

On 14 February 1917, Kiggell moved to standardize both the new platoon organization and infantry tactics within the BEF. His directive, entitled "OB/1919/T" was sent to all British and Empire divisions and issued down to the battalion and company levels.[28] Kiggell gave specific orders as to how infantry were to train for the attack. It read in part:

> The normal formation described below is one which has frequently been employed with success in recent fighting; it is simple and adaptable to the varying conditions of trench-to-trench attack. It should also prove suitable in most instances of open warfare. So far as the Platoon is concerned, the formation described should be applicable to most circumstances and it should seldom be necessary to depart therefrom, while as regards the Battalion it aims at elasticity…Each platoon will therefore normally be disposed in two lines, bombers and riflemen in the front line, rifle grenadiers and the Lewis guns in the second line. Further, it has been found convenient as a general rule for the

Company to be formed up on a two platoon frontage. The Platoon, therefore, should normally be formed in two lines, constituting one wave, and the company in two waves…As regards extensions between men, these should usually be from 4 to 5 yards. The distance between lines should be from 15 to 35 yards and that between waves from 50 to 100 yards.[29]

In effect, Kiggell adapted to the platoon the method of linear attack that had been used at the battalion level on the Somme. Instead of a battalion advancing in a uniform series of lines organized by companies, the individual platoons were to attack in a series of uniform lines organized by sections [see figure 1]. The platoons would still be lined up horizontally and, as a battalion, would still attack shoulder to shoulder [see figure 2]. As Kiggell pointed out, the purpose of the new formation was to provide battalion commanders, not platoon commanders, with more flexibility. It would appear that Kiggell believed that this standardization of tactics would make battalion commanders more trusting of their potentially inexperienced subordinates.

A subsequent manual, SS 143, *Instructions for the Training of Platoons for Offensive Action,* issued a few days after OB 1919/T discussed how the new formations were to be used on the battlefield. Kiggell explained the strength of the new doctrine:

[A] normal formation for the attack, of which the Platoon is the Unit, has been laid down. The adoption of a normal formation for the attack has been necessitated partly by the shortness of the time which is available for training, and partly by the lack of experience among subordinate commanders.[30]

For Kiggell, the use of a standard formation of attack compensated for the lack of experience and training among the new citizen-soldiers because the tactical concepts it was based on were easy to understand.

According to SS 143, the platoon was to close with the enemy in the "normal formation," and during the attack, the first objective of the platoon was to "push on to the objective at all costs and get in with the bayonet."[31] These tactics were based on the premise that an attack made in waves with men dispersed in a line at set distances, with bayonets fixed, would succeed most of the time. Only when these primary tactics broke down, as when the advance was held up by an enemy machine gun, was the platoon commander to deviate from the "normal formation."[32]

It was only in such a scenario that the platoon truly became an "army in miniature." According to Kiggell's directives, when the advance was held up or stalled the platoon commander was to employ the weapons at his disposal as he saw fit, but this freedom was intended as a last resort and was not to be a primary course of action.[33] In the final analysis, Kiggell defined the ultimate objective of the infantry as a charge made with the bayonet. If all went according to plan (and the new doctrine) the infantry would make its charge in standard linear formation. In this way, Kiggell's new doctrine was not a radical departure from past practice and was instead received by some British officers as a limited refinement of the type of linear tactics they had used on the Somme. For example, on 1 March 1917, the war diarist for the 1st Battalion, East Surrey Regiment, mused:

> In adopting this new organization the British are following the French example. The great success of the latter in their Verdun offensive has evidently impressed our staff and encouraged it to make these changes. Nevertheless, it is doubtful whether the decision to make the platoon the complete fighting unit, rather than the company or battalion really affects the issue in operations on a large scale such as those on the Somme. It will always be the work of the man with the rifle and bayonet to assault a position, and of the Specialist to follow, the Lewis Gunner to resist counter-attack and support further advance, the bomber to mop up etc.[34]

For the 1st East Surrey's war diarist, the new doctrine only retooled existing tactics which had little impact on the way that his battalion would fight; he also certainly did not view the lessons of Verdun as revolutionary.

This is perhaps because Verdun can be viewed as a tabula rasa on to which both Canadians and British officers projected their own conceptions of warfare. As Currie's biographer A.M.J. Hyatt reminds us, Currie used his report to put forward his own ideas. Although written as such, it was not a literal report on French tactics.[35] Likewise, it would appear that the anonymous First Army general staff officer saw in the French experience evidence of his own conceptualization of warfare, an understanding of the battlefield that happened to resemble closely the dominant view at British GHQ. While Currie had rejected this "cookie cutter" view of the battlefield, Kiggell's standardized, linear doctrine took precedence over Currie's ideas and it was in this doctrine that both the Canadians and British trained in the months leading to 9 April 1917.

The time and space allotted for training during the winter of 1916-17 was different in each division and was governed by both location and situation. Throughout the winter, Canadian and British brigades and divisions rotated in and out of the front line trenches. Generally activities were scheduled whenever a unit was out of the line for several days at a time. It would appear that between January and April 1917, Canadian and British battalions on average spent about two days out of five conducting training activities of one form or another.[36]

A typical training syllabus from January 1917 is provided by the 15th Canadian Battalion:

> 0800-0830 Physical Training
> 0830-0930 Extended Order Drill
> 0930-1015 Bayonet Fighting
> 1015-1030 Lectures
> 1030-1130 Rifle Exercises
> 1130-1200 Musketry[37]

These activities were designed to keep the basic skills of the individual infantryman sharp. Physical training ensured (in theory) a uniform level of fitness. Extended order drill taught soldiers the new formations. Bayonet fighting reminded the men of how the assault was to be carried home. Lectures focussed on military law, hygiene and other mundane topics. Rifle exercises encouraged discipline and adherence to orders, while musketry allowed for practice in marksmanship.

Other battalions followed similar schedules. On 14 January 1917, the 19th Battalion began one hour of physical drill at 0830 hours and then practiced saluting from 0930 until 1000 hours. This was followed by one hour of section drill, a half hour of rifle exercises and an hour of platoon drill. After a ninety-minute lunch break, the battalion reconvened for a half hour of gas drill from 1400 to 1430 hours, bayonet fighting from 1430 to 1530 hours and company drill from 1530 to 1600 hours. The day finished with two hours of lectures on a variety of topics.[38]

The most common activities during the winter of 1917 were geared toward the training of individual soldiers at the platoon or company levels. In the 2nd Battalion between 1 January 1917 and 8 April, thirty percent of all training consisted of squad or platoon drill, sixteen percent of physical drill and nine percent of bombing practice.[39] Likewise, in the 18th Battalion, twenty-four percent of the training time was devoted to company or platoon drill, while physical training accounted for sixteen percent and bayonet fighting eleven percent.[40] In the 22nd Battalion, the five most common training activities were gas drill, squad drill, platoon drill, lectures and physical training.[41]

The British battalions of First Army adhered to similar training programs. The 1st Battalion, Royal Fusiliers practiced parade drills, route marches and musketry, sometimes while wearing gas masks.[42] They also carried out several exercises designed to teach soldiers to contact airplanes using coloured panels and flares.[43] The 8th Battalion, East Kent Regiment (The Buffs) practiced physical drill, bayonet fighting and bombing,[44] while the 1st Battalion, King's Royal Rifle Corps, concentrated on specialist training.[45]

These types of training activities served several purposes. They taught individual soldiers to respond to orders and to act as a group and at the same time, imparted skills like bayonet fighting that soldiers needed in combat. Even parade ground drills taught the basics of manoeuvring on the battlefield in Kiggell's new formations. By early April 1917, at least half of every training day was spent on bayonet fighting, drill and similar activities. If a battalion was unsure of how long it had to train, or if facilities were unavailable, these types of activities were all that could be reasonably accomplished. During extended periods out of the line, however, it was possible to prepare a system of training intended to last several weeks.

In the third week of January, the 2nd Canadian Division moved out of the line for three weeks' training.[46] The first six days were devoted to individual training as described above. The second and third weeks of training continued such exercises in the mornings, followed by collective training in the afternoon that involved tactical schemes at the platoon level conducted over fields and practice trenches. On 16 January 1917, the 10th Battalion carried out a tactical exercise in which the battalion's commanding officer suggested that an attack be made against prepared enemy machine gun positions and strong points without artillery support. [47] The training order assigned objectives to each company and suggested the general direction for the advance, leaving much of the decision-making to the platoon commanders on the ground. Given the lack of even imagined artillery support, this was not intended to be a realistic operation. It did, however, provide both the men and the platoon commanders with the opportunity to cross ground in a trench-to-trench attack using Kiggell's formations.[48]

Realistic practice attacks also taught the proper use of the new formations in battle. On 15 February the 10th Battalion carried out a second, more realistic tactical exercise. The operational order called for the four companies to be arranged in four waves, each composed of two lines. The waves were to advance on the "enemy" trench behind an imagined barrage, with 45 metres between each wave. The first two waves were to take the first objective, a line of trenches and the third and fourth waves were to take the second objective. The practice attack demonstrated the ideal attack described by Kiggell, absent of any difficulties such as enemy strong points or machine gun nests. The principle taught by the exercise was that linear attacks were often successful.[49]

The British, too, practiced the use of Kiggell's formations in battle. The 1st Battalion of the East Surrey Regiment began an intensive, sixteen-day program of training when it left the front line on 20 March. The program started with physical drill, bayonet fighting, musketry, lectures and bombing but soon moved on to more complex exercises which, as the battalion's war diarist recorded, were designed to familiarize all ranks with "organization in the new formations [as] laid down in OB 1919/T."[50] The war diary records that these exercises were specifically based on Plate A of Kiggell's February directive (Figure 1)[51] and later in the month, the battalion carried out practice attacks at the company and battalion levels, similar to those conducted by Canadian units, to instruct soldiers in how to use the formations in battle.[52]

Throughout the winter British and Canadian soldiers behind the lines trained in specialist courses that lasted several days. Victor Wheeler of the 50th Battalion remembered:

> With a few other signallers, I was ordered to signal school to take special courses in one or more branches of telegraphy, trench-wireless, and other types of signalling. There, we also studied refined uses and operation of the Fullerphone, Popham panels, Power-Buzzer-Amplifier, Lucas Lamp, visual flag work, heliograph uses and interpretation of Codes.[53]

Similar courses were run for Lewis gunners, machine gunners, runners, rifle grenadiers and Stokes mortar teams. Yet Kiggell's directives still placed great weight on the bayonet as a primary weapon of the infantry. This lesson was driven home with frequent bayonet practice and a special individual assault practice designed to remind all soldiers that they were riflemen first. The instructions sent out from British HQ warned that "every man was to be put through it." They read in part:

> 1.   The purpose of this practice is to ensure that every soldier realizes that he must be trained to use his three weapons equally well, i.e. rifle, bomb and bayonet.

> 2.   Every recruit should be put through this practice on arriving in France, if not before, and every soldier again after having specialized in his section weapon, in order to counteract the tendency to think that he is merely a specialist in his section weapon.[54]

The actual exercise consisted of a lone individual soldier running an obstacle course to capture and consolidate an enemy trench using only a rifle, bombs and the bayonet. While the purpose of the exercise was to refresh basic skills in an interesting way, it also made the point that every soldier was a rifleman with a bayonet.

At the beginning of March, each formation in the BEF began to prepare for its specific role in the Arras offensive. When on 5 March 1917, Byng submitted the Canadian Corps' scheme of operations for its part in the operation to First Army, the focus of training shifted to preparing for the assault on Vimy Ridge.[55] The plan involved a massive, simultaneous advance by all four Canadian divisions, supported by the 51st Highland Division to the south and 24th Division to the north, to a successive series of objectives labelled from first to last as the black, red, blue and brown lines. Under a precisely timed artillery barrage, each battalion, company and platoon was responsible for the capture of specific objectives before the next phase of the advance was to begin. Halfway through the attack, fresh troops were to pass through the formations of tired soldiers to give the advance new impetus. Timing, discipline and preparation were crucial.

By 1917, the lead-up to a major engagement had become a familiar process. British historian Paddy Griffith explains:

> Before the end of 1915, the preparation for a deliberate attack had been reduced to a routine that was designed to leave as little as possible to chance. The terrain would be reconnoitred both visually and from maps and air photos. A small-scale model of it would be constructed for briefing, and then a life size replica would be taped out as a training area behind the lines. Everyone would be fully drilled in their roles during each of the phases — assembly, assault, mopping up and consolidation.[56]

To prepare for the northernmost part of the Arras offensive, this is the model that the Canadian Corps and British First Army set out to emulate.

More than 40,000 maps were disseminated with the intention that all soldiers were to become familiar with their battalion's specific task.[57] Air photographs were also circulated to the lower ranks for the same purpose. Air reconnaissance, nightly patrols by the infantry and raids helped form as complete a picture of the battlefield as possible.[58] A 1/10,000 scale model of the British and Canadian battlefield was prepared at First Army headquarters that, according to one British officer, gave "a fair, though exaggerated, idea of the slope of the ground, and the commanding position of the ridge."[59] British and Canadian officers and NCOs reviewed this model to familiarize themselves with the ground that they were to cover in the attack.

Behind the lines, reconnaissance was also used to construct training areas where replicas of each British and Canadian battalion's objectives were constructed on taped courses. D.E. Macintyre described the process for the 9th Canadian Infantry Brigade in his memoirs:

> A large open field with a gentle slope had been requisitioned for use as a training ground. On this had been staked out with tape, a replica of the trenches we were to capture. Over these tapes we put the men again and again, first by platoons and then by increasing numbers, until the day came when the entire brigade carried out the exercise together, one battalion following another in line, everyone walking, the officers timing the advance by their watches and the men with their rifles at the high port, bayonets fixed, ready to shoot or lunge. At each taped barrage line, all would halt and wait a few minutes until the barrage lifted to the next line. Mounted officers carrying flags represented the rolling barrage.[60]

The experience of British units was similar. Captain Robert Monypenny of the 2nd Battalion, the Essex Regiment remembered:

> [Before the Battle of Arras] a regular plan was made over the surrounding countryside to the exact formations, positions and defences of the German Army...The officers studied special maps issued to them and, more than once, the whole division advanced together in rehearsing its part. A line of runners in front, waving white flags, acted as the moving barrage.[61]

While the actual conditions of battle could not be recreated, the idea was to come as close as possible to replicating the attack as it existed in the plan of operations.

To this end, the training scheme of the 6th Canadian Infantry Brigade read in part:

> The disposition of companies for the three stages of the advance through Thélus should be practiced, in order that each section has various houses and cellars told off as definite tasks for a certain number of files [sic], and the practicing of reorganization [sic] of these companies after each task has been thoroughly completed, is necessary — as well as the manner in which they are to be moved forward east of the village after completion of their task.[62]

This type of collective training was very close to the tactical schemes employed earlier in the winter except that the scenarios on the taped course were designed to approximate reality. Some units were able to accomplish this goal better than others. The British battalions of the 95th Infantry Brigade began training on their special brigade ground in mid-March, with each battalion given several days to practice over the course.[63] Units in the 2nd Canadian Division, on the other hand, conducted their training on the tapes during the third week of March, without the barrage map and with no idea of the speed and timings of the barrage lifts.[64] Other units like the 73rd Battalion of the 4th Canadian Division had still not been on a taped course as late as 1 April.[65]

It was on these courses that the skills learned during individual training were most firmly connected to Kiggell's tactical doctrine. The endless drill exercises on the parade ground were intended both to familiarize soldiers with the new platoon formations and ensure that the section and platoon could act as one unit. These skills were vital when Kiggell's new doctrine was combined with a creeping artillery barrage, as the wall of shrapnel in front of the infantry could easily turn deadly if soldiers either fell behind the barrage or advanced too quickly.

The Battle of Arras, of which the Canadian and British operations around Vimy Ridge formed but one part, was the culmination of four months of extensive preparations. The process of tactical reassessment that began within the BEF after the Battle of the Somme was central to this period of preparation. Officers at British GHQ believed that the British Army could learn from the successes of the French at Verdun. But these lessons were not clear-cut and British and Canadian officers used the trip to put forward their own tactical ideas. For Arthur Currie, the most important lesson of Verdun was that a flexible doctrine employing self-reliant platoons could solve the riddle of the trenches, while a British GSO from First Army suggested that the standardization of French doctrine would hold the key to success. General Kiggell, faced with both a shortage of manpower and the influx of a large number of untrained troops, took the British GSO's suggestions which he felt could be most effectively implemented by inexperienced soldiers. Through a series of directives issued in February 1917, Kiggell refined the existing British linear doctrine of the attack, integrating the specialists into the platoon and standardizing the British Army's method of attack. British and Canadian soldiers both began to train in this doctrine which employed a "normal formation for the attack" that Kiggell believed was applicable to most situations on the battlefield.

British and Canadian soldiers not only employed a similar doctrine, but also trained for the Battle of Arras using Kiggell's linear formations in practice attacks and special training over taped courses. They were taught to be specialists but were reminded that the rifle and bayonet were still considered the most important tools of an infantryman. Similar courses of instruction meant that when Canadian and British soldiers went over the top on Easter Monday 1917, they were prepared to fight in a similar way.

Although the Canadian Corps played an important role on the Western Front, it did not have the capacity for independent action that some have suggested. While Canadian officers were able to make novel tactical suggestions, it was not always possible to bridge theory and practice. This reminds us that if we are to understand the experience of Canadian soldiers in the Great War, we must understand how the Canadian Corps functioned as part of a greater British Imperial Army.

Figure 1

The Platoon

Taking an average strength of 36 and HQ of 4
(Showing 2 Platoons in 2 Waves with the right the outer flank)

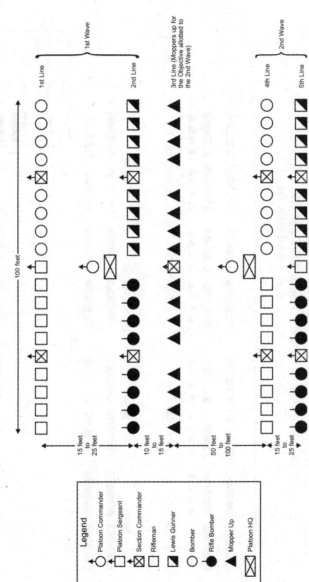

OB 1919/T, Plate A, folder 109, file 10, vol 3868, RG 9.

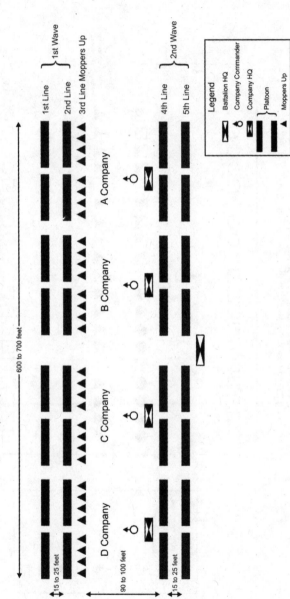

Figure 2

The Battalion

Taking 16 average Platoons of 36 Other Ranks, 4 Company HQ and Battalion HQ 70
(2 Objectives, 1st Wave to furthest objective)

OB 1919/T, Plate C, folder 109, file 10, vol 3868, RG 9.

Notes

1   See Martin Samuels, *Command or Control?: Command, Training and Tactics in the British and German Armies, 1888-1918* (London: Frank Cass, 1995); Paddy Griffith, *Battle Tactics of the Western Front: The British Army's Art of the Attack, 1916-1918* (New Haven: Yale University Press, 1994); Tim Travers, The Killing Ground: the British Army, the Western Front and the Emergence of Modern Warfare, 1900-1918 (London: Allen & Unwin, 1987); Shelford Bidwell and Dominick Graham, *Fire-power: British Army Weapons and Theories of War, 1904-1945* (London: George Allen & Unwin, 1983).

2   Griffith, 78.

3   Standard works on Vimy and the preparations for the battle include, G.W.L. Nicholson, *Canadian Expeditionary Force, 1914-1919: The Official History of the Canadian Army in the First World War* (Ottawa: Queen's Printer, 1962); Pierre Berton, *Vimy* (Toronto: McClelland and Stewart, 1986); H.F. Wood, *Vimy* (Toronto: Macmillan, 1967); Alexander McKee, *Vimy Ridge* (London: Souvenir Press, 1966); Brereton Greenhous and Steven J. Harris, *Canada and the Battle of Vimy Ridge, 8-12 April 1917* (Ottawa: Canada Communication Group, 1992).

4   Berton, 92.

5   Jeffery Williams, *Byng of Vimy: General and Governor General of Canada*, (London: Leo Cooper, 1983), 147.

6   "Notes on French Attacks North-East of Verdun in October and December, 1916," file 160, vol 35, Manuscript Group [MG] 30 E100, Currie Fonds, Library and Archives of Canada [LAC].

7   Ibid.

8   Travers, 37-55.

9   These views were reiterated by "A General Staff Officer from First Army" who authored "Notes on a Visit to the VII French Army," a report which was widely circulated in the Canadian Corps in January 1917. See file 1, folder 46, vol 4114, [Record Group] RG 9, LAC.

10 "Notes on French Attacks North-East of Verdun in October and December, 1916."

11 See Mark Humphries, "Myth of the Learning Curve: Tactics and Training in the 12th Canadian Infantry Brigade, 1916-1918," *Canadian Military History* vol 14, no 4 (Autumn 2005), 15-30; Griffith, 47-52.

12 Arthur Currie, quoted in Hugh M. Urquhart, *Arthur Currie* (Toronto: J.M. Dent and Sons, 1950), 142.

13 For a discussion of Currie's trip to Verdun see A.M.J. Hyatt, *General Sir Arthur Currie: a Military Biography* (Toronto: University of Toronto Press, 1987), 63-67; Daniel G. Dancocks, *Sir Arthur Currie: A Biography* (Toronto: Methuen, 1985); Urquhart, 141-45. For a discussion of the BEF in 1914, see Christopher Pugsley, "Learning From the Canadian Corps on the Western Front," *Canadian Military History* vol 15, no 1 (Winter 2006), 7-10.

14 See Bill Rawling, *Surviving Trench Warfare: Technology and the Canadian Corps, 1914-1918* (Toronto: University of Toronto Press, 1992).

15   BGGS, Radcliffe, "Canadian Corps G.340, 27 December 1916," file 1, folder 46, vol 4114, RG 9.
16   Ibid.
17   Initially there were differences in the organizations adopted within each Canadian division but by the end of January the platoon organization had been standardized in the Canadian Corps. See "Minutes of First Army Conference, 25 January 1917," files 27-22, folder 6, vol 3827, RG 9.
18   The Canadians too would face a manpower crisis in 1917 and were certainly beginning to feel the effects of decreased recruiting after the Battle of the Somme. However, the problem was mitigated by large numbers of troops in England who were earmarked for a 5th Canadian Division but instead were used as reinforcements for the existing divisions.
19   Douglas Haig, diary entry for 27 November 1916, in Robert Blake, (ed) *The Private Papers of Douglas Haig, 1914-1919* (London: Eyre and Spottiswoode, 1952), 183.
20   On the "new armies" see Peter Simkins, *Kitchener's Army: The Raising of the New Armies, 1914-1916* (Manchester: Manchester University Press, 1988) and Dominck Graham, *Against Odds: Reflections on the Experiences of the British Army, 1914-1945* (New York: St. Martin's Press, 1999), 22-47. On how tactics were affected by the destruction of the old contemptibles, see Pugsley.
21   The organization of platoons had been a concern in the British Army since October of 1916. See "Minutes of Conference held by G.O.C. First Army at First Army Headquarters, on 25th January 1917," files 17-22, folder 6, vol 3827, RG 9.
22   "Minutes of First Army Conference, 25 January 1917."
23   "Notes on a Visit to the VII French Army"
24   Ibid, 1.
25   Interestingly, the GSO does not critique linear, rigid tactics as Currie did.
26   Bidwell and Graham, 11.
27   For Kiggell's views on infantry tactics see Travers, 67-69, 179-183; Bidwell and Graham, 11-12.
28   "First Army No. 1115(G), 17 February 1917" file 10, folder 109, vol 3868, RG 9.
29   General Kiggell, British Army General Headquarters, "OE/1919/T the Normal Formation for the Attack, 14 February 1917, Ibid.
30   SS 143, Instructions for the Training of Platoons for Offensive Action, 3, Ibid.
31   Ibid, 7.
32   Ibid.
33   Ibid.
34   War Diary [WD], 1st Battalion, East Surrey Regiment, 1 March 1917, WO 95/1579, National Archives [NA].
35   Hyatt, 63-64.
36   This assertion is based on a systematic analysis of the war diaries of six Canadian infantry battalions and the war diaries of several British battalions found in WO 95, NA.
37   WD, 15th Battalion, 30 January 1917, file 478, vol 4951, RG 9.

38 WD, 19th Battalion, 14 January 1917, file 403, vol 4907, RG 9.

39 WD, 2nd Battalion, January-April 1917, part 1, file 354, vol 4913, RG 9.

40 WD, 18th Battalion, January-April 1917, part 2, file 398, vol 4926, RG 9.

41 WD, 22nd Battalion, January-April 1917, file 413, vol 4931, RG 9.

42 WD, 1st Battalion, Royal Fusiliers, March 1917, WO 95/2207.

43 Ibid.

44 WD, 8th Battalion, East Kent Regiment, January-March 1917, WO 95/2207.

45 WD, 1st Battalion, King's Royal Rifle Corps, March 1917, WO 95/1371.

46 2nd Canadian Division, "G.33/54 Training While in the Reserve Area, 14 January 1917" file 7, folder 26, vol 4031, RG 9.

47 "10th Canadian Infantry Battalion, Order Number 5, 16 January 1917," WD, 10th Battalion, Appendices, January 1917, part 2, file 373, vol 4919, RG 9.

48 Ibid.

49 "10th Canadian Infantry Battalion Order No. 15," 15 February 1917, WD, 10th Battalion, Appendices, February 1917, part 2, file 373, vol 4919, RG 9.

50 WD, 1st Battalion, East Surrey Regiment, 20 March 1917, WO 95/1579.

51 Ibid, 21 March 1917.

52 Ibid, 26-30 March 1917.

53 Victor Wheeler, *The 50th Battalion in No Man's Land* (Ottawa: CEF Books, 2000), 81.

54 While we cannot know if every man went through the exercise, copies of the instructions are found in many of the battalion and brigade records from each division. "Individual Assault Practice, 25 March 1917," file 11, folder 112, vol 3870, RG 9.

55 The actual document is undated, but Nicholson dates the submission of the document to 5 March 1917. See Nicholson, 224.

56 Paddy Griffith, "The Extent of Tactical Reform in the British Army," in Paddy Griffith (ed), *British Fighting Methods in the Great War* (Portland: Frank Cass, 1996), 3-4.

57 Hyatt, 67.

58 See, for example, Tim Cook, "A Proper Slaughter: the March 1917 Gas Raid on Vimy Ridge," Canadian Military History vol 8, no 2 (Spring 1999), 7-23 and Andrew Godefroy, "A Lesson in Success: The Calonne Trench Raid, 17 January 1917," *Canadian Military History* vol 8, no 4 (Autumn 1999), 25-34.

59 WD, 1st Battalion, East Surrey Regiment, 23 March 1917, WO 95/1579.

60 Macintyre, 84.

61 Captain Robert Monypenny, 2nd Battalion, Essex Regiment, interviewed 1978-1985, in Jonathan Nicholls, *Cheerful Sacrifice: The Battle of Arras, 1917* (London: Leo Cooper, 1990), 44.

62 6th Brigade Major, "C. 50/11, 16 March 1917," file 5, folder 4, vol 4124, RG 9.

63 WD, 1st Battalion, East Surrey Regiment, March 1917, WO 95/1579.

64 "C.50/11, 16 March 1917."

65 12th Brigade Major, "S.G.15/370 Training, 1 April 1917," file 2, folder 15, vol 4227, RG 9.

5

Julian Byng and Leadership in the Canadian Corps

PATRICK BRENNAN

Twenty-nine years after the great Canadian victory at Vimy Ridge in April 1917, William Ironside, a British regular who had served as a senior divisional staff officer in the Canadian Corps, attributed its success to the fact that it was not in the Canadian nature to get bored and "so they were magnificent when they [fought]."[1] A generation later, Alexander Ross, in 1917 a Prairie-lawyer-turned-battalion-commander, offered a more revealing explanation for the Canadian Corps' achievement: "We were up to strength, we had trained hard all winter whenever we could, we had adequate artillery..., we had adequate preparation, we had adequate reconnaissance and we knew what we were going to do and we did it."[2] Explanations of the sort offered by Ironside may still warm the hearts of Canadians, but Ross's observations get us closer to the truth. His explanation speaks of courage and initiative, too, but also of planning and preparation and direction. In hierarchical organizations like armies, and unforgiving environments like battles, where poor plans and desultory leadership defeat the best soldiers, and good plans and thorough preparation give even ordinary soldiers the prospect of success, Vimy Ridge suggests leadership of a high order. In 1917, much of the leadership upon which the Canadian Corps still depended was British.

There were few accolades in 1915 for brilliant generalship among the commanders at Gallipoli, but certainly Lieutenant-General Julian Byng, commander of the British IX Corps, deserved acknowledgement for planning and carrying out that ill-starred campaign's successful withdrawal. As his biographer rightly notes, "He had begun to study the problem shortly after his arrival in August [1915]. Alone of the senior commanders he believed the operation could be carried out without great loss and devised a plan to achieve the result. His optimism and enthusiasm were infectious and turned the outlook of the other commanders from an acceptance of the inevitability of disaster to a belief in the possibility of success."[3] Military reputations are not often made by evacuations, but Byng had been noticed.

Byng arrived on the Western Front in February 1916 to command the British XVII Corps, then facing Vimy Ridge. During his brief spell there, and "fascinated by...the problems it presented [to an attacking force, Byng] spent hours reconnoitring it until he knew every contour."[4] Abruptly, in May 1916, Byng was ordered by general headquarters to assume command of the Canadian Corps. Field Marshal Haig wired the 54-year-old Byng "heartiest congratulations on your promotion... and good luck."[5] Byng was understandably disappointed: "Why am I sent the Canadians?" he lamented. "I don't even know a Canadian." Nonetheless he was resigned: "I am ordered to these people and will do my best, but I don't know that there is any congratulations about it."[6]

Indeed, Haig's proffered "good luck" did have an ominous ring to it. The formation Byng inherited was demoralized and the officer corps faction-ridden and politicized. Only Arthur Currie's 1st Division was truly fit for battle. Richard Turner's 2nd Division had been bloodied at St. Eloi and Turner's ability, and that of some of his senior subordinates to command in the field was in serious question. The 3rd Division had yet to see battle, its senior officers remaining unknown quantities, while the 4th Division was still forming up in England. And there were deficiencies all round—the Canadians' competitiveness and excessive unit pride often resulted in only grudging cooperation between battalions and even brigades, the inadequate professional training of Canadian officers hampered effectiveness, and the enthusiasm of the officers and men, unfettered by discipline, too often led to high casualties.[7] Byng at least realized that the unique standing of the Canadian Corps—its component divisions remained the same—gave its commander a great advantage to control the training, administration and preparation for battle in a way not possible with a normal British corps, whose complement of divisions could change monthly and even in the middle of a battle. But it was an advantage only if he could gain control of its personnel.

Byng quickly seized on this crucial point—the absolute necessity of breaking the power of patronage and other forms of outside interference in the promotion of senior officers. Writing to a friend, Byng spelled out his reasoning: "The men are too good to be led by politicians and dollar magnates, and if the credit of the Corps is to be augmented, the men must be led by leaders. I don't want Imperial officers but I want to shove on the Canadians who have proved their worth and get rid of the Bumstunts…[I] have no axe to grind of my own…and am only trying to do my best for these men who have fought for 15 months."[8] A great many of the senior Canadian officers, Byng was quick to point out, were solidly behind him.[9] With the support of the British War Office and Haig, who recognized that substantial Canadian manpower would be wasted if such reforms were not implemented, Byng made it clear to the Canadian government that he must have full control over the Corps, specifically the authority to promote and remove officers, subject only to considerations of merit.[10] Otherwise he was prepared to resign, causing the government great embarrassment. Canadian Prime Minister Robert Borden, who was tiring of the chaos in the army, and its author, the egotistical minister of Militia and Defence, Sam Hughes, did not fight Byng's demands.[11] Over the next ten months, Byng's success in getting rid of the "bumstunts" would be a major factor in improving the fighting efficiency of the Canadian Corps.

An examination of the cadre of senior commanders and staff officers in place in the spring of 1917, from brigade up, tells the tale of Byng's achievement. Of the four divisional commanders, two were Byng appointments. Major-General Richard Turner had been found wanting on the Somme and was sent to England to bring order out of the chaos of army administration where, as it would turn out, his talents really lay. His replacement at the head of the 2nd Division was Major-General Henry Burstall, a stolid, capable, prewar regular who had been in France from the start and most recently had commanded the Corps artillery. Major-General Malcolm Mercer, another "original," had been killed at the outset of his first battle at Mount Sorrel in June 1916. His replacement was the very able, and as a divisional commander certainly Currie's equal, Major-General Louis Lipsett. A British officer who had been seconded to Canada for training before the war, he had performed brilliantly first as a battalion and then brigade commander. Lipsett was a fiery taskmaster, brave and respected by his men, but a difficult personality for his senior subordinates. Of the other two, Major-General Arthur Currie, commander of the 1st Division, was the best of the senior Canadian officers at this point, as Byng had clearly recognized, whereas Major-General David Watson of the 4th Division was still very much a work-in-progress, personally courageous but given to impetuosity and bouts of insecurity which made him rely either too heavily (or worse, too little) on his staff and subordinates. While Currie, Watson and Lipsett had at least commanded their divisions in the Somme fighting, at Vimy Burstall would be leading an infantry division in battle for the first time.

Of the twelve infantry brigadiers, six were Byng appointments, including one replacement for Brigadier-General Victor Williams, who had been taken prisoner at Mount Sorrel. The "Byng Men" included all three brigade commanders in the 4th Division: Edward Hilliam, a former British regular who had immigrated to Canada before the war; Victor Odlum, a militia officer and wealthy broker; and James MacBrien, a prewar regular with staff training who had not commanded men in the field before taking over the 12th Brigade. Three of Byng's other appointments were among the best brigadiers produced in the Canadian Expeditionary Force during the war: James Elmsley, a prewar regular; William Griesbach, a militia officer and lawyer-politician; and Frederick Loomis, a wealthy businessman and, like Odlum and Griesbach, a prewar militia officer. Hilliam and Griesbach had been promoted so recently that they had not led their brigades in battle before Vimy Ridge.

In the artillery arm, Major-General Edward "Dinky" Morrison had taken over from Burstall at the end of 1916 as commander of all Corps artillery, with Brigadier-General R.H. Massie, a British regular, appointed by Byng to command the Corps' heavy guns. Two of the four divisional artillery commanders were also Byng appointments: Brigadier-Generals William Dodds and Henri Panet.[12] The post of chief engineer had been held by the very able Brigadier-General William Lindsay since Alderson's time, and Byng had appointed only one of the four divisional engineering officers, Lieutenant-Colonel Thomas Irving.

Byng's mark on officer selection among the commanders of infantry battalions and comparably sized artillery brigades was even more pronounced. No fewer than forty of the forty-nine infantry battalion commanders on the Corps' strength at Vimy came to their positions during Byng's tenure as Corps commander.[13] One of the two garrison (heavy) artillery brigade commanders was a Byng appointment: Lieutenant-Colonel Frank Magee, as were the commanders of seven of twelve field artillery brigades then attached to the Corps: Lieutenant-Colonels Samuel Anderson, Russell Britton, Edwin Hanson, Edwin Leonard[14], John Mackinnon, Alexander Ogilvie and John Stewart. The newly created Corps machine gun officer, Lieutenant-Colonel Raymond Brutinel, was also a Byng appointment.

Byng had a similar impact on the Corps' senior staff appointments. Brigadier-General Percy Radcliffe, who had been selected by Haig to be the chief of staff of the Corps, would serve both Byng and Currie with distinction. The deputy adjutant and quartermaster general, Brigadier-General George Farmar, arrived about a month after Byng and, like Radcliffe, was picked by Haig's headquarters. Farmar gave the Canadian Corps outstanding service, masterminding its logistics through to the Armistice. All three general staff officers (GSO), 2nd grade serving at Corps headquarters were Byng-era appointments: Canadian Lieutenant-Colonel Johnson Parsons and two British officers, Majors Charles Linton and Francis Chalmer. Of the GSO 1's serving in the four divisions, one, Lieutenant-Colonel Norman Webber, who would ultimately replace Radcliffe at Corps headquarters, was posted to the Canadian Corps during Byng's tenure, and ten of the twelve brigade majors, the senior staff officers of a brigade, had either arrived from the British Army (Majors William Alston, Marmon Ferrers-Guy and Richard Read) or been promoted from within the Corps since Byng's arrival (Majors Hew Clark-Kennedy, Duncan MacIntyre, Allen Meredith, Thomas Morrisey, Richard Stayner, Hugh Urquhart and Paul Villiers).[15] Furthermore, three of the four senior divisional artillery staff officers had either been posted from the British forces (Majors Henry Boyd and Arthur Newland) or been promoted by Byng (Major Fortescue Duguid). Finally, the newly appointed Counter-Battery Staff Officer, Lieutenant-Colonel Andrew McNaughton and the staff officer Royal Artillery, the senior staff officer in the Corps' artillery, Major Alan Brooke, were promoted (in the former case) or arrived during Byng's tenure in command.

Among 118 senior command and staff appointments in the Corps on 9 April 1917, eighty-four of them had taken up their positions under Byng. Obviously not all of the eighty-four men replaced were "bumstunts" — some had been promoted, while others had been killed or badly wounded, or become seriously ill. Moreover, British staff officers, who tended to be of a uniformly high quality, were regularly cycled in and out of the Canadian Corps. After nearly a year at his post, Byng had clearly built his own relatively experienced team. By April 1917, the commanding officers of the infantry divisions and brigades had held their positions for an average of eleven months. For the Corps and divisional artillery commanders, the average was nine months, while for the commanders of the artillery brigades, it was ten. Senior Corps and divisional staff officers also held their jobs for an average of eleven months. On average, the infantry battalion commanders had held their current posts for just over seven months.[16]

As at Gallipoli, Byng spent a great deal of time amongst his officers and men, preaching the gospel of optimism and building badly needed élan. He "looked like a soldier; a compact, wiry man, with a firm chin and piercing gaze, he did not suffer fools gladly, but was always willing to listen to advice from any sensible source."[17] Moreover, he knew a great deal about soldiering and possessed a wealth of common sense, combining that with an obviously caring and approachable manner. Finally, in the words of the Australian Corps' chief of staff, Brigadier-General C.B. White, he was a man of "intense earnestness..., an unambitious man without any desire for personal fame—a very rare thing in generals and a very precious quality in the eyes of those under them."[18] Certainly he cut an impressive figure in the Canadian lines, particularly among men who had rarely seen their commanders, and did not expect to. Ordinary Canadian soldiers took to Byng's fatherliness and informality, proudly adopting the sobriquet "Byng Boys" which they used through the end of the war, long after its namesake was gone.[19] But the bonhomie was matched by a ruthless energy and obsession with the benefits of imposing badly needed discipline. Byng was a trainer and an inspector and his commitment to doing both thoroughly was not lost on his officers and men. Within weeks of his arrival, most had seen him or heard him speak.[20]

It was among the middle and senior ranks of the officer corps, however, where Byng exerted his greatest influence. Looking back, Ross, whom Byng had promoted to battalion commander in September 1916, remembered that Byng "...revolutionized the whole thing. [He] gave me new ideas. Things that appealed to my common sense...I always found that [he] was rational, reasonable, and [as] a regular soldier, [a] trained soldier...he was able to give us ideas...which helped us. It improved my morale and my battalion I'm sure...I never found [anyone] as easy to get along with as I did him. He would come into your dugout in the front line, you would take out your maps, you would discuss things, his ideas were reasonable, he was interested, would make suggestions and so on...."[21]

At Mount Sorrel, Byng's first battle in command of the Canadians and their largest engagement to that time, their new commander was able to show his mettle. Henry Burstall, the commander of Corps artillery, later described Byng's discussions with his Canadian subordinates on their initial counterattack plan, which was subsequently altered on Byng's advice: "I have always thought his action on this occasion showed most marvelous strength of character as well as military knowledge. He hardly knew us and yet he was willing to stake his professional career on a plan he believed to be faulty, rather than force a better one on [officers] who did not believe in it, and to whom he was a stranger."[22]

Byng preferred to hold frequent, comprehensive briefings, led by Radcliffe or another senior staff officer, which the Corps commander would follow up with penetrating questions and comments, leaving his headquarters staff and any field officers present in no doubt as to what he expected of them. He realized that all a senior commander on the Western Front could expect to do was to produce a sound plan, thoroughly prepare the men and officers who would carry out the attack, and then learn any lessons that could be gleaned from what happened. Byng knew that the day of the "Great Captain" was over.

He could not expect, save for rare circumstances, to make a difference once his men were engaged.

Under Byng's command, the Canadian performance on the Somme showed improvement though it was still far from uniformly good. Like their peers throughout the British Expeditionary Force, Byng and his abler senior officers of the Canadian Corps learned much from the Somme. Embracing what was becoming standard practice in the BEF, Byng authorized every formation in the Corps down to battalion to make detailed analytical studies of every aspect of the Somme offensives in which they had participated "...in order that the valuable experience gained there by the Corps may be turned to the best account in future operations."[23] Thus did institutionalized and universalized learning become the norm under Byng's and Radcliffe's methodical direction.[24] The adoption of new infantry tactics specified in BEF directives SS143 *Instructions for the Training of Platoons for Offensive Action* and SS144 *The Normal Formation for the Attack* were implemented in the Corps during the winter of 1916-17, and new artillery tactics were developed as well, both in barrage and counter-battery work.[25] Throughout the winter, Corps headquarters held frequent conferences which brought together Byng's staff with the commanding officers and senior staff from the divisions, brigades and battalions. Byng also invited small groups of his battalion commanders to spend a week at his headquarters with the Corps staff officers to study tactical problems and how to improve the administration and training of their units. Byng tried to be present as often as his schedule permitted to talk informally with these men, so that he got to know them and they him.[26] Although Byng wisely left the implementation of Corps headquarters' directives to his divisional subordinates, he diligently monitored the progress being made, whenever possible by meeting personally with the responsible officers. "The Corps Commander came to see me this afternoon to discuss the big operation and he gave me fuller particulars regarding same," Major-General David Watson recorded in his diary seven weeks before the attack, adding that "he was greatly pleased with the Division and all the work...that [we] had carried out."[27]

Byng also made a great effort to see his junior officers on their own ground. Captain J.F. McKay, a platoon commander at the time, remembered Byng's modus vivendi during a training exercise:

> General Byng had a way of coming down when you were training and he would ask you, the senior officer there, what you were doing. This senior officer would tell him what our plan was. Then he would say call in your officers, and...the senior officer would call in the officers. Then General Byng would say now you understand [what] you are supposed to do? Have you had a chance to tell your subordinate officers

and do they understand what's to be done? If they said they had he'd kill them right then. But if they hadn't he'd say I'd like you to go back to your subordinate officers and tell them what the scheme is and as soon as you have done that I want you back here. They'd tell their subordinate officers what the scheme was, see that they all understood it, [and] they'd come back. Well he'd kill you, and you, and you. Then the commanding and subordinate officer would have to carry on. Then he'd do this two or three times until he had corporals...or sergeants commanding companies and probably a Lieutenant commanding a battalion. The effect of this, we'd never seen anything like it before. All these schemes that you do with troops that are pretending that you are taking something and you have a suppositious enemy. It all seems so much like fairy land...Unless you are one with a responsibility [then] I can understand it's very hard for the man to keep awake. But when you did it this way, there wasn't one of them that didn't know but what he might be commanding the show before he was through. It had the effect of just electrifying every man in that whole show because he felt, well I've got to listen to my instructions, because I may have to take over and carry on. I think that you could see a change in...the interest that the men showed in these...field exercises, from the moment Byng came into the picture.[28]

The Corps commander's vigilance was not lost on the men or their own commanders. Byng's famous decision to disseminate thousands of topographical maps for the Vimy attack down to the level of non-commissioned officers (NCOs) had a profound impact far beyond these junior leaders receiving a useful tool; it meant they were trusted and given a share of responsibility for the entire enterprise. It should be said that this was neither a Byng nor Canadian Corps innovation, but established practice in the BEF after the Somme.[29]

When Byng was informed on 19 January 1917 that the Canadian Corps would assault Vimy Ridge as part of a larger British spring offensive, the transformation of the Corps then underway was given a practical focus that spurred on his headquarters. At a conference at Corps headquarters on 2 February, Byng announced the Vimy attack and the basic outlines of the plan to divisional commanders and staff officers. His staff, in consultation with Currie, Burstall, Lipsett, Watson and their staffs, drew up a scheme of operations which was submitted to General Henry Horne's First Army headquarters by 5 March and which, with relatively minor amendments, became the basic Canadian plan for the assault on Vimy Ridge.[30] The plan drew heavily on the reports of three Corps officers who were part of a larger group of British and Dominion officers nominated by general headquarters to attend a detailed briefing on the lessons learned at Verdun conducted by the

French Army in early January,[31] as well as on the latest British ideas and some uniquely Canadian insights. But as Currie's foremost biographer points out, Byng left his mark on the Corps' plan.[32]

While complex in detail, the plan was straightforward, indeed conservative, in its basic principles. Vimy Ridge was a limited objective and Byng dedicated little effort to planning any exploitation contingencies, focusing instead on consolidation. No record survives of his thoughts, but it is clear that Byng understood the limitations of breakthroughs on the Western Front under the prevailing conditions and accepted that all advances had to be patient and deliberate and well-supported by ample artillery.[33] Reaching the summit of the ridge with his infantry relatively unscathed remained his fixation. In that respect, he seemed to have absorbed Marshal Joffre's dictum offered earlier in the war about what would be required to wrest Vimy from the Boche: "sufficient artillery, heavy and field, to crush all resistance."[34] Simply put, there must be every possible support for his soldiers. With this in mind, no function which contributed to the Corps' effectiveness – the combat arms, of course, but also engineers, signals, supplies, transport and medical – escaped the personal scrutiny of Byng, Radcliffe and Farmar.

Not the least of Byng's achievements during this period was to keep senior British and Canadian officers working together so that egos and conflicting "professionalisms" did not take their toll. Similarly, the continuity in the Corps' make-up ensured divisional and corps staffs came to know each others' strengths and weaknesses very well, making for better performance all round.[35] This had not been the case in the faction-ridden officer corps of the Alderson period.[36] But Byng's warm personality, combined with his and Radcliffe's willingness to accommodate the Canadians as equals, was central to realizing this undoubted advantage.

It is understandable that the literature has paid little attention to the senior staff officers' successful preparations for Vimy Ridge.[37] As their battle plans and other vital contributions disappeared into the archives, the good work of the "Red Tabs" became less readily apparent. However, another factor was at work. As most of the senior staff officers in the Canadian Corps during the first thirty months of the war were British, their input into the critical development of the Corps' professionalization makes no contribution to the nationalist agenda of Canadian military history. Only one staff officer's contribution to Vimy has received any attention at all, and not surprisingly he was a Canadian who benefited from future fame and his own considerable self-promotional skills, namely Andrew McNaughton.[38] The same pressure contributed to the downplaying of the role of Julian Byng, but in the case of the staff officers, this is even more pronounced.

Brigadier-General Percy Pollexfen de Blaquiere Radcliffe was appointed by general headquarters only a week after Byng's own appointment took effect and served as brigadier-general, general staff, of the Canadian Corps through the spring of 1918. Tall, dapper and reserved, Radcliffe was highly intelligent. The son of a general, he had been commissioned a second lieutenant in the Royal Horse Artillery in 1893 and served in the South African War. Radcliffe was trained as a staff officer during the prewar decade and had been employed in this role in France with the BEF before being dispatched to the Canadians. He had turned forty-three two months before the attack on Vimy Ridge. Apart from his many administrative talents, in the intensely political arena of the general staff, he was a cunning ambassador for the Canadian Corps, with more useful personal connections than any Canadian officer would have possessed, even if one with equivalent professional qualifications had been available.[39] Without question, Radcliffe was the nerve center of Corps headquarters, far more than Currie, Byng's strong right hand and principal advisor.

Shortly after Radcliffe's posting to the Canadian Corps, he was joined by Brigadier-General George Jasper Farmar, another British regular, who, as deputy adjutant and quartermaster-general, would serve as the chief administrative officer and logistician of the Canadian Corps until the end of hostilities. During preparations for the Vimy attack, the Corps was allocated eight trains per day, each carrying 370 tonnes of stores: four for ammunition, one for engineering stores, one for road-building and tramway stores, one for general supplies and one split between animal fodder and spare capacity allocated at Farmar's discretion. Farmar requisitioned 24,000,000 rounds of small arms ammunition, 450,000 Mills bombs, and 1,005,000 rounds of eighteen-pounder gun ammunition. But the devil was in the details. His staff had to account for everything from tents, clothing and latrines to potatoes, razor blades, soap, pencils and typewriters, on which a small army of clerks banged out reams of reports that historians pore over today.[40] Farmar was pretty much a glorified clerk himself, but he performed superbly. With the needs of over 100,000 men, 25,000 horses and a mass of weaponry to attend to, the planning required of Farmar and his staff was daunting. Ultimately, the success of everything else the Corps attempted, from training, the prodigious engineering work, the massive artillery and machine gun barrages and the infantry attacks, depended on the timely performance of the logistical support Farmar masterminded.[41]

Despite being desperately short of experienced staff officers during the first two years of the war, the British army was nonetheless generous with the Canadians. One suspects this was done out of self-interest, for only the influx of some key men of professional ability offered any prospect of transforming the Canadian rabble into a modern army. In the spring of 1917, the senior staff officer in all four infantry divisions was a British regular,[42] including the Canadian born Lieutenant-Colonel Ross Hayter with Lipsett's 3rd Division.[43] Hayter was forty-two, a graduate of Upper Canada College and the Royal Military College in Kingston, who had served in the British army since 1895, and was attached as a staff officer with the Canadian Permanent Force when the war broke out. Lieutenant-Colonel Robert Kearsley, a thirty-seven-year-old graduate of Harrow, Sandhurst and like his fellows, Camberley Staff College, occupied the same position with Currie's 1st Division. Norman "Ox" Webber, aged thirty-six, an officer in the Royal Engineers and member of the last prewar Staff College graduating class, served with Burstall's 2nd Division.

Finally, Lieutenant-Colonel William Ironside, a thirty-six-year-old gunner with a burly six-foot-four physique and an opinion of his own merits that was equally towering, coordinated staff responsibilities in Watson's 4th Division. Indeed, Watson's many detractors felt that Ironside so intimidated the Quebec publisher-cum-major-general that Ironside effectively commanded the division. Certainly Ironside was ruthless, his ambitions boundless and his opinion of Watson low.[44] But his experience — he had been a staff officer since 1908 — and his abilities were exceptional. The process of Canadianization of staff appointments, which Byng had strongly supported, was bearing fruit by the spring of 1917, with seven of the senior staff officers of the Corps' twelve infantry brigades wartime-trained Canadians. Nevertheless, British officers still held twenty-one of thirty-two top staff appointments in the artillery, infantry or at Corps headquarters, including all but four of the most senior positions.[45]

Byng held a wide respect for the work of his staff officers, British and Canadian. When one of the young British GSO2s departed the Corps two months prior to Vimy to return to the BEF, the Corps commander penned him a hand-written note thanking him for his "...splendid work [which had] made it too easy for me...."[46] Many of the senior Canadian officers were similarly grateful for the invaluable contribution made by British staff officers during the preparations for Vimy. A battalion adjutant remembered Ironside as "a cracking good soldier" whose fiery temper with subordinates was matched by a willingness to explain.[47] Alexander Ross, commanding officer of the 28th Battalion, simply remembered that by Vimy "we were good, in every department. Staff work and all the rest. Everything was good. [And] our relations with the Corps staff were extremely good."[48] More specifically, Ross remembered Webber, with whom he most frequently dealt, as "most approachable and most cooperative and most helpful."[49] McNaughton, one of the few senior Canadian staff officers, always considered Radcliffe, Webber and Hayter to have made very great contributions to the Corps' success. "We had a wonderful group of staff officers around us, the pick of the British Army. They were absolutely superb...and they taught us much," he would later recount.[50]

One of Radcliffe's most valuable personnel decisions involved the appointment of McNaughton as counter-battery staff officer. General headquarters had been so impressed by the work of Lieutenant-Colonel A.G. Haig of the British V Corps to improve gunnery accuracy that counter-battery staff officers were authorized to disseminate his practices to every Corps. Major-General Morrison recommended McNaughton, an engineer in civilian life who was already responsible for many similar innovations in the Canadian Corps. Radcliffe stressed that McNaughton's role would be to explore all the scientific approaches to destroy or neutralize the enemy's guns to protect the infantry during the attack. He arranged for McNaughton to see Lieutenant-Colonel Haig and visit the French, and to have all the resources he thought McNaughton would need to neutralize German artillery in an attack.[51] McNaughton, whom Ironside colourfully described as having "that very mad look of genius in his eye that you see sometimes," copied Haig's work and improved on it where he could.[52]

Certainly one of the most unsung staff officers in the Canadian Corps during the preparation for Vimy was Major Alan Brooke, staff officer Royal Artillery (SORA) who was ultimately responsible for the barrage plans of the Canadian artillery, and the much larger numbers of British artillery temporarily attached by First Army in support of the Vimy assault. Brooke is rarely mentioned in Canadian accounts, except to say he was there and later went on to command the British Army in the Second World War.[53]

Before joining the Canadian Corps in early February 1917, Brooke had served with the 18th Division, where he had produced artillery barrage plans for Canadian attacks during some of the Somme fighting. Brooke met Currie as well as McNaughton during their tour of Verdun in January 1917. Hearing of Brooke's appointment the next month, Currie promptly sent him a welcoming letter and a request for the notes he had taken on French artillery practices.[54] Brooke found his introduction to the French approach fascinating, and considered the trip very valuable, whereas McNaughton dismissed the whole exercise as a junket.[55] Brooke was considered one of the more promising young

British artillery staff officers—he was twenty-nine, a year younger than McNaughton—with a reputation for industry and innovation, and he threw himself into his new job of adapting the plan already drawn up by his predecessor, Lieutenant-Colonel Edward Norton. "Am up to my neck in work at present," he confided to his mother on 16 February, "spent the whole of today and the day before yesterday tramping round the country examining positions and learning the ground."[56] And so it went without break for the next fifty-two days.

The requirements of Vimy would be the biggest barrage plan Brooke had attempted so far. With three times the artillery normally under the command of a Corps, he had to assign the batteries to the various divisional attacks, figure out the communications arrangements, establish the necessary transport lines and ammunition dumps, and of course, draw up bombardment and barrage plans which in turn had to be coordinated between numerous formations as well as the corps on either flank. In the end, the efforts of Brooke and his subordinates were crowned by success. "The whole thing went like clockwork," a justifiably proud Brooke confided to his mother in a letter rapidly scribbled on the 10 April, "the infantry delighted with the artillery preparation and support in the assault."[57] It was as effective in its role as McNaughton's more famous counter-battery plan. Once the fighting had ended, Brooke spent the next few weeks carefully exploring the battlefield, noting the impact of Canadian and British artillery fire on the German defences.[58] He was especially proud of the fact his barrage plan was being circulated to other corps as a model for future operations.[59] Byng, of course, was delighted with the artillery results.[60]

Brooke continued to hold the post of SORA, tutoring, among others, a promising young Canadian artillery staff officer named Harry Crerar. In March 1918, Brooke was offered and accepted the senior artillery staff officer position (and promotion to GSO1) with the First Army.[61] His performance during the thirteen months he spent with the Canadians, both as a staff officer and trainer of Canadian staff "learners," was judged uniformly excellent. "There is no one the Corps owes more to than you," Radcliffe consoled him when he failed to make the New Year's honours list in 1918.[62] Crerar, who ultimately replaced him as SORA, was generous in his praise. Brooke was also very popular with other officers, hardly the haughty Englishman suffering among the colonials alleged by McNaughton's biographer, John Swettenham. The portrayal of Brooke's association with the Canadian Corps, and particularly the dismissal of his role at Vimy and thereafter, seem primarily rooted in the Brooke-McNaughton hostility of the Second World War. But it was exacerbated by Brooke's dismissive attitude toward his nominal boss, Major-General Morrison. Brooke's predecessor, Norton, had in fact asked to leave the Corps because he could no longer get along with Morrison, whom he thought ignorant of modern artillery and very touchy. Brooke found that Morrison was "full of bravery and instilled the finest fighting spirit in the whole of the artillery under his command, but as regards the tactical handling of artillery, he knew practically nothing." Finally, Brooke arrived at a solution which, while unorthodox, nonetheless won Morrison's approval. Brooke would draw up artillery orders and ensure Morrison received a copy. Brooke doubted whether Morrison ever understood most of them, or even read them, but with a sympathetic Radcliffe's endorsement, Brooke controlled virtually the entire artillery component of the Corps. Even Byng got caught up in the charade. He talked to Morrison, who then passed on the requests to Brooke, who then sought out Byng to clarify what was required, and to inform the Corps commander in detail what was being done.[63] Morrison was otherwise a capable commander and, on the technical side, did not interfere and allowed the experts free rein. Currie even short-listed him for a divisional command in the spring of 1918. For his part, "Dinky" Morrison seems to have greatly admired and willingly relied upon Brooke's competence.[64]

Writing to his wife on April 15, Byng did not try to suppress his enthusiasm for what his army had achieved: "The Canucks are saying very nice things to me, and one informed me that they couldn't have done without the discipline and training which had been instilled into them for the last eight months. That is most satisfactory as it shews [sic] they are beginning to realize that bravery is not the only thing that is wanted and that without discipline it means loss of life without the compensating success. They are just bursting with bon-homie [sic] and grinning from ear to ear."[65] His final verdict on the Canadians with whom he had worked so amicably and productively over the previous year was expressed in the usual no-nonsense fashion of the man: "[The Canucks] are a real bright bunch and very easily handled."[66]

Julian Byng was no Arthur Currie, but the gap between the two was likely narrower than most Canadians prefer to think. Certainly no individual deserves more credit for the transformation of the Canadian Corps from a rabble of enthusiastic amateurs to battle-hardened professionals. Even Daniel Dancocks, arguably Currie's most adoring biographer, acknowledges that, "it was Byng who had moulded the Corps into a cohesive unit. He had made the Canadians realize what they were capable of achieving and had given them the self-confidence to do it. Because of Byng's efforts, Currie inherited a formidable fighting formation...." Even his qualification to that praise, that "it was also true that the Canadians would not have been as successful had Byng remained in command [because of his professional rigidity and lack of imagination],"[67] was more generous than General Hubert Gough's assessment that Byng's strength was "appealing to colonials" but that he otherwise lacked "military ideas" and possessed "no brain."[68] A.M.J. Hyatt fairly judges Byng when he concludes that "General Byng was responsible for most of the planning for the battle of Vimy Ridge and the credit for its success quite properly belongs to him."[69]

One could add that Byng's staff, a disproportionately British group, also deserves much overdue credit. As "Jumbo" Byng's biographer rightly concludes, "for the future a standard had been set in meticulous preparation, training and staff work, receptiveness to new techniques and [the embrace of] tactical innovations."[70] Alexander Ross, the gruff, no-nonsense Scot from Saskatchewan, was not far off when he offered in later life that, "General Currie was very fortunate in taking over the Corps after General Byng."[71]

Notes

1 Ironside to Lindsey, 23 Oct 1946, 92/40/1, Ironside Papers, Imperial War Museum [IWM].

2 Alexander Ross, Generals file, vol 21, BIII1, RG 41, CBC Papers, Library and Archives Canada [LAC].

3 Jeffery Williams, *Byng of Vimy: General and Governor General* (Toronto: University of Toronto Press, 1992), 108-09.

4 Ibid, 112.

5 Ibid, 115.

6 Byng to Blumenfeld, 29 May 1916, BY.14, BR-BY file, Blumenfeld Papers, House of Lords Records Office [hereafter HLRO].

7 Williams, 127.

8 Byng to Blumenfeld, 1 June 1916, BY.15, BR-BY file.

9 Byng to Blumenfeld, 7 July 1916, BY.19, BR-BY file.

10 Aitken to Hughes, 19 June 1916, BBK/E/1/44, Beaverbrook Papers, HLRO.

11 Stephen Harris, *Canadian Brass: The Making of a Professional Army, 1860-1939* (Toronto: University of Toronto Press, 1988), 115-21.

12 Brigadier-General James Mitchell had been appointed to command the 3rd Division's artillery only eight days prior to Byng's arrival.

13 The total is somewhat inflated when one realizes that eleven commanding officers who had held their positions when Byng had arrived at the Corps had been killed in action at Mount Sorrel, on the Somme or during the disastrous 1 March raid by the 4th Division on Vimy's Hill 145.

14 Leonard was killed in action on 9 April 1917, the most senior Canadian Corps officer to die in the attack.

15 All of these were Canadians. Another British officer, Major R. Partridge, had transferred to the Corps as senior staff officer of the 12th Brigade only two days prior to Byng's arrival.

16   Personnel information drawn from: *Canada in the Great World War,* vol VI (Toronto: United Publishers, 1921), Appendix I, 315-58; Officers Commanding Units, vol 473, RG 150, Canadian Expeditionary Force Personnel Papers; various personnel files, 1992-93/166, RG 150; G.W.L. Nicholson, *Canadian Expeditionary Force, 1914-1919: The Official History of the Canadian Army in the First World War* (Ottawa: Queen's Printer, 1962), Appendix A; *Nominal Roll of Imperial Officers Attached to the Overseas Military Forces of Canada,* HQ 54-21-1-203, vol 447, RG 24, LAC.

17   Robin Neillands, The Great War Generals on the Western Front, 1914-1918 (London: Robinson, 1999), 327.

18   Cited in Denis Winter, *Haig's Command: A Reassessment* (London: Penguin, 1991), 267.

19   This was a play on Byng's name and the popular 1916 London musical The Bing Boys are Here. Gary Sheffield and John Bourne (eds), *Douglas Haig: War Diaries and Letters, 1914-1918* (London: Weidenfeld & Nicholson, 2005), 227.

20   Williams, 131.

21   Alexander Ross, Generals file.

22   Cited in Williams, 125.

23   3 November 1916, file 3, folder 93, vol 3954, IIIC1, RG 9.

24   Patrick Brennan and Thomas Leppard, "How the Lessons Were Learned: Senior Commanders and the Moulding of the Canadian Corps after the Somme," in Yves Tremblay (ed) *Canadian Military History Since the 17th Century* (Ottawa: Department of National Defence, 2001), 135-44.

25   Bill Rawling, *Surviving Trench Warfare: Technology and the Canadian Corps, 1914-1918* (Toronto: University of Toronto Press, 1992) and Paddy Griffith, *Battle Tactics of the Western Front: The British Army's Art of Attack 1916-18* (New Haven: Yale University Press, 1994), 74-85. Brennan and Leppard, 138-39.

26   Williams, 147; Diary entries for 5-10 February 1917, file 5, vol 1, William Griesbach Papers, MG 30 E15, LAC; Alexander Ross, Generals file, vol 21, CBC Papers.

27   Diary entry, 22 February, 30 March, 1, 3, 5 April 1917, David Watson Papers, MG 30 E69; Diary entry, 12 March, 6 April 1917, file 5, vol 1, Griesbach Papers; Personal diary, 24, 30 March, 2 April 1917, file 194, vol 43, Arthur Currie Papers, MG 30 E100.

28   J.F. McKay interview, 28th Battalion file, vol 14, CBC Papers. In training exercises umpires 'killed' officers by removing them from the field

29   Alexander Turner, *Vimy Ridge 1917: Byng's Canadians Triumph at Arras* (Botley: Osprey Publishing, 2005), 39.

30   Nicholson, 247.

31   Rawling, 89-95, 111-12. Lieutenant-Colonel Andrew McNaughton and Major-General Arthur Currie attended these French briefings. So did Major Alan Brooke, the British artillery staff officer who a month later would lead the Canadian Corps' artillery staff.

32   A.M.J. Hyatt, *General Sir Arthur Currie: A Military Biography* (Toronto: University of Toronto Press, 1987), 67.

33   Turner, 89-90.
34   Neillands, 328.
35   Brereton Greenhous and Stephen Harris, *Canada and the Battle of Vimy Ridge, 9-12 April 1917* (Ottawa: Public Works and Government Services Canada, 1997), 56.
36   The Ross Rifle controversy still festered when Byng took over the Corps.
37   Kenneth Radley's *We Lead, Others Follow: First Canadian Division 1914-1918* (St. Catharines: Vanwell, 2006) focuses on the often neglected role of staff officers.
38   While Volume I of Swettenham's three-volume biography contains a great deal of useful material on McNaughton's Great War service, it is also as fine an example of hagiography as one can find in Canadian military historiography.
39   Turner, 33; *Who's Who, 1930* (London: A & C Black Ltd, 1930). After leaving the Canadian Corps in April 1918, Radcliffe was appointed director of military operations at the War Office, and by the mid-1920s was commanding a division in the peacetime army. Radcliffe is easily identified in group photographs, with a moustache and facial features that make him a dead-ringer for comedian John Cleese.
40   Turner, 33.
41   The perfection of logistics to supply massive armies is rightly now seen as one of the revolutions in military affairs characteristic of the Great War. See Ian Malcolm Brown, *British Logistics on the Western Front, 1914-1919* (Westport: Praeger, 1998), 161-62. The Canadian Corps was ultimately dependent on the BEF for logistical support, and greatly benefited from the dramatic improvements in the BEF's logistical capabilities during 1916-17.
42   As were their seconds–Majors Maurice Festing, C. Foss and A. Stericker, and Capt. T. Morgan-Grenville-Gavin. See *Nominal Roll of Imperial Officers Attached to the Overseas Military Forces of Canada.*
43   *Who's Who*, 1930.
44   Ironside to Lindsey, 15 March 1946.
45   Personnel information in this section is drawn from numerous sources, including CEF Personnel Papers, Officers Commanding Units and National Defence Papers and *Nominal Roll of Imperial Officers Attached to the Overseas Military Forces of Canada.*
46   Byng to Dill, 1 February 1917, I/2, John Dill Papers, Liddell Hart Centre for Military Archives [LHCMA].
47   Carmichael interview, 47th Battalion file, vol 14, CBC Papers.
48   Alexander Ross, Generals file.
49   Ibid.
50   John Swettenham, *McNaughton*, Volume I, (Toronto: Ryerson Press, 1968), 67, 70.
51   Ibid, 68, 74.
52   Ironside to Lindsey, 15 March 1946.

53   See Swettenham, 88-89, 132. The biography casts Brooke in a uniformly
     negative light as the pompous and not-quite-so-able British professional
     compared to the more innovative "colonial" part-time soldier.

54   Currie to Brooke, 31 January 1917 and Brooke to mother, 5 February 1917,
     2/1/10, Alan Brooke Papers, LHCMA. Major-General Ivor Maxse, one of the
     most innovative infantry commanders in the BEF, made a point of asking
     for Brooke's "quite excellent" notes, which he then circulated in his own
     corps. Maxse to Brooke, 19 January 1917, 2/1/10, Alan Brooke Papers. On
     Brooke's previous involvement with the Canadian Corps, see Webber to
     Metcalfe, 19 September 1916, 11/2, Alan Brooke Papers.

55   Brooke to mother, 11 January 1917, 2/1/10, Brooke Papers; Swettenham,
     69.

56   16 February 1917, 2/1/10, Brooke Papers.

57   10 April 1917 and Notes for Memoirs, 87-89, 5/2/1, Brooke Papers.

58   26 April 1917 and Brooke to mother, 15 April 1917, 2/1/10, Brook Papers.

59   2 May 1917, Brooke Papers.

60   Brooke's nephew (serving with the Canadian Corps as Byng's ADC) to
     Brooke's mother, 3 May 1917, 2/1/10, Brooke Papers.

61   The Canadian Corps would return to Horne's First Army after the Battle
     of Amiens in August 1918.

62   Radcliffe to Brooke, 8 Jan 1918, 2/1/11, and Notes for Memoirs, undated
     letter from Crerar to C.M. Long (researcher for Lord Alanbrooke
     autobiography), 11/2, Brooke Papers.

63   Notes for Memoirs, 5/2/1, 87-89 and 11/2, interview with Major-General
     Norton and Crerar to C.M. Long, Brooke Papers. Crerar shared Brooke's
     view that Morrison did not understand modern gunnery.

64   Morrison to Brooke, 17 Mar 1918, 2/1/10, Brooke Papers. Morrison was
     much admired by his subordinates. See John Stewart, Generals file, vol 21,
     CBC Papers.

65   Williams, 165.

66   Byng to Blumenfeld, 9 Jul 1917 BY-23, BR-BY file, Blumenfeld Papers.

67   Daniel Dancocks, *Sir Arthur Currie: A Biography* (Toronto: Methuen, 1985),
     177.

68   Cited in Gary Sheffield and Dan Todman (eds), *Command and Control on
     the Western Front: The British Army's Experience 1914-1918* (Staplehurst:
     Spellmount, 2004), 75. Gough's intense dislike of Byng dated to the South
     African War.

69   Hyatt, 67.

70   Williams, 166.

71   Alexander Ross, Generals file, vol 21, CBC Papers.

6

The Gunners at Vimy
"We are Hammering Fritz to Pieces"

TIM COOK

The Great War has often been called the gunner's war. "The artillery conquers and the infantry occupies," was how one French general dismissed the infantry.[1] Glib remarks like that are always too simplistic, but there was no doubt about the importance of artillery in shattering enemy defences and, by 1917, working in conjunction with other arms, primarily the infantry, to achieving victory on the Western Front.

At the Battle of Vimy Ridge, the role of artillery was essential in shooting the infantry onto its objectives. Several weeks of pre-battle fire annihilated the enemy defences, cleared barbed wire, and forced defenders to their protective dugouts. A week before the battle the rate of fire increased and was augmented by heavier guns. This plunging drumfire saturated the enemy front, further clearing obstacles for the infantry, killing the enemy, and reducing the survivors to a quivering mass.

On the morning of 9 April 1917, the day of battle, the artillery provided a complicated and innovative creeping barrage. This moving wall of flame and shrapnel fell in front of the advancing infantry and passed through the enemy lines, destroying strongpoints but also forcing the defenders to find refuge in their dugouts. Without the protection of the barrage, the attack on Vimy would have been little more than a frontal assault against the massed guns of entrenched enemy positions. Yet the gunners offered more than simply a creeping barrage. As part of their destructive fire plan, the new Canadian counter battery office (CCBO) systematically gathered and processed intelligence on enemy batteries, waiting to unleash concentrated fire to stop the opposing guns from launching a counter-barrage that could stop or slow the Canadian infantry assault against the ridge. The Canadian gunners, in the words of Lieutenant-Colonel Andrew McNaughton, the first commander of the CCBO, aimed to "exploit gun power to the limit for the purpose of saving the lives of our infantry."[2] Through improved tactics, doctrine, and weight of shells, the gunners at Vimy took and saved lives on the way to victory.

The image of the deadly machine gun, firing in methodical arcs as it mowed down troops, remains central to the popular memory of the Great War. But the artillery was the true killer, causing an estimated sixty percent of all wounds.[3] The crash of high explosives, whirling shrapnel and shell splinters proved early in the conflict that artillery would decide the fate of empires.

Artillery fire wreaked havoc on those caught in the open. Shrapnel shells exploded downwards in a shotgun-like blast, spraying the front with hundreds of lead balls. High explosive shells exploded like dynamite, killing through the force of a blast that could collapse lungs and kill a man without leaving a mark. The explosive charge that shattered the shell casing also created jagged shell splinters. The irregular wounds caused by artillery fire were deadly; a victim was three times as likely to die from a shell fragment wound to the chest as from a bullet wound to the same region.[4]

Yet the gunners were themselves vulnerable to small arms fire, and after several battles where crews took crippling casualties firing over open sights, the guns were withdrawn behind the thickening trench lines. Increasingly they began to fire indirectly on their targets from several kilometres away, sight unseen. The fire was inaccurate at first, but it could still be deadly against troops in the open. Even when guided by forward observers, a lack of communication ensured that gunners were slow to react to changing circumstances.

Throughout 1915, British and Canadian gunners continued to be plagued by an insufficient supply of shells. Except in extraordinary circumstances, gun teams were often limited to five or ten shells a day, restrictions that neither inspired confidence nor improved skills. Shell shortages were compounded by difficulties with fuses. To clear barbed wire, shells needed to explode on contact with the wire. But in 1915 and 1916, the fuses were often not sensitive enough to detonate on contact, and the shells buried themselves in the ground before exploding. The infantry suffered accordingly as they were held up on the uncut barbed wire and mowed down by enemy machine gunners.

As General Officer Commanding, Royal Artillery (GOC RA) for the Canadian Corps from late 1915 to 1916, Brigadier-General Henry Burstall realized his gunners had to improve. He encouraged experimenting with new techniques, like firing from a map. Forward observers directed the guns by telephone and were soon assisted by

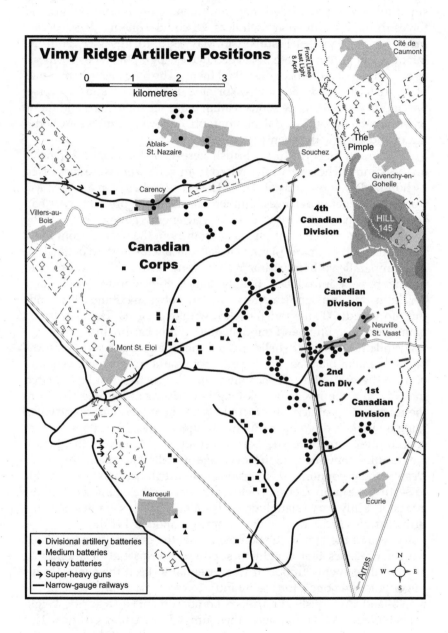

Vimy Ridge Artillery Positions

0   1   2   3
kilometres

Front Lines
Last Light
8 April

Cité de
Caumont

Ablais-
St. Nazaire

The
Pimple

Souchez

Givenchy-en-
Gohelle

Carency

Villers-au-
Bois

4th
Canadian
Division

HILL
145

**Canadian
Corps**

3rd
Canadian
Division

Neuville
St. Vaast

Mont St. Eloi

2nd
Can Div

1st
Canadian
Division

Maroeuil

Écurie

● Divisional artillery batteries
■ Medium batteries
▲ Heavy batteries
→ Super-heavy guns
— Narrow-gauge railways

Arras

N
W ⊕ E
S

aerial observers, who corrected the fall of shells using a clock system superimposed on a gridded map, and then communicated to ground forces through rudimentary wireless. Of course, one needed accurate maps. At the Battle of Festubert in May 1915, for instance, both the infantry and gunners were bedeviled by "cartographic monstrosities," as one artillery staff officer described them.[5] The maps were sometimes off by up to 400 yards (366 metres) printed upside down and in reverse. Special survey units were soon creating more accurate maps and these, when combined with aerial photographs, allowed gunners to better target and destroy the enemy.[6]

By the summer of 1916, the British were ready for their big offensive on the Somme. The new armies raised from volunteers were supported by hundreds of thousands of shells. The British relied on mass to smash through the enemy defences. Limited attacks in the previous year had been on too narrow a front and allowed enemy guns to respond by shelling the heavy concentrations of infantry in the packed front lines. The British at the Somme planned to saturate a wide portion of the front in an unparalleled bombardment for several weeks. New and heavier howitzers were introduced, like the 6-inch, 8-inch and 9.2-inch guns. Each gun fired, in a steep trajectory, shells of between 118 and 290 pounds (fifty-four and 132 kilograms) packed with explosives. The infantry on both sides faced limb- and mind-shattering bombardments.

While the howitzer shells crashed into the rear support areas, the high command planned that the infantry would simply walk over and occupy the shattered trenches after this destructive fire had cleared the way. But the intense week-long bombardment had alerted all to the forthcoming attack, and incredibly resilient German infantrymen hung on in their dugouts, ready to rise up and meet the attackers with concentrated fire once the barrage stopped. Moreover, the British ammunition contained a high percentage of shells that failed to explode.[7] Despite the cacophony of explosions, the British barrage was not able to destroy the entire German defensive system. The opening day of the attack on 1 July was a slaughter, with almost 60,000 casualties. Still, the British armies pressed on in the Somme for another 141 days.

Towards the end of the Somme battle, the gunners experimented with new tactics that sought to suppress fire instead of attempting to annihilate enemy troops. It was essential to keep the enemy in his dugouts long enough for the infantry to cross the killing zone of no-man's-land. Previously, the artillery bombardment laid a terrific weight of shell on enemy strongpoints, then jumped to the next position. This helped smash defences and defenders, but not all of them.[8] When the barrage jumped off to the next objective, the defenders rose from their dugouts and shot down the infantry still struggling through no-man's-land.

Learning from these failures, gunners began to fire a creeping barrage, or wall of fire, that slowly moved over the enemy lines in shorter leaps. The infantry were to stay close to the wall of shrapnel and, in the words of instructors, "lean into the barrage" for protection. The barrage would usually rest on an enemy position for a few minutes, and then leap forward 100 yards (91 metres). A.A. Bonar of the Princess Patricia's Canadian Light Infantry described how the creeping barrage worked:

> The infantry advance in long waves, the first wave keeping forty yards behind the barrage or as near it as comfortable. When the barrage lifts the waves of men jump forward a given distance, keeping close to the barrage until it lifts again, when the same tactics are repeated. The concentrated drumfire from artillery and machine-guns keeps the enemy in his deep dugouts. When the barrage lifts he hasn't time to come out of his subterranean galleries to work his machine-guns before our infantry are on top of him.[9]

The infantry tried to follow the barrage closely, aware that if they were slowed down by enemy strongpoints, they would be left defenceless in no-man's-land as the barrage moved away. The creeping barrage was a vast improvement on previous tactics, yet it was difficult to have several hundred guns fire in unison on the same target and then move forward at the same pace along different terrain across the front. As well, communication was so rudimentary that once a barrage started, it could not be called off or brought back to deal with obstinate defenders. There was little flexibility.

It was also dangerous. Even one gun firing short could drop shells into the forward lines of advancing troops. Although there were countless examples of friendly fire incidents, the infantry accepted this burden if it meant suppressing enemy small arms fire. By the end of the Somme battles, the creeping barrage showed promise in neutralizing enemy fire. But even if the barrage succeeded, too often barbed wire remained uncleared because of faulty fuses and dud shells. Furthermore, attackers always remained vulnerable to enemy counter-barrage fire, making any attack in the open costly. While the power of the guns reduced the landscape to a wasteland where only corpse-filled craters ran the length of the front, the enemy still found ways to hold on during the artillery onslaught. The attacking Canadian infantry paid dearly when they left their trenches.

In October 1916, the men of the Canadian Corps, now four divisions strong and with a strength of nearly 100,000 men, had limped off the Somme. The attritional battles had been devastating. With 24,000 casualties in the Corps, its commander, Sir Julian Byng, realized that the allies had to find a better way to wage war. He selected two of his most promising officers, Arthur Currie, GOC of the 1st Division, and Andrew McNaughton, the 29-year-old artillery expert, to investigate the lessons learned by British and French troops during the devastating battles of the Somme and Verdun.

McNaughton was to become one of the premier gunners of the war. Born in 1887 in Moosomin, Saskatchewan, he was commissioned in the Montreal field battery in 1910 while studying at McGill University. McNaughton graduated in 1912 with a Master's degree in electrical engineering. He had a keen scientific mind and was instructing at McGill before he went overseas in 1914. 'Andy,' as he was known to the men, was not above sharing a can of bully beef over a fire with the rank and file. He also kept a pet lion in his command headquarters, which was prone to chew on the shoes and puttees of alarmed guests. While he was becoming the stuff of legend, it was his embrace of scientific gunnery that would prove him one of the war's key innovators.

McNaughton's visit to the French was disappointing. Despite surviving the bloodbath of Verdun, the French had not codified their lessons into any sort of doctrine, with artillery tactics differing between armies, corps, and divisions. In fact, McNaughton later observed that the key lesson from the French was "what not to do" in organizing an efficient artillery service.[10] More important was McNaughton's discussion with British artillery officers, especially Lieutenant-Colonel A.G. Haig of V British Corps, a cousin of Sir Douglas Haig, who shared with McNaughton improved scientific gunnery principles relating to flash-spotting and sound-ranging to locate enemy guns. McNaughton even invited a number of British scientists who had been rebuked in other British divisions to share their findings with the Canadian Corps.

McNaughton emerged from the consultations with a better understanding of how artillery could support the infantry. The Somme had proven that despite millions of shells, total destruction of the enemy lines was not possible. It was more important to neutralize the enemy so that the foot soldier could be protected from enemy machine gun fire and counter-barrages. An improved creeping barrage would neutralize the machine guns and clear the barbed wire, but a new organization was needed to engage the enemy batteries.

The Canadian counter battery office (CCBO) was established in February 1917 to gather enemy intelligence so as to harass enemy operations and destroy opposing artillery forces. McNaughton had dedicated heavy batteries attached to his command to carry out the destructive shoots once the enemy was located. Pilots and observers in BE2 aircraft from the Royal Flying Corps (RFC) flew over the battlefield, spotting battery positions, spent shell casings and other tell-tale tracks, and then informed their headquarters with letter drops, primitive wireless radio or photographs. Aware of the importance of these aerial observers, the gunners sought to protect them from fierce ground defences. As the 2nd Division's war diary noted, "we put on a shrapnel barrage to keep heads down while the plane was over."[11] But the gunners could do nothing to protect the slow-flying aircraft from aggressive German fighters in mass formations, known as flying circuses. Led by Baron von Richthofen, better known as The Red Baron, the Germans made April one of the costliest months of the war for the RFC.[12] W.A. "Billy" Bishop, the Canadian air ace who flew over the Vimy battlefield, later paid special tribute to the aerial observers, who "take enormous risks and seldom get any glory."[13]

The CCBO's greatest strength was its ability to gather, analyze and process intelligence.[14] Experienced intelligence officers studied the aerial photographs, looking for telltale signs of camouflaged enemy batteries. These were combined with other forms of intelligence from forward observers and from infantry battle patrols that snatched prisoners in the hope of extracting information. The intelligence was collated on maps to create a target list of guns that would either be knocked out immediately or, to surprise the enemy, become targets for destructive fire at the time of the assault. While none of these intelligence techniques delivered victory on its own, McNaughton was fashioning an efficient system to locate and destroy enemy guns, which was essential to saving the lives of the Canadian infantry.

McNaughton and his seniors, especially the GOC, RA, Brigadier-General E.W.B. Morrison, a South African War veteran and prewar editor of the Ottawa Citizen, who had replaced Burstall, encouraged the study or incorporation of other scientific skills into the artillery. Daily meteorological reports were sent out to all brigades and batteries. Wind, rain and air pressure could throw off the flight of a shell by dozens of metres. While some gunners wondered at how deeply the 'boffins' (scientists) would intrude in their work, there was no point in knowing the location of enemy guns if weather conditions kept the gunners from hitting their targets. The wear on gun barrels also affected accuracy. Most guns were fired far beyond their life-span and prolonged periods of firing heated the barrel and turned the nose up slightly.[15] Acknowledging these constraints did not always lead to success, but it reduced the factors that had plagued the gunners in the two previous years.

Vimy Ridge had fallen to the Germans in October 1914, and they had repulsed three attacks over the next two and half years of battle. All the while the Germans had fortified the imposing ridge, digging deep concrete dugouts, laying rows of barbed wire, and expertly situating their machine gun posts. Some 10,000 German defenders manned the ridge, but the position was not held in much depth because the ridge dropped away on the eastern side. This was one of the few Canadian advantages, but they had to strike hard and fast to capture the ridge and hold it before counterattacks could throw them back.

The Canadians knew that preparation was an essential ingredient for victory. The stockpiling of ammunition, the digging of gun pits, the building of new roads and the establishment of underground subways to allow the infantry to move closer to the jumping-off points without losing men to stray enemy artillery fire, were all part of the pre-battle planning. Yet Byng had a difficult time situating his artillery, since the Canadians were under observation from the ridge, and nothing could be done during the day within 5,500 metres of the front.[16] At night, gunners and horses worked frantically to drag the guns into gun-pits built of corrugated iron and sandbags, protected by a top cover of sandbags or sod. Platforms of brick or stone stabilized the gun.

The concentration of guns into such a small area forced Byng to echelon the guns in a dangerously exposed arc around Vimy Ridge. Some of the light field pieces were camouflaged as close as 460 metres behind the lines. But since the Germans controlled the heights they called down devastating fire and a steady trickle of guns were lost.[17] The sleet and rain of March had also reduced the ground to a quagmire. "The mud grew deeper, more viscous, more ubiquitous every hour," wrote one gunner. "We forgot what it was to shave, to wash, to be dry. Mud crept into our ears, noses, eyes and food."[18] The 7th Siege Battery, which fired 200-pound 8-inch howitzer shells, had one gun sink so far into the mud that its barrel was only a few centimetres above the ground.

The artillery plan consisted of a four-phase artillery battle that was organized to run from 20 March to 9 April.[19] The artillery followed its plan with ruthless precision. Phase I ran from zero minus twenty (20 March) to zero minus seven (2 April). General Morrison ordered his divisional artillery commanders to silence half their guns in order to deceive the Germans as to the real intent of the operation, but it was still a devastating bombardment. The divisional artillery had twenty-four brigades of artillery at its disposal: 480 eighteen-pounders, 138 4.5-inch howitzers, ninety-six two-inch trench mortars, and twenty-four massive 9.45-inch trench mortars.[20] In addition, the Corps headquarters and McNaughton's counter-battery group had access to 245 siège guns and heavy mortars.[21] The Canadian infantry had never been supported by such overwhelming firepower.

The first guns that opened up on 20 March targetted enemy dugouts, trenches and known strongpoints that had been identified through aerial and ground intelligence. The incessant pounding by the guns, trench mortars, and indirect machine gun fire (not controlled by the gunners) was to "prevent the repair of trenches."[22] An extensive Canadian raiding program snatched dozens of prisoners, most of whom were willing to pass along information as they were interrogated. Throughout this first phase of the artillery battle, more batteries arrived at the front, were situated in their gun pits and joined in the methodical, punishing bombardment. However, this was not a one-sided battle, for the gunners dueled to knock out each other's guns. The Canadian Corps' six-inch howitzers were particularly effective in their counter-battery role, scoring many hits that were confirmed by aerial photography.[23]

Barbed wire remained Byng's greatest concern. Too many assaults on the Somme had been stopped by soldiers unable to advance, shot down as they looked desperately for gaps in the wire. The eighteen-pounders continued to soften up the enemy front lines and clear the obstacles that had been laid and fortified for more than two years. The two-inch trench mortars were also employed with the eighteen-pounders to clear wire. The 106 fuse, one of the most important inventions of the war, was used extensively at Vimy Ridge. This fuse and the new mushroom-shaped cap made shells explode on contact with the wire, which harnessed the shell's full power to clear the obstacle. One artillery report later noted that the "wire was nearly all destroyed, 106 fuses having proved most effective for the purpose."[24]

More than 200,000 eighteen-pounder shells were fired in the first phase, as well as another 143,000 larger calibre rounds.[25] Despite the hundreds of guns that were to pound the enemy fortifications, they would be useless without their shell allotments. In addition to ammunition dumps formed at the guns (which usually consisted of a few days' worth of shells), five enormous main dumps contained 25,000 tons of shells, the bulk of the 1.6 million shells allotted to the Canadian Corps.[26] After light rail and lorries carried them within a few kilometres of the front, the task of hauling the vast weight of the shells through the muck fell to the horses and mules. Although slowed by dissolving roads and interdiction fire, the logistical system never faltered, with drivers leading their four-legged friends back and forth through sleet and shell fire.[27] It was terribly stressful and William Ogilvie, part of an ammunition column, thought that the "drivers were out of the danger zone just long enough to realize how dangerous it was...many of them got shell-shocked [sic] just with the thought of going back up to the front."[28]

Once the shells were dropped off, the gunners cleaned them to reduce the chance of premature explosions in the gun barrel. Water barrels were kept filled to cool the guns during the expected period of rapid fire. In preparation for battle, the gun crews screwed off the caps and inserted the fuses, making live rounds. Yet there were still many dud shells. Shrapnel shells also had a tendency to explode in the barrel, the casing disintegrating from the force of the propellant charge. Sergeant Ernest Black recounted that the gunners tried sample shells from each batch that arrived and there were frequent premature bursts that sent hundreds of shrapnel balls from the gun barrel like a shotgun blast. Black's gun was in a particularly bad position, the front row of seven lines of guns: "all day and all night the air above us was filled with the whine of shrapnel bullets from premature burst and the howl of fuses and shell cases."[29] The building of thick sandbag parados behind gun pits protected the gunners, but the Canadian infantry ahead endured continuous friendly fire raining down on them.

The artillery plan moved into phase II on 2 April, a week before the battle. Intensified shoots involved all guns to soften up the enemy trenches: the eighteen-pounder guns were allocated 336,000 shells for the week leading up to zero hour on 9 April, roughly ten rounds per yard of front.[30] It was an enormous amount of ammunition, but intelligence estimated that there were some 37,000 yards (33,800 metres) of enemy fire trenches, 16,000 yards (14,600 metres) of communication trenches, and 10,000 yards (9,100 metres) of barbed wire.[31] The withering preliminary bombardment, called the "Week of Suffering" by German troops, consisted of high explosives and shrapnel. Machine gun fire was added to "thicken up" the barrage, although many gunners saw this as next to useless. There was, no doubt, some professional competition at work here. Putting aside rivalries, the barrage of shells and bullets created an inferno of fire that isolated front line troops and then shattered their morale. "We are hammering Fritz to pieces," wrote Lieutenant V.G. Tupper, only days before he was killed during the battle. "Our ammunition and guns now seem to be unlimited."[32]

German trenches were pounded hour after hour, day after day. Even in the dark there was no escape. Byng ordered his gunners to fire all night to interrupt reliefs and working parties and to keep the enemy in a "state of alarm" and "deny him rest."[33] The Germans went to ground in deep dugouts that offered good protection, but the psychological strain was terrible. A German account presented the barrage:

What the eye sees through the clouds of smoke is a sea of masses of earth thrown up and clouds of smoke rolling along…among all of these are spitting fuses, slow burning gas shells, exploding trench mortars, and the white vapour appears to consume everything until it obliterates the whole spectacle of dancing madness in impenetrable fog. How long did this nightmare last? The sense of time seems intensified so that every second is divided into one hundred moments of fear.[34]

Feint bombardments were fired during the last week. Targets were shelled, the guns moved off and then returned with a crash bombardment in the hope that the Germans had quit their dugouts and gone to their trenches waiting for an attack. Each time this happened, the enemy infantry waited longer in his dugout, unwilling to expose himself to a returning barrage. These precious minutes were often the difference between life and death for the Canadian infantry on the day of battle.

The Canadian and British gunners targeted the eight fortified villages behind the German lines with heavy and super heavy guns. The village of Thélus held a commanding view on the 2nd Division's front, and it was destroyed under the weight of 480 twelve- and fifteen-inch shells and 8,400 rounds from smaller howitzers. Thélus was wiped from the map, leaving little but rubble and corpses.[35] "The gunners back in their rough splinter-proof gun pits had become temporarily stone deaf, while blood oozed from their ears and noses," remembered one gunner. "Orders were passed in writing; the noise was too terrific for words."[36] The other villages were subjected to lesser, if still heavy, periodic fire to inflict casualties and demoralize the enemy.

Canadian infantry patrols went out every night to inspect the damage. When wire was not cleared, new arrangements were made to saturate those parts of the front with mortar or artillery fire. The Canadian Corps heavy artillery mortar batteries fired a punishing 130,000 rounds of plunging high explosive fire to clear wire and damaging fortifications in the final week.[37] Daily battery intelligence reports tracked the effectiveness of their shoots for headquarters.[38] Efforts were redoubled to locate and destroy enemy guns. Victory could be achieved only if every detail was observed.

Phase III of the operation was to occur on 9 April, the day of the attack. As the minutes ticked down to 0530 hours on 9 April, twenty-one battalions of more than 10,000 infantrymen lay in wait to 'go over the bags.' Many were in the protective shelter of the special assault tunnels, but thousands more lay out in the cold mud. Adjustments were made to equipment; last letters written; cigarettes were held in shaking hands; NCOs and officers offered a warming tot of battle rum.

Minutes before the assault, orders went out from hundreds of NCOs and officers to fix bayonets. And then they waited for the barrage.

The gunners had spent the night preparing for the furious opening barrage. The rate of fire had also been reduced along the front to allow them to rest and, it was hoped, to provide the enemy with a false sense of respite. But in the hour before the assault, all the gunners were at their posts, and all eyes were on synchronized watches. As high explosives left too many impassable craters for the final phase of the operation, the creeping barrage consisted of eighteen-pounders firing shrapnel. Each of the eighteen-pounders would fire three rounds a minute, with lifts of 100 yards (ninety one metres) every three minutes. On the 1st and 2nd Division's fronts, where the troops had to penetrate further than the two divisions on the left, the barrage was modified, lengthened and coordinated to allow for more pauses for follow-on troops to push into the enemy lines. Along the four-division Canadian assault, however, there would be an average of one eighteen-pounder for every seventeen yards (sixteen metres) of front, in effect nine rounds over a three minute period on a sixteen metre-front before moving off to the next objective. Another standing barrage kept pace 150 yards (136 metres) further on while a third heavy barrage was fired 300 yards (273 metres) beyond the second wave. In all, three sweeping fields of fire moved over the German lines.

In the seconds before zero hour, there was a strange, unearthly silence as all shell fire stopped. Then came the crash of artillery shells at exactly 0530 hours. The entire countryside lit up in flames as 983 guns and mortars fired in unison. J.A. Bain, a Canadian signaler, described the opening barrage:

> The din was terrific—deafening—indeed it is hard to find suitable words to describe the awful uproar made by thousands [sic] of our guns and the shells passing through the air, bursting on and over the enemy's trenches ahead of us. The rattle of machine guns, the detonation of hand grenades and bombs, and the enemy's counter-barrage which, although not very formidable, was bursting on our old front line, all joining in one vast volume of noise.[39]

With thousands of shells hurtling over their heads, the infantry advanced behind the moving wall of fire and steel.

The complexity of the barrage required the infantry to recall the measured bounds of the "barrages" under which they had advanced in their training. On the 3rd Division's front, for example, sixty eighteen-pounders were employed in a rolling barrage. Twenty-four additional eighteen-pounders were used in the standing barrage on strongpoints from zero to zero plus seventy-five minutes. An additional eighteen-pounder battery from each brigade fired over the front, superimposing its fire over earlier targets and responding to SOS calls or targets of opportunity from forward observers. At zero plus seventy-five, the twenty-four guns employed in the standing barrage then joined the rolling barrage to maintain the ratio of guns across the widening frontage. The 4.5-inch howitzers fired on selected strongpoints and targets behind the creeping barrage, lifting to stay 150 yards (136 metres) ahead of the first barrage to combat against short shells. Medium and heavy howitzers also laid down their bombardment on strongpoints behind the second barrage, 300 yards (273 metres) beyond, moving as the creeping barrage moved. Further complicating the fireplan was the fact that the 3rd Division's frontage was not parallel due to terrain, requiring the barrage to have twenty-five lifts on the right, but only thirteen on the left.[40] Sergeant Ernest Black testified that one German officer caught in the barrage remarked that "he had never seen anything like it in the whole war."[41] Indeed, along the Canadian front, the supporting artillery represented the greatest concentration of guns per yard of front to that point in the war.[42] "Nothing human could stand it," wrote Sergeant Percy Willmot.[43]

"The state of the country we went over is almost beyond description; simply a waste with no distinguishing marks," reported one Canadian forward observation officer (FOO) to headquarters. "Shell hole upon shell hole, some being enough to put a small house in, and most filled with water and mud. A tangled mass of old wire, iron, pit props, equipment, and, here and there, the bodies of friend and foe—a ghastly sight."[44] The FOOs had lived in brigade and battalion headquarters for a few days prior to the assault to strengthen the bond between the artillery and the infantry.[45] Morrison hoped that these forward eyes, with their links to artillery brigades in the rear, would help to reduce "short-shooting" and allow the artillery to respond more quickly to emergency calls.[46] The latter they were able to do, but there was no avoiding friendly fire. Worn barrels, faulty shells, and lack of skill all contributed to Canadians being killed by Canadian and British shells, but the barrage generally worked as planned, with enemy machine gunners knocked out or at least confined to their dugouts before the infantry overran their positions.

The Canadian guns pounded the enemy positions along the front, but the German batteries in the rear were not safe either. Counter-battery fire was devastating, although the attempt to use chemical shells was cancelled until better weather conditions arrived on 12 April.[47] In the week before zero, the counter-battery guns had fired 125,900 rounds, harassing eighty-three percent of an estimated 212 located guns.[48] At zero hour, McNaughton's counter-battery groups laid down destructive barrages on enemy guns that identified themselves by responding to the German infantry's distress calls. McNaughton's guns destroyed forty-seven additional guns after zero hour, providing immeasurable support to the infantry.[49] By 0550 hours, FOO dispatches filtered back to artillery headquarters reporting that the "Hun barrage [had] slackened off."[50] Black smoke from burning ammunition was observed rising from enemy gun pits. The German guns were largely silenced before the battle or knocked out as they opened fire after zero hour. Attesting to that success, the Canadian gunners had surprisingly low casualties. On 9 April, the 2nd Division's gunners lost only one gun, eight killed and eight wounded; the 3rd Division's gunners suffered only nine killed and fifty-eight wounded over the four-day battle.[51]

For the three divisions on the right, the attack was a success, if a costly one. The barrage had played an important, perhaps essential, part in supporting the attack, but it had not been perfect. On the 2nd Division's front, there were complaints that the soldiers were slowed by their barrage, which forced the troops to rein in their quick advance for fear of being torn apart by their own shells.[52] Yet more often there was praise for the gunners. "The enemy defences had been practically obliterated by the preliminary bombardment and the garrisons offered very little resistance," was the observation in the 3rd Division's final report of action.[53] Closer to the sharp end, the 1st Brigade reported that there was general agreement among the officers of its four battalions that "our artillery was good. It was sufficient in quantity and quality and absolutely bore down the enemy."[54] Brigadier G.S. Tuxford of the 3rd Brigade noted that the artillery was "excellent, and is spoken of by everyone in enthusiastic terms."[55] A report by the commanding officer of the 3rd Battalion observed that "the morale of the German infantry was found to be poor" on their front, but that this was "no doubt" because of the "severity of our barrage stunning them and rendering them stupid."[56]

However, on the far left, the 4th Division struggled against machine gun strongpoints on the highest point of the ridge that the barrage had not cleared. Deep dugouts and abandoned mines had allowed large portions of the German garrison force to escape unscathed. And as Andrew Godefroy relates later in this volume, a barrage was called off on one critical trench in front of the 87th Battalion, causing terrible casualties.[57]

General Morrison heard of the collapse of 4th Division's attacks by 1400 hours, and agreed to devote additional heavy guns to the sector to "smash up" the enemy positions. At 1515 hours, a well-timed barrage swept through the enemy lines followed by the attacking infantry. This time the coordination between infantry and artillery was described as brilliant.[58] A few captured German officers confessed that "they got hell from the heavies."[59] The highest point on Vimy Ridge eventually fell to the 4th Division on 9 April, and the remaining portion of the ridge was captured in the early hours of the next day.

With the ridge captured, the fear among Byng and his troops was that they would lose it in the expected counterattacks. Heavy snow on the 9th, combined with the bombardment, reduced the roads to mush. This complicated the final phase of the plan to move field batteries up the ridge. Horses and guns sank in the mud. Enemy fire targeted the known roads and there were casualties all day. In fact, Captain A.F. Duguid, a staff officer with 2nd Division and future official historian, noted that the Germans had brought up many new batteries to engage the infantry on and in front of Vimy, and they did so with "impunity, as they are out of range of all our batteries."[60] The mud was so bad on the 10th that the mules and horses carrying eighteen-pounder ammunition had to be turned back. Engineers, pioneers, and infantry struggled to lay new roads, often with fascines of branches bundled together and layered into the mud and slime.[61]

But the terrible weather conditions worked against both armies. The shock of the operation and failure to keep the reserves close to the front meant that the German counterattacks were too slow and disorganized. The German forces that moved forward on 10 April did so under full observation of Canadian machine guns, and Canadian gunners turned German guns against their former owners. Forward observers continued to coordinate the guns in the rear, even though many were out of range. Still, there were enough to cause terrible damage to enemy troops in the open. One of the 2nd Division's forward observers called back to headquarters at 1042 hours on 10 April to report that a German force was "advancing in mass...towards northern parts of Vimy thick as peas."[62] The observer tracked their movement through binoculars, reporting back every few minutes and vectored the division's guns on to map grids. The German force was shredded by shrapnel fire before it could even close with ridge's defenders. Clumsy German tactics combined with able forward observers broke up additional attacks during the day.

There was little fighting on 11 April, but on the next day, the 4th Division launched a final assault against the Pimple, a position on the far left of the ridge and initially outside of the corps boundary. It was heavily fortified and recently garrisoned with fresh, elite troops. But the Canadian gunners, including much of the heavy corps artillery, supported the limited two battalion attack to the hilt and the position was buried under a crescendo of fire. Yet the hurried nature of the battle meant that the attacking Canadian battalions went forward with gaps in the barrage. As always, the infantry had to fight its way forward. The Pimple was captured by the end of the day and all of fortress Vimy was in Canadian hands.

The Battle of Vimy Ridge was a well-planned and executed set-piece battle. The Canadians succeeded because they had studied their previous failures. The high command was far from the mindless, ossified donkey-generals of literature; instead, they were forward-thinking and willing to acknowledge and embrace the lessons of the past. The artillery made significant improvements from the battles of 1915 and 1916. The important evolution of guns, shells, fuses, intelligence-gathering techniques, operational analysis, refined doctrine and tactics led to victory in April 1917.

It is not often noted how much the Canadians depended on British guns for their victory. On the 1st Division front, ninety-four guns were Canadian and 102 were British; on the 2nd Division's front, ninety-three guns were Canadian while ninety were British; on the 3rd Division's front, 108 were Canadian and forty-eight were British; on the 4th Division's front, all of the guns, 177, belonged to British units.[63] The Corps' heavy guns and counter-battery work were more Canadian, but also consisted of British and Australian batteries. At the very least, such figures give pause to the oft-repeated claim that Vimy was solely a Canadian battle. While the four infantry divisions were largely composed of Canadian units (along with one British brigade), the units on the flanks, as well as much of the artillery and logistical staff were British.

The lessons of the successful set-piece battle at Vimy would contribute to the Corps' success over the last year and a half of war. Victories at Hill 70 and Passchendaele, the March Offensive and the Final Hundred Days were predicated on the combined arms battle that relied on the infantry and artillery working together. The artillery continued to refine its doctrine and tactics, further embracing the principles of scientific warfare. Destructive and neutralizing fire were combined to kill, harass and force the enemy to seek safety in deeper dugouts, which bought precious time for the assaulting infantry. New techniques, like firing from a map without pre-registered shots, or back barrages which moved backwards to forward, caused confusion in the enemy lines. The evolution of artillery tactics continued with counter-battery work that used high explosives, shrapnel, chemical, and smoke shells to exhaust or destroy the enemy.[64] Counter-battery work increased in importance: in August 1914, the BEF had 500 artillery pieces, of which only twenty-four sixty-pounders had the range to target enemy batteries; by war's end, the artillery had grown to 6,500 pieces, of which 2,000 were medium or heavy howitzers that suppressed enemy battery fire.[65] And all the while the weight of firepower increased, with hundreds of thousands of shells saturating objectives before, during, and after each battle. By the battles of the Final Hundred Days in the fall of 1918, the artillery arm could consistently harass and destroy enemy batteries to provide a protective screen of steel and shell.

Despite these vast improvements, artillery alone could not win the war. The artillery laid the ground work for victory, but ultimate success in battle fell to the infantry. Even the best barrages could not destroy all enemy strongpoints. Enemy positions that held out had to be knocked out by the infantry. It was they who conquered the battlefield, but they could not have done it without the support of the gunners.

Notes

1   Jonathan M. House, *Toward Combined Arms Warfare: A Survey of 20th-Century Tactics, Doctrine, and Organization* (U.S. Army Command and General Staff College, Fort Leavenworth, KS 66027-6900, 1984).

2   A.G.L. McNaughton, "The Development of Artillery in the Great War," *Canadian Defence Quarterly* vol VI, no 2 (January 1929), 164.

3   Desmond Morton, *When Your Number's Up: The Canadian Soldier in the First World War* (Toronto: Random House, 1993), ix.

4   Gary Sheffield, *Forgotten Victory: The First World War: Myths and Realities* (London: Review, 2002), 111.

5   Duguid to Burns, 2 April 1937, file 990.009 (D6), vol 20541, Record Group [RG] 24, Library and Archives of Canada [LAC].

6   See Jeffrey Murray, "British-Canadian Military Cartography on the Western Front," *Archivaria* vol 26, 52-65.

7   John Keegan, *The Face of Battle: A Study of Agincourt, Waterloo and the Somme* (London: Pimlico, 1976, reprint 1993), 204-42.

8   For artillery on the Somme, see Jonathan Bailey, "British Artillery in the Great War," Paddy Griffith (ed), *British Fighting Methods in the Great War* (London: Frank Cass, 1996), 28-35.

9   Robert Zubkowski, *As Long as Faith and Freedom Last: Stories from the Princess Patricia's Canadian Light Infantry from June 1914 to September 1919* (Calgary: Bunker to Bunker Publications, 2003), 251.

10 John Swettenham, *McNaughton, Volume I* (Toronto: Ryerson Press, 1968), 69.

11 War Diary [WD], 2nd Canadian Divisional Artillery, 7 April 1917, T-10776-10777, vol 4959, RG 9, LAC.

12 For the RFC at Vimy, see S.F. Wise, *Canadian Airmen and the First World War* (Toronto: University of Toronto Press, 1980), 398-408.

13 Bill Freeman, *Far from Home: Canadians in the First World War* (Toronto: McGraw-Hill Ryerson, 1999), 105.

14   For a technical analysis of counter-battery intelligence gathering, see A.G.L. McNaughton, "Counter Battery Work," *Canadian Defence Quarterly* vol III, no 4 (July 1926), 381-86; Notes on Counter Battery Work in Connection with the Capture of Vimy Ridge, file 4, folder 8, vol 3922, III, RG 9.

15   Robin Prior and Trevor Wilson, *Command on the Western Front: The Military Career of Sir Henry Rawlinson, 1914-18* (Oxford: Blackwell, 1992), 40.

16   Administrative Arrangements — Vimy Ridge Operations, file 8, folder 2, vol 3922, III, RG 9.

17   For enemy harassing fire, see intelligence reports. For example, WD, 4th Division, Appendix B, Weekly Summary of Operations, 29 March to 5 April 1917, T-1938, vol 4859, RG 9.

18   T.W.L. MacDermot, *The Seventh* (Montreal: privately printed, no date), 63.

19   For the plan, see Artillery Instruction for the Capture of Vimy Ridge [Artillery Plan], file 8, folder 3, vol 3922, III, RG 9.

20   Report of Operations of Canadian Corps against Vimy Ridge, file 5, folder 51, vol 3846, III, RG 9. It is interesting to note that the allotment of guns was not distributed equally: the 1st Division had 206 guns and mortars; the 2nd Division had 183 guns and mortars; the 3rd Division had 160 guns and mortars; the 4th Division had 197 guns and mortars. These figures did not include the corps heavy or counter-battery guns. See Artillery Plan, Appendix A.

21   For the breakdown of heavy and counter-battery groups, see Artillery Plan, Appendix B. The medium guns were classified as anything under six inches, while the heavies were largely composed of eight-inch howitzers and 9.2-inch howitzers, plus a few larger guns.

22   Artillery Plan, Section 2, Phase I-2.

23   WD, Canadian Corps, Heavy Artillery, 21-31 March 1917, T-10800, vol 4973, RG 9.

24   WD, Canadian Corps, Heavy Artillery, 9 April 1917.

25   Artillery Plan, Appendix G.1.

26   Report of Operations of Canadian Corps against Vimy Ridge, file 51, folder 5, vol 3846, III, RG 9; Administrative Arrangements — Vimy Ridge Operations, file 8, folder 2, vol 3922, RG 9.

27   John A. MacDonald, *Gun-Fire: An Historical Narrative of the 4th Brigade C.F.A. in the Great War (1914-1918)* (Toronto: Greenway, 1929), 78.

28   William Ogilvie, *Umty-Iddy-Umty: The Story of a Canadian Signaller in the First World War* (Erin: The Boston Mills Press, 1982), 25.

29   Ernest G. Black, *I Want One Volunteer* (Toronto: The Ryerson Press, 1965), 58.

30   Artillery Plan, Appendix G.5.

31   Artillery Plan, Appendix G.4.

32   Reginald Hibbert Tupper, *Victor Gordon Tupper: A Brother's Tribute* (Oxford University Press, 1921), 62.

33   Importance of Night Firing, 23 March 1917, file 17, folder 9, vol 4249, III, RG 9.

34 Elmer Jones, Translation of 'Battle of Arras, 1917' by the German General Staff, Manuscript Group [MG] 30 E 50, LAC.

35 Artillery Instructions, No. 2, WD, Royal Artillery, Canadian Corps, T-10773-10774, vol 4957, RG 9.

36 MacDonald, 56.

37 Expenditure during recent operations on wire, trenches and villages by CCDHA trench batteries, 11 May 1917, file 8, folder 1, vol 3922, III, RG 9.

38 See the examples in WD, 3rd Canadian Divisional Artillery, March 1917, T-10779, vol 4961, RG 9.

39 J. Alexander (Sandy) Bain, *A War Diary: A Canadian Signaller, My Experiences in the Great War* (Moncton: self-published, 1986), 57.

40 WD, 3rd Canadian Divisional Artillery, Report of Operations for Vimy Ridge, 27 April 1917.

41 Black, 59.

42 General Sir Martin Farndale, *History of the Royal Regiment of Artillery: Western Front 1914-18* (London: The Royal Artillery Institution, 1986), 175.

43 Brian D. Tenyson, "A Cape Bretoner at War: Letters from the Front, 1914-1919," *Canadian Military History* vol 11, no 1 (Winter 2002), 44.

44 "The Story of the Fourth Overseas Siege Battery in the Great War," (unpublished battery history), 8, 58 A 1 141.3, Canadian War Museum [CWM].

45 Liaison and Forward Observation, 1 April 1917, file 17, folder 10, vol 4249, III, RG 9.

46 Artillery Plan, Section 2, Phase III-4-4.

47 Instructions for Firing Gas Shells; Report on the Use of Gas Shells by Canadian Corps Vimy Ridge, file 8, folder 2, vol 3977, III, RG 9.

48 Swettenham, *McNaughton*, 90.

49 Notes on Counter Battery Work in Connection with the Capture of Vimy Ridge, file 8, folder 4, vol 3922, III, RG 9.

50 Information from F.O.O.'s and Officers, 9 April 1917, 5:50 am, WD, 2nd Canadian Divisional Artillery.

51 WD, 2nd Canadian Divisional Artillery, 9 April 1917; Report of Operations for Vimy Ridge, 27 April 1917, WD, 3rd Canadian Divisional Artillery.

52 Wallace to OC, 6th Brigade, CFA, 10 April 1917, file 17, folder 10, vol 4249, III RG 9.

53 3rd Division, Narrative of Operations file 51, folder 5, vol 3846, III, RG 9.

54 Report of the 1st Brigade, file 51, folder 1, vol 3846, III, RG 9.

55 Report of Operations by 3rd Brigade, G. 1307, file 51, folder 4, vol 3846, III, RG 9.

56 Report of Operations by the 3rd Battalion, file 51, folder 1, vol 3846, III, RG 9.

57 Report of 4th Division at Vimy, Appendix B, WD, 4th Division.

58 Report of 4th Division at Vimy, Appendix B.

59 Time Log, 2:29 am, WD, Royal Artillery, Canadian Corps, 9 April 1917.

60 WD, 2nd Canadian Divisional Artillery, 10 April 1917.

61   For logistics at Vimy, see Michael Ryan, "Supplying the Materiel Battle: Combined Logistics in the Canadian Corps, 1915-1918," Master's thesis, Carleton University, 2005.

62   Information from F.O.O.'s and Officers, 10 April 1917, 10:42 am, WD, 2nd Canadian Divisional Artillery.

63   These figures differ slightly from earlier ones, likely as a result of the attrition of guns, either through enemy shelling or mechanical failure.

64   For the success of chemical counter-battery fire, see Tim Cook, *No Place To Run: The Canadian Corps and Gas Warfare in the First World War* (Vancouver: University of British Columbia Press, 2000), 109-110.

65   Albert P. Palazzo, "The British Army's Counter-Battery Staff Office and Control of the Enemy in World War I," *Journal of Military History* vol 63 (January 1999), 58.

7

The Sappers of Vimy
Specialized Support for the Assault of 9 April 1917

BILL RAWLING

William Withrow was not a stereotypical warrior and his death was not what one would have expected of a soldier on the Western Front. On 4 May 1917, less than a month after the capture of Vimy Ridge, he was watching a baseball game when he collapsed and died; an autopsy concluded that he had succumbed to heart failure. He was forty-eight years old.

Withrow was not killed by artillery fire, the most common cause of death for Canadian soldiers in France and Belgium, and he was not in the infantry, the branch that suffered most in the course of the 1914-18 conflict, but he is an example of what a modern battlefield had become since the American Civil War initiated industrialized warfare. Having served in an infantry militia unit in Toronto in the late nineteenth century, Withrow joined the 3rd (Ottawa) Field Company in 1914 and then served in the 2nd Pioneer Battalion as the Lewis machine gun officer before being posted to Canadian Corps headquarters in early 1917 to take command of the topographical section. There he was responsible for the production of specialized maps showing German defences which could be used for planning, for setting up rehearsals and even for orientation in the assault itself.[1] As a post-war report noted, more than 40,000 such maps were issued at Vimy, enough to ensure that every NCO in the attack would have one.[2] William Withrow was a member of the Canadian Engineers, whose work at Vimy Ridge will be described in the pages that follow.

The Canadian Engineers, a corps since 1903, was something of a multi-purpose organization in that it incorporated those technical elements of the army that did not fit logically elsewhere. By 1917 it included light railway troops, which were responsible for the construction and operation of the tramways which brought supplies close enough to the front to be transported to the trenches by lorry, wagon or animal. It also incorporated surveyors and cartographers and sundry workshops. For the assault on Vimy Ridge, the chief engineer, Canadian Corps, Brigadier-General W.B. Lindsay, had under his command six army troops companies (normally answering to army headquarters), the Corps Light Railway Company, a composite railway company and a Canadian permanent base company. To ensure the necessary labour was available, Lindsay relied on the 1st through 4th Canadian entrenching battalions, several labour companies, the 67th Canadian Pioneer Battalion, the 5th Division Pioneer Battalion (the rest of the division was in England), the 123rd Canadian Pioneer Battalion and No. 2 Forestry Detachment, complete with sawmill.[3] Such were the personnel and material resources available at the corps level; none of these units, nor those listed below, could accomplish their tasks without working parties provided by infantry battalions, which would lead to no shortage of difficulties, as we shall see.

Within each division was a pioneer battalion of over a thousand men whose training gave them a combination of engineering and infantry skills. For the assault on Vimy Ridge the 1st Division incorporated the 107th Pioneer Battalion, the 2nd had the 2nd Pioneer Battalion, the 3rd Division had the 3rd, and the 4th Division had two, the 67th and the 124th. Each division could also count on three field companies averaging 218 sappers each, men recruited largely for their civilian skills. With the addition of an entrenching unit, those responsible for engineer tasks numbered between 2,402 and 3,310 per division, averaging almost thirteen percent of such a formation's strength.[4]

The field companies began arriving in the shadow of Vimy Ridge in the last days of 1916 and soon started work. Each field company was assigned to the infantry brigade that shared its number. Thus, the 11th Field Company arrived at the zone allotted to the 11th Brigade on 22 December and by the end of the month began executing a "scheme of development." Digging communication trenches and constructing dugouts allowed the concentration of troops and supplies for offensive operations, as well as improved forward trenches and barbed wire obstacles to protect the build-up.[5] Such work was not carried out in the most benign conditions, one officer noting that, "This is said to be the coldest French winter in twenty years. Coal is scarce, and costs 46 francs per 1000 kilos at the minehead." He also noted how "Frost coming out of the ground played havoc with roads and trenches," as his unit, 6th Field Company, carried out routine tasks, including enlarging galleries in tunnels that led up to the forward trenches, issuing materials from yards and shops and erecting bunks for the thousands of troops moving into the area.[6]

The engineers spent a great deal of time reconnoitering the battlefield. In January Lieutenant-Colonel G.C. Williams, the controller of mines, inspected nineteen craters and groups of craters on the Canadian Corps' front. "The conclusion arrived at is, that no crater is actually insurmountable and that craters are much less of an obstacle than would appear from observation from saps and through periscopes. However they should be negotiated by small parties who can take advantage of causeways and can skirt the actual bottom." The Canadian Corps, like the rest of the British Expeditionary Force, had given up on wave attacks after the carnage of the Somme, so Williams' advice fell on willing ears. In fact, in some previous attacks,

> the crater groups were avoided and the attacks carried over the open ground only between groups; these attacks were subjected to much enfilade fire and it appears that small parties could easily have pushed through the crater groups to deal with machine guns posted to enfilade the open spaces, and to form a link between the attacks on either side of the groups.[7]

Later, when some engineer units were told that they would go into the assault with the infantry, officers and non-commissioned officers (NCOs) studied the ground from the front trenches. A Lieutenant Weldon of 6th Field Company, for example, accompanied by two NCOs, used binoculars to pick out a route between craters for his section's advance.[8]

Not all engineers were pleased that their units were to join the infantry in the assault phase. On 23 March, the 11th Brigade issued its orders calling for seventy-two officers and sappers of the 11th Field Company to carry out the necessary engineering work the day of the attack. The company's commanding officer later "considered this to be an abnormal number of personnel for one operation," given that it might leave him short of troops to conduct subsequent tasks. Discussion with the brigade commander reduced the number assigned to the assault to forty-four. "This arrangement was satisfactory except that it called for 2 Officers and 29 OR [Other Ranks] to go over with the attacking Infantry," which the engineer officer felt placed his sappers[9] at too great a risk.

In fact, such tasks on the battlefield were entirely in keeping with the engineers' role. At Vimy, the only way to build strongpoints before the enemy launched counterattacks was for the engineers to accompany the infantry and put spade to dirt as soon as objectives were captured.[10] The 8th Brigade plan in La Folie sector included a field company to consolidate captured ground while a company of pioneers extended communication trenches to new positions.[11] Likewise, Major Halfdan Hertzberg's 1st Field Company worked with the 1st and 2nd Infantry Brigades, preparing defences on the right flank of the 1st Division.[12] As we shall see, this was dangerous but essential work.

With roles determined for the day of the assault, the Canadian Corps prepared for the upcoming battle, a process industrial in scope and complexity. For example, whether for reinforcing trenches or tunnels, repairing miles of roads, or constructing light railways, engineers required enormous amounts of timber. Number 2 Forestry Detachment drew its men from the infantry battalions and set up a sawmill in the Bois des Alleux: "[A]lthough of a crude description [the mill] was able to cut about 100,000 feet board measure weekly."[13]

The engineers also had to see to the troops' living conditions. Engineers built 460 huts behind the lines,[14] while closer to the front units such as 6th Field Company converted caves into something resembling barracks, complete with stairs, ventilation shafts, bunks and partitions.[15] The supply of water proved a most critical requirement. If lack of accommodation forced troops to sleep in uncomfortable surroundings, lack of water could lead to painful thirst and disability. The problem was not restricted to the troops, either. As a Corps after-action report noted:

> The sudden concentration of 50,000 horses within a restricted area where little water existed required a huge development of the existing sources of water supply. 600,000 gallons a day were necessary. To accomplish this 22 engines and 24 pumping installations were completed, 45 miles of pipe lines were laid, 16 reservoirs of varying capacities were constructed and the water was successfully distributed in sufficient quantities to all horse-watering, water-bottle, and water-cart filling points.[16]

Running a water supply point presented dozens of small challenges. When the 3rd Field Company took over from the 12th Field Company, it found a faulty pump: "owing to there being one piston ring missing, it is using a large quantity of coal." The company then requested "that 100 lbs more coal be delivered daily for running this pump." It was a temporary measure, as "We have to-day received advice that the piston ring ordered by us for this engine should be delivered in about two days."[17] Providing water could be rather capital intensive, at one site requiring the installation of engines and pumps at a spring, from which water traveled by pipeline to a farm where a reservoir was constructed. From there it flowed downhill to underground cisterns, where "deep dugout accommodation is being provided for an engine room and crew."[18]

The vast system of dugouts beneath Vimy Ridge not only offered places of refuge against German guns and mortars, but also provided a means of taking the war to the enemy. Specialized tunnelling companies prepared for the assault by digging galleries and packing them with explosives. On the day of the offensive, these mines were detonated, demolishing enemy strongpoints and creating openings through which infantry could emerge to outflank the enemy, or even creating communication trenches (called Russian saps) forward of one's front line. More famous were the subways and tunnels that helped move the attacking troops forward undetected. A report on operations boasted that

> 11 subways were constructed on the frontages concerned having a total length of approximately 6,500 yards or nearly 4 miles. The longest sub-way was 1500 yards. All of these subways had at least 25 feet of head cover, were lighted by electricity, and had the necessary water supply. Numerous dug-outs for Brigade and Battalion Headquarters, accommodation for the men, dressing stations, magazines for trench mortar and other ammunition etc were provided. Tramlines were installed in some of them. Buried cable and water mains were carried through selected sub-ways. Numerous exits were provided into our trench system and in some cases galleries or Russian saps were pushed forward to within a short distance of the German front lines, and exits broken out into shell holes and craters at the hour of attack.[19]

The four tunnelling companies of Royal Engineers found it relatively straightforward in the chalky soil to expand the many tunnels and galleries that were already in place.[20]

As one group of specialists worked below ground, another focused its activities above. Special companies, as they were called, prepared to deploy poison gas. First used by the Germans at 2nd Ypres in April 1915, chemical warfare was still an infant science two years later, as evidenced by heavy losses in a trench raid when the wind shifted and carried gas into the ranks of the 54th and 75th battalions. Of forty-two sappers assigned to the operation, thirty-one became casualties.[21] Gas remained part of the Canadian arsenal, however, with special companies attached to each of the four divisions. Unlike bullets and shells, chemicals worked through dugouts and other shelters where the enemy might take cover. Still, determining whether these attacks were successful was fraught with difficulty and required no little detective work after the fact. Following one gas bombardment on 5 April against the German 261st and 262nd Reserve regiments, observers saw "several men violently sick from gas, did not know whether these men were evacuated." A captured officer from the 3rd Battalion, 261st Regiment, insisted that "gas was no longer effective." The interrogator, perhaps self-servingly, reported that the prisoner "gave the impression of deliberately attempting to minimise the effects of gas."[22]

Evidence of casualties among members of the 262nd Reserve Regiment was more forthcoming, one prisoner relating how he had heard that sixty men had suffered from violent vomiting and had to be evacuated. Another, who remained in the trenches all night after shelling destroyed his shelter, watched gas casualties streaming rearwards. "They came from all sides," he told his interrogator. "It was terrible!" He counted more than fifty stretcher-borne victims in all.[23] Such results required constant vigilance, however. Firing gas-filled shells at the enemy instead of releasing gas from cylinders may have lessened the threat to friendly troops, but the wind still had to be blowing in the right direction. For one such operation scheduled for 6 April, the Officer Commanding F Special Company, RE, reported on the wind's direction and strength every hour. In the event, the attack had to be postponed.[24] Winds also prevented the special companies from deploying their deadly arsenal when the offensive started three days later.

Given their knowledge of explosives, sappers also played a substantial role in trench raids. For the 'minor operation' (as they were called) of 13 February, each battalion of the 10th Brigade, 4th Division supplied a company, with engineer support from 10th Field Company and the 67th Pioneer Battalion. "Bangalore Torpedoes will be used. These will be placed if possible the night of operation at several places in German wire...and exploded by Sappers. An Engineer Officer will superintend this" to ensure the desired result. At the time of the assault, artillery batteries opened up on schedule and "Numerous gaps were found in enemy wire giving entrance to raiding parties," which took prisoners, destroyed dugouts and inflicted casualties. Officers and sappers of the 176th Tunnelling Company came with the 47th Battalion. A thorough search of the trench lines uncovered three mine shafts which the engineers destroyed with mobile charges. Sapper parties also "freely used" P (phosphorous) bombs, "setting fire to woodwork" to destroy several more dugouts that contained a number of enemy who refused to come out.[25]

As the battle loomed, sappers continued their training to support the advance. The 11th Field Company received orders for the attack from brigade headquarters on 2 April. The following day those who would accompany the assault "were instructed in their duties and became acquainted with the trench system in the enemy's territory."

Also, "Each Sapper was taken carefully over the practice course and met the Infantry Officer and NCOs of the platoon with which he was to work...As a guide to the probable type of work to be done each party of sappers was given a card, on which was a sketch of the section of trench to which the party was going and an outline of the scheme of development...."[26]

With the assault only a few days away, the engineers began their final preparations. On 6 April, 10th Field Company, with 250 men of the 124th Pioneer Battalion, dug jumping-off trenches so attacking troops could assemble without crowding the forward defences.[27] That day the United States declared war on Germany, but according to one sapper officer the news "excited little comment."[28] Shellfire forced a working party of ten sappers from the 10th Field Company and 250 infantrymen to stop until a determined engineering officer, Lieutenant Whyte, "worked his party in front of enemy shell fire, completing his task." Seventeen infantrymen became casualties.[29]

Overall sapper losses were light in these final days before the attack, although one of the more poignant was an individual who had been "shell shocked" in August 1915 "and has suffered from same ever since. He has been employed as cook for the past five months and I find he is unable to stand even this employment. I now recommend that he be evacuated."[30] Another type of casualty to consider was, "Mortality among horses, due partly to shell fire and partly to exhaustion," which was "rapidly increasing. Dead bodies of the poor beasts lie all over the place. Strict orders have been issued, enjoining drivers to dismount during even the shortest halts."[31]

A speech by commanders to their soldiers in the days before the assault was a final ritual before going "over the bags." Brigadier-General Hilliam of the 10th Canadian Infantry Brigade wrote to Major Vilgar of the 10th Field Company that, "I wish you to convey to all ranks of your Unit my high appreciation of the splendid work they have been doing since I took over the Brigade, whilst holding the line... I fully understand the tremendous hardships that they have had to put up with owing to bad weather, bad trenches and other annoyances too numerous to mention, but the way they have carried out their duties cannot have been surpassed by any Unit in the Imperial Army." Having congratulated them for their accomplishments, the general reminded them of what lay in store and, "In the coming operations I shall still ask you and your men to do some very hard work and trying work and I know they will carry out the orders issued for them to do in the future as they have done in the past."[32] It was not a time for cynicism.

On 9 April, the first sappers at work were the tunnellers who detonated bags of ammonal which were packed into galleries dug beneath the front. In the 4th Division's sector on the left, the 176th Tunnelling Company set off three charges, one to destroy an enemy gallery, which itself had been charged with explosives, another to destroy enemy machine guns on the lip of a crater, and the third to create a crater on the formation's left flank which could be organized for defence.[33]

It was in a German tunnel that Lieutenant William Gordon McGhie of the 2nd Tunnelling Company earned the Military Cross "For conspicuous gallantry and devotion:"

> While reconnoitering with three officers he found the entrance to an enemy tunnel 500 yards in length. Calling on sixteen enemy in the tunnel to surrender, he drove them before him, forcing them to show the leads to the mines, the wires of which he cut, and finally he removed an electric battery for exploding all the mines, thereby saving many lives.[34]

The engineers' role above ground was equally crucial as the infantry moved out across the battlefield. On the right flank, small groups from the 1st Field Company went out with each of the assaulting battalions of 1st Division to construct "Machine Gun Strong Posts," while other sappers carried forward wire, pickets, shovels and picks. Those trying to prepare redoubts found, however, that in the midst of battle, the infantry simply could not be relied upon for engineering tasks.

> Considerable trouble was met with in organizing [working] parties and getting them to work as considerable confusion existed, and a great number of the Infantry had dropped their shovels, and...the Infantry Officer refused to accept responsibility for the sighting of the Trench. [The engineering officer] Lieutenant Neelands thereupon took charge of the situation, collected some shovels, got the party to work, and completed a most successful Line, on his Front, by 9.30 p.m.

One can empathize with the infantry, which might consider a shovel rather redundant in the middle of a firefight, and with an infantry officer who had just fought a brutal battle and was then expected to determine the outline for a defensive position. Not until the night of 10 April was the redoubt in question completed.[35] One of the other field companies of 1st Division reported that a work party of infantry needed to build a road to bring up artillery had not shown up.[36] A third engineering unit with the 1st Division was more fortunate, able to build an "overland route" and repair a water supply system and track for a tramline.[37]

The 6th Field Company assigned to 2nd Division left a detailed account of its operations that day. As soon as the leading infantry had reached their objectives, sappers began digging new defensive positions. Each man carried rifle and bayonet, helmet and gas mask, fifty rounds of ammunition, two water bottles, twenty-four hours' worth of fresh rations and some iron rations. Distributed among them were picks, shovels, sandbags, wire and stakes. Each of the two engineering sections had attached to it fifteen soldiers of the 6th Brigade. "Crossing No Man's Land between Pulpit and Stafford Craters, the parties came under fire from guns which had not yet been put out of action. Section 1 lost its sergeant, (Doc) Miller and Private Ellinson of the 31st Battalion and Section 4, Private McKane of the 27th; all being wounded by shrapnel." Such casualties were not severe, however, and the parties set to their tasks. "Each strong point was laid out in the form of several bits of trench about 25 ft long, radiating from a common centre and having machine gun emplacements at their outer extremities. Completely enclosed by wire, they were thus capable of all round defence," and able to defeat German counterattacks, or so it was hoped. At about 1630 hours the positions were handed over to the infantry and the sappers prepared to enjoy some of the fresh eggs they had found.[38] Overall, the sappers of the 2nd Division seemed to have better luck with their infantry work parties than did those of the 1st Division. The 4th Field Company successfully completed its two strongpoints while also building a light railway grading.[39] Its comrades in 5th Field also built two strongpoints and a mule track.[40]

The sappers of the 3rd Division were also busy on Vimy Ridge. The 7th Field consolidated three strongpoints and put up barbed wire obstacles between them while also constructing an overland route. Defences were in place in the afternoon and the other work was done by the end of the day.[41] The sappers of 9th Field were, if anything, busier. Alongside members of the 3rd Pioneer and the 116th Infantry Battalions, they extended two routes, dug two communication trenches and converted another trench that had been blown by the 172nd Tunnelling Company.[42] Setting up a headquarters for the 8th Field Company proved challenging; intended to be built in an old subway, it was found that "Practically all the Tunnel entrances were crumped in or were blocked with mud." Also responsible for building two strongpoints, its men also had to clear Fickle Trench so it could be put to immediate use. The task had to be postponed, however, as "Neither men nor shovels were available at the time." The infantry company commander charged to help with the work, Major Samuel Bothwell, was killed and his men scattered in the course of the attack. Instead, some sixty to seventy German prisoners "were rounded up and put to work digging." Often, however, the tactical proved more important than the technical. Part of one infantry work party had to be dismissed so it could establish an outpost in case of German counterattack. Start on another trench system was delayed as "Shovels were rather scarce as a great many were lost by the men in going forward."[43] Here was a lesson to be learned, which would have an impact on the later organization of the Canadian Engineers.

The 8th Field Company was not lacking in challenges, as its No. 2 Section tried to build the left-hand strong point (SP) on the brigade front.

> Tape was laid for this and work started, but a great deal of tape was lost on the way up and there would not have been enough to lay out connecting trench to Right Strong Point. As Major Taylor had very few men he withdrew the left party and put all to work on the Right. Later when work was recommenced on the Left SP again, the party was driven off by shell fire, chiefly 5.9's, and A/L/Cpl [Acting Lance Corporal] Hartland was killed and Sapper Speirs badly wounded in the face and neck. As this point was under direct observation [and] work was discontinued until after dark, when a continuous trench was dug from Right SP to 2nd CMR [Canadian Mounted Rifles] on left.

No. 1 Section had an even harder time:

> Just as the party were leaving the Assembly Trench for the assault a shell struck Sappers Quintin and Kirton, killing the former and wounding the latter (since reported missing). Sapper Fisher was wounded at the same time but did not make known the fact until the Final Objective was reached. When going through Artillerie Weg, Major Mackenzie, OC "D" [Company], with his runners and Lieut. Smith and Party, were surrounded by a score of Germans who came out of a dugout taking them in front and rear. Major Mackenzie was wounded, but in the fight that ensued the Germans were all disposed of. Lieutenant Smith and Sapper Fisher became separated from the rest of the Party, but during the wait at Swischen [sic] Stellung they reassembled. In the Zwischen Sappers McSweeney and Palmer were picked up and put at work consolidating Fickle [trench], after the completion of which work they went forward and rendered valuable assistance at the Final Objective.[44]

The Canadian Corps' left hand division was the 4th, which suffered the heaviest casualties on 9 April as it tried to capture the highest ground on Hill 145. Neither its infantry nor its engineers achieved their tasks that day. One section of 11th Field Company, detailed to dig the main communication trench, check dugouts, set up a brigade stores dump and construct barbed wire obstacles, "were not able to carry out their program on the day of the attack." Other parties responsible for laying out the line of a trench, putting in a "bathmat" route forward from the old front line and setting up dumps (complete with signs) took until the 10th and 11th of April to complete their tasks.[45] Initially, 11th Field Company reported that six of its members had been killed outright and a further six wounded and two missing. When on the 12th one of the missing sappers died,[46] the company's dead-to-wounded ratio was about one to one, an indication of the battle's brutality on the left flank. Other field companies of the Canadian Corps reported only one or two killed (four units reported no fatalities) and a handful of wounded each, although one, 6th Field, discovered that one of its missing men had been killed when someone saw the man's name on a cross over a freshly dug grave.[47]

Work continued in the days following the assault. An officer of 6th Field related how:

> Sections 2 and 3 were detailed to assist with the all important work of getting our lines of communication pushed forward across the hopeless looking morass of water-logged soil beyond our old front. Several officers and NCOs of the Company reconnoitered captured territory as far as the outskirts of Farbus which was still occupied by the enemy. Screened by a snow squall his guns opened up and, though their fire was wild and ineffective, it discouraged movement in the open. During clear intervals, an enormous stretch of country was visible, including Lens with its mining and industrial suburbs.

This was evidence of the nature of the Canadian Corps' victory. On the 11th the unit repaired roads, graded a route for a light railway and collected tools and equipment, undoubtedly including some of the shovels the infantry had dropped during the assault.[48]

With Vimy Ridge firmly in Canadian hands, the nature of sapper work came full circle, as engineers focused on road construction and the water supply. There was still, however, another task to perform, which was to glean whatever lessons could be learned from the events of early April. The most important was that sufficient labour for engineering work was only available under ideal conditions. If infantry battalions found it difficult to capture their objectives, or had suffered heavy casualties, or simply had lost their bearings, then working parties simply were not available and certain tasks had to be postponed, including the construction of defences to fend off German counterattacks.

The engineers applied the lessons of Vimy Ridge, but not for another year. Little was done while the Canadian Corps continued offensive operations through 1917, but the Canadian Engineers were reorganized early in 1918. Breaking up the nascent 5th Canadian Division in England provided the Corps with more field and tunnelling companies. Other units were disbanded and amalgamated to form engineer battalions that were gathered into engineer brigades. As Julian Byng's successor as commander of the Canadian Corps, Arthur Currie, later related, "We trained the infantry for fighting and used them only for fighting,"[49] while sappers relied on their own personnel and material resources to accomplish their tasks. The result was that in August 1918, at the beginning of the Final Hundred Days that ended the war, the Canadian Expeditionary Force boasted a strength of over 155,000 that included 62,000 infantry, 19,000 gunners and over 34,000 engineers.[50] One could find no better evidence of the technical nature of industrialized warfare.

Notes

1   "Withrow, William James," *Dictionary of Canadian Biography, Volume XIV* (Toronto: University of Toronto Press, 1998), 1077.
2   "The Battle of Vimy Ridge, 9th-14th April, 1917," GAQ 5-3, vol 1820, Record Group [RG] 24, Library and Archives Canada [LAC].
3   Report on Operations of Canadian Corps against Vimy Ridge, 51-5, vol 3846, RG 9.
4   Vols 3759-3761, RG 9.
5   War Diary [WD], 11th Field Company, April 1917, OC 11th Field Company to CRE 4th Canadian Division, 12 Apr 17, vol 5000, RG 9.
6   K. Weatherbe, *From the Rideau to the Rhine and Back: The 6th Field Company and Battalion Canadian Engineers in the Great War* (Toronto, 1928), 206, 213.
7   G.C. Williams, Controller of Mines, to HQ Canadian Corps, 29 January 17, 32-3, vol 3885, RG 9.
8   Weatherbe, 223.
9   The Oxford English Dictionary (Second Edition, 1989) defines a sapper as "a soldier employed in working at saps, the building and repairing of fortifications, the execution of field-works, and the like." "The non-commissioned officers and privates of the Engineers were formerly called the (Royal) Sappers and Miners, but in 1859 they became the Royal Engineers. (The privates are still unofficially called *sappers*.)"
10   WD, 11th Field Company, April 17, OC 11th Field Company to CRE 4th Canadian Division, 12 April 1917, vol 5000, RG 9.
11   Commander 8th Canadian Infantry Brigade to 3rd Canadian Division, 9 February 1917, vol 4163, RG 9.
12   Adjutant, 1st Canadian Divisional Engineers to Field Companies, 30 March 1917, LAC, 8-6, vol 4397, RG 9.
13   Report on Operations of Canadian Corps against Vimy Ridge, 8.
14   Ibid, 9.

15 Weatherbe, 222.
16 Report on Operations of Canadian Corps against Vimy Ridge, 9.
17 CRE 4th Canadian Division to DAQMG 4th Canadian Division, 3 January 1917, 20-6, vol 4377, RG 9.
18 "Administrative Arrangements," 12 March 1917, 32-3, vol 3885, RG 9.
19 Report on Operations of Canadian Corps against Vimy Ridge, 10.
20 "Canadian Corps, Scheme of Operations, Part I (Tactical)," Appendix G, 32-3, vol 3885, RG 9; E.L.M. Burns, *General Mud: Memoirs of Two World Wars* (Toronto: Clarke Irwin, 1970), 36.
21 Report on Co-operation by 11th Field Company, CE, in Operation G.52-9, 2-15, vol 4411, RG 9.
22 Monthly Return of Effect of Our Gas on the Enemy, 5 April 1917, 9-15, vol 3978, RG 9.
23 Ibid.
24 WD, 10th Field Company, 10th Canadian Infantry Brigade, First Army 1009 (G), 6 April 1917, vol 5000, RG 9.
25 10th Canadian Infantry Brigade, Orders and Report for Raid of 13 February 1917, 160, vol 35, MG 30 E100, LAC.
26 WD, 11th Field Company, April 17, OC 11th Field Company to CRE 4th Canadian Division, 12 April 1917.
27 WD, 10th Field Company, April 17, 10th Canadian Infantry Brigade, Capture of the Pimple Area, 1 April 1917, vol 5000, RG 9.
28 Weatherbe, 228.
29 WD, 10th Field Company, Report of Work Accomplished Night of 7th/8th April, 1917, vol 5000, RG 9.
30 OC 3rd AT Coy Canadian Engineers to MOAM Corps, 25 March 1917, 1-12, vol 4424, RG 9.
31 Weatherbe, 225.
32 WD, 10th Field Company, April 1917, BGen Hilliam, 10th Canadian Infantry Brigade, to Major Vilgar, 10th Field Company, 1 April 1917, vol 5000, RG 9.
33 Mine Explosion Report, 176th Tunnelling Company, 9 April 1917, 26-14, vol 3963, RG 9.
34 In 1938, McGhie admitted that an artillery officer named Cooper Bond discovered the tunnel and cut the leads. GAQ 5-80, vol 1826, RG 24, LAC.
35 WD, 1st Field Company, 9-10 April 1917, vol 4993, RG 9.
36 WD, 2nd Field Company, 9 April 1917, vol 4994, RG 9.
37 WD, 3rd Field Company, 9 April 1917, vol 4995, RG 9.
38 Weatherbe, 231.
39 WD, 4th Field Company, 9 April 1917, vol 4995, RG 9.
40 WD, 5th Field Company, 9 April 1917, vol 4996, RG 9.
41 WD, 7th Field Company, 9 April 1917, vol 4997, RG 9.
42 WD, 9th Field Company, 9 April 1917, vol 4999, RG 9.
43 OC 8th FCCE to CRE 3rd Canadian Division, 17 April 1917, 9-9, vol 4408, RG 9.
44 Ibid.

45   WD, 11th Field Company, April 1917, OC 11th Field Company to CRE 4th
     Canadian Division, 12 April 1917.
46   OC 11th Field Company to CRE, 9 April 1917, 3-1, vol, 4371, RG 9.
47   Weatherbe, 235; WDs, 1st-12th Field Companies, April 17, vol 4992-5000,
     RG 9.
48   Weatherbe, 234.
49   Quoted in Bill Rawling, *Technicians of Battle* (Toronto: Canadian Institute
     of Strategic Studies, 2001), 33.
50   Statistics compiled by Richard Holt, based on data in vol 3765, IIIB3, RG
     9.

8

The Canadian Army Medical Corps at Vimy Ridge

HEATHER MORAN

A total of 3,598 men of the Canadian Corps died during the Battle of Vimy Ridge, while another 7,004 were wounded.[1] The Vimy battlefield thus posed one of the most daunting medical challenges in Canadian military history. This chapter argues that the very features that made the battle a success in turn imposed enormous difficulties on those whose job it was to evacuate the battlefield and tend the wounded.

The basic medical system at Vimy Ridge had been in place from the beginning of the war. The main front line medical units were the regimental aid post, the field ambulance and the casualty clearing station. The regimental aid post served the wounded of every battalion, often from a large dugout in the trenches. It employed a medical officer, an orderly and a four-man water detail that helped treat the wounded. Each division had three field ambulances whose stretcher-bearers evacuated the wounded from regimental aid posts to the advanced dressing stations. The field ambulance staff generally consisted of nine medical officers and 238 other ranks including stretcher-bearers, orderlies, male nurses, a chaplain and a dentist. No 8. Field Ambulance, for example, supported General Lipsett's 3rd Division in La Folie sector of the front. The Acting Commanding Officer was Major John Nisbet Gunn, a thirty-eight-year-old doctor from Calgary trained at the University of Toronto. He organized two advanced dressing stations for each of the attacking brigades, one in a series of dugouts in the Pont Street trench, the other in a wine cellar beneath the ruined village of Neuville St. Vaast which lay less than two kilometres behind the line.[2]

Several features of this battlefield were to be especially important to the handling of medical cases. Because the Germans held the high ground overlooking the Canadian lines and rear areas, many of the medical units were located much further back than in previous battles.

No. 1 Canadian Casualty Clearing Station, for example, was at Aubigny near Amiens, a distance of over 80 kilometres from Arras. A casualty clearing station could treat 900 patients and had a staff of 22 medical officers, eight of whom were surgeons, and 29 nursing sisters to care for the wounded. By 1917 surgical teams from the base hospitals reinforced casualty clearing stations to improve efficiency and treat serious cases during battles. To that end eight to ten surgical teams joined each casualty clearing station in the days before the Vimy offensive. These stations marked the final echelon on the battlefield before ambulance trains evacuated the wounded to base hospitals.[3]

The crucial link in this evacuation system was the stretcher bearer, who trudged through the dirt and mud with little time to sleep or eat. In 1915 there were 16 bearers allotted to each regimental aid post, but fatigue among their ranks created a serious problem; in 1916 their numbers were doubled to 32, then to 60. For the Battle of Vimy Ridge each regimental aid post was provided with 100 bearers. Squads were arranged by height to make it easier to carry the wounded. Friends were often paired up "with the idea of gaining the best results from the services at our disposal."[4]

The bearers gained further relief from another innovation that was used at Vimy for the first time. Hand trucks on narrow-gauge railways between the regimental aid posts and the advanced dressing stations allowed two stretcher bearers to do the work of ten by transporting four stretcher or ten sitting cases.[5] To make better medical and triage decisions, one orderly from the field ambulances supervised each squad to ensure that dressings were applied properly and that the general state of trench medicine was improved.[6]

These innovations were just a few of the extensive preparations for Vimy. On 11 March 1917 the first advanced parties for No. 8 Field Ambulance arrived at the front under the supervision of Major Ernest Raymond Selby, a doctor from Bradford, Ontario. Their job was to prepare the medical units to handle the expected casualties. In the advanced dressing station in Neuville St. Vaast, several rows of wine racks were removed:

> This left a good open space, with sufficient room for 3 stretcher cases to be dressed, and also for a small dressing table in the centre. The left side was arranged with the dispensary at the immediate entrance, a small clerk's table next, and the remainder of this side was all cleared and forms provided for the accommodation of walking patients. Splints, Dressings, Bandages, etc. etc, were placed on shelves at the top of roof support beams. These were out of the way, but yet handy and within easy reach of Officers and Dressers in the course of their work.[7]

With the supplies delivered and sorted by 6 April, Major Gunn moved the remainder of his field ambulance to the front lines that night. The move in the cold and rain took five hours before his party left their horse ambulances and walked: "The roads were in a bad state,...traffic blocked most of the way, the darkness of the night, the roar of our guns and the occasional reply of the enemy made real the fact that the actual war zone was being approached."[8]

By 8 April the medical service was ready to take part in "the great attack which had been anticipated so long."[9] One medical officer wrote of the bombardment, "It is impossible to describe the intensity of this, as all efforts would fail to convey to the imagination what it resembled and one can only be satisfied with the general description that it surpassed anything previously seen or heard."[10] One of the first casualties treated by No. 8 Canadian Field Ambulance was one of their own when a sergeant walking from his sleeping quarters to the dressing room was hit in the neck by a stray bullet. He died later at the base hospital.[11]

The casualties began to arrive at the divisional dressing stations by 0700 hours, but the "rush period" began as objectives were reached and consolidated between 0900 hours and 1500 hours.[12] Throughout the battle, "The work at the Advanced Dressing Station proceeded satisfactorily. As the cases arrived by trucks, on narrow-gauge railway, across country, or down the main road," a non-commissioned officer (NCO) and his staff arranged all the casualties according to urgency of treatment.[13] The war diary of No. 8 Canadian Field Ambulance boasted that patients were well cared for. Their dressings and bandages were reinforced and their muddy, soaked clothing changed. Splints were applied to fractures and everything possible was done to keep the wounded comfortable.[14] Reports suggested a particularly cheery disposition among the Canadian wounded who seemed optimistic, proud and happy from the successful efforts of the day. One wounded soldier "laughingly remarked 'I wouldn't have missed this morning for anything!'"[15]

The Battle of Vimy Ridge was very different for those unable to get off the battlefield. The tactical gains won at Vimy Ridge often forced medical staff out of the relative security of the regimental aid posts. Carrying as many supplies as they could manage, medical officers and their staffs simply dressed the men out in the open or in trenches before flagging down bearer squads to evacuate the wounded to the field ambulances.

Captain Robert J. Manion, MC was a medical officer at Vimy Ridge. He later wrote, "After the Battle of Vimy Ridge my boys and I dressed our men for four days in an open, muddy trench, with the shells dropping about all the time. Dug-outs are simply holes in the ground, and may be most primitive dressing rooms."[16] Captain Arthur Chester Armstrong, a twenty-nine-year-old doctor from Drayton, Ontario managed to fit seven stretcher cases in his hole on the battlefield, but there was scarcely room for any other wounded.[17] Captain James Frederick Stewart Marshall, a thirty-year-old doctor who practised in Montana, moved to a post that was "a very small place, with practically no accommodation as a Dressing Station, and only just sufficient cover for himself."

Finding these improvised aid posts often proved difficult. On the night of 9 April, No. 8 Field Ambulance sent a bearer party to locate the new aid posts, but after several hours they returned with no idea where the posts were.[18] Meanwhile a runner reported to the same ambulance that some 40 to 50 wounded men were lying in shell holes in front of another aid post. With the help of the runner, stretcher-bearers found and evacuated the men. Not until 10 April did the stretcher-bearers of No. 8 Field Ambulance again go forward to find the missing regimental aid posts.[19]

Aid posts were hard to find because "the land...[stretcher bearers] traversed was simply one mass of shell-holes and ruined barbed wire, and it was a matter of impossibility to follow any given direction."[20] The war diary of No. 11 Canadian Field Ambulance of 4th Division described the terrain immediately after the battle:

A more desolate scene than this battle-field could scarcely be imagined. Every foot of earth had been up heaved time and time again during the furious bombardments from both sides, until the very bowels of the Ridge had been hurled on high and spread abroad, and clay, chalk and gravel had been so mingled together and compounded with the moisture as to resemble the contents of a giant haggis. The plateau was so flooded that it presented the appearance of a series of lagoons and in some places the only possible footing across the Ridge was afforded by narrow, slippery reefs of mud thrown up around the shell holes and dividing one lake from another. Amid this flood...lay the half-submerged bodies of the dead, whose blood had coloured to rusty red the stagnant water lapping around them.[21]

The work of the stretcher-bearers was long and difficult. Every tree around the advanced dressing station at la Folie Wood, for example, was destroyed, leaving a wild jumble of tree trunks, branches and barbed wire to be navigated. Groping in the dark with gas masks on, the bearers could barely see. Intense shelling forced the collecting post that the field ambulance bearers had established to be abandoned and set up further back.[22] The tram line that was to speed evacuations was destroyed. Road and field conditions made it impossible to traverse with a wheeled stretcher, so the area continued to be cleared by hand.[23] No wonder that the stretcher-bearers nicknamed the evacuation route by la Folie Wood "Death Valley." Nevertheless, most of the bearers worked for 48 hours, "ever anxious to continue so long as there were [sic] any wounded remaining to be brought in."[24]

No soldier with any chance of survival was left behind, but stretcher-bearers were often forced to make difficult decisions. At Vimy a private came across a group of wounded men lying in a crater. "One, a Scotsman, had shrapnel in him on the left side from head to foot." The stretcher-bearers were collecting the wounded, but none of them moved to assist the Scotsman. The private pulled a bearer aside and asked him why they were leaving without that wounded man. The bearer whispered that the Scotsman, "was fatally wounded and would peg out at any moment."[25] The private was upset by the reply, but did not interfere with the work of the stretcher-bearers.

Throughout the battle German prisoners were pressed into service as stretcher-bearers. By most accounts, the POWs were quite happy to help clear the wounded. For them the war was over. Armed guards ensured that the Germans did not try to escape or harm a wounded Canadian.[26] The Canadian soldiers and medical staff were receptive to the assistance of the German bearers, although the fact that these were the same men who were shooting at them earlier was not lost on the Canadians. One Canadian soldier commented that he "was impressed by the thought that here were men striving to save the lives of men they had tried to destroy a few hours before." He went on to say that, "The Germans worked hand in hand with us, dressing wounds, carrying stretchers over muddy, soaked ground...there was not a trace of hate in the heart of any [German] I worked with that day."[27]

As the battle continued, the poor weather, difficult terrain and the priority given to supplies going forward created enormous difficulties for those trying to get the wounded off the battlefield for treatment. No. 4 Canadian Field Ambulance in the 2nd Division area faced a four-to-five hour round trip to cover the six kilometres between its advanced dressing station in Aux Rietz and its main dressing station in les Quatre Vents. The motor ambulances could not keep up with the number of wounded, so the field ambulances overflowed with wounded men.[28] No. 4 Canadian Field Ambulance reported, "As we had only space for about 100 men under cover a number varying from 100-200 men were lying out on a field near the road most of the afternoon and evening."[29] Some chaplains complained of inhumane treatment, but the medical officers faced terrible choices.[30]

Hubert Morris, a twenty-one-year-old Canadian school teacher from Lambton, Ontario, was a stretcher-bearer during the Vimy battle.

His advanced dressing station became over-crowded and, like the others, had rows of stretchers lying in the snow. Morris followed his medical officer, Major Herbert Wadge, a forty-year-old doctor from Winnipeg, Manitoba who gave the bearers a slight nod when he came across a soldier too badly wounded to survive treatment. The bearers then placed them within the row of stretchers outside and covered them with blankets. The medical officer checked on the wounded outside the station often and gave whatever medical aid he could.[31]

The first train of casualties from the Vimy battlefield arrived at No. 1 Canadian Casualty Clearing Station at Aubigny at 1145 hours, six hours after the attack began. Midday reports that XVII Corps of the British Third Army to the south of the Canadian Corps was suffering very heavy casualties prompted a decision to place this unit at the disposal of Third Army.[32] By 2000 hours, the dressing room at the clearing station was completely full, forcing ambulances to leave wounded soldiers along the roadside. Not until 0230 hours on the morning of 10 April were the last of the wounded brought into the station.[33]

During the course of 10 April, No. 1 Canadian Casualty Clearing Station saw 1,234 cases, including 165 wounded Germans. It managed to evacuate 523 men, but still had 711 cases in the station at midnight. Twenty-six soldiers died there that day, while others died on the journey to the station. The mortuary was filled beyond its capacity and rows of bodies lay on the ground outside.[34] The sustained cost of the Battle of Arras can be measured in part by the numbers of men who passed through No. 1 Canadian Casualty Clearing Station. Between 9 April and 9 May, its staff treated 7,773 cases, the majority of whom were stretcher cases. In that period 1,315 major operations were performed at No. 1 Casualty Clearing Station on 1,119 patients, along with 723 minor operations performed in the dressing room.[35] Between 9 and 10 April, the heaviest part of the fighting, Canadian medical units admitted 5,962 Canadian wounded along with 7,350 British wounded and 706 wounded German prisoners, a total of 14,018 patients in two days.[36]

On the treatment of German prisoners, Canadian brigade instructions were clear that they "Will be treated in every way similarly to our own wounded."[37] Two German interpreters attached to No. 1 Canadian Field Ambulance were joined by two captured German medical officers on 10 April who began treating German casualties in a separate ward and kept working until the last patients were evacuated.[38] Allied intelligence officers kept close watch of German prisoners as they gathered information on German lines, positions and plans. At No. 1 Canadian Casualty Clearing Station, intelligence officers were making great progress with one wounded prisoner until he realized the value of what he was saying and refused to say another word. A German-speaking Canadian intelligence officer was then bandaged and placed on a stretcher beside the reticent German. Thinking that he was talking to a fellow German soldier, the prisoner spoke freely about many topics and told the intelligence officer the date and time of a German relief.[39]

While this chapter is a brief overview of the medical service actions at Vimy Ridge, the information included suggests that the medical services were extremely well prepared for the thousands of expected casualties. Hundreds of stretcher bearers worked almost to exhaustion, aided by tram lines and German prisoners who were pressed into service.[40] But, as always, there were unexpected problems. A battlefield destroyed by artillery fire was a bewildering place. A shortage of stretchers noted after the battle was partly caused by the German prisoners/stretcher bearers who did not return to the battlefield. Adding to the shortage was the observed ratio of stretcher cases to walking wounded at Vimy (1:1) that was dramatically higher than it was in previous engagements (1:3). No one was then able to explain why the wounds were more severe in this battle than they had been previously, though it may have been due to the higher concentration of artillery fire. In future "new preparations to accommodate large numbers of stretchers" were required at the various units.[41]

Traffic congestion was also a serious problem at Vimy Ridge. The guns and ammunition columns going forward limited the speed of the motor and horse ambulances to a walking pace. At one point the 8th and 13th Motor Ambulance Convoy units each sent forward their trucks, but the vehicles only added to the road congestion. The Canadian Army Medical Corps offered no solutions to the traffic congestion; the army controlled the traffic, not the medical corps, so there was little that the medical directors could do beyond informing headquarters of the problem.[42]

There was much to learn from treating the casualties of Vimy Ridge. The long efforts to set up regimental aid posts and main dressing stations behind the lines were not as effective on a battlefield of such dramatic movement. In later battles, these arrangements were abandoned. Before they were evacuated to the field ambulance, most of the wounded were first treated in open fields at gathering points marked with large strips of white bandages.[43] In addition, forward surgical and resuscitation centres allowed timely intervention. Soldiers in shock, unconscious, or requiring immediate surgery were rushed to these units to receive blood transfusions and other treatment without the long wait for transport to the casualty clearing stations.[44] Such innovations eased traffic congestion in later battles, as did the use of thousands of German POWs, who often outnumbered the Canadian wounded, as stretcher bearers.

It is difficult for modern historians to assess how over 10,000 casualties were treated in a two-day battle. By the measures of the time, the experience of the Canadian Army Medical Corps at Vimy Ridge proved valuable during the open warfare of 1918. Ultimately Vimy Ridge demonstrated a systematic willingness to grow, adapt and improve the medical service based on battle experience and medical advancement.

Notes

The author would like to thank the Associated Medical Services for their support. *Associated Medical Services Inc. (AMS) was established in 1936 by Dr. Jason Hannah as a pioneer prepaid not-for-profit health care organization in Ontario. With the advent of Medicare AMS became a charitable organization supporting innovations in academic medicine and health services, specifically the history of medicine and health care, as well as innovations in health professional education and bioethics .*

1   Major-General Sir W.G. Macphearson, *History of the Great War Based on Official Documents: Medical Services, General History*, Volume 2 (London: His Majesty's Stationary Office, 1921), 110.

2   War Diary [WD], No. 8 Canadian Field Ambulance, April 1917, Appendix 1, sheet 1, T-10919, volume [vol] 5030, Record Group [RG] 9, Library and Archives of Canada [LAC].

3   Thomas Brenton Smith, "Clearing: The Tale of the First Canadian Casualty Clearing Station, British Expeditionary Force, 1914-1919," Manuscript Group [MG] 30 E31, LAC.

4   WD, No. 8 Canadian Field Ambulance, April 1917, Appendix 1, sheet 7.

5   WD, ADMS, 2nd Division, May 1917, Report to ADMS 2nd Division, T-10910-10911, vol 5025, RG 9; WD, No. 8 Canadian Field Ambulance, April 1917, Appendix 1, sheet 7 and 5.

6   WD, No. 8 Canadian Field Ambulance, April 1917, Appendix 1, sheet 3.

7   Ibid, April 1917, Appendix 1, sheet 6.

8   Ibid, April 1917, Appendix 1, sheet 4.

9   Ibid, April 1917, Appendix 1, sheet 7.

10 Ibid, April 1917, Appendix 1, sheet 8.

11 Ibid, April 1917, Appendix 1, sheet 8.

12 Ibid.

13 Ibid, April 1917, Appendix 1, sheet 10.

14 Ibid.

15 Ibid, April 1917, Appendix 1, sheet 13.

16 R.J. Manion, quoted in Lawrence J. Burpee, "The Canadian Army Medical Corps," *Canada in the Great War, Volume VI: Special Services, Heroic Deeds, Etc.* (Toronto: United Publishers of Canada Limited, 1921), 103.

17 WD, No. 8 Canadian Field Ambulance, April 1917, Appendix 1, sheet 1 and 14.

18 Ibid, April 1917, Appendix 1, sheet 12.
19 Ibid.
20 Ibid.
21 "Diary of the Eleventh: Being a Record of the 11th Canadian Field Ambulance (Western Universities) Feb. 1916 - May 1919," (Winnipeg, 1919), 62.
22 "The Period of Preparation for the Vimy Offensive," file 4-3, vol 3752, III-B-2, RG 9.
23 WD, No. 8 Canadian Field Ambulance, April 1917, Appendix 1, sheet 1 and 9.
24 Ibid, April 1917, Appendix 1, sheet 13.
25 Reginald Roy, *The Journal of Private Fraser, 1914-1918, Canadian Expeditionary Force* (Victoria: Sono Nis Press, 1985), 268.
26 WD, No. 8 Canadian Field Ambulance, April 1917, Appendix 1, sheet 10 and 11.
27 William Mathieson, *My Grandfather's War: Canadians Remember the First World War, 1914-1918* (Toronto: Macmillan Canada, 1981), 119.
28 WD, No. 4 Canadian Field Ambulance, 9 April 1917, T-10914, vol 5027, RG 9.
29 Ibid.
30 "The Period of Preparation for the Vimy Offensive."
31 Hubert Morris, "The Story of My 3½ Years in World War 1," November 1978, MG 30 E379.
32 Thomas Brenton Smith, "Clearing: The Tale of the First Canadian Casualty Clearing Station, British Expeditionary Force, 1914-1919." LAC, MG 30 E31.
33 Ibid.
34 Ibid.
35 Ibid.
36 WD, No. 8 Canadian Field Ambulance, April 1917, Appendix 1, sheet 10.
37 WD, 7th Canadian Infantry Brigade, Appendix A, "Prisoners of War, Arms, Documents, Etc.," April 1917, T-10688-10689, vol 4893, RG 9.
38 WD, No. 1 Canadian Field Ambulance, 9 April 1917, T-10913, vol 5027, RG 9.
39 Smith.
40 "Report on Collection and Evacuation during Vimy," MG 30 E 53.
41 Ibid.
42 Ibid; see also Report to ADMS 2nd Division.
43 "New Features in Evacuation, Amiens, August 8 to 10," file 3, folder 1, vol 3753, III-B-2, RG 9.
44 Smith; Norman Guiou, *Transfusion: A Canadian Surgeon's Story in War and Peace* (Yarmouth: Stoneycroft Publishers, 1985), 47-48.

When Lieutenant-General Julian Byng took over the Canadian Corps in 1916, he lamented: "Why am I sent the Canadians? I don't even know a Canadian." But Byng left his mark. Canadians proudly referred to themselves as the "Byng boys" well after Byng left the Corps in 1917.

As Minister of Militia and Defence, Sam Hughes was instrumental in shaping the Canadian Expeditionary Force, but his increasingly erratic control of recruiting, training and appointments led to his dismissal in October 1916.

Colonel W.E. Ironside, the General Staff Officer 1, 4th Canadian Divison, was one of many superb British staff officers who helped organize the Canadian Corps for the battle of Vimy Ridge.

Lieutenant-General Byng confers with Canadian staff officers in May 1917: "I don't want Imperial officers but I want to shove on the Canadians who have proved their worth and get rid of the Bumstunts."

Left: "At the Battle of Vimy Ridge, the role of artillery was essential in shooting the infantry on to its objectives." Canadian gunners load 18-pounder shells into the limbers of their guns.

Below: Moving the guns was not easy. Crews push their 18-pounders onto the Corps tramway.

An anti-aircraft gun moves along a submerged road during the Battle of Vimy Ridge.

Heavy guns firing at Vimy Ridge. An artillery summary before the battle noted, "All selected targets have been systematically bombarded and much damage has been done to the enemy's defences."

Pack horses taking up ammunition to guns of 20th Battery, CFA, April 1917. The toll on animals was high: "Dead bodies of the poor beasts lie all over the place. Strict orders have been issued, enjoining drivers to dismount during even the shortest halts."

Shell casings stacked along the roadways behind Vimy Ridge. With twice the artillery as was used on the Somme in 1916, the gunners at Vimy Ridge targetted German guns, trenches and wire.

LAC PA 1208

Top & Centre: Prior to the battle, light railway troops built tramways which brought supplies close enough to the front to be transported to the trenches by lorry, wagon or animal. These trams then helped evacuate wounded during the battle.

LAC PA 1215

Bottom: Soldiers of the 28th Battalion establish a signals headquarters during the advance of 9 April 1917. The flags signalled the infantry's progress to aircraft.

LAC PA 1096

Canadian soldiers laying road near Vimy Ridge. One engineering officer noted: "This is said to be the coldest French winter in twenty years....Frost coming out of the ground played havoc with roads and trenches."

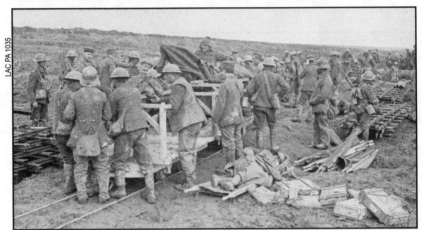

German prisoners help Canadian Red Cross men carry wounded to a light railway for evacuation during the battle.

Both Canadian and German stretcher cases await evacuation, Vimy Ridge, April 1917. These men owed a great deal to the hundreds of stretcher-bearers deployed during the battle.

No.3 Field Ambulance, July 1916. Each division had three field ambulances with a staff of nine medical officers and 238 other ranks including stretcher-bearers, orderlies, male nurses, a chaplain and a dentist.

Canadian stretcher bearers and German prisoners help evacuate the wounded. A Canadian soldier remembered that "The Germans worked hand in hand with us, dressing wounds, carrying stretchers over muddy, soaked ground…there was not a trace of hate in the heart of any [German] I worked with that day."

Tending to a German soldier at Vimy Ridge. Canadian brigade instructions were clear that German soldiers "Will be treated in every way similarly to our own wounded."

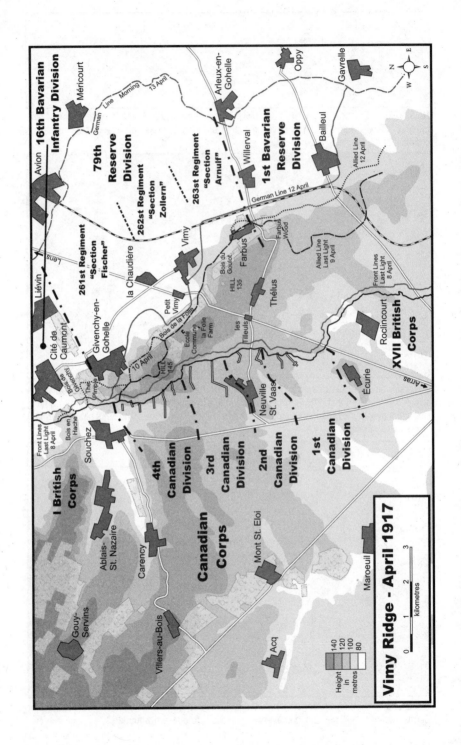

Vimy Ridge - April 1917

16th Bavarian Infantry Division

Méricourt

Avion

79th Reserve Division

German Line Morning 13 April

262st Regiment "Section Zollern"

263st Regiment "Section Arnulf"

Arleux-en-Gohelle

Oppy

Gavrelle

N
W E
S

Willerval

1st Bavarian Reserve Division

Bailleul

Allied Line 12 April

Lens

German Line 12 April

261st Regiment "Section Fischer"

Liévin

Vimy

Farbus Wood

Farbus

Bois du Goulot

HILL 135

Allied Line Last Light 9 April

Front Lines Last Light 8 April

la Chaudière

Thélus

Cité de Caumont

Givenchy-en-Gohelle

Petit Vimy

Bois de la Folie

la Folie Farm

École Commune

les Tilleuls

Roclincourt

XVII British Corps

Bois de Givenchy

The Pimple

HILL 145

10 April

Écurie

Arras

I British Corps

Bois en Hache

Front Lines Last Light 8 April

Souchez

Neuville St. Vaast

1st Canadian Division

4th Canadian Division

3rd Canadian Division

2nd Canadian Division

Ablais-St. Nazaire

Carency

Mont St. Eloi

Canadian Corps

Gouy-Servins

Villers-au-Bois

Acq

Maroeuil

Height in metres

140
120
100
80

0   1   2   3
kilometres

9

The 1st Canadian Division
An Operational Mosaic

ANDREW IAROCCI

In May 1935 the official Canadian Army historian, Colonel A.F. Duguid, delivered a paper on Canada's operational record in the Great War to the Canadian Historical Association. Duguid explained to his audience that Vimy Ridge was important not because it was the "hardest fought" battle, nor the most "fruitful of immediate results," but because it was "almost exclusively" a Canadian show, one in which the Canadian Corps "was consolidated into one homogenous entity; the most powerful self-contained striking force on any battlefront." Duguid described a corps that functioned almost flawlessly at Vimy, with keen coordination among the different branches of service and a confidence that stretched from the Corps' commander, Sir Julian Byng, down to the ordinary privates in the firing line.[1] Over seventy years later, Duguid's interpretation of Vimy Ridge continues to dominate Canadian historical imagination. Yet to celebrate Vimy Ridge as a unifying epic for the nation does not help us to realistically understand the experiences of those who fought on the battlefield. An examination of Major-General Sir Arthur Currie's 1st Canadian Division suggests that no single narrative can adequately describe the complexity of the battle. The 1st Division's fight, like the broader Canadian experience, was far from uniform.

A recent study of 1st Division's complete war record portrays Vimy as a thoroughly planned operation that "incorporated the lessons of 1916," resulting in an assault on 9 April 1917 that "was virtually textbook perfect."[2] One cannot help but wonder if the troops who advanced over the shattered ground that Easter Monday would have something to add to such a tidy statement; several of Currie's battalions encountered serious difficulties during their respective advances, suffering casualty rates of nearly fifty percent in some cases.

Despite careful training and planning, individual platoons, companies, battalions, batteries and brigades met with widely differing fortunes, often beyond anyone's control. While technological innovation and new tactics and organization played important roles, there was also a great deal in common with earlier battles. The infantry at Vimy variously used mortars, machine guns and rifle grenades to capture their objectives, but they relied on the rifle and bayonet just as often. Sophisticated staff work helped situate the people and material at the right place and time, but no effort could save men and horses from a stray shell, an untouched machine gun position, or even the mud and miserable weather that marked so much of the Western Front. This chapter, tempered with an awareness that much of what transpired at Vimy was dreadfully familiar to the veterans of 1915 and 1916, highlights some of the contrasts and variations that constituted 1st Division's experience in early April of 1917.

A review of the divisional war diaries for the first week of April makes it hard to believe that a major offensive was in the offing. As 9 April approached, the daylight hours were filled with routine activities: officers and other ranks were dispatched on or returned from courses; soldiers practised battle drill behind the lines while commanders inspected their troops. At night it was a different story. Under cover of darkness, small parties of troops ventured into no-man's-land in search of fresh intelligence on the enemy's activities and whereabouts.[3] Sometimes these forays escalated into intense skirmishes. On the night of 4-5 April a patrol from the 2nd Infantry Battalion crossed no-man's-land and found a trench unoccupied. The interlopers waited for several hours before meeting a handful of Germans. In the ensuing melee an enemy officer was wounded. He did not survive the trip back to 2nd Battalion's lines, but his epaulettes showed that he belonged to the 3rd Bavarian Reserve Infantry Regiment, one of three regiments in the 2nd Bavarian Reserve Brigade of the 1st Bavarian Reserve Division.[4] This division, together with the 14th Bavarian and 79th Reserve, constituted I Bavarian Corps (Group Vimy), which was responsible for defending the area along the Canadian frontage between Givenchy-en-Gohelle and the Scarpe River.

Raids and patrols continued until the last hours before battle, when all of Currie's divisional formations were finally deployed to their start positions. On the right flank of the divisional frontage was Brigadier-General Frederick Loomis's 2nd Infantry Brigade, with the 5th, 7th and 10th battalions in the first wave and 8th Battalion in reserve. To the left was the 3rd Brigade, under Brigadier-General George Tuxford, with 15th, 14th and 16th battalions in line and 13th Battalion in reserve. These two brigades were responsible for capturing the Black and Red lines.

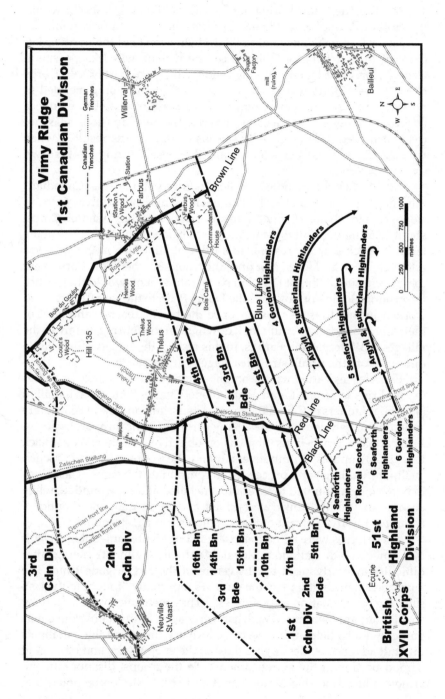

The 1st Brigade, under Brigadier-General William Griesbach, would then follow through and advance as far as the Blue and Brown lines.

Major-General Henry Burstall's 2nd Division held the north or left flank of the 1st Division. On the southern flank was Major-General George Harper's 51st Highland Division, which was part of XVII Corps of the British Third Army. The progress of 1st Division depended in no small part on the performance of Harper's troops. The evidence suggests, however, that liaison between the two divisions was not easily achieved, and potentially serious complications resulted when the right flank of 1st Division remained exposed during the first two days of the offensive.

As Michael Boire noted earlier in this volume, the Canadians inherited an "asymmetrical" battlefield. This meant that Currie's troops had to advance further than any division of the Canadian Corps, about 3,560 metres. But this challenge was balanced by the nature of the terrain, which scarcely resembled a ridge at all. Much of the area was relatively open and level. Not until the troops reached Bois Carré, near the current site of the 1st Division battle monument, would they notice the ground sloping off towards the Douai Plain to the east. This ground worked in the division's favour once the troops reached the limit of their advance, for they could look down upon the retiring enemy in the villages of Willerval and Farbus. In this respect the 1st Division's battle differed from the uphill struggles waged further north.

Experiences varied widely among Currie's three infantry brigades. On 3rd Brigade's front, Lieutenant-Colonel Charles Bent's 15th Battalion (48th Highlanders of Canada) launched its assault on time at 0530 hours and immediately captured the enemy's front line and support trenches. The battalion reached its first major objective, Zwolfer Weg (Black Line) in 40 minutes. Within several hours, the troops overran Zwischen Stellung (Red Line) and proceeded to consolidate the gains.[5] Casualties that morning amounted to three officers killed and six wounded, while at least sixty other ranks were killed and more than 100 wounded, about twenty-five percent of the battalion's combat strength.[6]

These losses were by no means light, but Lieutenant-Colonel Gault McCombe's 14th Battalion (Royal Montreal Regiment) met greater difficulty as it advanced up the centre of the 3rd Brigade front. The Bavarian riflemen and machine gunners reportedly "fought to the last, showing no inclination to surrender."[7] They were overcome largely by small groups of men armed with hand grenades. Indirect fire from Lewis gun crews also helped, but accurate artillery fire eased the battalion's difficult advance by destroying most of the enemy wire and damaging a good portion of the entrenchments. To the troops' disappointment, armour played no role on the battalion's front. McCombe noted that a token showing of tanks "would have brightened up the troops considerably, even if [the tanks] had done little damage to the enemy." McCombe was most disappointed by the medical services, later lamenting that a shortage of stretcher-bearers delayed the evacuation of his wounded. This was understandable, for of McCombe's 701 officers and men, 287 became casualties on 9 April, almost double the number suffered by the 15th Battalion on adjacent frontage.[8]

Lieutenant-Colonel Cy Peck's 16th Battalion (The Canadian Scottish) found that the artillery barrage had failed to stop heavy small arms fire from a trench line known as the Visener Graben. Peck's men simply rushed the position with hand grenades and "at the point of the bayonet."[9] It was here that twenty-four-year-old Private William Milne earned the Victoria Cross posthumously for destroying two machine gun positions with grenades. Regardless of how much planning preceded an attack, lone soldiers or small parties were often the only means of overcoming stubborn resistance on Great War battlefields.

On 2nd Brigade's frontage, Lieutenant-Colonel William Gilson's 7th Infantry Battalion (1st British Columbia Regiment) advanced up the centre. In close coordination with the artillery barrage, the troops reached the Black Line just after 0600 hours with very few casualties, but opposition from enemy machine gunners and grenadiers grew more intense as the battalion continued to the Red Line. With Canadian casualties mounting, reinforcements from the 8th Battalion moved up to the Black Line so that the remaining men from 7th Battalion could concentrate their strength against the Red Line.[10] Unlike their counterparts in 14th Battalion, Gilson's men found that rifle grenades proved useful against German strongpoints. The grenadiers from A Company under Major A.L.W. Saunders used their weapons to good effect against a machine gun position. In common with 3rd Brigade units, Gilson's battalion suffered heavy casualties on 9 April: four officers and sixty other ranks killed and four officers and 257 other ranks wounded.[11]

The frontage of Saskatchewan's 5th Battalion (Western Cavalry) was especially crucial, as it bounded that of 51st Highland Division on the Canadian Corps' right flank. The fighting of 9 April proved to be highly intense, and the first casualties were suffered well before zero hour when a German shell killed one soldier and wounded five others. Immediately before zero hour a second shell killed about ten more men, including twenty-four-year-old Lieutenant William Broad, a British-born officer who had volunteered for the Canadian Expeditionary Force in December 1916.[12] By the time the two forward assault companies reached the Black Line at 0610 hours, they had already lost 200 men, mostly to German machine guns. The artillery had not silenced every

German strongpoint, so the men of the 5th Battalion relied on every weapon they could carry: Mills bombs, smoke grenades, rifle grenades, as well as the standard-issue 1907 Pattern bayonet with its frightening forty-centimetre-long blade fixed to the muzzles of their rifles. Consider this excerpt from a 5th Battalion report:

> The tactics of the enemy, as usual, consisted in the use of his machine guns to the very last, and our most effective weapon against them was undoubtedly the rifle grenade. At one or two places, there were smart bayonet fights, in which our men proved much superior. Several cases of treachery on the part of the enemy were summarily dealt with.

As this passage and others in the battalion records suggest, Canadian soldiers may not have always accepted the surrender of German machine gunners who put up their hands after exhausting their ammunition. According to the 5th Battalion's operational summary, "after suffering many casualties, the enemy showed a tendency to surrender, but the fight was pushed to the finish, the position was captured, the advance sweeping on...."[13] The fight may indeed have been pushed to the finish, but success was not a foregone conclusion for the 5th Battalion. Due to heavy resistance, A and B companies were forced to deviate from the operational plan by "bombing their way down a trench," possibly to bypass or outflank an especially heavy point of resistance. This diversion drew fire from the follow-up troops of C and D companies. Such action demanded initiative, not only from platoon and company officers, but also from the sergeants and corporals who took their places when officers were killed or wounded. This was especially true for the 5th Battalion, which lost fourteen of twenty-four officers on 9 April, five of whom were killed. The battalion lost about half of its fighting strength, 350 casualties among the other ranks. Even with the late arrival of twenty-five inexperienced stretcher bearers, the many wounded of the 5th Battalion still endured a long wait before evacuation.[14]

With the 2nd and 3rd Brigades on their objectives, it was up to the troops of Griesbach's 1st Brigade to pass through the newly captured positions and advance to the Blue and Brown Lines. The 3rd Battalion (Toronto Regiment), advanced up the centre of the brigade frontage towards the Red Line at 0730 hours. The 4th Battalion (Central Ontario) was on the left and 1st Battalion, whose troops were mainly from eastern Ontario, was on the right. Lieutenant-Colonel J.B. Rogers commanded the 3rd Battalion. He was reassured by the steady progress of the first assault wave, the heavy weight of the Allied barrage and the increasingly large groups of German prisoners who passed his battalion headquarters carrying wounded Canadians on stretchers. For some, however, the anticipation was too much. Early that morning a lieutenant reported to Rogers' headquarters "rather badly shaken up and slightly gassed." After being calmed down, the officer returned to his company.[15]

Rogers' battalion suffered relatively few casualties in the early going, with one officer killed and ten men wounded by 0930 hours. But a friendly barrage that lingered too long near the Thélus-Roclincourt road delayed the advance to the Blue Line until just before 1100 hours. Casualties remained light until this point, and the Brown Line was captured at 1420 hours; by midnight, however, the battalion had lost about 150 men. Again some weapons were more useful than others. No trench mortars were available until 10 April, and when two Stokes mortars finally arrived, they were supplied with just twenty bombs. The Stokes, consequently, were "practically useless throughout the operations." Lewis and Vickers machine guns were of much greater value, both during the assault and in the consolidation phases. The 3rd Battalion used only a small number of hand grenades, and according to Rogers, "under similar conditions such a large number of bombs need not be carried in the assault." The same was true of rifle grenades, for scarcely any were fired during the attack "or afterwards as the distance from which we fought the enemy automatically increased as soon as we carried out the operations which...one might describe as semi-open warfare."[16] The value of infantry weapons largely depended on immediate circumstances.

Upon the 3rd Battalion reaching the Brown Line, Major Reid immediately dispatched patrols from his D Company into Farbus Wood, where German gun emplacements lay hidden. Although the battalion had reached its objectives in good time, Reid was alarmed that his right flank was vulnerable to counterattack from German reinforcements massing along the railway embankment. The 1st Battalion (Western Ontario) had initially covered Reid's flank that morning, but its instructions had kept it at the Blue Line. The 1/4th Gordon Highlanders of the 51st Highland Division were to have continued to the Brown Line, but when Reid reached Farbus Wood, the Gordons were nowhere to be found. Ominously, Reid had tried to liaise with the Gordons three days before, but "no definite information could be received from [the Gordons] as to their intentions in this operation."[17] What had happened to the Gordons?

The British official history shows that the 1/4th Gordon Highlanders advanced beyond the Blue Line on 9 April, but in a southeasterly direction, away from the inter-corps and inter-army boundary.[18] This may explain why the troops of 1st Canadian Brigade were unable to find any of their British counterparts. Canadian records suggest that the Highlanders' advance may have been stalled rather than redirected. The 3rd Battalion narrative mentions in several instances that the Gordons were expected to "recommence" their attack, but that the promised action was never delivered. Just before 1900 hours on 9 April, Reid reported that the flank was still dangerously exposed. By 0900 hours on 10 April, enemy troops had reappeared in Farbus Wood, but still the Gordons had not been contacted. Rogers blamed the loss of a reconnaissance officer, Captain Arthur McCormick, on the right flank remaining "in the air" until the afternoon of 11 April when scouts confirmed that British troops were on the move toward the Brown Line.[19] Maintaining contact across divisional, corps and army boundaries was a problem that even the planning of Vimy Ridge could not overcome.

Major Walter Towers' 4th Battalion advanced on the left of Rogers' troops, but its experiences differed considerably from those of the 3rd Battalion. At 0730 hours on 9 April the men of the 'Mad Fourth' crossed into the German lines with little difficulty and scarcely any casualties. A shell killed Lieutenant Bill Gregory, an Anglican church minister, as well as Lieutenant Gordon Minchinton, the liaison officer from 27th Battalion (2nd Canadian Division). At about 1000 hours the assault troops crossed the Red Line to the sound of the 16th Battalion's pipers. Shortly after noon Towers' Colt machine gun teams fired into groups of retreating Germans, and several prisoners were taken when the Canadians reached Bois Carré; ultimately about 100 Germans gave up the fight in the wood. Uncut wire held up the troops beyond the trees, but three men managed to clear a path under cover of Colt fire. At this point battalion machine gun crews fired down on German transport along the road between Vimy and Willerval. By 1400 hours the battalion entered Farbus Wood and discovered the enemy withdrawing beyond the railway embankment. A number of Germans hidden in dugouts were overcome by Towers' men, who then helped themselves to hot lunches that had just been served on German mess tables. By 1600 hours, with the battalion headquarters set up in Bois Carré, the only cause for concern was German machine gun fire sweeping across the 3rd Battalion's front from the Canadians' exposed right flank. In the meantime 4th Battalion patrols toward the railway embankment found it defended in strength, but the Germans mounted no counterattacks.[20] With its flanks secure, and the Germans unwilling to put up much resistance, the 4th Battalion was lucky at Vimy Ridge, suffering only about thirty casualties.[21]

There was much more to an infantry division than three brigades of infantry. Indeed, a division's versatility came from its own supporting arms and ancillary troops: artillery, engineers, transport, cyclists, signallers and medical personnel. This book includes chapters on some of these branches of service, but something should be said of their roles at the divisional level. During the early part of April 1917, the 1st Division was supported by its own organic artillery brigades and trench mortars, as well several British brigades. The artillery and mortars were organized into three groups under Brigadier-General Herbert Thacker, the Commander Royal Artillery for 1st Division, to support each of the division's infantry brigades.

Among the artillerymen there was no mistaking that a "big push" was in the offing for early April, but even before the battle began, the going was tough. In the 2nd Brigade, Canadian Field Artillery (CFA), the cold and wet snow was made worse by a shortage of rations and rum in the week before the battle; it is unlikely that any of the crews stripped down to their bare chests as war artist Richard Jack depicted them in his painting *The Taking of Vimy Ridge, Easter Monday, 1917*. The weather and heavy pace of work was especially hard on the horses of the gun batteries and ammunition columns. The weather aggravated the animals' kidneys and livers, and there were not enough veterinary personnel available to treat all of the afflicted animals.[22] The appalling mud surrounding the battery emplacements proved too much for sick and exhausted horses, which were dying at an alarming rate, and officers worried that shells might actually run out at a crucial moment.[23] In addition to the loss of horses, general weather conditions and enemy activity interrupted artillery fire plans. On 2 April the eighteen-pounders of 2nd Brigade, CFA were able to fire only half of their allotted ammunition due to high winds and snow.[24]

Throughout the battle the 1st Division's artillery resources engaged in a full range of missions, including suppression, counterbattery and interdiction. To preserve an element of surprise, some of the batteries and brigades remained silent until a few days or hours before the attack. When they opened fire to register their assigned targets between 7 and 9 April, they camouflaged their positions under the cover of other batteries.[25] Like the infantry, the gunners' experience varied. Despite a clear superiority in guns, Allied counterbattery fire was unable to suppress every German emplacement, and British and Canadian artillerymen suffered casualties. In Hinton's Group, which supported 1st Infantry Brigade, a gun of the 5th Brigade, Royal Horse Artillery was put out of action during the morning of 9 April by a 4.2-inch German shell.[26]

During the first two years of trench warfare, offensive operations were limited because of the difficulty of moving artillery batteries forward behind the infantry. Infantry assaults that had been able to penetrate the first and second lines of German defences usually ran into trouble once their advance exceeded the ranges of their guns. Various solutions had been implemented throughout the war, and at Vimy special arrangements helped the guns keep pace with the infantry. In 3rd Brigade, CFA, Major Harry Crerar (future commander of First Canadian Army in the Second World War) was in charge of a working party that followed the infantry assault and built bridges across the German trenches so that guns could be pulled forward. Thanks to the efforts of Crerar's men, all of the batteries in the brigade advanced to new emplacements by 1630 hours on 9 April.[27] Crerar's success was not matched everywhere else. Impassable roads trapped the guns of the 72nd Brigade, Royal Field Artillery in their original firing positions for four days, until 13 April.[28]

Artillery officers attached to the infantry as forward observation officers (FOOs) served as the gunners' eyes, forming the crucial link between the guns and the foot soldier. Accurate fire depended on reliable communications. The war diary of 3rd Brigade, CFA, firing in support of 3rd Brigade, boasted that

> Lieutenant F.C. Betts acted as FOO and remained in constant communication 3rd CFA Brigade. Lieutenant J.J. Campbell was stationed as FOO near Ecurie. Communications from him were also uninterrupted throughout the day. A great deal of valuable intelligence information reached brigade headquarters due to the vigilance and care of these officers.[29]

The 2nd Brigade, CFA, also supporting 3rd Brigade, was less fortunate. At zero-hour, German shells cut the telephone wires leading from the infantry battalions into brigade headquarters. A crucial thirty minutes went by before signal troops repaired the lines.[30]

The 1st Canadian Divisional Signal Company and other signal units worked tirelessly to keep lines open prior to and during the battle. As of 8 April, buried cable connected all battalion headquarters with brigade and divisional headquarters. Brigade signal sections followed closely behind the first wave of the assault, burying "laddered" telephone lines up to advanced brigade reporting centres.[31] These parallel rows of cable allowed messages to get through should one cable break. This precaution was in place as early as 1915, but there was never any guarantee that lines would remain open, so signallers were constantly searching for breaks. This meant that traditional means of communication, visual signal panels and runners, were still used on Vimy Ridge, especially across the battlefront. By most accounts, lateral and forward communications within the 1st Division were relatively effective at Vimy. Major Towers reported the following experience for 4th Battalion:

> The system of communicating with brigade and other units was quite satisfactory. Touch was maintained practically constantly and when anything came up we were always able to get through in a reasonable time.

> An advanced Brigade Report centre well forward is of great value in affording speedy communication and saving Battalion runners. It should however be marked in some easily distinguishable manner...as our runners has [sic] some difficulty finding it at first, especially at night.[32]

As Bill Rawling's chapter reminds us, offensive operations would not have been possible without the work of divisional engineer and pioneer units, which performed a broad range of difficult and dangerous work, including the construction of road and light railways, excavation of tunnels, trenches and earthworks, snow removal and the bridging of obstacles in no-man's-land. Building materials were always in short supply. Timber and steel were in especially high demand, and engineer officers routinely salvaged discarded materials to get the job done.[33] Engineer officers also had to contend with a shortage of workers. Infantry battalions usually supplied much of the manpower for large digging or roadwork projects, but organising working parties in the middle of a major attack was no easy feat.

Captain E.F. Lynn's 2nd Field Company initially encountered few difficulties, but trouble ensued during the consolidation phase when the infantry battalions were weakened by casualties. On the evening of 9 April a working party from 10th Battalion tasked to assist with the construction of artillery roads failed to show up. Lieutenant William Pennock, the twenty-three-year-old engineer officer in charge of the work, went to 10th Battalion headquarters where he was bluntly informed that no troops were available for roadwork at that particular time.[34] Given the experiences of 1st and 2nd Field companies, it is not surprising that sappers from 3rd Field Company collected in excess of 1,300 discarded shovels by 12 April.[35]

Working in conjunction with the divisional engineers was Lieutenant-Colonel Glen Campbell's 107th "Timber Wolf" Pioneer Battalion. Campbell, a veteran of the Northwest Rebellion and former inspector for the Department of Indian Affairs, raised the 107th in Winnipeg back in 1915; more than fifty-five percent of the battalion's original recruits were Aboriginal Canadians.[36] Based at Ecoivres in

April 1917, the pioneers of the 107th Battalion repaired trenches, dug tunnels and buried telephone cable during the lead up to "Z" Day. Although some of this work was completed in rear areas, there was always the danger of German shelling. At least four officers were evacuated during the first five days of April, and ten men were killed or wounded by gunfire on 5 April. After 9 April, emphasis shifted to the construction of a light railway line running east of Thélus toward the Commandant's House, and later, the men repaired the road leading from the house to Farbus Wood.[37] This infrastructure was vital to the defence of the newly captured ground, and would also reinforce the Canadians' offensive activities later in the month.

Vimy was a great operational success for 1st Canadian Division. By the evening of 9 April the three infantry brigades advanced 3,500 metres into enemy territory, capturing more than 1,200 prisoners, seven artillery pieces, forty machine guns, twenty mortars and 900 rifles.[38] But much unpleasant work remained, for the dead and wounded needed to be removed from the battlefield. About 110 officers from 1st Division became casualties on 9 April, at least thirty percent of whom were killed or died of wounds; probably twenty-five more officers were killed or wounded between 10 and 12 April.[39] At mid-day on 10 April, 1st Infantry Brigade reported thirty-two men killed, 285 wounded and seventy-five missing.[40] By evening of 9-10 April, 2nd Brigade lost 214 men killed, 775 wounded and seventy-five missing. These figures represented approximately forty percent of the brigade's infantry combat strength.[41] Third Brigade lost in excess of 1,000 other ranks by 12 April. Among these were many specialists: 166 Lewis gunners, 226 grenadiers, 103 rifle grenadiers, fifteen signallers and five snipers.[42]

While the divisional field ambulances shuttled casualties to the rear, the division's pioneers and sappers retrieved discarded weapons, kit and equipment. Building materials and supplies were salvaged and stockpiled for another day. By the end of 9 April, Lieutenant-Colonel James Sutherland-Brown, 1st Division's assistant adjutant and quartermaster general, reported confidently that:

> practically all the wounded were evacuated within twenty-four hours. The salvage work and the burial of the dead under the divisional salvage officer and the officer in charge of graves location, was carried out with great expedition and in a few days we had one of the cleanest battlefields yet recorded in this war.[43]

Perhaps it was small consolation for the high price of a hard fought battle.

Vimy Ridge was a battle of contrasts for the 1st Division. Fortunes varied widely among the infantry battalions and other divisional elements. The 2nd and 3rd brigades generally suffered the heaviest casualties in the first wave of the attack, but losses fluctuated dramatically from battalion to battalion. The impact of various weapons and tactics also differed. Rifle grenades, for example, proved invaluable at one point, but quite useless at another. One's position along the front line also influenced outcomes. In the second wave, the 4th Battalion reached its objective with remarkably few casualties, while 3rd Battalion fared much worse along the boundary it shared with another corps and army. Careful preparation, coordination and training before the battle contributed to the Canadian success between 9 and 12 April, but exigencies demanded quick thinking. Even the impressive logistical build-up could not save the division's horses or working parties from exhaustion, circumstances which left some artillery batteries short of ammunition or threatened the success of the consolidation phase. No plan survives first contact with the enemy, and improvisation saved the day at many points along 1st Division's front. Fortunately most of the divisional objectives lay on the forward slope of the ridge, terrain which offered less advantage for the Germans than was true of the 3rd and 4th Divisional areas, where Canadian casualties were the heaviest.

Finally, although new weapons and tactics were employed successfully at Vimy Ridge, more traditional approaches also played an important part. Battalion runners, a presence on the battlefield for millennia, were crucial. So was the bayonet, and so was heroism. Sometimes it was up to men like Private William Milne to overcome strong points, armed only with courage and a few grenades. Countless individual stories comprised the mosaic of 1st Division's operational experience at Vimy Ridge.

Notes

1   The paper was later published as A.F. Duguid, "Canadians in Battle, 1915-18," *Canadian Defence Quarterly* vol XIII, no 1 (October 1935), 17-18.

2   Kenneth Radley, *We Lead, Others Follow: First Canadian Division, 1914-1918* (St. Catharines: Vanwell, 2006), 156-159.

3   War Diary [WD], 1st Canadian Division [Cdn Div] General Staff, 1-7 April 1917, T-1913-1914, volume [vol] 4831, Record Group [RG] 9, Library and Archives of Canada [LAC].

4   WD, 2nd Battalion, 4-5 April 1917, T-10705, vol 4913, RG 9.

5   WD, 15th Battalion, 9 April 1917, T-10718, vol 4924, RG 9.

6   Kim Beattie, *48th Highlanders of Canada, 1891-1928* (Toronto: Southam Press, 1932), 225-226.

7   WD, 14th Battalion, Report on Operations, 25 April 1917, T-10716-10717, vol 4923, RG 9.
8   WD, 14th Battalion, Report on Operations.
9   H.M. Urquhart, *The History of the 16th Battalion (Canadian Scottish) in the Great War, 1914-1919* (Toronto: Macmillan, 1932), 214.
10 WD, 2nd Canadian Brigade [Cdn Bde], 9 April 1917, T-10669, vol 4871, RG 9.
11 WD, 7th Battalion, Report on Attack of Enemy's Positions, Battle of Arras, 9 April 1917, T-10709, vol 4917, RG 9.
12 Accession 1992-93/166, Box 1082—49, RG 150, LAC.
13 WD, 5th Battalion, Summary of Operations, 9 April 1917, T-10708, vol 4916, RG 9.
14 WD, 5th Battalion, 5 April 1917.
15 WD, 3rd Battalion, Narrative of the Offensive on Vimy Ridge, 9 April 1917, T-10706-10707, vol 4914, RG 9.
16 WD, 3rd Battalion, Narrative of the Offensive on Vimy Ridge.
17 Ibid.
18 Map #6, XVII Corps, Attack, 9 April, J.E. Edmonds, *Military Operations, France and Belgium, 1917, Maps* (London: Macmillan, 1940).
19 Arthur Beamer McCormick was twenty-two years old and held the Military Cross when he was killed. His remains were never found and he is commemorated on the Vimy Memorial.
20 WD, 4th Battalion, Operations carried out between 8 and 12 April 1917, T-10707, vol 4915, RG 9.
21 W.L. Gibson, *Records of the Fourth Canadian Infantry Battalion in the Great War, 1914-1918* (Toronto: Maclean Publishing, 1924).
22 WD, 1st Division DADVS, 7-9 April 1917, T-10933-10934, vol 5042, RG 9.
23 WD, 2nd Canadian Field Artillery [CFA] Brigade [Bde], 1 April 1917, T-10785, vol 4965, RG 9.
24 WD, 2nd CFA Bde, 2 April 1917.
25 WD, 26th Royal Field Artillery [RFA] Bde, 1-7 April 1917, T-11131, vol 5067, RG 9.
26 WD, 5th Royal Horse Artillery [RHA] Bde, 9 April 1917, T-11132, vol 5068, RG 9.
27 WD, 3rd CFA Bde, 9 April 1917, T-10787-10788, vol 4966, RG 9.
28 WD, 72nd RFA Bde, 9-13 April 1917, T-11131, vol 5067, RG 9.
29 WD, 3rd CFA Bde, 9 April 1917.
30 WD, 2nd CFA Bde, 9 April 1917.
31 WD, 1st Canadian Divisional Signal Company [Cdn Div Sig Coy], 8-9 April 1917, T-10851-10852, vol 5004.
32 WD, 4th Battalion, Operations carried out between 8 and 12 April 1917.
33 WD, 1st Canadian Engineer Brigade [Cdn Eng Bde], 10-18 April 1917, T-10824-10825, vol 4990, RG 9.
34 WD, 2nd Fd Coy, 9 April 1917, T-10832, vol 4994, RG 9.
35 Work Reports, 3rd Fd Coy, 10-12 April 1917, T-10834, vol 4995, RG 9.
36 Steven A. Bell, "The 107th Timber Wolf Battalion at Hill 70," *Canadian Military History* vol 5, no 1 (Spring 1996), 73-78.

37   WD, 107th Battalion, April 1917, T-10859, vol 5010, RG 9.
38   WD, 1st Cdn Div General Staff, 9 April 1917.
39   WD, 1st Cdn Div AA & QMG, April 1917, App D, Officer Casualties, T-1922, vol 4838, RG 9.
40   WD, 1st Cdn Bde, 11 April 1917, T-10666, vol 4868, RG 9.
41   WD, 2nd Cdn Bde, 9 April 1917.
42   WD, 3rd Cdn Bde, 12 April 1917.
43   WD, 1st Cdn Div AA & QMG, 11 April 1917.

10

The 2nd Canadian Division
A "Most Spectacular Battle"

DAVID CAMPBELL

It was by no accident the Vimy Ridge was won. It was carried by the same methodical process by which a piece of land is farmed, a dinner party made a success, or a stage performance a triumph.

Captain Andrew Macphail[1]

For the 2nd Canadian Division, as for the rest of the Canadian Corps, the battle for Vimy Ridge set the standard for offensive set-piece operations for the remainder of 1917, if not the rest of the war. Hard lessons in tactics, training and organization learned throughout 1916, especially during the Battle of the Somme, laid the groundwork for the division's successful attack at Vimy on 9 April 1917. But for 2nd Canadian Division in particular, the battle also stood as its first unqualified operational success. Although the division's capture of Courcelette on 15 September 1916 largely erased the stigma of its earlier defeat at St. Eloi in April 1916, the glow of victory was shrouded by the difficulties and heavy casualties experienced during its subsequent tour at the Somme.[2] While the 2nd Canadian Division's performance at Vimy was not flawless, the inevitable mistakes were minimized due to an unprecedented degree by weeks of meticulous preparation and training. The result was the capture and retention of all of the division's assigned objectives on the first day of operations.

In late March 1917, the Canadian Corps commander, Lieutenant-General Sir Julian Byng, anticipated that "the sector of the 2nd Canadian Division...is likely to have the heaviest fighting."[3] Here lay the villages of les Tilleuls, Thélus, and Farbus, several wooded areas, and a height known as Hill 135. German troops, mainly from the 79th Reserve Division, had turned these positions into formidable obstacles.[4]

Although Major-General Henry Burstall's 2nd Canadian Division would commence its assault on a frontage of 1,400 yards (1,280 metres), its final objective line expanded to approximately 2,000 yards (1,830 metres). To reach their destination, Burstall's men would have to advance 2,300 yards (2,100 metres) along the division's left section and roughly 3,000 yards (2,750 metres) along the right.[5] This was too much for the division's three infantry brigades. Two of them, Brigadier-General R. Rennie's 4th Brigade from Ontario and Brigadier-General A.H. Macdonell's 5th Brigade from Quebec and the Maritimes, would be needed to punch through the enemy front line and seize the Black and Red objective lines running along the Zwischen Stellung and Turko Graben trench systems. This left only Brigadier-General H.D.B. Ketchen's 6th Brigade of Western Canadians to fight its way through Thélus to the Blue Line, then on to the ridge's steep wooded eastern slopes to the western outskirts of Farbus, where lay the Brown Line, the final objective. Brigadier-General L.O.W. Jones' 13th Infantry Brigade of the 5th British Division, temporarily attached to the Canadian Corps for the operation, would be needed to cooperate with 6th Brigade during the second half of the division's advance, beyond the Red Line.[6]

Additional British units also worked with 2nd Canadian Division on 9 April. Eight tanks of No. 12 Company, D Battalion, Heavy Branch, Machine Gun Corps, were detailed to support 2nd Division's advance. This was the entire complement of tanks allotted to the Canadian Corps for the operation at Vimy. Byng concluded that the heavy belts of barbed wire situated northeast of Thélus "cannot be very accurately ranged on by the artillery, and it is hoped that the Tanks will clear the obstacles."[7]

Despite Byng's concerns, the artillery resources earmarked for 2nd Canadian Division would prove more than a match for the German defence system. The field batteries and trench mortars of the 2nd Canadian Divisional Artillery were joined by the 5th British Divisional Artillery, the 28th and 93rd Army Field Artillery Brigades, and a battery of medium trench mortars from 7th British Division. In all, the division was backed by 183 field guns, howitzers, and mortars, with additional heavy artillery support from three heavy and six medium howitzer batteries of the 64th and 70th Heavy Artillery groups.[8] The field batteries' chief task was to fire the creeping barrage that would roll ahead of the advancing infantry.

Machine gun support was impressive as well, with 102 guns available for barrage work and infantry support duties. Some machine gun crews would lay down a rolling machine gun barrage supplementing the artillery bombardments. Other crews would move forward to protect the flanks of attacking battalions and brigades, fire on targets of opportunity, assist with consolidation and, if necessary, repel counterattacks.[9]

The attacking infantry were also backed by their division's full array of support services, particularly the engineering, labour, supply and transport and medical branches. Some sections of the 4th, 5th and 6th field companies of the divisional engineers would follow the infantry into battle and construct strongpoints to anchor the division's new defensive positions on the ridge. Others would extend the tramline and water systems forward to keep the fighting men supplied with munitions, food and badly needed drinking water. Companies of the 2nd Canadian Pioneer Battalion would also follow up to bury the telephone cables that would keep headquarters in touch with units at the front.[10]

The 2nd Canadian Divisional Train and the 2nd Canadian Divisional Ammunition Column were responsible for transporting artillery and small arms ammunition, Mills bombs, water and other supplies to the fighting units. Both organizations would receive additional assistance from a divisional pack company — a temporary organization comprising drafts of men and mules from the infantry and pioneer battalions. Should the forward tramline in 2nd Canadian Division's sector be damaged, the pack company would fill the gap by ferrying supplies from the advanced divisional dump at Aux Rietz (about 2.4 kilometres behind the Canadian front line) to the forward brigade dumps.[11]

Casualties evacuated from the battlefield and from regimental aid posts would be transported by stretcher, trolley, or tramline back to the Advanced Dressing Station (ADS) at Aux Rietz. After being treated at the ADS, the wounded would be moved by motor and horse ambulance convoys to main dressing stations at Villers au Bois and Les Quatre Vents.[12]

On the afternoon of 8 April, less than twenty-four hours before the assault was scheduled to begin, the division commander, Major-General Burstall, moved his headquarters forward to Aux Rietz Cave, where he and his staff would monitor the division's progress the next day.[13] Since early February, Burstall and his chief of staff for operations, (GSO I) Lieutenant-Colonel N.W. Webber, had conferred with their brigadiers, heads of services, and staffs to formulate the division's plan of attack. In March, Burstall encouraged his brigadiers to hold daily conferences to discuss fresh intelligence on enemy dispositions gathered from a variety of sources, including battalion patrol enterprises and trench raids. Conference results were reported to division headquarters, which revised its operational plans accordingly and assigned new tasks and targets to the field and heavy artillery groups supporting the division.[14]

During the weeks preceding the operation, the infantry conducted practice attacks behind Canadian lines on training grounds that simulated the enemy-held territory over which they would advance. Platoons that were restructured earlier in the winter to incorporate all of the major types of infantry weapons (rifles, Mills bombs, rifle grenades, and the Lewis gun) were drilled in the tactics of fire and movement to enable them to overcome enemy positions that survived the preliminary artillery bombardments and the creeping barrage.

The division's preparations and final assembly for the attack were made in the kilometres of tunnels available along the Vimy front. In 2nd Canadian Division's sector, the subways, caves and tunnels around Neuville St. Vaast, the largest of which were the Zivy and Lichfield subway systems, sheltered entire units of infantry as well as brigade and battalion headquarters, medical units and communications details.[15]

Between 0325 and 0450 hours on 9 April, the infantry of the leading and supporting brigades assembled in their jumping-off positions. Immediately in front of the first waves was a shell-torn and brutally cratered no-man's-land. Some of the larger craters, products of huge mines that had been detonated in earlier operations, were given codenames like Phillip, Stafford, and Pulpit, and were big enough to contain a house. These had been well reconnoitered, however, and would not seriously impede the attacking troops.[16]

In the pre-dawn hours of 9 April 1917, as the leading waves of infantry shivered in their cold and muddy jumping-off trenches, they could take some comfort, however small, from the thoroughness of their training and the diligence with which supporting arms and services had been organized. "Nothing was left to chance and nothing kept secret," remarked Major D.J. Corrigall, a veteran of the 20th Battalion.[17] Claude Craig, a signaller with the 28th Battalion, noted, "We were all very tired and muddy but in good spirits as we were to go over all right and for the most of us this was to be the first time. Looking around the dugout at the fellows sitting and lying around, one couldn't help wondering who was to come back and who wasn't."[18] About an hour before the attack, nerves were soothed and the chill was warded off by a rum ration "judiciously administered so as not to diminish fighting effectiveness."[19]

At precisely 0530 hours the artillery opened fire along the length of the Canadian Corps front. The eighteen-pounder guns pummelled the German front line with deadly shrapnel for three minutes before adjusting their range and making the first of forty-six lifts that morning. According to Lance-Corporal Donald Fraser, "A constant stream of eighteen-pounder shells was sent pouring down on to the enemy front line...Our eyes were glued in wonderment to the line and we felt that

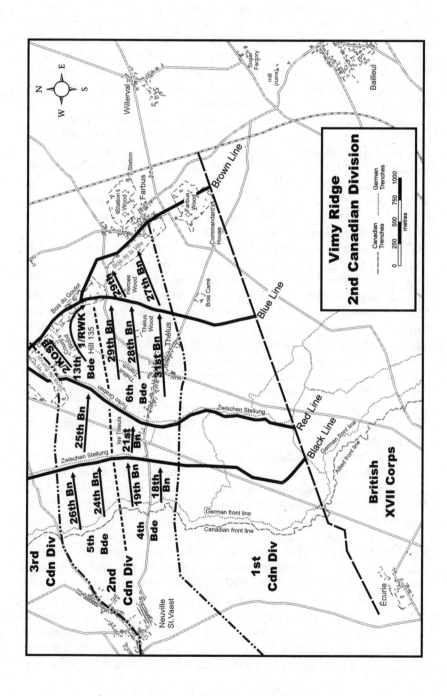

ungodly havoc was being wrought on the Hun. The shelling was so intense that the line was illuminated nearly all the time."[20] The attacking infantry rose from their jumping-off positions under the barrage, squinted through the early morning sleet and snow, and trudged towards their objectives. Following the glare of the shell explosions, the troops kept "well close to the protective [creeping] barrage, as they had been instructed in their pre-battle training."[21]

The division commenced its assault on a two-brigade front with each brigade advancing on a two-battalion front. On the right, the attacking units of 4th Brigade were the 18th Battalion (Lieutenant-Colonel G.F. Morrison) and the 19th Battalion (Lieutenant-Colonel L.H. Millen), while the 24th Battalion (Major C.F. Ritchie) and the 26th Battalion (Lieutenant-Colonel A.E.G. McKenzie) executed the 5th Brigade's advance on the left. These four battalions were to capture and consolidate their division's portion of the Black Line, which ran mainly along the Zwischen Stellung and a small portion of the Zwolfer Stellung. Once the Black Line was taken, the reserve units of each brigade—the 21st Battalion (Lieutenant-Colonel E.W. Jones) of the 4th Brigade, and the 25th Battalion (Lieutenant-Colonel D.S. Bauld) of the 5th Brigade—were to leapfrog ahead to capture the Red Line along the Turko Graben. Extra companies from the 20th Battalion (Major H.V. Rorke) and the 22nd Battalion (Lieutenant-Colonel T.L. Tremblay) accompanied the attacking battalions in both brigades to mop up the captured ground and ensure that each trench line was free of Germans.[22] The assaulting battalions dispatched their troops in five waves, with platoons of the first three waves deployed in two lines. The first line featured riflemen and rifle grenadiers, followed by a line of Lewis gun and bombing sections.[23]

From his headquarters in Zivy Cave, Brigadier-General Rennie carefully monitored his 4th Brigade's progress. Just three minutes after zero, the leading waves of infantry overran what remained of the German front line defences; five minutes later they reached the German support line. German artillery responded, but only weakly. "At no time during the attack could enemy shelling be considered very heavy," the 4th Brigade reported, "certainly not heavy enough to prevent our attacking waves from getting through it." Surviving machine gun nests posed a greater problem.[24] The 19th Battalion, attacking on the brigade left, encountered heavy enemy machine gun fire from Balloon Trench. While the assault platoons dove for cover, flanking parties worked around both sides of the position and destroyed the machine guns with volleys of rifle grenades. By 0600 hours, the 19th Battalion resumed its advance. Flares fired eleven minutes later confirmed the brigade's arrival at the Black Line, the Zwischen Stellung.[25] Training in fire and movement had paid off.

Occasionally, a single soldier could clear the way for a platoon or an entire company. On the 18th Battalion's front, Lance-Sergeant Ellis Wellwood Sifton single-handedly attacked a machine gun crew that was holding up his company. For this daring feat, Sifton would earn posthumously 2nd Canadian Division's lone Victoria Cross of the day.[26] It was through numerous acts of courage and initiative that small groups, or individuals like Sifton, managed to overcome enemy strongpoints to open the way for their comrades.

Brigadier-General Macdonnell's 5th Brigade assault proceeded with equal success, but the Germans exacted a heavy payment. The 24th and 26th battalions, with the help of Stokes mortar crews, took the German front and support lines in twelve minutes. Then resistance grew, forcing the 24th Battalion to fight "hard to maintain the speed of its advance and the continuity of its attacking front...Enemy machine-guns by this time were sweeping the front and were subdued only after sharp encounters, sometimes by rifle grenades...sometimes by counter machine-gun fire...sometimes by bombing with Mills grenades...and again by straight driving bayonet attacks in which many of the men participated."[27] The field guns' barrage rolled onward in 100 yard (90-metre) lifts every three minutes until it reached the Black Line at 0559 hours. Along the way, it "practically obliterated" Furze Trench, situated half way between the German support trench and the Black Line. Fighting behind the shrapnel screen, the attacking companies of the 24th and 26th Battalions reached the Black Line between 0602 and 0614 hours, igniting three white Very lights for the benefit of observation personnel straining to follow events from the rear.[28]

Mopping-up parties from the 20th and 22nd Battalions faced the hazardous work of clearing dugouts and trenches, from which they secured large numbers of prisoners. Some Germans willingly surrendered, but others fought to the bitter end. Occasionally, the artillery barrage and the assault waves virtually eliminated any remaining resistance. Some of the 22nd Battalion men "felt that their assignment gave them too little to do, so they simply joined the assault waves."[29] Many 20th Battalion men also helped overcome strong points that opposed the leading platoons from the 18th and 19th Battalions. While the artillery barrage paused beyond the Black Line for thirty-seven minutes, advance posts found a few surprises. Troops from the 18th Battalion discovered "large straw-stacks" situated "just ahead of the Black Objective" that concealed abandoned "concrete [machine gun] emplacements."[30]

The next stage of the attack began at 0645 hours, when the creeping barrage continued forward in a succession of lifts toward the Red Line, which lay about 500-600 yards (460-550 metres) ahead, just east of the Lens-Arras road.[31] This was the objective of the 21st and 25th battalions. F. MacGregor of the 25th Battalion recalled years later that, "The nerve strain in an attack like Vimy ends when you're away...They were piling the gunfire ahead of us, plowing up everything ahead of you. A rat couldn't live on that ridge."[32] An anonymous Prince Edward Islander serving in the 25th Battalion described the initial dramatic moments of the advance:

> At last hell breaks loose and the good old [25]th Nova Scotians with their comrades from all over Canada on either flank, leapt over the parapet with a yell. Two of our pipers have volunteered to play the battalion over and with their pipes shrieking "Bonnie Dundee" and ribbons flying the breeze they strut over the shell swept ground and again the boys cheer and yell. Now some of Canada's best are starting to fall and everybody sees red and nothing can stop us now.[33]

On the 25th's right, the 21st Battalion made for the tiny hamlet of les Tilleuls, quickly bombing machine gun nests in the ruins before reaching the Red Line just east of the little village at 0715 hours. "The enemy machine guns and trench mortars were the chief resistances [sic] encountered," reported the battalion war diarist, "as [the German] artillery was outclassed at every point. Wire was conspicuous only by its absence...our artillery having completely demolished same. Further proof of the thorough manner in which our artillery has done their work was demonstrated by the state of the Hun Trenches, only the outline of same remaining." Along the way, the battalion captured one field gun, five machine guns, three minenwerfers (mortars), and a number of prisoners. A half-hour after arriving at their objective, the Canadians discovered a large cave under the rubble of les Tilleuls, where the Germans had established two battalion headquarters. After flushing out the occupants with bombs, the 21st Battalion added a further six officers and 100 other ranks to their list of captures for the day.[34]

The prizes were equally impressive on the left, where the 25th Battalion reached the Red Line at 0714 hours and occupied the Turko Graben. In the process, it had seized two seventy-seven millimetre field guns, eight machine guns, six trench mortars, and scores of prisoners. B and D companies of the 22nd Battalion were particularly busy, fighting alongside the assault waves. In the Grenadier Graben, 125 Germans were captured after being outflanked by parties of French-Canadians, and a further 271 prisoners were taken through similar manoeuvres in

Dump Trench. In one shell hole, the Canadians found a dozen defenders on their knees praying.[35]

Despite their success, the 4th and 5th Brigades had not had an easy time taking the Red Line. The 21st and 25th Battalions reported 215 and 253 casualties, respectively. Major J.A. DeLancey, who led the 25th Battalion's attack, was killed while clearing enemy troops from a series of shell holes, and Lieutenant-Colonel E.W. Jones of the 21st Battalion was wounded by shrapnel as he moved up to establish his advanced battalion headquarters.[36]

Casualties, bad weather, and smoke that "blotted out landmarks" caused several problems. Some 5th Brigade troops on the divisional left reportedly "lost direction and swung across the front of the 1st Canadian Mounted Rifles (1st CMR), causing considerable confusion" along the right portion of 3rd Canadian Division's front.[37] More difficulties came with the eight tanks that lumbered forward from their assembly point along Elbe Trench, south of Neuville St. Vaast. By 0715 hours, just as the 21st and 25th Battalions were occupying the Red Line, the tanks reportedly crossed the old Canadian front line. Four of them were earmarked to support the 6th Brigade's attack on Thélus, with "two passing round either end of the village." The other section of four tanks was to support the 13th British Brigade.[38] All of the machines eventually broke down or wallowed in the thick mud. Some sources claim that none of the tanks made it past the German support line, while others indicate that a few of them got as far as the vicinity of les Tilleuls. Although they failed to make any material contribution to the advance, the ditched tanks succeeded in "drawing and localizing the enemy fire to a certain extent," thereby giving some relief to the infantry in the third phase of the division's attack. The tank crews reportedly removed the machine guns from their "land ships" and went on with the infantry.[39]

Shortly after 0900 hours, the 6th Brigade, the "Iron Sixth" from Western Canada, crossed the Red Line through 4th Brigade's positions to await the next series of lifts by the artillery barrage. Brigadier-General Ketchen allotted three of his battalions to the assault, disposing from right to left the 31st Battalion (Lieutenant-Colonel A.H. Bell), the 28th Battalion (Lieutenant-Colonel A. Ross), and the 29th Battalion (Lieutenant-Colonel J.M. Ross). Their objective would be the portion of the Blue Line that lay just northeast of the village of Thélus. On the way to their jumping-off positions, they beheld terrible sights left in the wake of 4th Brigade's attack: "wounded men sprawled everywhere in the slime, in the shell holes, in the mine craters, some screaming to the skies, some lying silently, some begging for help, some struggling to keep from drowning in [water-logged] craters, the field swarming with stretcher-bearers trying to keep up with the casualties."[40]

At the same time, the 1st Battalion, Royal West Kent Regiment and the 2nd Battalion, King's Own Scottish Borderers of the 13th British Brigade, passed through 5th Brigade's positions and formed up on the 6th Brigade's left flank, preparing to tackle the German defences around Hill 135 and in Bois du Goulot. On their path to the Blue Line, both the 6 and 13th brigades would have to punch through the strongly wired Thélus Trench, which cut through the western end of Thélus and stretched northward toward Bois de Bonval.[41]

At 0935 hours, the scheduled artillery barrage crept eastward toward the Blue Line, about 1000 yards (915 metres) ahead. The previously silent batteries of the 5th British Divisional Artillery now joined in from their positions within 500 yards (457 metres) of the old Canadian front line to cover the latter stages of the operation. Unfortunately, some of the batteries were not properly ranged and fired short, causing casualties among the attacking battalions. Troops of the 31st Battalion quickly fell back to avoid the worst of the short shelling. The 29th Battalion would later claim that most of the casualties it suffered in this phase of the attack "were caused by 'shorts' from our own barrage."[42]

In spite of this deadly mishap, by 0955 hours the 29th Battalion captured its section of the battered Thélus Trench, while companies of the 28th and 31st battalions pushed through stubborn resistance into the western outskirts of the village of Thélus. Special heavy artillery bombardments had blasted the village into rubble. Covered by watchful Lewis gunners, bombing sections picked their way along the trenches on either side of Thélus' main street. By 1040 hours, the 29th Battalion had pushed on over the southern slopes of Hill 135 and driven through Thélus Wood, while the 28th and 31st battalions secured the eastern section of Thélus. East of the village, the 31st Battalion even managed to take a large dugout containing a fully stocked German officers' bar staffed with waiters.[43]

At around 0955 hours, the 1st Battalion, Royal West Kents and the 2nd Battalion, King's Own Scottish Borderers charged into Thélus Trench on the divisional left. They found the wire well cut by the artillery and the defending garrison reasonably easy to overcome. However, the Scottish Borderers on the left began to suffer from heavy sniper fire from a series of dugouts on the north side of Bois de Bonval. According to the 13th Brigade's after-action report, these dugouts "should have been captured by 3rd Canadian Division as part of their Red Objective." A bombing party silenced the snipers' nests, capturing three officers and thirty-three other ranks.[44] Both British battalions then pushed around the northern slopes of Hill 135. While the Royal West Kents pressed through the smoking stumps of Count's Wood and the Bois du Goulot to the southeast, the Scottish Borderers pushed through Bois de Bonval where they captured 200 Germans, two twenty-one centimetre howitzers, and four machine guns, two of which they turned on enemy parties retreating toward the village of Vimy.[45]

The Blue Line in the 2nd Canadian Division's sector was in Canadian and British hands between 1050 and 1110 hours. For almost an hour and a half, the artillery barrage remained stationary while the 6th and 13th brigades reorganized for the fourth and final stage of the division's assault. The ultimate objective was the Brown Line, which stretched along the eastern portions of Bois du Goulot and Bois de la Ville, the latter being on the western outskirts of Farbus. Throughout this wooded region, along the steeper eastern slope of Vimy Ridge, lay the German artillery lines which gave immediate support to their garrisons on the ridge.[46]

The advance on the 6th Brigade front would be carried out by the 29th Battalion on the left and the 27th Battalion (Lieutenant-Colonel P.J. Daly) on the right. To 6th Brigade's left, the 1st Battalion, Royal West Kents Regiment and the 2nd Battalion, King's Own Scottish Borderers would continue sweeping southeast through the enemy gun positions along Bois du Goulot. In moving up to the Blue Line, the 27th Battalion suffered around twenty casualties from German artillery barrages, and at one point its members were forced to don respirators in response to gas shelling. Nevertheless, the troops deployed in good order, forming up in a series of shell holes.[47]

Owing to the contours of the terrain, the layout of German defences, and the Canadian divisional boundaries, the battalions from 6th Brigade had to wheel to the left and advance in a northeasterly direction toward the Brown Line. The artillery barrage had to shift accordingly, lifting "by sections from right to left." At 1242 hours, the barrage began to creep ahead on the divisional right, with the 27th Battalion's right-hand company (A Company) moving off behind it. As the barrage ploughed onward to the northeast, successive companies followed suit from right to left. By 1300 hours the 27th Battalion's entire line was in motion.[48]

The formerly silent batteries of field guns that first came into action during the assault of the Blue Line were the only ones in range to fire this final creeping barrage. Their shells cut gaps in the two heavy wire belts that screened the final German defences along the ridge. But, as the 6th Brigade later reported,

a great deal of wire in coils and stretches still standing made the advance a most difficult one...This was, however, surmounted by all the waves of the 27th (City of Winnipeg) and 29th (Vancouver) Battalions. Stiff opposition was met with from here on, as the German gunners held their ground and did the utmost to check our troops, by firing their guns point blank and using machine guns, rifles and revolvers.[49]

Amid this maelstrom, Bandsman P.M. Smith of the 27th Battalion drew a piccolo from his tunic pocket and played his unit's regimental march. His coolness under heavy fire was inspiring. After volleys of well-aimed rifle grenades overcame a German machine gun nest, the men of the 27th "charged the last 50 yards with a cheer and leaped into the gun pits where the gunners put up a stout fight." The German artillery crews managed a spirited defence until they were shot down, bayoneted, or captured with their guns. At 1355 hours the 27th Battalion shot white flares to signal that their objective was secure. "Fritz lambasted us right till we got right up to him," recalled W.J. Sheppard, "and they threw their hands up and said 'Mercy, Comrade' but I don't think they got much mercy." Bandsman Smith was killed by a shell just as he reached the objective.[50]

On the left, the 29th Battalion cleared its portion of Bois de la Ville and reached the objective by 1415 hours. The Scottish Borderers and the Royal West Kents of 13th Brigade also finished clearing Bois du Goulot, capturing nine field guns and howitzers in the bargain. Two of the captured seventy-seven millimetre guns had fired on the British troops over open sights as they advanced, but the German crews were driven off by bursts of Lewis gun fire and showers of rifle grenades.[51]

By the mid-afternoon of 9 April 1917, 2nd Canadian Division held the Brown Line.[52] That night Major-General Burstall issued the following message to his commanders:

> GOC wishes you to convey to all ranks under your command his hearty congratulations on the magnificent success obtained today and his thanks for the splendid work and cooperation of all arms throughout the Division. The Division has gained the whole of its objectives and has penetrated the enemy's defences to a depth of 2 miles. Some 1,500 prisoners and probably 15 guns in addition to Machine Guns and Trench Mortars have been captured by the Division and attached troops.[53]

But the battle was not yet over. German counterattacks threatened, and the Canadian and British battalions lost no time consolidating new defensive positions and seeking intelligence on the enemy's movements. On the afternoon of 9 April, the 6th Brigade was at work establishing an outpost line on the eastern edge of Bois de la Ville, where a further 250 prisoners were rounded up. The 27th and 29th Battalions dispatched small patrols into what remained of Farbus, where the former unit captured a German artillery colonel, two other officers, and "six large sacks of documents," all of which would keep brigade and divisional intelligence officers well occupied for some time to come.[54]

The division established its main line of resistance along the west side of the German wire belt, labelled "Point du Jour — Farbus Line" on the maps. Manned by the 6th and 13th brigades, this line would anchor the division's defences on Vimy Ridge. Engineers from the 4th, 5th and 6th field companies constructed a series of six strongpoints behind the line, each of which "was laid out in the form of several bits of trench about 25 feet long, radiating from a common centre and having machine gun emplacements at their outer extremities. Completely enclosed by wire, they were thus capable of all round defence." The 4th and 5th brigades, meanwhile, still held firm on the Black and Red lines.[55]

The condition of the battlefield made the essential task of hauling the artillery forward extremely difficult. By dusk on 9 April, only two eighteen-pounder and two 4.5-inch howitzer batteries had been registered for further action.[56] Captain Duguid of 2nd Canadian Divisional Artillery headquarters (and future Canadian official historian) noted with frustration: "It is clear that unless adequate provision is made for clearing and repairing roads and laying light railways, it is impossible to get field guns forward across a heavily shelled area and keep up ammunition supply. It will be several days before the heavies can come up."[57] Captain Andrew Macphail of No. 6 Canadian Field Ambulance framed the problem in more vivid terms:

> The history of war should be written in terms of farming. Let any one who supposes that we might continue the advance make the attempt to haul a load of potatoes over a ploughed field, sodden with rain. When horses have no footing they are helpless. If the officer in charge of 'Tanks' had ever tried to operate a potato-digger in heavy ground he would know that his tanks were impossible...The fact is we are held up by the elements of nature, and there is a point in the contest beyond which mere men are powerless.

"The terrain is much worse than on the Somme," Macphail had concluded. "Mile after mile not an inch of ground remains undisturbed. It is like a tumultuous sea suddenly turned to earth."[58]

The Germans made several attempts to counterattack the division's positions, but the attacks were poorly coordinated and broken up by the Canadian artillery batteries that managed to get forward. Captured enemy guns, re-sighted and crewed by Canadian gunners, also defended the division's gains. By 11 April, the German high command was finally reconciled to the loss of Vimy Ridge. The Germans completed their withdrawal to the Oppy-Méricourt Line and the Avion Switch on the night of 12-13 April, leaving the Canadians to consolidate their defences and extend their supply and transportation network to units that were pushing over the eastern side of the ridge. Aggressive patrols maintained contact with German rear guards, but it would be some time before 2nd Canadian Division and the rest of the corps would marshal enough resources for further offensive operations.[59]

The year 1916 had been frustrating for 2nd Canadian Division. Months of dismal trench warfare, punctuated by operational setbacks like the fighting at St. Eloi in April, and even rarer successes like the capture of Courcelette in September, had cost thousands of casualties for little gain. This left many weary veterans, like the 19th Battalion's Fred Stitt, convinced that the war "was going on and on forever."[60] But with the capture of all of its assigned objectives on 9 April 1917, the men of 2nd Canadian Division had gained the sense that they could be masters of the battlefield. The division's advance through German defences of notorious strength stood not only as a great tactical and technical achievement, it also represented an important psychological turning point.

By almost every measure, General Burstall's division had won an impressive victory. Earlier that winter, the Canadians had recognized that this was essentially a "platoon commander's war."[61] Senior commanders and staffs formulated the tactical plans, logistical schemes, and operation orders but it was up to company and platoon commanders to carry out those orders. When asked about the quality of infantry tactics, Burstall concluded:

> The platoon organization has fully justified its introduction. Whenever preparations for an attack have been complete, i.e. wire properly cut and trench destruction thoroughly carried out, the Infantry have been able to advance with comparatively small casualties as the new organization has enabled them to overcome opposition with the weapons at their own disposal. This organization does not, however, enable Infantry to overcome the obstacle of wire which has not been properly cut.[62]

What Burstall did not mention was that, in a war dominated by artillery and automatic weapons, there was still a place for traditional soldierly virtues like initiative, courage and leadership.

Certainly the gunners received great praise. Summing up the majority opinion, 4th Brigade reported that, "Our artillery was most effective, wire being cut and trenches demolished, and a large part of the success of the operation is no doubt due to this thorough artillery preparation as well as to the excellent creeping barrage which was laid down."[63] Duguid pronounced the operation, "a perfect success. In 8 hours barrage — the longest on record to date — only one 18 pdr of all the field guns covering the 2nd Canadian Division went out of action."[64] Aside from the regrettable incident of short shelling, the artillery's biggest difficulty came with its attempt to move forward over the broken ground.

Communications functioned as well as could have been expected. Division and brigade headquarters maintained contact with subordinate commands on 9 April. Telephone lines were judged "the most satisfactory" while visual signals such as semaphore flags were used "extensively between Companies and Battalions, and proved of great value." Wireless sets established at the various brigade headquarters before the attack, "were [not] used to any extent." "Buried cable is of the utmost importance," declared Lieutenant J.E. Gennet, the 6th Brigade's signals officer, "and for the rest, resolute linemen, and good runners I have found will always carry one through."[65]

The human cost was substantial: between 9-14 April, the division suffered approximately 2,547 casualties, all ranks (including 381 casualties from the 13th British Brigade). Of these, twenty-seven officers and 597 other ranks were killed.[66] Still, Colonel H.M. Jacques, the divisional assistant director of medical services (ADMS) considered the speed of evacuation at Vimy to be "unprecedented. Hundreds of walking cases, having been dressed, had reached Ambulance Corner, 5000 yards to the rear, within 2 hours from commencement of the attack." The tramlines that carried stretcher cases to the rear "were utilized to the fullest extent, especially as the nature of the terrain made stretcher carrying exceedingly slow and laborious." Jacques admitted that locating regimental aid posts in deep dugouts "would have proved of great value in an unsuccessful attack, but on account of the rapidity and depth of the advance were of little use, the majority of cases being treated in the open." Traffic congestion contributed to overcrowding at the division's advanced dressing station at Aux Rietz. Nevertheless, within a twenty-three-hour period, 5,112 wounded men were evacuated through Aux Rietz alone, some of whom came from the neighbouring 1st and 3rd Canadian divisions.[67]

Logistical arrangements also had worked well. By 10 April, it was estimated that 2nd Canadian Division had captured forty-nine officers and 1,740 other ranks, exclusive of the numbers of wounded Germans evacuated through Canadian dressing stations.[68] The divisional assistant provost marshal (APM) and his staff had few difficulties handling these men in the "divisional cage." Traffic control personnel worked under "high pressure," dealing with congestion, keeping ammunition and supplies moving forward to the fighting troops, and ensuring that convoys of wounded and injured personnel made it to the appropriate dressing stations. The APM reported that the workload of his battle straggler posts was

> exceedingly light there being only 12 names sent in and in all cases they were men who had missed the forward dressing stations and were proceeding direct to the rear hospitals with slight wounds. This is a fact which redounds greatly to the credit of the whole Canadian Corps and particularly to this division and further emphasises the high standard of discipline and morale which has always been shown by the Canadian Soldier.[69]

Survivors of the victory on 9 April 1917 had mixed reactions. H.R.H. Clyne of the 29th Battalion recalled, "It was hard to realize that Vimy Ridge had been captured and on schedule. There were no cheers and no gleeful shouts." As they gazed out over the Douai Plain from the summit of the ridge, the men "looked over the great expanse of new country silently." On the other hand, the 31st Battalion's medical officer, Harold McGill, was more effusive in his praise of the operation. "...It was by all odds the most spectacular battle I have seen," McGill wrote shortly afterward. "One of our officers remarked that a show manager would require to charge 10 dollars a seat to put on as good an exhibition." F. MacGregor of the 25th Battalion maintained that the attack at Vimy was "a wonderful successful thing and a lot was made of it through journalists, but as far as actual hardship and killing [went] it wasn't to be compared with the Somme and Ypres...I would rather go over [the top at] Vimy any morning than go on some of those big raids, or [hold] the line and [be] pounded continuously day and night...."[70]

Perhaps even more telling was the contemporary reaction of Major Georges Vanier of the 22nd Battalion. In October 1916, reflecting on his unit's recent terrible losses in the Battle of the Somme, Vanier wrote, "It is hard to be very merry under these circumstances but it is necessary not to be downhearted, so we try to think of the present and of the living and not of the past and of the dead." However, in the afterglow of events on 9 April 1917, Vanier cheerfully informed his mother: "You know of course that things are going with a tremendous swing and that we are pursuing the Boche. The morale of our troops is magnificent. We cannot lose—what is more we are winning quickly and the war will be over within six months."[71] Vanier's predictions were wildly optimistic, inflated perhaps for the benefit of his family. But the future governor-general's clear expression of confidence and hope in April 1917 suggests that the memory of Vimy Ridge was firmly grounded in the belief that the Canadians had won a remarkable victory.

Notes

1. Andrew Macphail, "The Cavendish Lecture on A Day's Work," reprinted from *The Lancet*, 30 June 1917, 7.

2. David Campbell, "The Divisional Experience in the C.E.F.: A Social and Operational History of the 2nd Canadian Division, 1915-1918," PhD Thesis, University of Calgary, 2003, Chapters 3 and 5.

3. "Minutes of Conference of Corps Commanders Held by G.O.C., First Army, at Chateau Philomel, 29th March, 1917," files 23-26, folder 6, volume [vol] 3827, [Series] III-C-1, Record Group [RG] 9, Library and Archives Canada [LAC].

4. Brereton Greenhous and Stephen J. Harris, *Canada and the Battle of Vimy Ridge, 9-12 April, 1917* (Ottawa: Minister of Supply and Services, 1992), 94 and folding map; Alexander Turner, *Vimy Ridge, 1917: Byng's Canadians Triumph at Arras* (Osprey Publishing, 2005), 62-63; Captain Cyril Falls, *History of the Great War: Military Operations, France and Belgium, 1917, Vol. 1: The German Retreat to the Hindenburg Line and the Battle of Arras* (London: Macmillan, 1940), 353; Generalleutnant Alfred Dieterich, "The German 79th Reserve Infantry Division in the Battle of Vimy Ridge, April 1917," trans. Christopher and Ute Wilde-Linnell; introduction by Andrew Iarocci, *Canadian Military History*, vol 15, no 1, 2006, 69-70, 72.

5. Falls, 307, 323; D.E. Macintyre, *Canada at Vimy* (Toronto: Peter Martin, 1967), 95.

6. "Summary of Operations for the Capture of Vimy Ridge by 2nd Canadian Division," Appendix 760, War Diary [WD], 2nd Canadian Division General Staff, May 1917, T-1928, vol 4845, III-D-3, RG 9; Falls, 335.

7. Corps Commanders' Conference, 29 March 1917.

8. Appendices A and C, Canadian Corps Artillery Instructions for the Capture of Vimy Ridge, file 1, folder 21, vol 4089, III-C-39.

9. WD, 4th Canadian Machine Gun Company, 8-9 April 1917, T-10813, vol 4982, III-D-3, RG 9; WD, 6th Cdn MG Coy, 9 April 1917, T-10813-10814, vol 4983, III-D-3, RG 9.

10. "Instructions for the Offensive No. 3," 24 March 1917, App 676, WD, 2nd Cdn Div Gen Staff, March 1917, T-1927, vol 4845, III-D-3, RG 9; K. Weatherbe, *From the Rideau to the Rhine and Back: The 6th Field Company and Battalion Canadian Engineers in the Great War* (Toronto: Hunter-Rose, 1928), 229.

11. 2nd Canadian Division S/68/264, Instructions for the Offensive No. 3, 26 March 1917, App A, WD, 2nd Cdn Div AA & QMG, March 1917, T-1931, vol 4849, III-D-3, RG 9.

12. Medical Arrangements, 2nd Canadian Division, 5 April 1917, Appendices, WD, 2nd Cdn Div ADMS, April 1917, T-10911, vol 5025, III-D-3, RG 9; untitled "report upon the part performed by the Medical Service of the 2nd

Canadian Division" at Vimy, 18 May 1917, Appendices, WD, 2nd Cdn Div ADMS, May 1917, T-10911, vol 5025, III-D-3, RG 9.

13   WD, 2nd Cdn Div Gen Staff, 8 April 1917, T-1927, vol 4845, III-D-3, RG 9.

14   WD, 2nd Cdn Div Gen Staff, 4 February 1917; 2nd Cdn Div G.S. 1551/756, 17 March 1917, file 10, folder 4, vol 4083, III-C-3, RG 9; Colonel G.W.L. Nicholson, *Canadian Expeditionary Force, 1914-1919: The Official History of the Canadian Army in the First World War* (Ottawa: Queen's Printer, 1962), 247; Canadian Corps Scheme of Operations, Appendix VIII, WD, Canadian Corps General Staff, March 1917, T-7176, vol 4814, III-D-3, RG 9; Instructions No. 3, 24 March 1917, App 676, WD, 2nd Cdn Div Gen Staff, March 1917; "Outline Scheme for the First Stage of the Attack and Capture of Vimy Ridge, 'Y' Division of Southern Corps," folder 44-2, vol 4098, III-C-3, RG 9.

15   Turner, 51; Nicholson, 250.

16   "6th Canadian Infantry Brigade, Narrative of Offensive Operations on 9th and 10th April 1917," M 4791, H.D.B. Ketchen fonds, Glenbow Museum Archives [GMA]; 4th Infantry Brigade report on operations, 9 April 1917, File 9, Folder 19, vol 4105, III-C-3, RG 9; Macintyre, *Canada at Vimy*, 64-65; Appendix A to Instructions No. 3, 24 March 1917, App 676, WD, 2nd Cdn Div Gen Staff, March 1917.

17   Major D.J. Corrigall *The History of the Twentieth Canadian Battalion (Central Ontario Regiment) Canadian Expeditionary Force in the Great War, 1914-1918* (Toronto: Stone and Cox, 1935), 114.

18   Claude C. Craig Diary, 9 April 1917, E 351, Claude C. Craig Papers, Manuscript Group [MG] 30, LAC.

19   J. Clinton Morrison, Jr., *Hell Upon Earth: A Personal Account of Prince Edward Island Soldiers in the Great War, 1914-1918* (Summerside: J. Clinton Morrison, Jr., 1995), 111.

20   Reginald H. Roy (ed), *The Journal of Private Fraser, Canadian Expeditionary Force, 1914-1918* (Nepean: CEF Books, 1998), 262-263.

21   Operation Order No. 114, 6 April 1917, App 3, WD, 2nd Cdn Div Artillery, April 1917, T-10777, vol 4959, III-D-3, RG 9; 4th Bde report, 9 April 1917.

22   4th Bde report, 9 April 1917; 5th Infantry Brigade, "Summary of Operations, 8th April to 18th April, 1917," App 5, WD, 5th Infantry Brigade, April 1917, T-10682, vol 4885, III-D-3, RG 9.

23   "Formation for Battalions of 4th Brigade Attacking Black Objective," 19th Battalion, App I, Preparations for the Offensive on Vimy Ridge, WD, 19th Battalion, March 1917, T-10725, vol 4928, III-D-3, RG 9; "Formation of Battalion of 5th Brigade Attacking Black Objective," App 3, WD, 26th Battalion, April 1917, T-10737, vol 4934, III-D-3, RG 9.

24   4th Bde report, 9 April 1917.

25   WD, 4th Infantry Brigade, 9 April 1917, T-10678, vol 4881, III-D-3, RG 9; Corrigall, 118-119.

26   Nicholson, 254.

27   5th Bde Summary, 8-18 April 1917; R.C. Fetherstonhaugh, *The 24th Battalion, C.E.F., Victoria Rifles of Canada, 1914-1919* (Montreal: Gazette Printing Company, 1930), 131.

28   5th Bde Summary, 8-18 April 1917; WD, 24th Battalion, 9 April 1917, T-10733, vol 4932, III-D-3, RG 9; WD, 26th Battalion, 9 April 1917.
29   5th Bde Summary, 8-18 April 1917; Serge Bernier, *The Royal 22e Régiment, 1914-1999* (Montreal: Art Global, 2000), 53.
30   Table A1, Operation Order No. 114, 6 April 1917, App 3, WD, 2nd Cdn Div Artillery, April 1917; 5th Bde Summary, 8-18 April 1917; WD, 18th Battalion, 9 April 1917, LAC, T-10721, vol 4926, III-D-3, RG 9.
31   Operation Order No. 114, 6 April 1917, App 3, WD, 2nd Cdn Div Artillery, April 1917; 5th Bde Summary, 8-18 April 1917; H.C. Singer and A.A. Peebles, *History of Thirty-First Battalion C.E.F.* (Calgary: privately printed, 1939), 198.
32   Excerpt of interview with F. MacGregor, transcript of broadcast episode, "The Battle of Vimy Ridge," episode 9, vol 6, *Flanders Fields*, B-III-1, RG 41, Records of the CBC, LAC.
33   Morrison, 115.
34   Falls, 324.
35   5th Bde Summary, 8-18 April 1917; WD, 25th Battalion, 9 April 1917, T-10735, vol 4933, III-D-3, RG 9; WD, 22nd Battalion, 9 April 1917, T-10732-10733, vol 4931, III-D-3, RG 9; Pierre Berton, *Vimy* (Toronto: McClelland and Stewart, 1986), 234.
36   5th Bde Summary, 8-18 April 1917; WD, 25th Battalion, 9 April 1917; WD, 21st Battalion, 9 April 1917.
37   Falls, 325. The 1st Canadian Mounted Rifles' war diarist remarked that, "only one officer of the 2nd Division was met with in our area," and that the other ranks seemed "hopelessly lost and without ideas of their flanks." WD, 1st Battalion CMR, 9 April 1917, T-10754-10755, vol 4946, III-D-3, RG 9.
38   Summary of Operations, 2nd Cdn Div, App 760, WD, 2nd Cdn Div Gen Staff, May 1917, T-1928, vol 4845, III-D-3, RG 9; Falls, 335.
39   4th Bde report, 9 April 1917; Nicholson, 248; Greenhous and Harris, 96; Singer and Peebles, 201.
40   6th Bde Narrative, 9-10 April 1917; Berton, 235.
41   6th Bde Narrative, 9-10 April 1917; "Report on Operations of 13th Infantry Brigade Carried Out When Attached to 2nd Canadian Division," File O-1-28, vol 2226, III-B-1, RG 9; Falls, 333.
42   Table A1, Operation Order No. 114, 6 April 1917, App 3, WD, 2nd Cdn Div Artillery, April 1917; 6th Bde Narrative, 9-10 April 1917; Singer and Peebles, 198, 204; WD, 29th Battalion, 9 April 1917, T-10740-10741, vol 4936, III-D-3, RG 9; H.R.N. Clyne, *Vancouver's 29th: A Chronicle of the 29th in Flanders Fields* (Vancouver: Tobin's Tigers Association, 1964), 31-32.
43   6th Bde Narrative, 9-10 April 1917; WD, 29th Battalion, 9 April 1917; Falls, 333-335; Singer and Peebles, 204-205.
44   Report of 13th Bde.
45   Falls, 335-336; Report of 13th Bde.
46   WD, 6th Infantry Brigade, 9 April 1917, T-10685, vol 4889, III-D-3, RG 9; 6th Bde Narrative, 9-10 April 1917; Falls, 336; Nicholson, 257; Operation Order No. 52, 8 April 1917, App 1, WD, 6th Cdn MG Coy, April 1917.

47 Nicholson, 257; 6th Bde Narrative, 9-10 April 1917; WD, 27th Battalion, 9 April 1917, T-10738-10739, vol 4935, III-D-3, RG 9.

48 Falls, 336; 6th Bde Narrative, 9-10 April 1917; WD, 27th Battalion, 9 April 1917; WD, 29th Battalion, 9 April 1917.

49 Nicholson, 257; 6th Bde Narrative, 9-10 April 1917.

50 "Narrative of Offensive, 9-4-17," App M, WD, 27th Battalion, April 1917; Transcript of interview with W.J. Sheppard, tape 1, vol 11, 27th Bn, *Flanders Fields*, B-III-1, RG 41.

51 WD, 29th Battalion, 9 April 1917; Report of 13th Bde.

52 According to the schedule for the operation, the eastern escarpment of the ridge would be in Canadian hands by 1318 hours. Nicholson, 248.

53 2nd Cdn Div headquarters, 9 April 1917, file 4, folder 21, vol 4089, III-C-3, RG 9.

54 6th Bde Narrative, 9-10 April 1917; "Narrative of Offensive, 9-4-17," App M, WD, 27th Battalion, April 1917.

55 6th Bde Narrative, 9-10 April 1917; "Narrative of Offensive, 9-4-17," App M, WD, 27th Battalion, April 1917; Report of 13th Bde; Summary of Operations, 2nd Cdn Div, App 760, WD, 2nd Cdn Div Gen Staff, May 1917; description of strongpoints quoted from Weatherbe, 231; Instructions No. 3, 24 March 1917, App 676, WD, 2nd Cdn Div Gen Staff, March 1917.

56 WD, 2nd Cdn Div Gen Staff, 9 April 1917.

57 WD, 2nd Cdn Div Artillery, 12 April 1917.

58 Sir Andrew Macphail Diary, 11-15 April 1917, vol 4, D 150, Sir Andrew Macphail Papers, MG 30.

59 Summary of Operations, 2nd Cdn Div, App 760, WD, 2nd Cdn Div Gen Staff, May 1917; Greenhous and Harris, 98; Nicholson, 263-264.

60 Transcript of interview with F.A. Stitt, tape 1, vol 10, 19th Bn, *Flanders Fields*, B-III-1, RG 41.

61 Canadian Corps G.340, 27 December 1916, file 3, folder 24, vol 4136, III-C-3, RG 9.

62 2nd Canadian Division to Canadian Corps, 10 May 1917, file R-1-28, vol 2227, III-B-1, RG 9.

63 4th Bde report, 9 April 1917.

64 WD, 2nd Cdn Div Artillery, 9 April 1917.

65 "Report on Communications, 2nd Canadian Division, April 1st — May 15th, 1917," App 730, WD, 2nd Cdn Div Gen Staff, Apr 1917; D.E. Macintyre Diary, 269, vol 1, E 241, D.E. Macintyre Papers, MG 30.

66 "Casualties By Days — France and Belgium," vol 496, RG 150, LAC; Summary of Operations 2nd Cdn Div, App 760, WD, 2nd Cdn Div Gen Staff, May 1917; Report of 13th Bde.

67 Reports from the ADMS, 2nd Cdn Div, 18 May 1917, Appendices, WD, 2nd Cdn Div ADMS, T-10911, vol 5025, III-D-3, RG 9.

68 WD, 2nd Cdn Div Gen Staff, 10 April 1917.

69 WD, 2nd Cdn DivAPM, 9 April 1917, T-10942-10943, vol 5050, III-D-3, RG 9.

70 Excerpt of interview with H.R.H. Clyne, transcript of broadcast episode, "The Battle of Vimy Ridge," episode 9, vol 6, *Flanders Fields*, B-III-1, RG 41;

Harold W. McGill, personal correspondence, 23 April 1917, GMA, M 742, file 7, box 2, Harold W. and Emma G. McGill fonds; transcript of interview with F. MacGregor, tape 4, vol 11, 25th Bn, *Flanders Fields*, B-III-1, RG 41.

71 Vanier to his sister, Frances, 15 October 1916, quoted in Deborah Cowley (ed), *Georges Vanier: Soldier, The Wartime Letters and Diaries, 1915-1919* (Toronto: Dundurn, 2000), 173; Vanier to his mother, 14 April 1917, quoted in, 190.

11

The 3rd Canadian Division
Forgotten Victory
GEOFFREY HAYES

Several hundred metres south of the Grange tunnel in the Vimy Ridge memorial park stands a white stone cross. Marked on the roadway by a humble signpost and hidden by the years, it is a silent and nearly forgotten testament to the men of 3rd Canadian Division who fought nearby.

Major-General Louis Lipsett's division fought two battles at Vimy Ridge. The first, the division's initial advance, succeeded through careful planning, rehearsal and the intricate timings and overwhelming force of the division's artillery. The division's second battle is too often forgotten, but the Canadians' fragile hold against German counterattacks left the outcome uncertain through most of 9 April 1917. That the division prevailed suggests a battlefield where details mattered. Supplies mattered, as did the carrying parties that hauled them forward. Picks and shovels mattered. So did leadership.

Will Bird was a private reinforcing Montreal's 42nd Battalion, the Royal Highlanders of Canada, when he first saw Vimy Ridge early in 1917. He was billeted in the village of Neuville St. Vaast, which shellfire had "reduced...to rubble.

> Soldiers occupied the cellars. We were divided into groups and eleven of us were shunted into a cellar, in which were timbers holding shreds of wires. They had been bunks once. Rats ran into holes as we lit candles and then came boldly back and stared at us. It was a cold and wet-smelling place.

Bird heeded signs that warned, "Keep low. Use trench in daytime." Soon assigned to a working party, he helped build the vast labyrinth of trench works, saps and dugouts that crossed the ridge. Beneath the light of a flare, Bird first saw no-man's-land. He recalled the scene years later: "Jumbled earth and debris. Jagged wreckage: it looked as if a gigantic upheaval had destroyed the entire surface and left only a festering wound. Everything was shapeless, ugly and distorted."[1]

Will Bird joined 3rd Canadian Division when it was just over a year old. Formed in France at Christmas 1915 under Major-General Malcolm Mercer, the division was hit hard at its first sustained action defending the most easterly part of the Ypres salient near Mount Sorrel in June 1916. One of its infantry battalions, 4th Canadian Mounted Rifles (4 CMR) suffered eighty-nine percent casualties in the gunfire that also killed Mercer.[2] Louis Lipsett, a British professional officer who had served in Western Canada before the war, took over the division and fought it at the Somme in September. At the time of Vimy Ridge, Lipsett was the only British regular officer leading a Canadian division. Bird shared a forward observation post one night for several hours with Lipsett. For someone who seldom spoke well of senior' commanders, Bird was impressed.[3]

Lipsett's brigade and battalion commanders also made an impression. Brigadier-generals F.W. Hill, A.C. Macdonell and James Elmsley were all professional officers. Both Macdonell and Elmsley were veterans of South Africa, where Elmsley was twice wounded.[4] Of the three, Macdonell ("Batty Mac") held the widest reputation. His fondness for the front lines and his generous notes of praise won him a loyal following among the battalion commanders in 7th Brigade. In Lieutenant-Colonel C.H. Hill, who commanded the Royal Canadian Regiment (RCR) at Vimy Ridge, Macdonell likely found a kindred spirit for Hill had taken over the RCR in April 1916 from Macdonell's cousin. Agar Adamson, who was fifty-one-years-old when he led the Princess Patricia's Canadian Light Infantry (PPCLI) onto Vimy Ridge, admitted to his wife early in 1916 that Macdonell "seems to know his job and is most considerate." The war diary of the 42nd Battalion also spoke well of Macdonell.[5] In early 1917 that battalion was commanded by a thirty-five-year-old banker from Ingersoll, Ontario, Major Stanley Counter Norsworthy.[6] Edmonton's 49th Battalion was also under new leadership at Vimy Ridge when former Edmonton mayor William Griesbach took over 1 Canadian Infantry Brigade in February. He left the 49th to R.H. Palmer, a battalion original who brought the unit home at war's end.[7] Macdonell asked a great deal of these men at Vimy Ridge.

The impact of Mount Sorrel was especially important to 8th Brigade's commanders, for Brigadier-General Elmsley and three of his four battalion commanders earned their commands there. Ralph Craven Andros described himself as a rancher living in Esquimalt when he enlisted in Winnipeg. He took over the 1st Canadian Mounted Rifles

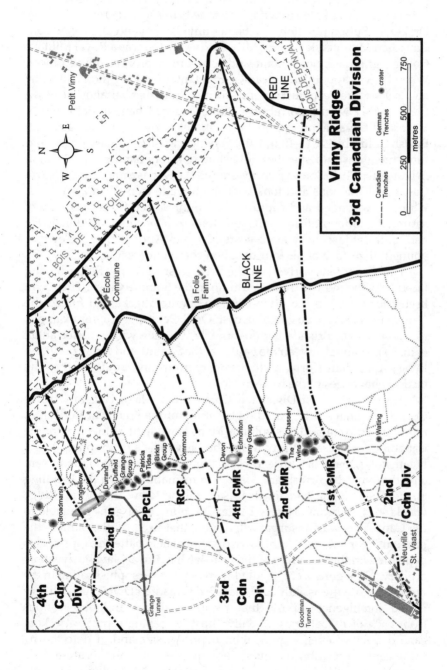

(1 CMR, raised in Manitoba and Saskatchewan) when his predecessor, Alfred Shaw, was killed in action on 3 June 1916. On that same day, Denis Draper, of Sutton Junction, Quebec assumed command of Quebec's 5th Canadian Mounted Rifles (5 CMR). Harry Gordon was a Royal Military College graduate, accountant and long-time Toronto militia officer. When he was appointed to lead Central Ontario's 4 CMR on 7 June, he had to start afresh, for just seventy-six men from that battalion survived the ordeal of Mount Sorrel unscathed. George Chalmers Johnston of Victoria, BC was another pre-war militiaman who went overseas with British Columbia's 2 CMR in 1915. Having earned a Military Cross[8] and three mentions-in-dispatches, Johnston took command of his battalion in November 1916. James Elmsley started the war as a major in the Royal Canadian Dragoons and took over the brigade from Victor Williams, who was wounded and captured at Mount Sorrel. Elmsley no doubt assumed a different leadership style than someone like Macdonell. He had to, for at just thirty-eight years of age in April 1917, Elmsley was younger than each of his four battalion commanders.[9]

The Canadians arrived in the area west of Vimy Ridge having faced a costly and frustrating autumn in the Somme valley. There had been successes, but too often German counterattacks had forced the Canadians back at considerable cost. On 8 October 1916, for example, Macdonell's 7th Brigade had lost nearly 950 men with no substantial gain.[10] The pause between the battles of the Somme and Arras provided Byng's Canadian Corps a chance to regroup and study further the tactical challenges of the battlefield.

The report of 1st Divisional Commander Major-General Arthur Currie in January 1917, based on his study of the French at Verdun, is referred to throughout this volume. Many consider it a blueprint for the Canadians' success at Vimy Ridge, but as Currie's biographer, A.M.J. Hyatt, notes, many of Currie's observations and recommendations were already in use by British and Canadian formations.[11] On the handling of the guns Currie had much to say, for he knew that Vimy Ridge was largely to be an artillery battle. The number of guns available to the Canadians was unsurpassed, double that used on the Somme the previous year.[12] As well as his own divisional field batteries, Lipsett also depended on the resources of the British 63rd (Royal Naval) Divisional artillery.[13] The guns were handled with impressive sophistication in the months before the assault. Each day, 3rd Canadian Divisional Artillery issued intelligence reports that recorded shoots and observations from each of its batteries. A daily "hostile shelling report" also kept careful track of enemy guns, their quantity, size and, if detected by the recent innovation of sound ranging, their specific location.[14] As the intensity of the barrage increased in late March, divisional field batteries (reorganized from four to six guns each) rehearsed timed barrages across the front. With X day[15] drawing near, the larger calibre guns of the No. 3 Group Canadian Corps Heavy Artillery were called on to destroy the German trench lines and the wire. A summary of operations for the week ending 4 April noted confidently, "Destructive bombardment by heavy artillery has been carried on in accordance with programme. All selected targets have been systematically bombarded and much damage has been done to the enemy's defences."[16]

The divisional staff had by then finalized the plan of attack across a front of 1.5 kilometres. The landmarks to which they referred held rather common and familiar names. Macdonell's 7th Brigade on the left or northern portion of the front was committed from Lasalle Avenue south past the Durrand, Duffield and the Grange group of craters, beyond Grange Avenue, Patrick and Tidza craters to the Vernon Sap; Elmsley's 8th Brigade front ran another 700 metres further south past the Devon and Edmonton craters, Goodman Avenue and two craters known as the Twins. A crater known as B.4 marked the boundary with General Burstall's 2nd Division.

Today the divisional advance of about 1,200 metres can be walked in several minutes. Even by the measures of 1917, the 1st and 2nd Divisions faced advances that were much deeper, but Lipsett's division still anticipated an imposing challenge. Aerial photographs from the time showed a very open battlefield. At its centre hedgerows bounded small fields near the remains of la Folie Farm, a former chateau, and a small collection of buildings, l'Ecole Commune. The longest of a series of German trench lines, the Staubwasser Weg, ran diagonally across the left or northern half of the advance through stands of fruit and fir trees that marked the divisional flank. Hill 145, the highest point of Vimy Ridge, lay 200 metres north of the boundary with General David Watson's 4th Division.

On the divisional right, elaborate lines of German trench works and tunnels formed a corridor into which three of Brigadier Elmsley's battalions were to enter. The most elaborate trench system, the Zwischen Stellung, lay about 700 metres from the start line. Past Fickle Trench and la Folie Farm was the division's final objective (the Red Line) La Bois de la Folie (Folie Wood), a battered stand of trees that lay on the reverse slope of the ridge overlooking the village of Le Petit Vimy.

The infantry's challenge of occupying, consolidating and holding this square of ground was enormous and it prompted what one historian has referred to as a "revolution in tactical doctrine."[17] In March 1917 the 42nd Battalion was in Divion when its four companies were each divided into three platoons, "according to the new platoon organization." The battalion war diary described the routine for the month:

> The training consisted of tactical exercises over taped trenches in the morning, the afternoon being devoted to Squad Drill, Platoon Drill, Route Marches, and Specialists' training. Lewis Gunners were trained at Eaton Machine Gun Co[mpan]y range La Cauchiette, and Bombers and Rifle Grenadiers had practice on alternate days at bombing pit dug in rear of our Transport Lines.[18]

The combination of new organization, tactical training, infantry weapons and an elaborate artillery program were all to play a crucial role in la Folie sector of Vimy Ridge.[19]

The raiding programs before the battle provide some idea of how small groups of well-armed men could dominate ground. On 23 March, at 0300 hours the enemy exploded a large mine beside Durand crater on the divisional left in front of the 42nd Battalion. Immediately Lieutenants Charles Topp and Douglas Small rushed a party of Lewis gunners to the highest lip of the crater. Scouts found that the explosion had linked four other craters in a line that ran about 208 metres to the north. It was an opportunity the Canadians worked hard to exploit. Will Bird was among the working parties ordered to build what became known as Longfellow trench. "The mud was deep and we did not know our location. Each man worked feverishly. All around us in the dark was a deafening clamor of shellfire and rattling of machine guns. Flares were soaring in quick succession, illuminating the area where we dug." For three nights Bird's platoon helped deepen saps and trench lines, lay wire, build assembly trenches and install metal plates through which the muzzles of snipers' rifles could be aimed. General Lipsett sent his congratulations.[20]

On 1 April, Longfellow trench became the jumping off point for a successful raid to "obtain identification and inflict...casualties" led by Lieutenant Ralph Willcock, MC and thirty men from the 42nd Battalion. It was a brutal business. As a box barrage sealed off the objective, snipers, machine gun and mortar crews supported four parties of raiders as they lumbered through the mud: "all encountered dugouts. In two cases enemy sentries attempted to excape[sic] down dugout entrances and were shot; in a number of other cases enemy had been driven into dugout entrances by our shrapnel barrage. They were all killed by the raiding party and dugouts wrecked with Mills and Stokes bombs." This time Macdonell, Lipsett and Corps Commander Julian Byng all sent their congratulations. The raid earned Willcock, a teacher from Hamilton, Ontario, a bar to his Military Cross.[21]

Brigadier Hill's 9th Brigade continued these raids into the first week of April during which time operation orders were issued for what were effectively two battles. The first task to occupy the ridge was to be measured by precise timings and organized advances. A three-minute artillery barrage was to overwhelm the German forward line before six companies from three of Macdonell's battalions moved to the Black Line, a collection of German trenches.[22] Three of Elmsley's battalions were to push just one company to the largest of these trenches, the Zwischen Stellung, in thirty-five minutes. For another forty minutes the barrage was to remain fixed beyond the trench lines so that reinforcements from 49th Battalion on the left and 5 CMR on the right could haul forward ammunition, water, barbed wire, picks and shovels, as well as machine guns and trench mortars. The barrage would then lurch forward to "shoot" the last waves of troops over the final several hundred metres past l'Ecole Commune and la Folie Farm onto the Red Line at the western edge of Folie Wood.[23]

Here began the division's second battle. The task of 'consolidation' meant holding and preparing a newly captured position against a counterattack. This had always proved difficult, but to consolidate on the edge of Folie Wood posed its own problems. The artillery could fire the troops onto their objectives; it could also disperse any observed threats beyond the ridgeline, but in the woods themselves, shellfire was liable to kill Canadians. This meant that the forward platoons, together with divisional engineers and machine gunners, had to secure their strongpoints with whatever they could carry. A grim contest loomed. At issue was whether the Canadians could dig their forward trenches before German snipers and counterattacks overwhelmed them from the woods.[24]

In the final days before battle, the troops tended to details large and small. Lieutenant-Colonel Harry Duncan Lockhart Gordon was not happy when he set up 4 CMR headquarters in the Goodman Tunnels on the night of 5-6 April. He complained that the trenches were "in a very dilapidated condition" and only 75,000 rounds of ammunition had been brought forward.[25] Men bailed the forward trenches. They also filled supply dumps with more ammunition, wire-cutters and bombs that were carried in canvas bomb-buckets that regimental tailors had sewn quickly. Shovels, picks and barbed wire came forward until the very last minute. Wary that the German wire remained uncut on the afternoon before the battle, Lieutenant-Colonel Andros ordered his Stokes guns and trench mortars to fire 200 rounds onto the German front line and support trenches. Gordon sent two parties under Lieutenants Aitkin and William Eric Dixon to cut wire in front of the Albany, Devon and

Vernon craters. The moon was bright, but the men returned without incident.[26]

The final movements to the front took several nights. The scouts who led the men forward kept watch so that they did not become too crowded and vulnerable to stray German gunfire. Two companies of the RCR were led to the Wedd Street entrance of the Grange subway on the night of 6-7 April. There Hugh Walkem (a Montreal insurance broker before the war) was the tunnel's traffic manager.[27] He banned smoking in the tunnels after 2000 hours each night. Lieutenant-Colonel Lang in the Goodman Tunnel ordered the men to sit on the damp tunnel floors to keep the air circulating. Each soldier was fitted with one water bottle, enough rations for twenty-four hours, a forty-eight hour iron ration, a box respirator and gas helmet, an entrenching tool, five sand bags, a field dressing and a steel helmet. In their haversacks, each was to carry four bombs, with two flares and a cardigan jacket rolled in a rubber sheet. Platoons carried a Very pistol and twenty-four cartridges, as well as a flag to mark objectives. Officers and NCOs carried a message book and three maps on which they could mark their positions.[28]

At 1800 hours on Sunday, 8 April 1917, Brigadier Macdonell signaled forward that the battle would begin at 0530 hours, Monday, 9 April 1917. From the Machine Gun Fort where he shared his brigade headquarters with the divisional machine gun officer and a large dressing station, Macdonell sent on the following message at midnight: "I cannot go to bed without wishing you & your gallant lads good speed, best of good luck and victory." Readied in their assembly trenches by 0430 hours, the Patricias took some food and a shot of rum. Only the war diarist of 5 CMR reflected on the day to come: "This is y/z day—tomorrow will make history. Everything possible has been done…All ranks calmly confident."[29]

Lieutenant-Colonel Draper's war diarist captured a remarkable description of the battle's opening minutes:

> Intense artillery bombardment—one continuous roar. The ground trembled and there is mingled with the roar of the guns the swishing and screeching of the shell-filled air. 60 guns are covering our own advance, forming a "rolling barrage." Smoke and debris thrown up by the bursting shells, give the appearance of a solid wall.[30]

Thirty seconds later the forward troops braced themselves as the 172nd Tunneling Company detonated charges to open a series of communications trenches across the 8th Brigade's front. German guns replied, but the men of the Canadian Mounted Rifles climbed from their wet trenches, saps and tunnels and struggled across the first crater lines through the broken wire towards the German support trench. Reports across the front showed steady progress. Just before 0600 hours, the Germans in the Zwischen Stellung fired white flares. A German barrage replied, causing "a considerable number of casualties" among the men of 1 CMR who had little choice but to push through it. These men also discovered German troops emerging from the Prinz Arnolf Tunnel behind them, but a company following on from 5 CMR killed several and took twenty-three others prisoner. Soon parties of dazed German prisoners were moving through the crater lines back to the Canadian positions. The 1 CMR proudly claimed 350 German prisoners by day's end, but complained that 2nd Division units to their right had unfairly tallied some as their own.[31]

Lieutenant Alex McIntyre was the 42nd Battalion's scout officer. From his observation post in Longfellow crater on the division's left flank he watched the initial advance and reported that "everything was going well." Agar Adamson of the PPCLI was in the Grange subway when he heard from Lieutenant Haggard that the Patricias' No. 1 Company had reached Famine trench "with few casualties." Lieutenant-Colonel Hill's RCRs also made good progress through the first hour. Despite the uneven ground, his first two companies advanced in waves twenty paces distant, the soldiers three paces apart. Hill himself went forward and reported, "The Hun trenches and the ground is in a terrible condition; the trenches practically cease to exist."[32] Major Godfrey's company from 2 CMR first reported reaching the Zwischen Stellung by 0600 hours. The guns had done their job. The German lines were "practically obliterated" and the "garrisons [had] offered very little resistance." As follow-on companies came forward for the final push, signalers laid telephone line so that forward battalion headquarters could report on the attacks to the final objectives. Observers in the rear areas noted that "our men could be seen moving freely overland along the whole front."[33]

At 0645 hours the curtain of artillery fire continued on, leading the follow-on companies to their final objectives along the western edge of la Folie Wood. Lieutenant-Colonel Johnston's 2 CMR advanced in the middle of the 8th Brigade. At 0650 hours, Lieutenant George Patrick Heinkey reported that la Folie Farm was occupied; an hour later Captain Gray announced the capture of final objective. Johnston later boasted,

> In every case the advance being in accordance with the artillery curtain fire, and each objective being reached and captured in accordance with our artillery time table. Owing to the rapid advance behind our curtain fire, enemy machine guns had no time to get into action, and of the two that made an attempt to do so, both were wiped out immediately by our infantry.[34]

Johnston's account was an exception, for the battle to hold the division's forward positions was hard-fought for the rest of the day. Lieutenant-Colonel Hill's Royal Canadian Regiment was hit hard by a German strongpoint that had survived the barrage on the forward slope. Sniper fire took its toll, especially on officers whose revolvers in hand made them obvious targets. At least seven officers were reported wounded by 0745 hours. By 0920 hours the RCR's B Company reported losing all of its officers "and on that account did not get on so quickly with the digging."[35] The battle of supply was beginning.

Soon the RCRs began to lose touch with the battalions on either side of them. To their right, two platoons of Gordon's 4 CMR were busy digging strongpoints in the woods when Gordon dispatched a small party under Lieutenant Benjamin Pierce to extend the battalion's left flank towards the ruins of l'Ecole Commune. At 0900 hours, Pierce reported that some of his troops had been "driven back and that they needed more men." Gordon went forward with his scout officer, Lieutenant Thomas William Eric Dixon, to find that his men had "suffered severe casualties" holding a line that was becoming increasingly porous. Brigadier Elmsley then ordered 5 CMR forward, telling the company commanders "to decide for themselves where their troops were most needed."[36]

At 1100 hours Major Algernon Edward Willoughby, the RCR's second-in-command, reported that a shortage of men had left another "small gap" between his A Company and the Patricias to the left. Willoughby's dispatch was grim: "We command the whole situation at present, but unless reinforcements and supplies of every sort, more especially... [small arms ammunition], available machine Guns, Shovels etc., are sent up at first opportunity, it will be difficult to withstand another counter attack."[37]

Three hours before the battle of Vimy Ridge, Greg Clark had been a self-described "baby lieutenant" with the Royal Canadian Regiment. He recalled that by 0830 hours, he was the only officer left in his company. "Now I was alone with 200 men." At 0900 hours, Clark was ordered to lead a party of six others into the gap towards the Patricias. "It was a pretty dreadful time. It was sleeting. The air shook with shellfire, whistled and spat with machine-gun fire." Hauling canvas buckets full of bombs, Clark's party began a desperate scramble, "Down into shell craters, up over crater lips, down into the next craters, pools, mud; fresh hot holes, charred and new-burned, big holes, we slithered and slid and crouched...Two or three times, [Clark's sergeant] had to slide the nozzle of the Lewis [gun] over the lip of craters and spray half a pan of fire into brush clumps."[38]

Brigadier Macdonell's brigade faced opposition from two directions by late morning. To the front, patrols from both the RCRs and the Patricias tried but failed to reach Bracken Trench at the foot of la Folie Wood. Lieutenant-Colonel Adamson of the Patricias understood that his patrols had taken some prisoners, but the Germans continued to be "fairly strong in front." The Patricias then laid wire and waited for the 49th Battalion to haul up more ammunition. Two platoons from the 49th later tried to reach Bracken Trench, but machine guns, sniping and a German charge forced them back.[39]

The Brigade's other difficulties lay to the north, where Major-General Watson's 4th Division was stalled, leaving the highest point of the ridge, Hill 145, in German hands. Hearing that sniping and rifle fire was causing casualties on the divisional left, Major Norsworthy dispatched Major Edson Raymond Pease of A Company, a thirty-two-year-old electrical engineer from Montreal, and a party of rifle grenadiers to "see what we could do."

> [Pease] could see numbers of the enemy on the skyline about 200 yards distant. The rifle grenadiers took cover and opened up fire at the enemy and I moved down to the left, warning everyone I could find towards the flank. To our left a Machine Gun and a number of men presumably 54th (Battalion) also engaged this party, and after a brisk exchange of fire the enemy withdrew leaving only a few snipers who took positions in the wood on the brow, and just below the slope.

Pease soon called for Lewis gunners and ammunition, as "the Hun was attempting to turn our flank 100 yards left of the re-entrant." The fighting only worsened, but the liaison officers still kept a diplomatic tone, promising cooperation as small parties of infantry worked through a series of trenches named Blunt and Blue. By 1100 hours, the 42nd Battalion had counted about 200 casualties trying to hold the divisional flank.[40]

By mid-day, the division's hold on its gains remained tenuous. On the right flank, two companies of 1 CMR reached their objectives in about forty-five minutes and, with the help of the brigade machine guns and engineers, began to build strongpoints that were to secure the 2nd Division's advance further down the slope. It was tough going, mainly because only about forty men from A Company had reached the wood. At 1235 hours, Lieutenant-Colonel Andros heard that the men were too tired to be used as carrying party.

> The trenches were unrecognizable, mud beyond belief. The whole of our Battalion frontage was alive with men of the 2nd Division…who had swung right across our front. Situation was then being cleared up

and these men were being sent back to their own areas. It was noted that only one officer of the 2nd Division was met with in our area, and that these men were hopelessly lost and without ideas of their flanks.

One can only imagine the severity and the chaos of the fighting that day. Andros sounded desperate but firm when he ordered forward 100 reinforcements from 5 CMR to support his weakened companies on the divisional right. Andros urged that more reserves be sent if needed, even if he "used every available man in the Battalion."[41]

The Canadians continued to cling to their forward positions in the afternoon. By 1500 hours patrols had reinforced Lieutenant-Colonel Andros' forward companies, which "seemed to be badly used up."[42] Lieutenant-Colonel Gordon of 4 CMR returned to the front at that time and "found the situation well in hand" since the enemy "did not intend to make an immediate counterattack, but we were suffering severely from snipers and machine gun fire in the STRONG POINT." Realizing that this position could not be held "without very heavy casualties" Gordon asked Brigadier Elmsley for permission to withdraw his men. "This was granted, and the garrison was withdrawn after dark."[43]

On 7th Brigade's front, the fighting for the forward positions was equally heated. "Active" sniping throughout the afternoon kept the RCRs from digging in "as all our men are engaged trying to combat them." Not until 1615 hours did Major Willoughby report that the situation was "good" but he still needed more men, Lewis guns and ammunition. All three arrived in the evening. A double Lewis gun post between B Company and 4 CMR began to deal with snipers. By 2300 hours two platoons from the 58th Battalion carried up more ammunition, bombs, flares, water and rations. By midnight, 9 April 1917, "everything was satisfactory."[44]

The difficulties faced by Major-General Watson's 4th Division are well recounted in Andrew Godefroy's chapter, but from the perspective of Macdonell's 7th Brigade, Watson's attack on Hill 145 could not come soon enough. While Major Norsworthy remained forward through much of the day with his 42nd Battalion, his second-in-command, Major Ewing, sent a firm message to Macdonell in the afternoon: "I consider it urgent that 4th Division advance and occupy Hill 145."[45] One had to be patient. Norsworthy was told to expect a brigade attack on his left by 1630 hours. Not until 2228 hours came unconfirmed reports that the 85th Battalion had taken Hill 145. The next morning found 150 of Norsworthy's men still held out in the woods, their flank still "in the air" while 4th Division continued to fight for its objectives.[46] One company of the Patricias was nearby with six machine guns and their understrength crews holding a quarter of the 42nd Battalion's line. It had been a long night for the Patricias. Enemy shelling began the previous afternoon and 'flattened out' their forward strongpoints, causing seventy-five casualties, including thirty-seven dead in one company alone. Agar Adamson's after-battle reports showed the strain: "Excuse lack of continuity, but blame Germans for keeping me up."[47]

On the afternoon of 10 April, Brigadier Elmsley sent out patrols to locate German positions beyond the eastern slope of the ridge. Their fortunes were mixed. It was snowing heavily when a patrol of fifty men from 1 CMR found almost no opposition, losing just one killed and two wounded to snipers. Other patrols from 2 and 4 CMR came upon "heavily manned" positions. A patrol of twenty-five men under scout officer Lieutenant Dixon of 4 CMR ran into about forty-five men and two machine guns in a shallow trench that extended onto the RCR's front. Anticipating resistance, a barrage was arranged to precede a two-battalion attack the next morning. But before the attack went in, Dixon again moved forward through the woods and found the trench "badly knocked about...and no enemy in sight."[48]

The relief of 3rd Division began on Wednesday 11 April. Lieutenant-Colonel Gordon's 4 CMR "had great difficulty in getting out [of the forward trenches], owing to condition of ground & men having held the line for 65 hours after the attack." Having complained about the state of the forward trenches before the attack, Gordon had even worse things to say about Dumbell Camp behind the lines. It was "the worst camp the Battalion has ever been billeted in during the 18 months they have been in France."[49]

General Lipsett rotated his brigades in and out of the line for the rest of the month. Baths, divine services, parades, the occasional sports event and more training took up the time. Officers and NCOs won promotion; reinforcements were inspected and trained. Back in the line the patrolling continued, as did the raiding. So did the casualties. The call for working parties was endless, in part to salvage the tools that had been left on the battlefield.

General Lipsett addressed Lieutenant-Colonel Gordon's 4 CMR on 15 April. In his thanks to the battalion, he boasted that the battle "was the most complete victory in the history of the British Army." But Lipsett also made a sobering admission: "The Artillery preparation was splendid, and we expected few casualties, I am sorry to say they were rather heavy."[50] As regimental padres retrieved the dead and their commanding officers oversaw burial parties, the brigade staffs tallied nearly 2,000 divisional casualties. The distribution of those casualties is noteworthy, for the fighting on the divisional right flank was the most costly. Lieutenant-Colonel Andros' 1 CMR suffered 336 casualties, the most in the division; next was Lieutenant-Colonel Johnston's 2 CMR

206   GEOFFREY HAYES

with 327 casualties. In 7th Brigade, Lieutenant-Colonel Hill's Royal Canadian Regiment lost 307 men, with nearly seventy missing. Major Norsworthy's 42nd Battalion sustained 277 casualties, with seventy-four missing.[51]

Vimy Ridge demonstrated that the Canadian Corps could wrench ground from the Germans. The massive weight of artillery and materiel available to the Canadian Corps was crucial to the victory at Vimy Ridge. Reorganization, training and meticulous preparations were also important. Details mattered. But there was no easy way to do it. Success still required men to occupy and hold la Folie sector. And as General Lipsett admitted, the cost was greater than the planners expected.

In this battle we should not forget that leadership also mattered. Lipsett demonstrated it and found it among his subordinates. It was in the endless notes of congratulations and encouragement sent by Brigadier Archie Macdonell. Battalion commanders like Norsworthy, Gordon and Andros showed firm leadership (and a great deal of guts) going forward to organize their battalions against German counterattacks.

And then there were the battalions' junior leaders, both the NCOs and commissioned ranks. Consider Lieutenant Thomas William Eric Dixon of 4 CMR. The Bayliss family of Toronto had adopted Devon-born Thomas and his brother Gerald. The young men left their jobs to enlist in 1914, and both were among the few survivors of the battalion's disaster at Mount Sorrel, where Thomas won the Military Medal. The brothers were then commissioned in the field. Lieutenant-Colonel Gordon depended a great deal on Thomas Dixon at Vimy Ridge. Indeed, Dixon seemed to be everywhere: he cut wire in no-man's-land the night before the attack; he reported on the forward troops during the fighting, and then led two daring patrols in the days following. Lieutenant-Colonel Gordon later acknowledged Dixon's "coolness and courage in leading battle patrols which brought in such valuable information."[52] For his actions at Vimy Ridge, Thomas Dixon earned the Military Cross. He had reached the rank of captain by the time he was killed on 3 August 1918. He was twenty-five years old.[53]

Richard Coupland Spinks was born in Liverpool, England, but was a lawyer in Vancouver when he enlisted in 2 CMR. As the scout and sniping officer for Lieutenant-Colonel Johnston's battalion, he "rendered splendid service" on 9 April 1917. The next day Lieutenants Gordon Patrick Heinekey and Spinks led the patrol into Bloater Trench that ran into "heavily manned" defences: "severe casualties resulted from rifle and machine gun fire." Heinekey, a South African-born fruit grower in Victoria before war, was badly wounded, but survived. Spinks, then forty-one years old, was killed.[54]

Or consider Benjamin Clifford Pierce. Born in Gaspé, Quebec, he lived at 58 Victoria Street in Kingston when he joined the CEF in February 1916. A graduate of Kingston Collegiate and Vocational Institute and Queen's University, Pierce was a Dominion land surveyor with some militia experience. On the morning of 9 April 1917, Lieutenant Pierce led a platoon to fill the gap between his 4 CMR and the Royal Canadian Regiment. "The quick action, and presence of mind, of Lieut. Pierce, undoubtedly helped to prevent the enemy breaking through at this point." Some time that day, Pierce was also killed. He was twenty-seven years old. He is buried at Ecoivres Cemetery.[55]

Notes

1   Will Bird, *Ghosts Have Warm Hands* (Toronto: Clarke, Irwin & Company, 1968), 12-13. A case of mumps kept Bird out of the actual battle of Vimy Ridge.

2   G.W.L. Nicholson, *Canadian Expeditionary Force, 1914-1919: The Official History of the Canadian Army in the First World War* (Ottawa: Queen's Printer, 1962), 132.

3   Desmond Morton, "Louis James Lipsett," *Dictionary of Canadian Biography* (1911-1920, Volume XIV) Toronto: University of Toronto/Université Laval, 2000, (http://www.biographi.ca/EN/ShowBio.asp?BioId=41658&query=Lipsett); Bird, 20-21. One month after taking over the British 4th Division, General Lipsett was killed in action, on 14 October 1918.

4   Attestation Papers, James Harold Elmsley, Box 2894–13, Accession 1992-93/166, Record Group [RG] 150, Library and Archives of Canada [LAC]. Macdonell took command of the 7th Infantry Brigade in December 1915, Hill was appointed to lead 9th Brigade a month later, while Elmsley led 8th Brigade as of June 1916. For appointments, see "Commanding Officers Overseas," *Canada and the Great World War, Volume VI, Special Services, Heroic Deeds, Etc.* (Toronto: United Publishers of Canada Limited, 1921), 318.

5   See Ian McCulloch, "'Batty Mac': Portrait of a Brigade Commander of the Great War, 1915-1917," *Canadian Military History* vol 7, no 4 (Autumn 1998), 14.

6   Attestation Papers, Major Stanley Counter Norsworthy, Box 7372–23.

7   G.R. Stevens, *A City Goes to War* (1964), 395.

8   The Military Cross was the third-highest award for bravery in the British Empire.

9   Attestation Papers, Ralph Craven Andros, Box 186–6; Attestation Papers, Denis Colburn Draper, Box 2660–22; Attestation Papers, Harry Duncan Lockhart Gordon, Box 3647–16; Nicholson, 132; Attestation Papers, George Chalmers Johnston, Box 4869–29. At the time of Vimy Ridge, Brigadier Elmsley was 38 years old. Andros was 46; Draper 42; Gordon, 44; Johnston, 42. I am grateful to Professor Pat Brennan for providing me with information about these men from his research.

10   Bill Rawling, *Surviving Trench Warfare: Technology and the Canadian Corps*, (Toronto: University of Toronto Press, 1992), 219.

11   A.M.J. Hyatt, *General Sir Arthur Currie: A Military Biography* (Toronto: University of Toronto Press/Canadian War Museum, 1987), 63.

12   Cyril Falls, *History of the Great War: Military Operations, France and Belgium, 1917* (London: Macmillan, 1940), 307.

13   War Diary [WD], 3rd Canadian Division, Appendix 301, "Narrative of Operations in Connection with the Attack and Capture of the Vimy Ridge—From April 9th to 14th, 1917," T-1934, vol 4853, RG 9, LAC.

14   See for example, Appendices, WD, 3rd Canadian Divisional Artillery, January 1917, T-10778-10779, vol 4961, RG 9; Rawling, 107.

15   X day (9 April 1917) was kept secret until the very last hours before the attack.

16   "Summary of Operations for week ending, April 4th 1917" WD, 3rd Canadian Division, General Staff April 1917, T-1934, vol 4852, RG 9.

17   Christopher Pugsley, *The Anzac Experience: New Zealand, Australia and Empire in the First World War* (Auckland: Reed Publishing, 2004), 172.

18   WD, 42nd Battalion, March 1917, T-10743, vol 4938, RG 9.

19   On the development of tactical doctrine, see Rawling, 87-113 and Mark Osborne Humphries, "The Myth of the Learning Curve: Tactics and Training in the 12th Canadian Infantry Brigade, 1916-1918," *Canadian Military History* vol 14, no 4 (Autumn 2005), 22.

20   War Diary, 42nd Battalion, March 1917; Bird, 27.

21   "Report on Raid by 42nd Canadian Battalion on Enemy Front and Second Line Trenches in Rear of Longfellow Crater, April 1st, 1917," Appendix 585, WD, 3rd Canadian Divisional April 1917; WD, 42nd Battalion, 1 April 1917; Attestation Papers, Lieutenant Ralph Willcock, Box 10349—61.

22   "7th Canadian Infantry Brigade, Operation Order No. 70," 7 April 1917, WD, 7th Canadian Infantry Brigade, T-10688-10689, vol 4893, RG 9.

23   "Instructions to Units of the 8th Canadian Infantry Brigade for the Attack and Capture of Vimy Ridge," WD, 8th Canadian Infantry Brigade, April 1917, T-10690, vol 4895, RG 9.

24   WD, Princess Patricia's Canadian Light Infantry [PPCLI], "Operation Order No. 8," 7 April 1917, T-10703, vol 4912, RG 9.

25   WD, 4th Canadian Mounted Rifles [4 CMR], 5-6 April 1917, T-10756, vol 4947, RG 9.

26   WD, Royal Canadian Regiment, [RCR] April 1917, T-10702-10703, vol 4911; WD, 1st Canadian Mounted Rifles [1 CMR], April 1917, T-10755, vol 4947, RG 9; WD, 4 CMR, April 1917.

27   Attestation Paper, Hugh Crawford Walkem, Box 9999—5.

28   "8 Brigade Instructions," WD 8th Canadian Infantry Brigade, April 1917; WD, RCR, April 1917; War Diary, 2nd Canadian Mounted Rifles [2 CMR], T-10754-10755, vol 4946, RG 9; War Diary, 1 CMR, 8 April 1917; "Preliminary Instructions for Attack and Capture of Vimy Ridge,"; WD, 4 CMR, April 1917.

29   WD, PPCLI, 8 April 1917; War Diary, 5th Canadian Mounted Rifles [5 CMR], 8 April 1917, T-10760, vol 4949, RG 9.

30   WD, 5 CMR, 9 April 1917.
31   "Report on Operations Carried Out by the 1st CMR Battalion on the 9th April 1917," WD, 1 CMR, April 1917; WD, 5 CMR, 9 April 1917.
32   WD, 42nd Battalion, 9 April 1917; WD, PPCLI, 9 April 1917; "Summary of Operations, RCR," WD, RCR, 13 April 1917.
33   "Summary of Operations for week ending, April 4th 1917," WD, 3rd Canadian Division.
34   "Operations Against Vimy Ridge," Appendix B, WD, 2 CMR, 9 April 1917.
35   "Summary of Operations of The Royal Canadian Regiment," WD, RCR, April 1917.
36   "Report by Lt.-Colonel H.D.L. Gordon, DSO On action of the 4th CMR Battalion, On Assault and Capture of Vimy Ridge by the Cdn Corps, 9-4-17," WD, 4 CMR, April 1917.
37   Attestation Paper, Algernon Edward Willoughby, Box 10424 – 38; "Summary of Operations of The Royal Canadian Regiment," 18.
38   For his actions at Vimy Ridge, Lieutenant Greg Clark won the Military Cross. Greg Clark, "The Bully" in *Gregory Clark War Stories* (Toronto: The Ryerson Press, Toronto, 1964), foreward, 71-72.
39   "Report on Operations of the 7th Canadian Infantry Brigade in the Attack on Vimy Ridge…from April 9th to April 12th 1917," 15; WD, 7th Brigade, April 1917.
40   Attestation Papers, Edson Raymond Pease, Box 7691 – 28; WD, 42nd Battalion, 9 April 1917.
41   WD, 1 CMR, 9 April 1917; See also "Report on Operations Carried Out By the 1st CMR Battalion on the 9th April 1917," Ibid.
42   WD, 1 CMR, 9 April 1917.
43   "Report by Lt.-Colonel H.D.L. Gordon," 5.
44   "Summary of Operations of The Royal Canadian Regiment…"
45   WD, 42nd Battalion, 9 April 1917.
46   Ibid, 15.
47   "Princess Patricia's Canadian Light Infantry, Narrative of Operations, April 8-11 1917," 14.
48   WD, 1 CMR, 2 CMR, April 1917; "Report by Lt.-Colonel H.D.L. Gordon," 5.
49   War Diary, 4 CMR, 12-13 April 1917.
50   "Speech by Major-General L.J. Lipsett, CMG, 3rd Canadian Division," 15 April 1917, Appendix, War Diary, 4 CMR, April 1917.
51   "8th Canadian Infantry Brigade, Summary of Operations on April 9th, 10th, and 11th 1917," Appendix D: 5, War Diary, 8 Canadian Infantry Brigade, April 1917: 1CMR, 336 casualties; 2CMR, 327 casualties; 4 CMR, 181 casualties; 5CMR, 92 casualties; 8 Brigade total casualties: 1027; "Casualties, Noon 8 April, Noon 14 April 1917," War Diary, 7 Canadian Infantry Brigade, April 1917: RCR, 307 casualties; PPCLI, 223 casualties; 42nd Battalion, 277 casualties; 49th Battalion, 110 casualties; Machine Gun company, 28 casualties; 7 Trench Mortar Battery, 2 casualties. 9 Brigade Total Casualties 946. 3 Division Casualties: 1973.

52   "Report by Lt.-Colonel H.D.L. Gordon," 2.

53   See Thomas William Eric Dixon, Commonwealth War Graves Commission,
      http://www.cwgc.org/search/casualty_details.aspx?casualty=432249,
      (accessed 12 March 2006). Captain Dixon is buried at Lijssenthoek Cemetery.
      See also, Canadian Virtual War Memorial, Veterans Affairs Canada, http://
      www.vac-acc.gc.ca/remembers/sub.cfm?source=collections/virtualmem/
      Detail&casualty=432249 Thomas William Eric Dixon, (accessed 12 March
      2006). An obituary for Captain Dixon appears on the website, *Toronto Daily
      Star*, 19 August 1918.

54   "Operations Against Vimy Ridge," Appendix "B", WD, 2 CMR, April 1917;
      Attestation Papers, Richard Coupland Spinks, Box 9198–13. Lieutenant
      Spinks is buried at Ecoivres Military Cemetery, Mont St. Eloi; Attestation
      Papers, Lieutenant George Patrick Heinekey, Box 4235–6.

55   Attestation Paper, Benjamin Clifford Pierce, Box 7820-18. Lieutenant Pierce
      is buried at Ecoivres Military Cemetery; "Report by Lt.-Colonel H.D.L.
      Gordon," 1.

12

The 4th Canadian Division
"Trenches Should Never be Saved"

ANDREW GODEFROY

"G[eneral] O[fficer] C[ommanding] reports to Division that the
attack is going well"
— War Diary of 11th Canadian Infantry Brigade,
0610 hours, 9 April 1917[1]

At 0530 hours on 9 April 1917, Canadian soldiers stormed out
of their assembly trenches to assault Vimy Ridge. This was it. After
months of difficult and meticulous calculation and preparation, the
soldiers of the 4th Canadian Division surged forward to execute their
well-rehearsed scheme and overwhelm the German positions they
faced before the enemy could organize any sustainable defence. The
plan was surprisingly simple and its tenets would form the foundations
of success for the Canadian Corps for the rest of the war.

Yet when the 4th Canadian Division executed its attack on the
morning of 9 April, nothing seemed to go as it should. Within minutes
of its start the assaulting battalions of the 11th Canadian Infantry
Brigade were smashed to pieces, decimated by sustained enemy fire
that ripped through the brigade's leading elements and jeopardized the
12th Canadian Infantry Brigade advancing on its flanks. While other
Canadian divisions were reporting slow but sure success all along the
line, the 4th Division's attack quickly became confused and appeared
to stall; towards the end of the day there was even speculation that it
was in complete jeopardy. The Canadian battalions in this division had
suffered severe casualties right at the start of the attack, the situation on
the ground was unclear to the commanders, and at the end of the day
the enemy still held vital ground on the ridge. What went wrong?

Despite the unquestionable importance of the Battle of Vimy Ridge
to Canadian military history, questions such as these have received

surprisingly little attention from scholars and academics. The most complete official overview of the battle remains chapter eight of Colonel G.W.L. Nicholson's, *Canadian Expeditionary Force: The Official History of the Canadian Army in the First World War*, which was published in 1962. Other early interpretations include Alexander McKee's 1966 publication, *Vimy Ridge*, and the 1967 book, *Vimy Ridge!* by Herbert Fairlie Wood.[2] Pierre Berton's popular history appeared in 1986, but since then the battle has seldom enjoyed centre stage in academic or popular works. As a result, assessments of the battle made decades ago remain the accepted version of events. The reason is obvious: Canadians consider Vimy Ridge an icon of national achievement.

This chapter reexamines the battle on the left and most dangerous flank where the 4th Canadian Division was at the apex of the Battle of Arras and held the lynchpin to success for the entire Canadian Corps. It first examines the version of events from the official history and then suggests that a much more complex set of circumstances contributed to the initial difficulties of the 4th Canadian Division, as well as its subsequent hard-earned victory.

The reputation of no other major unit at the battle of Vimy Ridge suffers more than that of the 4th Canadian Division. Much of Colonel Nicholson's four pages on the division's assault was consumed in identifying senior Canadian commanders, naming the units and citing the circumstances surrounding the awarding of two Victoria Crosses.[3] The rest is devoted to describing what appears to have been a challenging but ultimately successful engagement against a nebulous group of German defenders with no identifiable leadership or defensive plan. The reader may also be left with the impression that "things did not go so well" initially on the north flank because

> A portion of German trench had been left undestroyed by the heavy artillery at the request of the Commanding Officer of the left assaulting battalion (the 87th), [Major Harold LeRoy Shaw] who hoped to put it to good use when captured. From this position machine-gun fire cut down half the 87th's leading wave and pinned the right of the supporting 75th Battalion to their assembly trenches. Those who could pressed on, though harassed in flank and rear by machine-gun fire from the uncaptured sector, and from Germans who emerged from mine shafts and dugouts after the attacking wave had passed. Then came murderous fire from the second trench, whose garrison had been given ample time to man their positions. The entire left wing of the 11th Brigade's attack broke down, and the 54th Battalion, its open flank under counter-attack, was forced to withdraw.[4]

Nicholson's account, suggesting as it does that Shaw's decision brought the 11th Brigade's assault to a complete halt while threatening the rest of the division's advance, is open to criticism. First, this telling of events suggests that both sides are winning and losing at the same time. This may have reflected the chaos of battle on 9 April but it obscures the complexity of the engagement and gives too much weight to specific details to explain the ebb and flow of battle. For example, at the outset of the divisional narrative, Nicholson wrote that "Major-General Watson hoped to overrun the forward slope position [of Hill 145] by surprise"[5] as if this was the centre of gravity of his plan. Given the weeks of Canadian pre-bombardment and other obvious preparations prior to the attack it seems absurd to suggest this as the key influence in Watson's decision cycle. In fact, one has little sense of how Watson sought to execute his plan, or if there was any sort of command and control once the assault began.

There are other parts missing from the story. The official history offers no detailed assessment of leadership and command in either Brigadier-General Victor Odlum's 11th or Brigadier-General MacBrien's 12th brigades, or of the plan these two assaulting brigades were assigned to execute. One is again left to assume that the critical decision of the 87th Battalion commanding officer to order parts of the German front line spared somehow eclipsed all the planning and efforts by teams of staff officers. Other evidence suggests that Shaw may not have had any role in the decision. As well, one must look beyond the human element, for both technology and geography also played important roles. If the assaulting battalions were broken apart, how did the surviving junior leaders employ ground to their advantage and utilize local fire support, machine guns, snipers and bombers to shape the tactical situation and relieve pressure on those who survived the initial assault? What other tactical and technical considerations might have influenced the battle and allowed the Canadians to reach their objective? A new examination of the war diaries and after-action reports allows us to reevaluate these questions from the bottom up.

The youngest of the Canadian divisions, the 4th was organized at Bramshott Camp, Hants, in the spring of 1916 under the command of Major-General David Watson. The newspaper editor-turned-soldier brought considerable experience to the job, having previously commanded the 2nd (Eastern Ontario) Canadian Infantry Battalion at the start of the war and later 5th Canadian Infantry Brigade from September 1915 until his appointment as General Officer Commanding (GOC) 4th Canadian Division in April 1916. His new command was well supported with a staff of veteran soldiers, including the very able Lieutenant-Colonel W. Edmund Ironside, who acted as his General

Staff Officer (GSO) I, Majors K. Digby Bold Murray and A.G. Turner serving as his GSO IIs, and Major Gordon G. Morriss and Captain Alan Anderson Aitken, son of Sir Max Aitken (later Lord Beaverbrook), as his GSO IIIs.

Ironically nicknamed "Tiny," the six-foot-four-inch Ironside was an experienced soldier, a solid planner, forceful, self-confident, multilingual and at times outspoken.[6] He was a strong presence in the divisional headquarters, some officers later speculating that Ironside, not Watson, was truly in charge.[7] The thirty-six-year-old Digby Murray was of a similar character. Originally from Dublin, Ireland, Murray was a confident and outspoken field man on loan from the Indian Army, with extensive campaign experience in both South Africa and the Northwest Frontier. Turner was also a well-known quantity, for he had served under Watson in the 2nd Canadian Infantry Battalion. Gordon Morriss, born in Japan to British parents, had served only briefly with the Royal West Kent Regiment before coming to Canada and serving in the militia. Aitken, meanwhile, had previously served with the Royal Naval Division. These men were the nucleus around which divisional command and control evolved over the next several months.

For approximately four months, the division organized and trained in preparation for its eventual deployment to France. These were trying times for the new command, constantly straining for personnel and resources while making poor attempts to guard its own. In June 1916 nearly 8,000 men from the division became reinforcements to the Canadian Corps in France.[8] Many of these men were experienced, vital, junior and mid-level leaders whose loss hurt the fledgling division, which reached the continent in August 1916. From there, the 4th Canadian Division moved into the line near Ypres and took over the Ypres-Comines Canal up to the point opposite Messines. There it remained for a little over a month, before heading to the Somme on 23 September. Another few weeks were spent training before Major-General Watson was given orders to deploy again into the line in front of Regina Trench on the Somme.

In the next several weeks, the 4th Canadian Division incurred 4,311 casualties in the treacherous fighting for Regina and Desire trenches at the end of the Somme campaign.[9] It was a terrible introduction to warfare, but after-action reports suggest that despite the poor conditions, the division acquitted itself rather well. Watson moved the division out of the line on 28 November, and went into refit in the Bruay-Divion area before joining the rest of the Canadian Corps immediately south of the Souchez River opposite Vimy Ridge. It was here that the division fought next, suffering hardships comparable to those endured the previous autumn.

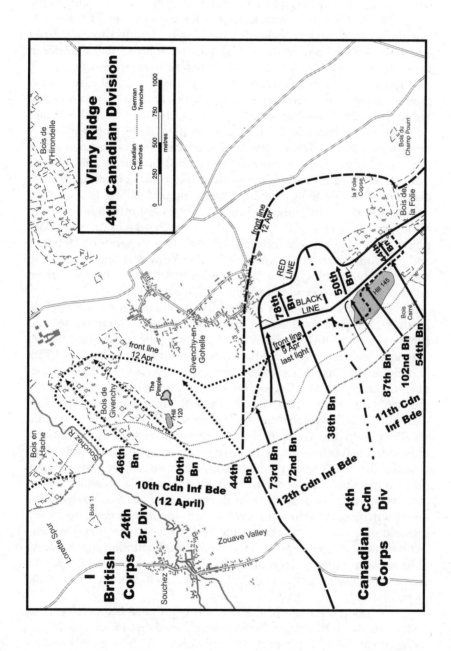

Vimy Ridge
4th Canadian Division

Canadian Trenches
German Trenches

metres
0 250 500 750 1000

To understand better how the 4th Division acquitted itself at Vimy Ridge, it is important to examine the influences that shaped the organization prior to its attack. Except for the German 79th Reserve Infantry Division, which defended the heights, the division's greatest adversary was the terrain itself. Attacking from Broadmarsh Crater in the south to Givenchy in the north, Watson's division had to cover a frontage of 1,950 yards (1,800 metres) and advance 1,300 yards (1,200 metres) across badly broken ground up the eastern slopes of Vimy Ridge and capture two pieces of key terrain, Hill 145 (the highest point on the ridge) and another height known as the Pimple. Unlike the other divisional lines of advance, the land here was already churned into a lunar landscape from previous fighting, and the soupy mud slowed the infantry to a crawl while affording them little or no cover from defensive fire. For the Germans it was a natural killing ground. The heights afforded them commanding views of the entire Souchez-Zouave Valley and the whole of the road between Souchez and Carency.[10] Both points were also heavily fortified. Hill 145 was ringed with defences and dugouts down its slopes, and the Pimple was strengthened with two concrete machine gun emplacements that flanked the entire front and sides of Hill 145 and the adjoining Hill 120.

The 4th Division's men learned just how effective the Germans' mutually supporting defences were when they attempted to raid enemy positions on 1 March 1917.[11] Launching the largest raid to date with approximately 1,700 soldiers from the 54th, 72nd, 73rd, and 75th Battalions, the Canadians sought to reconnoitre and sack the German positions atop Hill 145. Defending this key terrain in Section Fischer of their front line were units of the German 79th Reserve Infantry Division, with the 16th Bavarian Infantry Division holding the line around the Pimple on the German right. Despite all possible preparations, unfavourable weather, uncooperative winds and poor communications doomed the attack from the start. Neither poisonous gas nor artillery fire had dislodged the Germans from their trenches and, with surprise lost, the Canadians were mowed down as they tried to navigate the uncut wire and the withering fire of their opponents. Only one small incursion was achieved, against the 16th Bavarian Infantry Division, but it came at a terrible price. Two experienced battalion commanding officers were killed in the attack and the four attacking battalions suffered 687 casualties for very little, if any, intelligence or operational gain.[12]

Certainly the morale of the division must have been shaken, but neither of the 11th Brigade's assaulting battalions (87th and 102nd) took part in the 1 March raid, and only one of 12th Brigade's raiding battalions, the 72nd, showed fatigue in the assault on 9 April. Thus it is difficult to suggest any direct relationship between the two, especially considering that other large-scale raids were subsequently carried out by the division later that month.[13] Some have also explained the poor performance of the 87th Battalion on 9 April by their role in the March gas raid. However, between 1 January and 6 April 1917 the battalion suffered few casualties, with only four officers wounded, and thirty-one other ranks killed and sixty-three wounded. Of those four wounded officers, two immediately returned to duty and fought on 9 April. Other battalions in the division fared equally well. Reinforcements were available to those commanders who needed them and units were rotated with enough frequency that no one battalion suffered the brunt of main engagements. Casualties certainly impaired the division's fighting units prior to the Vimy battle, but did not paralyze them. Other simpler factors helped stop the division's advance on the morning of 9 April.

After the 1 March debacle there is little doubt that Watson and Ironside realized that the German commander in this sector, the experienced veteran Oberst Wilhem von Goerne, held the vital ground on the ridge and that any attempt to take it from him would be messy. The critical question was how to do it. There was no hope for surprise, no positions to cover any advance against either Hill 145 or the Pimple, and no easy terrain that would allow the infantry to overwhelm the position quickly before the defenders could react. Even in their own assembly trenches the Canadians were not entirely out of harm's way. The 10th Brigade reported that on the night of 31 March/1 April, German artillery destroyed trench lines and caused casualties. As a final touch of misery, poor weather before the assault turned much of the ground into a sea of mud, and one report noted that, "in many places men were up to their waists [in muck]."[14]

Divisional staff considered a number of plans, but in the end only substantial suppressing artillery and machine gun fire against the German positions would afford the Canadian soldiers the means of reaching their objectives alive. Knowing this, why then would anyone in the division be allowed to withhold such critical support in front of their own advance? Surely Brigadier-General Odlum or Lieutenant-Colonel Ironside would have denied such a careless request, unless, of course, the request originated above the level of battalion.

Within minutes of the start of the 4th Division battle at Vimy Ridge one of its two brigades had disintegrated. When Odlum sent his initial status report to division that the attack was going well, he could not have known the full extent of the disaster that had befallen his leading battalions. His battalion leadership had evaporated within the first hour of the fight, leaving his remaining troops scattered, largely leaderless, and left to fend for themselves.

The 102nd Canadian Infantry Battalion assaulting on the right was commanded by Major A.B. Carey, who took over in February 1917. His ·four company commanders were Major R.G.H. Brydon and Lieutenants J.H. Wilson, E.J. Peers, and H.G. Dimsdale. The three lieutenants had all replaced majors who had commanded the companies prior to the assault, though the regimental history offers no explanation for these replacements.[15] The battalion went over the parapets on time and immediately ran into resistance at the German front line trenches after successfully navigating the enemy wire. Here it suffered its first casualties, including Lieutenant Dimsdale, who was wounded in the hand and leg just moments after he had left his own trench. By 0640 hours other officers reported fierce resistance and heavy casualties inflicted by the 9th and 11th companies of the 261st Reserve Infantry Regiment, but the battalion had breached the final objective.[16]

Still, no word on the situation had arrived from any of the other three assault company commanders and none would be coming. Major Brydon was killed leading his company and both Wilson and Peers were seriously wounded (Wilson later died of his wounds). Command of the battalion had by default fallen to Company-Sergeant-Major Russell of C Company who was holding a strongpoint at Broadmarsh crater with about 30 men from the 102nd Battalion. He was receiving increasingly heavy enemy fire from his front left where survivors from the Germans' 2nd and 3rd battalions, 261st Reserve Infantry Regiment, had linked up in the Bitter.communication trench. At approximately 0740 hours Lieutenant Everett Fallis, 102nd Battalion's scout officer, was sent out to report on the consolidation of the captured German trenches and take over from Russell who was seriously wounded soon after he arrived.[17] Fallis did what he could to take control of the situation but it was not long before one of von Goerne's snipers found his mark, killing Fallis just as Major Carey and Scout Sergeant Fredrick Vogel were making their own way forward to assess the situation. Vogel was killed by enemy fire on the way, but by approximately 1230 hours Carey completed a personal inspection of his new forward line. His situation was secure for the moment but his soldiers were still suffering severe harassment from enemy still entrenched on Hill 145.[18] It appeared to Carey that the 87th Battalion had yet to secure the high ground and, due to the withering fire pouring into his position, he was barely able to get ammunition and reinforcements forward to his own beleaguered troops. Little did even Carey realize at the time, however, just how perilously open his left flank remained.

The 87th Battalion fared even worse in its initial assault. The enemy's 1st Battalion, 261st Regiment, under command of Major Zickner, shook off the initial bombardment and emerged from dugouts to stop the Canadians struggling towards them. Of the eleven Canadian officers and one sergeant commanding the four companies in the initial advance, only one officer and the sergeant remained in action after the first few minutes. The history of the German Army in Arras suggests that perhaps as few as two machine guns from 5th Company, 261st Infantry Regiment were involved in the annihilation of the 87th Battalion's entire right flank.[19] Withering fire cut through this third of the battalion, immediately wounding Captain P. Law and Lieutenants J.G. Planche and J.F. Simmons, along with several dozen soldiers. When Major Arthur Ross moved forward to lead the survivors of this group onwards he was instantly killed by the sweeping machine gun fire.

The centre of the 87th was also quickly smashed. Here Lieutenant James Rooke was shot through the head and killed just after leaving his own parapet while Lieutenant Rupert Taylor was killed just a few feet away. Major Edward Joy was also killed here but Lieutenant Isadore Yonkles was able to get through and lead his soldiers into a section of the enemy's first line of trenches just as the Canadian artillery finished pounding it. Portions of the 87th's left flank also managed to reach the German front line. Lieutenants Taylor and Sinclair were down (Sinclair later died of his wounds) as were dozens of soldiers, but Lieutenant Alfred Hannaford and Sergeant Sutherland and a handful of others had miraculously completed the first rush unscathed. Diving into the enemy line, Hannaford took fifteen men to seize the junction of Batter and Basso trenches, while Sergeant Wilford and another group of men bombed down the front line trench and turned captured machine guns onto the enemy.[20] Despite these footholds, the attack quickly dissolved into a series of deadly firefights. Major Harry Sare, officer commanding the assault, was shot in the head and could not carry on, and Lieutenant Edwin Savage was killed trying to take a German strongpoint. Yonkles had by this time been shot through the arm but he stayed in the fight and survived the day.[21]

Of the two assaulting battalions of Odlum's Brigade, the 87th and 102nd, the latter suffered the worst. The 87th sustained 303 casualties by this time: seven officers and 110 men killed or died of wounds, four officers and 157 men wounded, and twenty-five men reported missing, some of whom later were reported as prisoners of war. The 102nd suffered 314 casualties: six officers and 119 other ranks killed or died of wounds, and nine officers and 180 other ranks wounded. A number of other ranks were reported missing, some of whom, again, were later discovered to have become prisoners.

The 12th Brigade battle played out in equal desperation. Despite "an encouraging start" with exploding mines engulfing many of the German front line defenders, the 73rd Battalion, Brigadier-General J.H. MacBrien's vanguard, became bogged down while crossing the swampy broken ground. Some troops wounded in the assault later drowned in shell holes. The 72nd Battalion history reported that the battalion "could be seen moving in small groups that twisted their way among the shell craters" as they fired at their attackers.[22] Bumping straight into remaining elements of the 11th Bavarian Infantry Regiment, still holding a portion of the first and second line, hand-to-hand fighting broke out as the Canadians wrestled for control. The 38th Battalion fared no better. After losing touch with the opening barrage, soldiers were trapped in the open and cut to pieces by Germans emerging from their well-protected dugouts. On more than one occasion, individual acts of heroism saved Canadian soldiers from disaster. In one example, Captain Thain Wendell MacDowell of the 38th Battalion earned the Victoria Cross after he convinced a superior enemy force to surrender despite the fact that only he and a comrade were challenging them.[23]

The assault soon bogged down as scattered detachments of Canadians and Germans began to link up and form fighting units, but the situation was so confused by mid-morning that no organized advance was possible. After the divisional assault stalled around noon, Major-General Watson called forward Brigadier-General Edward Hilliam, commanding 10th Brigade, to mount an attack against the Pimple and secure 11th Brigade's remaining directives. A supporting attack by the untested 85th Battalion (North Nova Scotia Highlanders) late in the day without artillery support managed to overwhelm and defeat what remained of the German defence on the west side of Hill 145, preparing the ground for the follow-on attacks the next day. Fresh units of the 4th Division finally forced the remnants of von Goerne's regiment from the northern end of Hill 145 by 1515 hours on 10 April, and operations by 44th and 50th battalions overwhelmed the undermanned German positions east of Hill 145.[24] A short brutal contest in blowing snow on 12 April decided the final ownership of the Pimple, and with nothing left to defend the ridge, the remnants of the German 79th Reserve Infantry Division abandoned both their trenches and the village of Givenchy completely. It was, as a great captain once observed of another struggle, a near run thing, but despite terrible setbacks the 4th Canadian Division achieved a hard earned tactical success.

Major Harold LeRoy Shaw, the commander of the 87th Battalion, who allegedly decided not to destroy the German trench, remains a mystery. Shaw survived the attack on 9 April but the 87th Battalion war diary makes no note of his actions that day, whereas we know that Major Carey of the 102nd went forward to take command of his battalion after all other officers in the initial advance had become casualties. Likewise, the official history of the 87th Battalion (Canadian Grenadier Guards) contains no details of Shaw's actions, except to note that he was replaced as battalion commander on 8 May.[25] No other mention is made of him in the official history.[26]

The source of Colonel Nicholson's claim about Shaw is an anonymous official report found in the appendices of the 4th Canadian Division's war diaries for March-April 1917, dated 21 April.[27] The only paragraph in the ten page summary to be check-marked states that:

> Trench destruction by the Heavy Artillery was excellent, and only in one place was a portion of the trench allowed to remain, and that by the desire of the infantry who proposed to use it afterwards. This was a mistake, which should not have been allowed to occur. After an attack, lines of shell-holes are easier to occupy than any lines of trenches. Trenches should never be saved from destruction for the purpose of use after an assault.[28]

The same report then suggests some confusion about the initial assault:

> Only at one point in the line, that opposite Black Trench did the infantry fail to get forward. The portion involved was about 100 yards in length, and the trench and wire had not been properly destroyed.

> Either the barrage did not cover this point, or the men did not follow it closely enough, for the enemy stood his ground and inflicted severe casualties on our men. The 87th and the 75th were formed up, each in two lines, the latter behind the former. The two lines of the 87th were stopped dead, losing 60% of their strength from machine gun fire, and apparently, the men of the 75th did not start from the jumping off trenches of the 87th over which they should have gone.[29]

Was the barrage called off, did it miss this portion of the trench, or did the barrage lift onto the next line, losing the infantry who were to follow just behind? These are unanswerable questions. Major Shaw's operation order for Vimy Ridge clearly stated that, "the attack will follow the creeping barrage...[the] barrage will be a double one, standing and creeping; the standing barrage jumping to the next objective just before the creeping barrage reaches the line before the former is waiting. The creeping barrage will lift approximately 100 yards [91 metres] every three minutes...," theoretically giving his infantry plenty of time to reach the first German trenches.[30]

Canadian Corps artillery barrage maps for Vimy Ridge support the operation order, but suggest that the distance between the Canadian and German front line positions may have been greater than previously suggested. Barrage line Alpha (German front line positions from Broadmarsh crater past Gunner crater to Cluny trench) is noted to last from H Hour to H+six minutes, before moving onto barrage line Bravo (Clutch, Basso, and Batter trenches) where it would saturate German targets from H+six minutes to H+seventeen minutes. Nowhere does the map show a break in the barrage lines, but it appears that the opposing front lines may have been much farther apart than estimated at the time, supporting the claim that the barrage simply advanced away from the leading assaulters.[31]

More frustrating is that none of the 4th Division war diaries make any other mention of this apparently critical decision or provide any grid references for what strongpoint or portion of German trench is even being described. Nor is there any obvious record in the artillery war diaries or the Royal Canadian Artillery official history; it cites the same anonymous report as its reference. Given that other less critical locations, such as road intersections, are well identified in reports, one is at a loss to find corroborating evidence to support the contention that Major Shaw somehow altered the artillery plan.

The issue is further clouded when one considers a statement found in the personal papers of Brigadier-General Odlum, who commanded 11th Brigade on 9 April 1917. In the margin of what appears to be a draft chapter in 1938 of either the unpublished Canadian official history or the British official history then in preparation by Captain Cyril Falls,[32] titled "Battle of Vimy Ridge," Odlum noted:

> This section of the trench was directly opposite and commanded at 400 yards range the exit of the British tunnel (Tottenham) under the Zouave Valley leading up to the brigade front. It had been destroyed earlier in the bombardment but air photographs taken on the 11th [March] showed it again intact. Requests were made for the heavy artillery to destroy this position on the 8th [April surely] but in compliance with the wishes of Brig. General Odlum who hoped to make it his headquarters during the advance, the bombardment was not carried out.[33]

Here then it appears that Odlum assumed responsibility for the decision not to bombard the German trenches.

The 4th Canadian Division battle was perhaps the most difficult and confused fighting to take place on 9-12 April at Vimy Ridge. Though this chapter touches on only a few select issues, it suggests that the recognized interpretation is questionable at best. Even a brief reexamination of available primary and secondary evidence reveals that contemporary official histories leave a great deal unexplained. Given the terribly confused nature of the battles for Hill 145 and the Pimple, nothing short of a full scale study will do justice to the history of the engagement. Such a study is important, not only to better understand the battle itself but also the actors who took part in it. Surprisingly little is still known about senior officers such as Major-General Watson and Brigadiers Hilliam, Odlum, and MacBrien. And what of critical players like Major Harry Shaw? How can the history of this battle be complete without knowing more of these and other men who fought there?

Notes

1   War Diary [WD], Headquarters 11th Canadian Infantry Brigade [Bde], 9 April 1917, T-10696, volume [vol] 4904, Record Group [RG] 9, Library and Archives Canada [LAC].
2   G.W.L. Nicholson, *Canadian Expeditionary Force, 1914-1919: The Official History of Canada's Army in the First World War* (Ottawa: Queen's Printer, 1962); Alexander McKee, *Vimy Ridge* (Aberdeen: Souvenir Press, 1966). This is one of the best unofficial operational histories of the battle; McKee had the opportunity to interview several eye-witnesses and direct participants in the assault on Vimy Ridge; Herbert Fairlie Wood, *Vimy!* (Toronto: Macmillan of Canada, 1967).
3   Nicholson, 258-63. The division's Victoria Crosses were awarded to Captain T. W. MacDowell of the 38th Battalion and Private J.G. Pattison of the 50th Battalion.
4   Ibid, 259.
5   Ibid.
6   Brian Bond, "Ironside," John Keegan (ed), *Churchill's Generals* (London: Warner Books, 1991). Ironside was later Chief of the Imperial General Staff.
7   Lieutenant (later Lieutenant-General) E.L.M. Burns noted in his memoir, "the general opinion was that Ironside was the real commander of the division." E.L.M. Burns, *General Mud* (Toronto: Clarke, Irwin & Company, 1970), 15.
8   *The Story of the Fourth Canadian Division, 1916-1919.* (Aldershot: Gale and Polden), 5.
9   Casualties, file 11-11B, vol 1844, RG 24, LAC.
10   WD, 4th Canadian Division, March-April 1917, Appendix B, T-1938, vol 4859, RG 9.
11   WD 4th Canadian Division, March 1917, Appendix A. For an analysis of this engagement see Tim Cook, "A Proper Slaughter: The March 1917 Gas Raid at Vimy Ridge," *Canadian Military History*, vol 8, no 2 (Spring 1999), 7-23.
12   Cook, 18.

13 Report on raid carried out by 10th Canadian Infantry Brigade on the night 31st [March] and 1 April, WD 4th Canadian Division, March-April 1917. The raid included 615 men drawn from the 46th, 47th, and 50th battalions. On the 1 March raid, see Bill Rawling, *Surviving Trench Warfare: Technology and the Canadian Corps, 1914-1918* (Toronto: University of Toronto Press, 1992), 128-29.

14 Report on raid carried out by 10th Canadian Infantry Brigade.

15 L. McLeod Gould, *From B.C. to Basieux: Being the Narrative of the 102nd Canadian Infantry Battalion* (Victoria: Thos. R. Cusak Presses, 1919), 41-58.

16 *Oberschlacht bei Arras.* Cited in A.F. Duguid, *History of the Canadian Grenadier Guards, 1760-1964* (Montreal: Gazette Printing Company, 1965), 500-01.

17 WD, 102nd Battalion, 9 April 1917, T-10752, vol 4944, RG 9.

18 Ibid. See also Gould, 49-51.

19 Duguid, 500-01.

20 WD, 87th Battalion, April 1917, Appendix A, file 455, vol 4944, RG 9.

21 Lieutenant Isadore Benjamin Yonkles was killed in action at Hill 70, 15 August 1917.

22 Bernard McEvoy and A.H. Finlay, *History of the 72nd Canadian Infantry Battalion, Seaforth Highlanders of Canada* (Vancouver: Cowan and Brookhouse, 1920), 50.

23 Nicholson, 260.

24 For a detailed account of the 85th battalion attack see Lieutenant-Colonel Robert S. Williams, "The 85th Canadian Infantry Battalion and First Contact with the Enemy at Vimy Ridge, 9-14 April 1917," *The Canadian Army Journal,* vol 8, no 1 (Spring 2005), 73-82.

25 Duguid, 146-47.

26 An examination of the individual honours and awards presented to officers of the 87th Battalion during the First World War reveals that Major Shaw was the only commanding officer of the 87th Battalion not to receive any special recognition for his war services, suggesting that he may have been ostracized as a result of the 9 April debacle. The author is currently investigating the full details of Major Shaw's military career for a separate publication.

27 Report on Operations, Appendix B, 4/24, WD, 4th Canadian Division, March-April 1917.

28 Ibid.

29 Ibid, 6/26.

30 Operation Order No.33, 22 March 1917, Appendix A, WD, 87th Battalion.

31 Canadian Corps Artillery Barrage Map for Assault on Vimy Ridge, prepared by 1st Field Survey Company, Royal Engineers, author's collection.

32 See Cyril Falls, *History of the Great War: Military Operations, France and Belgium, 1917,* (London: Macmillan, 1940). Odlum's comment closely resembles text appearing on pages 328-29.

33 Draft chapters 11 and 12 (Battle of Vimy Ridge Parts I and II), vol 20, Victor Odlum Papers, Manuscript Group [MG] 30 E300, LAC. Notes cited in the margin, dated 1938.

13

The German Army at Vimy Ridge

ANDREW GODEFROY

"At last! Now the fight will be man to man, with the same weapons."
—Oberschlacht bei Arras[1]

Assessing military effectiveness and conceptual change in an army often begins at its defeat. However, Canadian military historians have suggested that the victory at Vimy Ridge was the catalyst for adaptive tactical and operational maneuvre that one historian has called "not glamorous but effective."[2] Still, any study of how the Canadian Corps won the battle should also include the German Army's perspective on how it lost the battle.

What was the German view of the Battle of Vimy Ridge? This is hard to know with certainty for tremendous amounts of German First World War primary records were lost during the Second World War. The allied bombing of Berlin in February 1945 destroyed the personnel rosters and card indices of the Prussian Army, the transition army (Uebergangsheeres), and the Imperial Army (Reichswehr).[3] Another allied raid at Potsdam on 14/15 April 1945 burned the German First World War official archives (Reichsarchiv), leaving only remnants of related records in other places.[4] Second, eyewitnesses to the event are effectively lost. Third, modern historians face some language barriers, as surviving German official histories of the First World War are written in Old German whose Latin-style romanticism makes interpretation difficult. German First World War unit histories and biographies, some of which appeared as early as 1919, were detailed but often selective about those battles that were covered. In the era of post-war accusation and apologia, turgid German official military histories often portrayed defeats as near victories or they simply absolved their commanders of any responsibility for the outcome.[5] These views certainly contrast sharply with Allied accounts of the same battles, making the matter of discerning actual events much more problematic.

In the wake of the failed offensives of 1914, the German High Command adopted a largely defensive strategy in the west, designed to hold on to ground already won, while the war on the Eastern Front was decided. Yet by 1917 the situation remained fluid. Though the German High Command felt confident in its eastern campaigns, the situation there was not stable enough to release large forces to the western theatre. Germany's allies were becoming less dependable, especially the Austro-Hungarians. Feeling the strain of his alliance with Germany, Austro-Hungarian Emperor Charles IV[6] even instructed his senior leaders in 1917 to distance the army from German influence wherever possible.

The German Army itself was also worn out after the bloody battles of the previous year and both reserves and munitions were in short supply. A typical army group of 140,000 men, for example, expended six or seven trainloads of heavy artillery munitions daily, requiring 26,000 horses to transport shells from railheads to the guns at the front. Seldom were there adequate resources to bring sufficient munitions or other critical supplies to the soldiers doing the fighting.[7] Food was also beginning to run low. In 1916 heavy rains had badly damaged the potato harvest in Germany, adding potatoes to the growing list of rationed items. One estimate suggests that the average German adult citizen was subsisting on as little as 1200 calories a day, the normal intake for a three-year-old. Soldiers at the front could expect little better for their sacrifice.[8]

The end of 1916 marked the beginning of the "turnip winter" for most Germans and despite steps to ease the army's logistical nightmare, many of its 154 front-line divisions were simply exhausted and not well supported. Given this situation and the unresolved hostilities in the east, Germany looked to a year of only defensive operations on the Western Front. As the blockaded Germans grew more isolated and weaker, the initiative passed to the ever-strengthening Allies.[9]

With their front lines seriously strained, the Germans began in late 1916 to withdraw to a fresh belt of defences on much better ground. Named the Siegfried Stellung (the Allies called it the Hindenburg Line), German commanders General Paul von Hindenburg and General Erich Ludendorff created a new wall of defence from Vimy Ridge down to the River Aisne west of the Chemin des Dames, reducing the overall German Western Front by forty kilometres and freeing thirteen infantry divisions desperately needed to reconstitute their reserve. The Siegfried Stellung was ready by the end of January 1917. On 22 February 1917, the Germans launched Operation Alberich and withdrew to the new line of defence, destroying anything of military value behind them.[10] As one historian has noted, "having established superiority over the enemy by an intellectual operation,"[11] Ludendorff judged the operation a complete success.

Now situated along their new defensive line, Hindenburg and Ludendorff brought forward fresh troops where possible and reorganized their army groups, replacing recalcitrant commanders and encouraging others to seek new tactics focused on an in-depth rather than traditional linear defence. The Germans continued to rely on the division as the core of their army in the defence, it being the smallest self-contained combined arms unit of tactical maneuvre available to commanders on the Western Front.

A German army division numbered, on paper, approximately 11,650 men organized into five groups—infantry, cavalry, artillery, pioneers and divisional support such as medical, transport, labour and communications. The divisional headquarters staff was manned by twenty to twenty-five officers and officials and further supported by approximately eighty to ninety men.[12] The commander's right-hand men consisted of the infantry brigade commander and the divisional artillery commander, both of whom did most of his fighting.

At approximately 19,772 all ranks, the Canadian division by comparison dwarfed its German competitor. But whereas Canadian divisions consisted of three infantry brigades, German divisions contained only a single infantry brigade along with a pioneer battalion, cavalry squadron and a field artillery regiment. Apart from the lone pioneer battalion, the German infantry brigade contained three regiments of 2,789 officers and men each (including headquarters) formed into three battalions of approximately 910 officers and men each; each of these battalions in turn was divided into four companies plus a machine gun company.[13] By comparison, Canadian infantry brigades (including headquarters) consisted of approximately 5,200 officers and men with the four infantry battalions each totalling approximately 1,240 all ranks.[14] At every tactical level, the Germans were decisively outmanned; however they were on the defensive and made every effort to compensate for the lack of personnel with firepower.

If nothing else, German divisions had a good supply of machine guns, which provided a simple yet effective means of defence against attacking infantry. In 1914 a German Landwehr infantry regiment had twelve companies of riflemen and one machine gun company (six machine guns) and no other supporting units. By 1917, the number of machine gun companies in a regiment had tripled. In many cases German regiments could also obtain additional defensive support around key terrain with machine gun sharpshooter detachments.[15] At Vimy Ridge, the Germans employed the 120 pound (54.5 kg) 1908-pattern water-cooled Maxim machine gun as well as the 50 pound (22.7 kg) Maxim 08/15 machine gun. Properly sighted, these machine guns could fire between 400 to 500 rounds a minute at ranges of up to 1,100 yards (1000 metres) making it possible for a single crew to stop a battalion of attacking infantry caught in the open.

The Germans also increased the number of trench mortars, so that by 1917 they could form a platoon of two light trench mortars in each infantry battalion. In a defensive battle, the German infantry battalion commander controlled four infantry companies, a machine gun company plus machine gun sharpshooter detachments and a light trench mortar platoon.[16] Additionally, he could call on artillery units supporting his part of the line. Local commanders had access to immediate support from eight-inch howitzers, 4.2in and 5.9in field artillery, and even seventy-seven millimetre anti-tank guns.[17] With this much firepower and the application of new tactics the Germans felt they could repel any challenge.[18]

The disposition of major German formations at Vimy Ridge down to the regimental level is well known and is readily accessible in most literature on the battle.[19] The German force at Vimy Ridge came under the command of Generaloberst Freiherr Ludwig von Falkenhausen, a 73-year-old Bavarian traditionalist who led German Sixth Army. Favouring the gruppe system of battlefield command, in which corps headquarters formed the nucleus of flexible formations organized and resourced as necessary, he created four such gruppes in his army: Gruppen Loos, Souchez, Vimy and Arras. Of these, two played a role defending Vimy Ridge, Gruppe Vimy and Gruppe Souchez.

The 65-year-old General der Infanterie Ritter Karl von Fasbender commanded Gruppe Vimy, which consisted primarily of units of the I Bavarian Reserve Corps and defended the front line from the River Scarpe north to Givenchy-en-Gohelle.[20] The four divisions within Gruppe Vimy were the 1st Bavarian Reserve Infantry Division, the 14th Bavarian Infantry Division, the 18th Bavarian Infantry Division (this division was detached and held in the Sixth Army strategic reserve) and the 79th Prussian Reserve Infantry Division. Fasbender, like Falkenhausen, was also a veteran Bavarian reservist who had served with distinction since the Franco-Prussian War and had been highly decorated for his command both in the 1914 and 1916 campaigns on the Western Front.[21] The two understood each other when it came to tactics and Fasbender would fight the lion's share of Falkenhausen's battle against the Canadians at Vimy Ridge.

Gruppe Souchez covered the front line from the Givenchy area northwards and was made up of the VIII Reserve Corps under the command of the 66-year-old General der Infanterie Georg Karl Wichura, previously commander of the 5th Bavarian Infantry Division until he assumed his corps command in September 1916.[22] During the battle, only one of his sub-elements, the 16th Bavarian Infantry Division, situated in the Givenchy area on the northern end of the ridge, saw action against the Canadians. The other two divisions in the gruppe, the 56th Bavarian and the 80th Bavarian Reserve, reinforced the front line troops.

Thus from north to south on 9 April, the Canadian Corps faced the 16th Bavarian Infantry Division's 14th and 11th Bavarian Infantry regiments, the 79th Prussian Reserve Infantry Division's 261st, 262nd, and 263rd Prussian Reserve Infantry regiments, and the 1st Bavarian Reserve Infantry Division's 3rd and 1st Bavarian Reserve Infantry regiments. Each regiment was responsible for approximately one kilometre of frontage and for manning a series of defensive lines known as Stellung. The I Stellung normally consisted of parallel fire trenches at the front line; II Stellung was a support line approximately one to 1.5 kilometres behind the first; while III Stellung consisted of reserve lines about six kilometres behind the front line. At Vimy Ridge, another intermediate position existed between I and II Stellung, resulting in divisional reserve battalions manning II Stellung and the Sixth Army reserve units manning III Stellung in the Douai Plain to the east of the ridge. In addition, each Stellung was reinforced further with several strong points armed with machine guns and mortars.

With the advantage of such defence on ground of their own choosing, perhaps the Germans should have won the battle. But despite these preparations and plenty of warning of an imminent attack, the defenders were unable to repulse the initial Canadian Corps assault on 9 April or even challenge it for control of other key terrain during the follow-up and pursuit on 10-12 April. How did the Germans lose the Battle of Vimy Ridge? The German defeat at Vimy Ridge was so unexpected that Hindenburg later ordered the German Great General Staff (OHL) to conduct a court of enquiry into what he called the "debakel" of Arras. The battle had made a mockery of evolving German defensive doctrine. Certainly the Allies acknowledged the damage left in the wake of the withdrawal to the Hindenburg line, but it took them only a few days to seize the abandoned ground and to begin probing the new line of defence.

Proponents of German operational and tactical genius make much of their transition from fixed lines to defence in depth in late 1916, but as the Canadian Corps demonstrated at Vimy Ridge and after, even this operational design and tactical doctrine could be soundly defeated. Weaknesses in the German defensive model are worth examining more closely.

The German command and control was almost a complete failure. The German Sixth Army had plenty of warning that an attack against Vimy was inevitable, but its senior commanders disagreed on how soon it would come. The OHL court of enquiry noted that, "Sixth Army headquarters did not consider the offensive to be imminent." The result was that reserve units were held too far back to execute an immediate counterattack against any possible breakthrough.[23] This conclusion suggests that Fasbender and even Falkenhausen disregarded "ground truth" reports from subordinate commanders such as General der Infanterie Ernst August Max von Bacmeister, the commander of the 79th Prussian Reserve Infantry Division, whose regiments defended most of the ridge.[24] A report signed by Bacmeister and later captured by 4th Canadian Division troops on 9 April revealed the extent of knowledge that the Germans had about both Canadian unit dispositions and preparations for the battle. Bacmeister concluded, "Even if there are no signs of an immediate attack, still it is very certain that the Canadians are planning an attack on a large scale in the immediate future, and both flanks of the division can be considered as the chief points where an attack will be pushed home."[25] Bacmeister's concern was apparently ignored by his superiors.

The Germans well knew both the threat and the ground they defended. Post-war German official histories seldom identify British or Canadian units engaged, but wartime reports and other captured documents show that commanders at the divisional level and below were reasonably well aware of who they were facing.[26] Bacmeister noted in his February-March assessment:

> Opposed to the division are Canadian troops. The 3rd Canadian Division on the right flank of the division came into the line about the middle of March. Recent identifications placed the 2nd Canadian Division on the left divisional flank. The extreme flanks of the Canadian Corps have closed in towards the center so that the Canadian Corps now occupies a narrower front than it did a few weeks ago.[27]

Bacmeister concluded that the Canadian Corps had formed into an echelon that would soon launch a major attack. The Germans knew this ground very well. They had fought over this terrain and knew the approaches, the lines of communication and also the ground conditions at different times of year. Overall, their situational awareness of both the ground and enemy afforded them some advantage, but it was not exploited to their success.

It appears that Falkenhausen's overconfidence led him to prepare for the last battle. He and his chief of staff, Oberst von Nagel, may have concluded that any attack against Vimy Ridge would play out in a fashion similar to that experienced on the Somme, with fighting in the battle zone lasting days or even weeks. Indeed Falkenhausen had issued orders to his reserve divisions on 3 April 1917 to be "ready to relieve the front divisions during the course of a long drawn-out defensive battle."[28] Combined with the decision to ignore the intelligence preparation of the battlefield received from subordinates, one might argue that Falkenhausen had forfeited the fight even before it started.

Ludendorff and his staff may have espoused the notion of mission command through decentralized execution in late 1916, but it does not appear to have been readily embraced at the German operational and tactical level. The German defence at Vimy Ridge was still organized around a series of unmoving strong points and hard lines of resistance, many of which were first isolated, then destroyed, by Allied artillery and attacking infantry. German fire support faced a similar fate. Canadian and British artillery curbed the Germans' ability to manoeuvre in their battle zone by pummelling lines of advance, crossroads and built-up areas where reserves formed up to counterattack. Once the Canadians took the crest of the ridge, rapidly deployed machine guns discouraged uncoordinated German counterstrikes. One such attempt, on the night of 9/10 April when the 1st Battalion, 14th Bavarian Infantry Regiment attacked from the Pimple and tried to retake the northern slope of Hill 145, was four hours late. After it bogged down in the mud a single Canadian machine gun repulsed the advance.[29]

Even astute subordinate commanders such as Bacmeister were slow to react to the rapidly deteriorating situation and get their reserves moving.[30] The commander of the 79th Prussian Reserve Infantry Division issued his first orders for a counterattack at 1100 hours, by which time only the 4th Canadian Division had yet to secure its objectives on Vimy Ridge. Most counterattacks did not materialize until well after nightfall, by which time the Canadians were secure in temporary defences atop the ridge and prepared to repel attacks from a position of advantage. By the night of 11/12 April, the Sixth Army had conceded defeat on the battlefield and made its retreat east to a new line of defence around Gavrelle, Mericourt, the Avion Switch and the western suburbs of Lens.

German defence and logistics were equally deplorable. Much has been written about the cleverness of German active and passive defences at Vimy Ridge, but without the logistics to create and sustain these defences they were doomed to fail against any prepared assault. Except for the failed Canadian raid on 1 March 1917, the Germans lost every contest for no-man's-land and were subjected to repeated harassment by Canadian troops in the weeks before the assault. While Canadian confidence over the terrain and the objective increased, German confidence was slowly sapped as they came to depend on their passive defences such as wire, dugouts and strong points. [31] Even these were poorly developed, as Generalleutnant Alfred Dieterich, commander, 79th Reserve Infantry Brigade, noted in his own post-war history of the material defence of Vimy Ridge:

> On top of the ridge the 1st position had three insufficiently planned lines whose shelters, which mostly lay mistakenly in the first line,...could not withstand any heavy calibre bombardment. The 2nd position was out of the question for a longer defence, due to its unfavourable position at the foot of the eastern slope. [32]

Though the defensive plans were completed on paper, poor weather and a chronic shortage of labour had prevented their completion. Aerial reconnaissance quickly spotted telltale piles of chalk and moved earth and quickly triggered a British or Canadian artillery barrage. The cold and wet meant that the ground could not be drained. Poured concrete could not properly set. Thinning out the front lines to secure extra hands for construction invited a possible attack if the reduced garrisons were discovered, and the units stationed in the rear rest areas were not enough to complete the work on their own. The men were constantly tired, rations were poor, and other critical supplies such as ammunition were also in short supply. The supplies that were available to Gruppe Vimy and Gruppe Souchez had to survive the perilous journey forward and the British and Canadian artillery made every effort to ensure that this did not happen.

Unable to sustain themselves properly, the German defenders of Vimy Ridge required massive and timely reinforcement, which Falkenhausen and Nagel held too far away to be of immediate assistance on 9/10 April. This meant that the defence of the ridge lay in the hands of the front line units, which were often driven to cover by artillery. As a result, with notable exceptions on the 4th Division front, Canadian infantry were able to overrun enemy positions before the Germans could emerge to fight. These tactics were critical to the overall success of the battle, as defenders who did manage to man their weapons inflicted serious casualties among the assaulting Canadian battalions in a very short period of time. [33]

THE GERMAN ARMY AT VIMY RIDGE   233

Despite the fact that the Canadian Corps won a decisive victory at Vimy Ridge, it is noteworthy that the official German record did not present the battle as a decisive defeat, but rather a draw or in some cases, a victory. The Germans learned few lessons from the battle that would improve their operations later on that year. The responsibility for the loss of Vimy Ridge, according to known German sources, appears to rest squarely with Sixth Army commander Falkenhausen and his chief of staff, Nagel. Even they, however, are blamed only for not committing enough reserves and artillery to the counterattack, as if this alone would have ensured a swift and successful recapture of the high ground.[34] Aside from the Germans' lack of command and control, as well as logistics to support such counterattacks on 9/10 April, the Canadians by then controlled the high ridge and the ground conditions around them were very poor. The German counterattacks launched against the Canadians on 9/10 April were uncoordinated and miserable failures, with soldiers getting lost, stuck in the mud, or simply unable to deliver sufficient force to recapture any vital ground. Other German official unit histories suggest that even if reserves had been at hand, a better plan would have been not to counterattack at all but to block the flanks of the break-through and force the assault into a narrowing pocket.[35] This was the tactic employed on the Somme and it again demonstrates that the Germans, despite their good ideas, had yet to successfully implement their new doctrine on the battlefield.

Still, a survey of contemporary German sources such as awards citations suggests that the affair was, at worst, viewed as some sort of draw. Despite his loss of both the ridge and Givenchy-en-Gohelle, General Wichura, the commander of VIII Reserve Corps (Gruppe Souchez) was awarded the Croix de l'Ordre Pour le Mérite for his command at Vimy Ridge. A few of the regimental commanders were also recognized for their "victories." Oberstleutnant Wilhelm von Goerne, the commander of the 261st Prussian Reserve Infantry Regiment, also received the Croix de l'Ordre Pour le Mérite. His citation for the award stated:

> For outstanding leadership and distinguished military planning and successful operations during the 1917 British offensive. The award was also given in recognition of distinction in action during the battle of Arras and especially the fierce fighting at Vimy Ridge when the 261st Reserve Infantry Regiment prevented a British [Canadian] breakthrough of the German lines between April 9 and 13 April 1917.[36]

The 261st Prussian Reserve Infantry Regiment undoubtedly stopped the 11th Canadian Infantry Brigade's initial assault in its tracks, but it certainly did not prevent the 4th Canadian Division from pushing through and ultimately capturing the vital ground.

In the immediate aftermath of the battle, and in post-war histories, the Germans maintained they had achieved some sort of defensive victory at Vimy. Alfred Dieterich named parts of the engagement 'The Battle for the Newly Won Defensive Front' and ended his account of the German battle at Vimy Ridge, stating:

> The fierce battle over Vimy Ridge was fought to a standstill. To be able to call oneself a Vimy fighter, was from then on a high honour! With justice the Division Commander could extend his Thanks and highest Recognition in front of the assembled troops. But in the hearts of the fighters and their loved ones, who restlessly, with deep yearning lived through it all in the Homeland; the memory of the days of heroic glory and deepest sorrow glows indelibly at the Battle of Vimy Ridge, that patch of earth sanctified by the rivers of noble blood and uncountable heroic graves.[37]

Clearly from this and other similar contemporary accounts Vimy Ridge was by no means perceived as a defeat for the German Army at the time, but simply a draw, and perhaps even considered a victory given the German defensive posture adopted on the Western Front in 1917. After all, no massive breakthrough followed this attack and perhaps to the German Army the loss of a few kilometres of vital ground meant little in the grand scheme of things. How different the perception was for the Canadian Corps, who, some have argued, forged not only a victory but also the very nation of Canada itself at this place some ninety years ago.

Notes

1   Cited from the annotated translation found in Colonel A.F. Duguid, *History of the Canadian Grenadier Guards, 1760-1964* (Montreal: Gazette Printing Company, 1965), 499-502.

2   Ian M. Brown, "Not Glamorous but Effective: The Canadian Corps and the Set-Piece Attack, 1917-1918," *Journal of Military History*, vol 58 (July 1994), 421-44.

3   Fortunately, some German regimental histories contain complete lists of the casualties. For an example see the regimental history of the 79th Reserve Infantry Regiment von Voigts-Rhets (3rd Hanoverian), which contains a detailed biographical sketch of its casualties.

4   Some material on Bavarian units survived in Munich. See also the Bavarian Army Museum online at http://www.bayerisches-armeemuseum.de/. The

surviving Potsdam files are now housed in the Federal Military Archive in Freiburg.

5 Senior German military leaders such as Field Marshal Paul von Hindenburg and General Erich Ludendorff led this trend through their adroit transference of the blame for military defeat to the German civilian government, industry, and population which failed to properly support their strategies. This is discussed briefly in Robert Asprey, *The German High Command at War: Hindenburg and Ludendorff and the First World War* (London: Warner Books, 1991), 9-12.

6 Charles IV of Hungary, also known as Emperor Karl I of Austria, (1887-1922), was the last emperor of Austria-Hungary.

7 Holger Herwig, "The Dynamics of Necessity: German Military Policy during the First World War," Allan Millet and Williamson Murray (eds), *Military Effectiveness Volume 1: The First World War*, (Boston: Cambridge University Press, 1988), 94-95.

8 Peter Graf Kielmansegg, *Deutschland und der Erste Weltkrieg* (Frankfurt: a.M., 1968), 181. Even the highest classes suffered from the food shortage. English-born Princess Evelyn Blucher noted the gaunt appearance of her immediate family in her post-war memoir, adding, "...our thoughts are chiefly taken up with wondering what our next meal will be." See Princess Evelyn Blucher, *An English Wife in Berlin*, (London: 1920), 158.

9 Asprey, 255-322.

10 Ibid, 303-12. Operation Alberich was so named after the King of the Dwarfs and the leader of Nibelungs so dear to Richard Wagner's heart. Alberich was cunning and cruel as was the German operational withdrawal.

11 Karl Tschuppik, *Ludendorff: The Tragedy of a Military Mind* (New York: 1932), 232.

12 David Nash (ed), *German Army Handbook, April 1918* (London: Arms and Armour Press, 1977). This publication was originally issued by the British Expeditionary Force General Staff as *Handbook of the German Army in War, April 1918*, having been amended and updated from the March 1917 edition.

13 Ibid, 33-35.

14 For Canadian war establishment tables circa 1915-1917, see G.W.L. Nicholson, *Canadian Expeditionary Force, 1914-1919: The Official History of Canada's Army in the First World War* (Ottawa: Queen's Printer, 1962). Reproductions of original British War Establishment tables for the division and battalion (1915-1916) are reprinted in Norm Christie, *For King and Empire: The Canadians at Ypres, 22nd-26th April 1915* (Ottawa: CEF Books, 1996), 10-12.

15 B.I. Gudmundsson, *Stormtroop Tactics: Innovation in the German Army, 1914-1918* (New York, 1989), 96-97.

16 Ibid, 97.

17 For technical specifications of German artillery see Herbert Jager, *German Artillery of World War One* (Wiltshire: The Crowood Press, 2001).

18   Brown; see also Andrew B. Godefroy, "Fighting to Win: Canadian Military Effectiveness in the First World War," Bernd Horn (ed), *The Canadian Way of Warfare* (Toronto: Dundurn Group, 2006).

19   In German official histories the 79th Reserve Infantry Division was credited with participation in the *Frühjahrsschlacht bei Arras 1917*, or what the German Army referred to as the Spring Battle at Arras 1917 (2 April-20 May 1917). See *Die Schlachten und Gefechte des Großen Krieges, 1914-1918* (Berlin: German Great General Staff, 1919), 268.

20   Ritter Karl von Fasbender (1852-1933) commanded the 9th Bavarian Infantry Brigade from 1905-1907, served briefly as Chief of Staff of the Bavarian Army between 1907 and 1908, and then commanded the 4th Bavarian Infantry Division until his retirement in 1912. He was recalled to active duty at the outbreak of war.

21   For details of honours and awards to Fasbender and other senior Prussian and Bavarian commanders see *Bayerns Goldenes Ehrenbuch, Den Inhaber der höchsten bayerischen Kriegsauszeichnungen aus dem Weltkrieg 1914/1918* (Bayerisches Kriegsarchiv, 1928), and Willam E. Hamelman, *The History of the Prussian Pour le Mérite Order, Volume III: 1888-1918* (Dallas: Matthäus Publishers, 1986). Often containing important details about specific events, award citations remain an underutilized source of evidence in military history and biography.

22   Georg Karl Wichura (1851-1923) was commander of 8th Reserve Corps from 7 September 1916 until the end of the war. He retired from military service in 1919.

23   OHL Court Enquiry as cited in Capt. Cyril Falls, *History of the Great War: Military Operations, France and Belgium, 1917* (London: Macmillan, 1940), 354.

24   Born in 1853, Bacmeister was a Prussian aristocrat serving as the director of the German Red Cross Committee in Berlin at the outbreak of war. He was recalled to military service, eventually assuming command of the 79th Reserve Infantry Division on 7 August 1916. The division had been raised in the 4th Corps District (Prussian Saxony) in the winter of 1914-1915 along with the 80th Reserve Infantry Division as part of the 40th Reserve Corps. After training at Doeheritz Cantonment the division deployed to East Prussia where it fought at the Battle of Masurian Lakes (7-17 February 1915). The 79th later took part in the Siege of Kovno as well as the action at Ochmiana, just south of Smorgoni. The division still occupied this sector of the Eastern Front when Bacmeister assumed command the following year. In November 1916, the 79th Reserve Infantry Division was transferred to the Western Front where it took up the defences at Vimy Ridge. For more details on Bacmeister see Wegner, *Stellenbesetzung der deutschen Heere: 1815-1939, band 1.*

25   War Diary [WD], 4th Canadian Division, March-April, 1917, Appendix B, 21, file 159, T-1938, volume [vol] 4859, Record Group [RG] 9, Library and Archives of Canada [LAC]. The full report is reproduced in Duguid, *History of the Canadian Grenadier Guards*, 138-139.

26 It is interesting to note that where British and Canadian official histories will refer to German forces by their unit identification where possible, German studies tend towards more nebulous identifiers for the Allies such as English, Tommies, or Khakis.

27 Cited in Duguid, 138-39.

28 Falls, 354.

29 Ibid, 355.

30 In some cases command and control elements were overrun before they could react. For example, the 6th Canadian Infantry Brigade captured the commander and staff of the 3rd Bavarian Reserve Infantry Regiment along with 250 prisoners, decapitating this unit before it could execute any sort of tangible defence.

31 This may also explain the increased displays of chivalry towards the Canadian Corps on 2-3 March 1917, including ceasefires so that the 4th Canadian Division could recover the bodies of their dead. Subsequent offers to extend the truce further may have simply been a ploy to buy time and perhaps a reprieve from harassing artillery fire.

32 See Generalleutnant Alfred Dieterich, "The German 79th Reserve Infantry Division in the Battle of Vimy Ridge, April 1917," Christopher and Ute Wilde-Linnel (trans), Andrew Iarocci (ed), Canadian Military History, vol 15, no 1 (Winter 2006), 69-85.

33 One must not forget that the battle of Vimy Ridge cost the Canadians over 10,000 casualties including 3,600 killed.

34 Falls, 354.

35 Ibid. In his report, Dieterich noted that "the difficulty for the defence was the shallow depth of the position of only 700-1000 meters. If the attacker was able to push back the defender off the small ridge by their first onslaught, then the re-capture by a counterattack was unlikely."

36 Awarded on 20 May 1917. Citation and related details are available in Hamelman.

37 Dieterich, 85.

14

In the Shadow of Vimy Ridge
The Canadian Corps in April and May 1917

MIKE BECHTHOLD

The 9th of April is marked officially in Canada as Vimy Ridge Day, a celebration of the achievements and sacrifices made by the Canadian Corps in 1917. This victory was an impressive accomplishment for a young nation, but it did not mark the defeat of Kaiser Wilhelm's Imperial Germany. The war continued for another nineteen months before the Armistice was signed on 11 November 1918. For the Canadian soldiers involved in the attack, Vimy was a proud moment, but they were not given long to rest on their laurels. Within days the men were back in the line, and 1st Canadian Division was committed to a series of costly operations in late April and early May.

This chapter will look at the attack on the village of Arleux-en-Gohelle, some three kilometres east of the ridge, carried out on 28 April 1917. Accounts of the Canadian Corps in April 1917 rightly focus on Vimy, but it is important to remember that the fighting in the Arras sector did not end with the capture of the ridge. The Canadian success of early April was followed with a return to static warfare. Field Marshal Douglas Haig, commander-in-chief of the British Expeditionary Force (BEF), continued to press the Germans around Arras in support of the French offensive to the south.[1] Through this period the Canadians held the positions they had captured and conducted two major set-piece attacks that were part of larger British offensives: at Arleux-en-Gohelle on 28 April and at Fresnoy on 3 May. The Canadians achieved their objectives, but lost 1,000 men in each attack. Remarkably little is known about these operations. They remain in the shadow of Vimy Ridge.

The literature on Canadian operations after Vimy Ridge in April and May 1917 is meagre. The best account of this period is found in the *France and Belgium, 1917* volume of the British official history of the Great War, which provides a good overview of the Battle of Arras but only brief descriptions of tactics. Less than a third of the volume deals with operations after Vimy with limited coverage about the Canadians.[2] The official history of the Canadian Army in the First World War contains just a few pages about the attacks at Arleux and Fresnoy.[3] The only recent book-length study of the Battle of Arras, *Cheerful Sacrifice* by Jonathan Nicholls, devotes one paragraph to the events of 28 April and scarcely more to the much larger offensive of 3 May in which three British armies took part.[4] Canadian sources do not provide much greater illumination. Most accounts make only passing reference to Canadian operations immediately after Vimy Ridge and no source explores the full battles in any detail.[5]

The loss of Vimy Ridge forced the Germans to reassess their defences north of Arras. Much to the surprise of the Canadians, who had interpreted increased German activity on their front as preparations for a major counterattack, the Germans withdrew to the Oppy-Méricourt line. As the Canadians moved to occupy the ground recently abandoned by the Germans, they discovered that the Germans had destroyed scores of farmsteads, livestock and crops during their withdrawal to the Hindenburg Line in March.

On 16 April, French General Robert Nivelle opened his long-awaited offensive south of Arras along the Chemin des Dames ridge. This ambitious offensive, known as the Second Battle of the Aisne, was intended to break through the German defensive line in the first two days and then destroy the German reserves. The battle did not go as the French had planned. Losses were appalling. In the first ten days the French suffered 134,000 casualties while German casualties were even higher at 163,000.[6] The limited gains made by Nivelle's armies were not enough to offset the perceived failure of the offensive and Nivelle was subsequently sacked. This created a strategic dilemma for Haig. The British role in the campaign had been conceived as a diversion for the main French effort. Haig now had to decide between continuing offensive operations around Arras or refocusing his efforts to the north in Flanders, his favoured course of action. Haig explained his decision later in the year:

> In order to assist our Allies [the French], I arranged that until their objective had been attained I would continue my operations at Arras. The necessary readjustment of troops, guns and material required to complete my preparations for my northern operations was accordingly postponed, and preparations were undertaken for a repetition of my attacks on the Arras front until such time as the results of the French offensive should have declared themselves.[7]

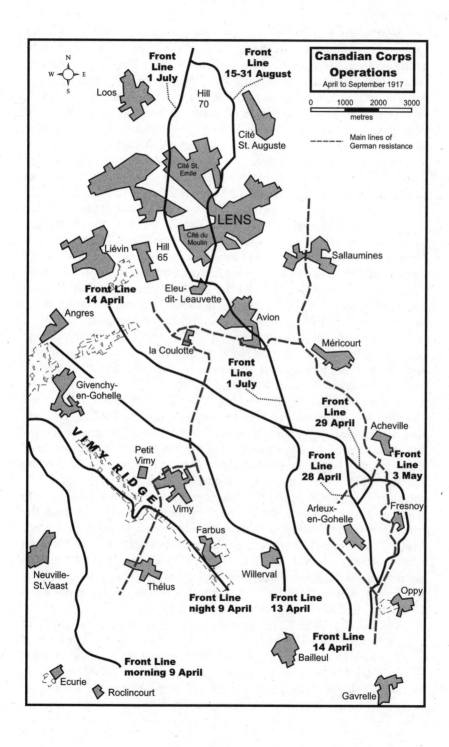

N
W—⊕—E
S

Front Line 1 July

Front Line 15-31 August

Canadian Corps Operations
April to September 1917

0   1000   2000   3000
metres

Main lines of German resistance

Loos

Hill 70

Cité St. Auguste

Cité St. Emile

LENS

Cité du Moulin

Liévin

Hill 65

Sallaumines

Front Line 14 April

Eleu-dit- Leauvette

Angres

Avion

la Coulotte

Méricourt

Givenchy-en-Gohelle

Front Line 1 July

Front Line 29 April

Acheville

Petit Vimy

Front Line 28 April

Front Line 3 May

VIMY RIDGE

Vimy

Arleux-en-Gohelle

Fresnoy

Farbus

Neuville-St.Vaast

Willerval

Thélus

Oppy

Front Line night 9 April

Front Line 13 April

Front Line 14 April

Bailleul

Front Line morning 9 April

Ecurie

Roclincourt

Gavrelle

Electing to continue operations astride the Scarpe River,[8] Haig resumed his offensive a week after Nivelle's attacks. On 23 April, eight divisions from Third Army and one division from First Army attacked south of the Canadian Corps, while two divisions of First Army attacked to the north. Gains of up to two kilometres were made in the south, while the northern attack made no progress because the artillery did not cut the German wire. The British suffered about 10,000 casualties in this operation, known as the Second Battle of the Scarpe.[9]

Haig's next push came five days later, on 28 April, when he launched a limited offensive aimed at capturing the Fresnes-Boiry switch, an intermediate German defensive line between the current German front line and their next major position, the Drocourt-Quéant Line. The plan saw three divisions from Third Army attack east of Arras while three divisions from First Army—63rd Royal Naval, 2nd British and 1st Canadian—tried to reduce the German salient around the villages of Oppy and Arleux-en-Gohelle. Four German divisions faced the British across a 9.5 kilometre section of the front. Overall, this assault again made minimal gains. The divisions of Third Army were not up to the task. Understrength, with many battalions only able to muster 200 men, and let down by the artillery, the 12th, 34th and 37th divisions made minimal gains while suffering heavy losses. The British official history records that the fighting had "reduced the 37th Division to a shadow and virtually destroyed its 63rd Brigade."[10]

The divisions of the British First Army fared little better. The 63rd Division tried to expand its hold on Gavrelle, the small village its units had captured at such a high cost on 23 April. The fighting was savage, but unsuccessful. At the end of the day the Royal Marines had captured the Windmill, but otherwise remained in their original positions.[11] The 2nd British Division, attacking to the right of the 63rd Division, was to capture the village of Oppy. The objectives were ambitious for a division that could only muster 3,500 riflemen, for they had to fight through the main German line to capture Oppy Wood before assaulting the village itself. Good progress early in the day was later checked by German counterattacks. Second Division did not achieve its objectives, but the advance gave the Canadians some protection while they assaulted the villages of Arleux, Fresnoy and Acheville, which formed part of the German defences called the Oppy-Méricourt Line.[12]

The 1st Canadian Division then held the northernmost sector in Haig's limited offensive. The instructions issued on 18 April called for a two-brigade attack to capture all three villages,[13] but divisional commander Major-General Arthur Currie believed he did not have enough artillery to breech the defensive belts that separated Arleux and Fresnoy. Currie made his point and the objectives were split into two discrete operations. The revised plan limited the initial attack to the village of Arleux.[14]

The attack on Arleux was built on the success of the Vimy operation. Brigadier-General F.O.W. Loomis' 2nd Brigade would attack on a three-battalion frontage: 8th Battalion (Major John Percival MacKenzie) on the right, 10th Battalion (Major Alexander Thomas Thomson) in the centre and 5th Battalion (Lieutenant-Colonel Hugh Marshall Dyer) on the left. Two battalions, the 7th Battalion (Lieutenant-Colonel William Forbes Gilson) on the right and the 16th Canadian Infantry Battalion (Major Roderick Ogle Bell-Irving) seconded from 3rd Brigade and on the left were held back in support. In addition, the 2nd Canadian Machine Gun Company and the 2nd Canadian Trench Mortar Battery each supplied six guns to advance with the rear waves of the assaulting battalions. Protection of the left flank would be supplied by the 25th Canadian Infantry Battalion (Lieutenant-Colonel D.S. Bauld) of the 2nd Canadian Division, while on the right flank 2nd British Division would be engaged in operations against the village of Oppy.[15]

The battalions of 2nd Brigade had done a masterful job of rebuilding after the heavy losses suffered at Vimy, where the Brigade's three infantry battalions had each suffered over 300 casualties. In less than three weeks, each battalion drew on experience gained at the Somme and Vimy to carry out section and platoon drill as well as rifle practice. Skirmishing and attack drills were followed by a full-fledged practice attack. By the time of the battle for Arleux, reports boasted that the fighting efficiency of the units was not affected in the slightest.[16]

The tactical formations for the attack were the same as those on 9 April. The lead battalions were committed on a three-company frontage with two platoons forward for each company. The first two waves were to clear the Arleux Loop trench (the German front line) before consolidating the eastern edge of Arleux. The second two waves would then push through to the final objective between Arleux and Fresnoy. As Arleux was known to be a rest billet that was "certain to contain numerous deep dugouts" the troops in the assault were to be followed by 'moppers up' to deal with any German troops that the first waves had overlooked.[17]

The decision to limit the operation to Arleux allowed the guns to concentrate on a limited area. Divisional and heavy artillery targeted German trenches and commenced wire cutting bombardments on the Arleux sector on 25 April.[18] The artillery of 1st and 2nd divisions supported the infantry with both standing and creeping barrages while the heavy artillery fired on more distant targets to screen the battlefield and make it difficult for German artillery or counterattacks to intervene. An indirect machine gun barrage was to fire on the German defences ahead of the assaulting troops.[19] In addition, the Headquarters Royal Artillery Canadian Corps devised a program to simulate an attack away from the actual objective. The deception program continued on 28 April when the Reserve and 3rd Canadian Divisional artilleries fired a feint barrage on their respective fronts starting at Zero hour. The results were mixed. While the deception program was considered successful, much would depend on the success of the guns to cut the wire that lay before the assaulting troops.[20]

Plans for the Arleux operation reflected the understanding that the Germans almost always launched counterattacks to regain lost territory. Immediately after capturing the village, Canadian troops were to "DIG IN, as hard and as fast as possible." A main resistance line built in and wired along the eastern edge of Arleux was to be anchored on a serious of strongpoints, each equipped around a Vickers or Lewis machine gun and a detachment of infantry. Should the enemy regain a footing in any part of the line, the Canadians were to deliver counterattacks from the strongpoints.[21]

At 0425 hours, 28 April 1917, the barrage opened across the entire front. Almost immediately the Germans sent up red SOS flares, resulting in a counter barrage three minutes later. As was the case at Vimy Ridge, many factors determined the fate of the assaulting battalions. On the left flank, the 25th Battalion had to advance to a sunken road midway between Arleux and Acheville to hold the flank of 2nd Brigade. The Battalion war diary states that, "Owing to wire and stiff opposition on part of opposing troops considerable time elapsed before situation could be cleared up and our new front line definitely located." At the time nobody held a clear idea of what was happening to the 25th Battalion. The clearest picture emerges from the war diary of the 5th Battalion, which fought on the immediate right. It states, "The Battalion on our left [the 25th] had, unfortunately, mistaken a sunken road some 300 yards in front of their jumping-off trench, for their final objective, which was a sunken road some 600 yards further on. As a result of the open left flank, the 5th Battalion was forced to withdraw its left-hand company back to the first German front line in order to link up with the 25th."[22] Screening the northern edge of the Canadian attack over featureless ground had cost the 25th Battalion dearly. High casualties resulted.[23]

The 5th Battalion was to clear the open ground north of Arleux. Shortly after the battalion began its attack, "the enemy threw a curtain of fire" at the Canadian start line. Fortunately, the three lead companies missed the German barrage that landed behind them on the Canadian start line, causing some casualties among A Company. Both C and B

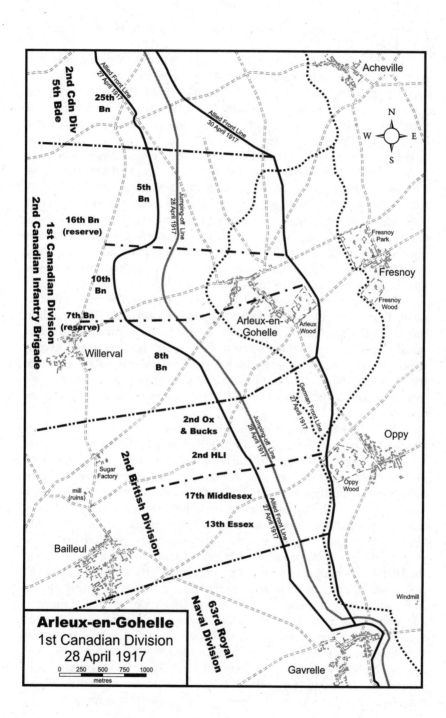

2nd Cdn Div
5th Bde

25th
Bn

Allied Front Line
27 April 1917

Allied Front Line
30 April 1917

Acheville

N
W — E
S

5th
Bn

Jumping-off Line
28 April 1917

16th Bn
(reserve)

1st Canadian Division
2nd Canadian Infantry Brigade

Fresnoy
Park

10th
Bn

Fresnoy

7th Bn
(reserve)

Fresnoy
Wood

Willerval

Arleux-en-
Gohelle

Arleux
Wood

8th
Bn

2nd Ox
& Bucks

German Front Line
27 April 1917

Jumping-off Line
28 April 1917

2nd HLI

Oppy

2nd British Division

Sugar
Factory

Oppy
Wood

mill
(ruins)

17th Middlesex

Allied Front Line
27 April 1917

13th Essex

Bailleul

Windmill

Arleux-en-Gohelle
1st Canadian Division
28 April 1917

0   250   500   750   1000
metres

63rd Royal
Naval Division

Gavrelle

companies found the wire well cut and were able to clear the German front line trenches.

The Battalion's D Company had a tougher time, finding only one path through the wire in its sector. As the men tried to close with the enemy, they found "the enemy's parapet lined with Germans and a great many machine guns which accounted for a large number of men, especially those who were unfortunate enough to have become entangled in the grass covered trip wire." The company was in danger of being decimated. Its commander was a thirty-year-old farmer from Belleville, Ontario, Major Kenneth Campbell, who had enlisted in the CEF as a private less than a month after the outbreak of the war. A natural soldier, he rose quickly through the ranks and took over D Company after its former commander, acting Captain E. Day, was wounded at Vimy. Knowing that "it was a case of getting through at once, or not at all, [Campbell] bravely attempted to rush the gun and bomb the crew." His actions inspired his men and the machine gun was knocked out by grenades, but Campbell was killed.

Having captured the front line trench, 5th Battalion proceeded to its next objective, the sunken road leading out of Arleux. The battalion then moved on to the final objective, where German machine gun fire raked its position from the northeast. This situation, as discussed above, was only rectified by retiring the left flank of the unit to join up with the 25th Battalion.[24] Not until an artillery barrage was organized the next day could the 25th and 5th Battalions consolidate their original objectives.

The village of Arleux was the objective of the 8th Battalion, which attacked to the south, and the 10th Battalion, advancing to the north. Like the flanking battalions, the early success of the attacking companies was related to how well the gunners had cut the German wire. The 10th Battalion faced difficulties even before the assault was launched. Heavy shelling delayed the battalion as it moved forward and Major Thomson, acting as the battalion's commanding officer during the attack, was only able to report his unit ready a scant sixty minutes before Zero hour. The shelling during the approach march caused a number of casualties. Then the battalion's support company was hit just thirty minutes before the attack when a single shell burst in the assembly trench, killing eleven men, including the company commander, Major Alfred Trimmer, and one of his platoon commanders, Lieutenant Stanley Jackson. The reserve officer sent forward to take over the company, Lieutenant Stanley Robertson, was also fatally wounded.[25]

Thomson's B and C companies "found the wire was completely destroyed" and passed into the village where the troops "encountered considerable resistance from enemy infantry, also from snipers, but they were overpowered by our troops, the bayonet, and rifle grenade, being used to good advantage."[26] Captain Wilfred Romeril's D Company on the left found the wire uncut. Caught in the open against prolonged rifle, machine gun and artillery fire, the company soon lost all of its officers, including its commander. Temporary Lieutenant Francis Costello, a twenty-nine-year-old accountant from Liverpool, England, took over the company and organized attacks on two machine guns that were holding up the advance and succeeded in getting his men through the wire.

Costello was aided by the extraordinary efforts of Private Frank MacMackin, from Albert County, New Brunswick. MacMackin had enlisted in Moncton in the 145th Overseas Battalion in early April 1916 at the age of fourteen. As a tall, fit lad just under six feet in height, nobody questioned his declared age. His ruse was later discovered and a handwritten note at the top of his attestation form read, "Minor— not to be sent overseas until nineteen years of age." Just over a year after he enlisted, and three months before his sixteenth birthday, he found himself in the thick of the fighting at Arleux. A 10th Battalion report commended MacMackin for helping his company through the wire, stating "he showed the greatest coolness and initiative. When his Company ran into uncut wire, and were held up by two machine guns, his No. 1 of the Lewis Gun having been killed, he engaged the enemy gun with his Lewis Gun, and when it jammed, he used a rifle, and succeeded in keeping the enemy gunners heads down, while they were outflanked and killed." MacMackin was awarded the Military Medal for his actions that day. Not bad for a fifteen-year-old kid.[27]

A similar story emerges for Major MacKenzie's 8th Battalion, where success again depended on cut wire. The left and right companies made good progress, but then faced resistance in the village that was overcome by remarkable individual effort. Lance-Corporal Harry Cranston, a twenty-seven-year-old picture framer from Merrickville, Ontario, was instrumental in clearing a number of machine guns in the wood behind Arleux. He sent his section of C Company to eliminate one of the guns while he bombed the other gun himself. He and his men then captured twenty prisoners. For his actions Cranston was also awarded the Military Medal. In the centre, B Company was held up by uncut wire and suffered accordingly. Once clear of the wire, the company met further resistance southwest of the village when it attempted to pass a sunken road that the Germans had turned into a strongpoint. The men knocked out the German position, but by this point B Company had lost all its officers and had ceased to function as a unit. The company's survivors were later collected by Captain Eric Michelmore who was bringing a platoon of A Company forward to establish the strongpoints behind the forward companies. Two Stokes Mortars and six machine guns from 2nd Brigade were in place to help defend the newly captured village.[28]

After ninety minutes, Arleux was under Canadian control. As 10th Battalion reached the eastern edge of the village, its men saw a large body of troops heading east. Major Thomson reported,

> When the first few men emerged from the village, they could see the enemy retreating very rapidly, but in such good formation, (being more or less in waves), that our men, owing to the very bad light, were undecided as to whether some of the attacking force had crossed ahead of them. They did not hesitate long, but fired into them, apparently causing many casualties.[29]

Lieutenant-Colonel Daniel Ormond, the commanding officer of the 10th Battalion, believed the German garrison had been pushed aside too easily. "If the enemy had made a determined resistance," the Canadians would not have been able to capture the village. He continued, "All officers are satisfied that if we had been holding the village with the same number of men that the enemy had, and were attacked by a force equal to that used by us, that we would have had no difficulty holding the village."[30]

The Canadian Corps artillery continued to support the troops in Arleux throughout the day, targeting known and suspected German positions behind the front line. The guns also shelled crossroads and other communications lines to seal off the battlefield. Lieutenant-Colonel A.G.L. McNaughton, the Canadian Corps' counter-battery officer, ordered the heavy guns to fire high explosive and gas shells on Fresnoy Wood and the Oppy-Méricourt Line to neutralize the German batteries and stop any counterattacks from those areas. As Tim Cook relates, "The aim of the gas was not to kill the enemy — although that certainly occurred — but, rather, to delay and encumber him so that attacks were slow and uncoordinated, soldiers arrived at the front exhausted from having to wear respirators, and artillery support was desultory."[31]

Judging by the German response on the 28th, the artillery did its work well. Ernst Jünger was a lieutenant in the 73rd Hanoverian Fusilier Regiment. On 28 April he commanded an intelligence clearing station in Fresnoy. The day before the attack he had been warned that the British were planning a major operation the next day. The shelling of Fresnoy was devastating:

A shell hit the house and blew in the wall of the cellar stairs and threw masonry into the cellar...in the middle of it there was a heap of wreckage...we pulled out the dead bodies. One had the head struck off, and the neck on the trunk was like a great sponge of blood. From the arm stumps of another the broken bones projected and the uniform was saturated by a large wound in the chest. The entrails of a third poured out from a wound in the belly.[32]

The artillery fire completely disrupted German communications behind the line. Jünger received a report at 0700 hours that he was to relay to his battalion headquarters, "Enemy has taken Arleux and Arleux park. Ordered 8th Company to counter-attack." Jünger lamented that, "This was the only message that my tremendous apparatus of transmission had to deal with during all three weeks of my time in Fresnoy...And now that my activity was of the utmost value, the artillery fire had put nearly the whole organization out of action."[33]

As was the case at Vimy Ridge, this battle was a two-phase affair: the first involved the capture of the objective; the second its defence. Two reserve battalions, the 7th and 16th, provided fresh troops to reinforce the line as well as carrying and working parties for 1st Field Company, Canadian Engineers.[34] The engineers needed labour, but in the middle of an operation, the infantry were often too busy or tired to provide the necessary working parties. Major H.F.M. Hertzberg, commander of 1st Field, reported, "the three Sapper parties became somewhat broken up on account of casualties and because they were ordered by senior Infantry N.C.O. to act as stretcher bearers, and to fight with the infantry. In spite of this some of them managed to get through and successfully complete consolidation of Front Line."[35]

The main task of the six machine gun companies committed to the operation was to provide indirect support as the attack went in. Approximately forty Vickers guns took part in the initial barrage on the enemy front line trenches. The amount of ammunition expended was impressive. The 3rd Machine Gun Company reported firing 50,000 rounds during this initial barrage, while the 5th Machine Gun Company fired a total of 162,000 rounds. Six guns of the 2nd Machine Gun Company then went forward with the assaulting troops to strengthen the main strongpoints built in Arleux by the battalions of 2nd Brigade.[36]

As it happened, the Germans were unable to mount any serious counterattacks on their lost territory. The British official history states that the commander of the German 111th Division responsible for the Arleux-Fresnoy sector accepted the loss of Arleux and forbade any counterattacks since the defences at Fresnoy had not yet been breeched and the integrity of the German line remained intact.[37] It may be true that the German commander made this assessment eventually, but the Germans were trying to mount counterattacks to retake Arleux. That such attacks did not occur had more to do with the Canadian response to the impending attacks than the unwillingness of the Germans to carry them out.[38] The Germans were unable to mount any significant threat to the Canadians in the Arleux sector.

Elsewhere, the 2nd British Division could not capture its objectives. The Germans holding the village of Oppy put up a spirited defence and launched repeated counterattacks throughout the day. Canadian Corps artillery fired in support of the British numerous times during the day to help smash attempted German counterattacks. None of the British battalions was able to reach its final objective. It appears that the artillery support during the early stages of the battle was insufficient. The war diaries of the 2nd Battalion Oxfordshire and Buckinghamshire, and the 2nd Battalion Highland Light Infantry both note their dissatisfaction with the supporting artillery. A series of breakdowns in the south at Gavrelle meant that the assaulting battalions in 63rd and 2nd divisions had to deal with open right flanks. A final factor concerned the state of the under-strength British battalions before the attack, which had a definite impact on their battlefield success.[39]

The capture of Arleux by 1st Canadian Division was a small success on a day characterized by general failure. It was not a striking victory on the scale of Vimy, but it was another in the series of attritional battles that would eventually wear down the German Army in the west. The British official history puts the accomplishment in perspective: "It was only a local success, but at this stage of the battle even local successes were hard enough to win, and it must be accounted a fine feat of arms." The Canadian victory, as at Vimy, was the product of a thorough, comprehensive plan carried out by well-trained, well-led and well-motivated troops. Though it was once again the infantry that had to do the heavy lifting, they were fully supported by all the resources at the disposal of the Canadian Corps. Heavy and field artillery, trench mortars and machine guns, as well as engineering and logistical support, ensured that the men at the sharp end were given every opportunity to succeed. The one recurring setback during the operation was the inability of the artillery to cut the German wire. The relative success of the assault companies was directly related to how completely the wire was cut on their front. However, the way the men dealt with the uncut wire shows the quality of their leadership and training. Even in the face of extreme adversity and mounting casualties, the men were able to find ways to overcome the German defences and accomplish their mission.

Bill Rawling points out that from Vimy onwards, success on the battlefield was common for the Canadian Corps, but every yard captured came at a price.[40] The battle for Arleux was no different. Casualties suffered by the Canadian Corps on 28 April were 1,255: 295 killed, 805 wounded and 155 missing.[41] To put these numbers in perspective, each of the assaulting battalions suffered at least thirty-five percent casualties. The 10th Battalion sustained 299 casualties out of 639, nearly forty-seven percent of the troops committed to battle. The 2nd Brigade committed 2,741 men to the operation and suffered casualties of 1,016. This casualty rate of thirty-seven percent is significant enough, but it must be remembered that the vast majority of the casualties were suffered by the assault battalions with much lower totals in the supporting units.[42]

Before the Battle of Arras ended on 17 May 1917, Field Marshal Haig made one last attempt to capture the Drocourt-Quéant Line so as to improve the position of the BEF in the Arras sector with territory that would be equally well suited "for a renewed offensive or for defence."[43] On 30 April, Haig met with his army commanders, General Sir Henry Horne (First Army), General Sir Edmund Allenby (Third Army), and General Sir Hubert Gough (Fifth Army), to discuss the offensive. They agreed that Third Army would launch an attack in the centre along the Scarpe River with support to the north and south by First and Fifth Armies. The attack, known as the Third Battle of the Scarpe, was launched on 3 May by fourteen divisions along a twenty-six kilometre front.[44]

The outcome of this offensive replayed Haig's attacks of 23 and 28 April. The battle was over in twenty-four hours with few tangible gains and considerable casualties. There were only two small successes in the operation. The 1st Anzac (Australian and New Zealand Army Corps) of Fifth Army captured the village of Bullecourt in the south, creating a small breach in the German lines. In the north, 1st Canadian Division built on its success at Arleux and captured the village of Fresnoy, creating a major problem for the Germans. As the British official history relates, "The capture of Fresnoy was the culminating point of the series of brilliant successes by the Canadian Corps during the Arras battles, and the relieving feature of a day which many who witnessed it consider the blackest of the War."[45]

The Canadian plan called for the 1st Canadian Infantry Brigade, led by the 1st, 2nd and 3rd battalions, to attack the village of Fresnoy with its flank protected by the 31st and 27th battalions of 6th Canadian Infantry Brigade. The attack, like the rest of the British offensive, was timed to start before first light. Planners hoped that the element of surprise and inaccurate German defensive fire would compensate for the difficulties in finding the gaps in the wire. Though casualties were high, 1st Brigade captured Fresnoy quickly and was already preparing its defensive positions as the sun began to rise. Against uncut wire and strong German resistance, the 6th Brigade did not reach its final objectives on the flank, but its advance was enough to cover the newly won positions in Fresnoy.[46]

Unlike Arleux, the Germans were desperate to regain Fresnoy. A German regimental history likened the strategic loss of the village to "a stone [that] had been knocked out of the German defensive wall which had to be replaced without delay if the whole neighbouring position to the north and south were not to be gravely threatened."[47] The first German counterattack, delivered at 1030 hours, was broken up by Canadian artillery, machine gun and rifle fire before it even reached Fresnoy. An even larger counterattack in the afternoon met the same fate. German losses at Fresnoy were the highest along their entire front on 3 May. One of the counterattacking German regiments admitted to suffering 650 casualties and some 500 Germans were captured during the operation. However, Canadian casualties were also high, approaching 1,300. Success had been dear.[48]

Unfortunately, the gains at Fresnoy were to be short-lived. On 5 May 1917, the 5th British Division relieved General Currie's 1st Canadian Division. The German desire to regain Fresnoy had not diminished since its loss and on the morning of 8 May they launched an attack, well supported by artillery, to recapture the village. The British battalion in Fresnoy, the 1st Battalion, East Surrey Regiment, was almost annihilated as its men were pushed out of the village to the outskirts of Arleux. The British counterattacks to regain the village were unsuccessful. The hard-won gains of the 1st Canadian Division were lost.[49]

The fighting in the Arras sector did not end with the capture of Vimy Ridge and its environs on 12 April. The overall campaign ran from 9 April to 17 May and included significant elements of three British armies. By the time the fighting shifted to other fronts, the BEF had suffered a total of 158,660 casualties.[50] For 1st Canadian Division, the events in late April and early May 1917 were significant and costly. Casualties for 2nd Brigade at Arleux and 1st Brigade at Fresnoy were proportional with the losses suffered at Vimy. The battalions fully appreciated their sacrifices at the time. The war diaries for the units involved in the Arleux attack were as detailed regarding their experiences of 28 April as they were of Vimy.

Ultimately, this study raises as many questions as it answers. First and foremost is the question of why the Canadians were successful and the British were not. The British official history suggests that the quality of reinforcements was a major contributing factor. While British units suffered a decline in efficiency after prolonged exposure to combat, Canadian units "appeared to deteriorate very little after taking part in several engagements at short intervals of time," because Canadian reinforcements had, "as a rule undergone more training but were also rather older men and often of better physique."[51] This statement cries out for further research. What other differences existed between the Canadian and British 'ways of war'? Some evidence suggests that the Canadians benefited from artillery support of greater quantity and accuracy than did their British counterparts.[52] What effect did morale have? Canadian casualties at both Arleux and Fresnoy were higher than those suffered by many of the unsuccessful British units. Were the Canadians more willing to sustain higher casualties to achieve their goals? Were the British troops more sensible and willing to call off an attack if the cost proved to be too high? What about the density of attack? Did the Canadians mass greater numbers of troops on a given frontage in order to overwhelm the German defenders? Though these questions remain to be answered, there can be no doubt that 1st Canadian Division remained a very effective formation in the month after Vimy. The capture of Arleux and Fresnoy, though costly, were notable successes in otherwise failed operations. They deserve to emerge from the shadow of Vimy Ridge.

Notes

1   BEF operations around Arras (including the Canadian Corps at Vimy) were of a secondary nature aimed at providing a diversion for the main Allied offensive, the French attack centred on the Chemin des Dames Ridge.

2   Cyril Falls, *History of the Great War: Military Operations, France and Belgium, 1917, Vol. 1; The German Retreat to the Hindenburg Line and the Battle of Arras* (London: Macmillan, 1940).

3   G.W.L. Nicholson, *Canadian Expeditionary Force, 1914-1919: The Official History of the Canadian Army in the First World War* (Ottawa: Queen's Printer, 1962), 269-79.

4   Nicholls makes only a brief statement about the Canadians on 28 April, "The only bright spot of the day was the capture of Arleux by Currie's 1st Canadian Division, its losses of 9 April repaired with reinforcements." Jonathan Nicholls, *Cheerful Sacrifice: The Battle of Arras 1917* (London: Leo Cooper, 1990), 195.

5   Daniel G. Dancocks, *Gallant Canadians: The Story of the Tenth Canadian Infantry Battalion* (Markham: Penguin, 1990) provides the most complete examination of a single battalion at Arleux, but does not examine the larger operation. Most other standard works on the Canadian Expeditionary Force devote no more than a few pages to the battle.

6   Nicholson, 242-43, 265-66.

7   Douglas Haig's 4th Despatch (1917 Campaigns), 25 December 1917, found on www.firstworldwar.com, last accessed 10 May 2006.

8   The Scarpe River follows an easterly course just to the north of Arras and marked the approximate boundary between British First and Third armies.

9   Nicholson, 269-70.

10 Falls, 413-18.

11 K.D. Tallett, "The Royal Marines at the Gavrelle Windmill, 28 April 1917: Triumph or Tragedy?" *RND - Royal Naval Division*, Issue No. 3, December 1997.

12 Falls, 418-22.

13 Appendix 4, "Instructions for the Attack Upon the Oppy-Acheville Line," 18 April 1917 and Appendix 91, "10th Canadian Infantry Battalion, Order No.39," 20 April 1917, War Diary [WD], 2nd Canadian Brigade, April 1917, T-10669, vol 4871, Record Group [RG] 9, Library and Archives of Canada [LAC].

14 "Report on the Vimy Ridge-Willerval-Arleux-Fresnoy Operations, April 9 to May 5, 1917," quoted in Daniel Dancocks, *Sir Arthur Currie: A Biography* (Toronto: Methuen, 1985). A revised order issued on 27 April 1917 stated that the intention was still to capture Arleux and Fresnoy, but the final objectives were clearly shown to be no further than the eastern edge of Arleux. See Appendix 115 for "Order No. 41" and "After Order No. 41," 27 April 1917, WD 10th Battalion, April 1917, T-10712, vol 4919, RG 9.

15 "Report of 2nd Canadian Infantry Brigade Operations, April 26th to April 30th, 1917 - Capture of Arleux-en-Gohelle, April 28th, 1917," [2nd Brigade Report] 11 May 1917, WD, 2nd Brigade, May 1917, T-10668, vol 4870, RG 9.

16 Major A.T. Thomson, "Report on the Attack on the Village of Arleux en Gohelle on April 28th 1917," [Thomson Report] WD, 10th Battalion, April 1917; WD, 5th Battalion, April 1917, T-10708, vol 4916, RG 9; WD, 2nd Brigade, April 1917.

17 Appendix 9, "2nd Canadian Infantry Brigade Instructions for the Attack on Arleux (No.2)," 27 April 1917, WD, 2nd Brigade, April 1917; Order No. 41, WD, 10th Battalion, April 1917.

18 WD, 1st Canadian Divisional Artillery, April 1917, T-10775, vol 4958, RG 9.

19 Appendix 9, "2nd Canadian Infantry Brigade Instruction for the Attack on Arleux (No. 2), 27 April 1917, WD, 2nd Brigade, April 1917; Artillery Order No. 17 (25 April 1917) and No. 18 (26 April 1917),WD, Royal Artillery Canadian Crops, April 1917 T-10773-10774, vol 4957.

20 Artillery Order No. 17 (25 April 1917) and No. 18 (26 April 1917), WD, Royal Artillery Canadian Corps; WD, HQ Reserve Divisional Artillery (Lahore), April 1917, T-11130-11131, vol 5067 RG 9, WD, HQ 3rd Canadian Divisional Artillery, April 1917, T-10779, vol 4961.

21 Appendix 9, 2nd Canadian Infantry Brigade Instructions for Attack on Arleux (No. 2).

22 WD, 5th Battalion, May 1917, T-10708, vol 4916, RG 9.

23 2nd Brigade Report; WD, 25th Battalion, April 1917, T-10735, vol 4953, RG 9.

24 WD, 5th Battalion, May 1917. Personal details of individual soldiers are from RG 150 (attestation records), the Canadian Virtual War Memorial (www.vac-acc.gc.ca) and the Commonwealth War Graves Commission (www.cwrg.org).

25 WD, 10th Battalion, April 1917; Thomson Report; 2nd Brigade Report.

26 Thomson Report; 2nd Brigade Report.

27 Thomson Report; 2nd Brigade Report.

28 WD, 8th Battalion, June 1917, T-10711, vol 4918, RG 9; 2nd Brigade Report.

29 Thomson Report.

30 Letter from Ormond to R.H. Kearsley, 30 April 1917, quoted in Daniel Dancocks, *Gallant Canadians: The Story of the 10th Canadian Infantry Battalion, 1914-1919* (Markham: Penguin, 1990), 118.

31 Cook, *No Place To Run: The Canadian Corps and Gas Warfare in the First World War* (Vancouver: UBC Press, 1999), 112.

32 Ernst Jünger, *The Storm of Steel: From the Diary of a German Storm-Troop Officer on the Western Front* (London: Chatto and Windus, 1929, reprint 1975), 134-35.

33 Jünger, 136-37.

34 2nd Brigade Report.

35 WD, 1st Field Company, Canadian Engineers, April 1917, T-10829-10830, vol 4993, RG 9.

36 WD, 2nd Machine Gun Company, April 1917, T-10812, vol 4982, RG 9; WD, 5th Machine Gun Company, April 1917, T-10813, vol 4983, RG 9.

37 Falls, 424.

38 WD, HQ Canadian Corps, April 1917, T-7176, vol 4814, RG 9; WD, 1st Canadian Division General Staff, April 1917, T-1913-1917, vol 4831, RG 9; WD, Royal Artillery Canadian Corps, April 1917; WD, 1st Canadian Divisional Artillery; WD, 5th Battalion, May 1917; WD, 8th Battalion, May 1917; WD, 10th Battalion, April 1917; WD, 2nd Machine Gun Company, April 1917; WD, 3rd Machine Gun Company, April 1917; WD, 5th Machine Gun Company, April 1917; WD, 13th Machine Gun Company, April 1917; WD, 14th Machine Gun Company, April 1917.

39 WD, 2nd Battalion, Oxfordshire and Buckinghamshire Light Infantry, April 1917, WO 95/1348, National Archives [NA]; WD 2nd Battalion, Highland Light Infantry, April 1917, WO 95/1347; Falls, 418-22.

40 Bill Rawling, *Surviving Trench Warfare: Technology and the Canadian Corps, 1914-1918* (Toronto: University of Toronto Press, 1992), 221.

41 This figure was compiled by examining the war diaries for each of the units involved in the attack on Arleux. It breaks down as follows: 5th Bn, forty-nine killed in action (KIA), 153 wounded in action (WIA) and forty-four missing; 7th Bn, ten KIA, sixty-seven WIA, five missing; 8th Bn, fifty-six KIA, 183 WIA, forty-nine missing; 10th Bn, eighty-seven KIA, 191 WIA, twenty-one missing; 16th Bn, twenty-six KIA, forty-one WIA, twelve missing; 25th Bn, fifty-one KIA, 119 WIA, twenty-four missing; 26 Bn, two KIA, eleven

WIA, 2nd Cdn MG Company, three KIA, ten WIA; 5th Cdn MG Company, one KIA, three WIA. 14th MG Company, one KIA; 2nd Cdn Trench Mortar Battery, two KIA, six WIA; 1st Field Company, CE, two KIA, nine WIA. Casualties for other units, such as artillery, medical, and other support are not known.

42   2nd Brigade Report; Thomson Report.

43   Quoted in Nicholls, 195.

44   Nicholls, 195-96.

45   Falls, 450.

46   Nicholson, 274-77; Falls, 448-450; WD 1st Canadian Division, May 1917, T-1914-1915, vol 4832, RG 9; WD 1st Canadian Brigade, May 1917, T-10666, vol 4868, RG 9; WD 6th Canadian Brigade, May 1917, T-10685, vol 4889, RG 9; WD 1st Battalion, May 1917, T-10704-10705, vol 4913; WD 2nd Battalion, May 1917, T-10705, vol 4913, RG 9; WD 3rd Battalion, May 1917, T-10706-10707, vol 4914; WD 27th Battalion, May 1917, T-10738-10739, vol 4935 RG 9; WD 31st Battalion, May 1917, T-10742, vol 4937, RG 9.

47   Quoted in Falls, 451.

48   Nicholson, 277.

49   Falls, 520-21.

50   Nicholls, 211. This breaks down as 87,226 for Third Army, 46,826 for First Army and 24,608 for Fifth Army.

51   Falls, 450-51.

52   10th Battalion reported that, "The barrage, throughout the attack, was quite satisfactory, except that compared with April 9th, 1917, its intensity was very disappointing." See Thomson Report. The war diaries of the 2nd Battalion Oxfordshire and Buckinghamshire, and 2nd Battalion Highland Light Infantry both complain about the artillery support they received during the attack on Oppy.

Major-General Arthur Currie
General Officer Commanding (GOC)
1st Canadian Division.

Major-General Henry Burstall
GOC 2nd Canadian Division.

Major-General Louis Lipsett
GOC 3rd Canadian Division.

Major-General David Watson,
GOC 4th Canadian Division.

"The terrain is much worse than on the Somme," Andrew Macphail observed. "Mile after mile not an inch of ground remains undisturbed. It is like a tumultuous sea suddenly turned to earth."

"The artillery conquers and the infantry occupies." **Above**: Men of the 29th Battalion, 2nd Canadian Division advance over no-man's-land. With landmarks destroyed, some Canadian troops lost their way. **Below**: Once they reached their objectives, the Canadians quickly dug in and prepared for German counterattacks.

Canadian soldiers prepare their Vickers medium machine guns for action at Vimy Ridge.

Julian Byng hoped that tanks would clear obstacles for the 2nd Division's advance towards Thélus, but all eight either broke down or "wallowed in the thick mud."

Canadians from either the 1st or 2nd divisions occupy the ridge crest near the German first trench line. Unlike the 3rd and 4th divisions to the north, their advance took them down Vimy Ridge.

Canadian officers, likely from the 3rd Division, look over the ridge towards the village of Vimy and the Douai plain beyond.

The relaxed posture of these Canadian support troops in advance suggests that the explosions were later added to the photograph.

Two patrols of 20 men and horses from the Canadian Light Horse advanced on Willerval in the afternoon 9 April 1917. According to the Canadian official history, "One patrol captured ten Germans in the village, but was in turn engaged by a machine-gun and lost half its men and horses; the other was all but wiped out by rifle fire."

A Canadian officer explores one of a network of German gun emplacements and shelters concealed in Farbus Wood, April 1917.

LAC PA 994

LAC PA 882

A German emplacement near the village of Thélus (**above**) and the ruined village of Farbus (**below**) shortly after its capture. "We are hammering Fritz to pieces," wrote Lieutenant V.G. Tupper, who was killed during the battle. "Our ammunition and guns now seem to be unlimited."

LAC PA 1084

LAC PA 1160

Under the watchful eye of civilians, mounted soldiers escort to the rear some of the 4,000 German prisoners who were captured at Vimy Ridge.

LAC PA 1189

"Within days [of Vimy Ridge] the men were back in the line." Canadian artillery observers direct gunfire during the capture of Arleux, 28 April 1917.

LAC PA 1941

A memorial service was held in September 1917 for the men of the 87th Battalion (Grenadier Guards) who fell at Vimy Ridge. The Battalion suffered over 300 casualties in its attacks on Hill 145.

PART III

Aftermath and Memory

15

Battle Verse
Poetry and Nationalism after Vimy Ridge

JONATHAN VANCE

As dusk fell on 9 April, the battalions of the Canadian Corps were consolidating their gains along the Brown line. They had achieved almost all of the first day's objectives — most of Vimy Ridge was firmly in their hands. The news from the battlefield reached Canada by wire in time to appear in the final editions of that day's major newspapers, but it was not until the next day that the full story hit the front pages. "Whole German Line Wavers Under First Spring Attack," proclaimed the Edmonton *Journal*. "Canada's Troops Have Won Biggest Victory of Career in Taking Vimy Ridge." Moncton's *L'Acadien* was even more effusive: "Brillant fait d'armes canadiens. La fameuse crête Vimy, théatre de tant de combat meutriers, est enlevées aux allemands par un irrésistible assaut des gars du Canada." "Progress Made in Offensive More Extensive Than Was First Indicated," announced the Toronto *Daily Star*, "Canadians Thoroughly Secure Vimy Ridge."[1] Inspired by the news, Canada's legion of amateur poets was probably at work by the end of that day. A great event in the nation's history occurred: the only thing to do was to celebrate the victory in verse.

Over the next twenty years, Vimy Ridge became the Great War's most popular battle with poets of every stripe, from the amateur versifier to Canada's most well-known writers. Its popularity lay in the fact that it was more than just a stunning military success of the kind that had inspired many a classic narrative battle poem.[2] The special appeal of Vimy Ridge rested in its ability to bring together the religious and the nationalist. Easter Monday, the holiest day in the Christian calendar, was chosen as the offensive's opening day for reasons that had nothing to do with religious symbolism, but that reality was irrelevant to Canadian poets. For them, Easter Monday 1917 brought together two events of tremendous import: the celebration of the resurrection of

Christ and the birth of a nation. The spiritual and the secular meshed so completely that the poet could not help but be drawn to it. Besides, Vimy Ridge was much easier to rhyme than Drocourt-Quéant.

That Canadians turned to verse to celebrate such a momentous event should come as no surprise, for Canada was then a society in which poetry mattered. Because it was used so widely in schools to teach reading, grammar, composition and history to even the youngest of children, it was an idiom that most Canadians found comfortable and familiar.[3] It was also much more widely disseminated at the time of the First World War than it is in the early twenty-first century. Virtually all of Canada's newspapers printed poetry in every issue, as did high-circulation magazines like *Maclean's* and *Saturday Night*. Nor was it the cultural preserve of the middle class and the idle rich. Labour newspapers like Winnipeg's *The Voice* and agricultural newspapers like *The Weekly Sun* regularly printed poetry, although the rough doggerel in such publications contrasted strongly with the refined verse that graced the pages of *The University Magazine* and *Queen's Quarterly*. Given the sheer amount of verse that was published (and we can assume that much more was written without ever making it into print) it is beyond question that poetry was the primary literary form where the memory of the Great War was negotiated and expressed. Even more importantly, it was a form occupied by soldiers and civilians, men and women, famous poets such as Sir Charles G.D. Roberts and people who are now nothing more than a name in an old newspaper. No other mode of public expression drew such a wide range of practitioners.

There is an enormous range, not only in authorship but in quality, in the body of Vimy Ridge verse. Ironically, the most famous poem on the subject is not even Canadian: it is "To E.T.," by the American poet Robert Frost, a tribute to Edward Thomas, the English poet who was killed at Beaurains, south of Vimy on 9 April 1917 while serving with the Royal Garrison Artillery.[4] There is nothing in the Canadian canon that reaches the aesthetic standard of Frost's poem:

> You went to meet the shell's embrace of fire
> On Vimy Ridge; and when you fell that day
> The war seemed over more for you than me,
> But now for me than you -- the other way.

Indeed, much of Canada's Great War poetry is dreadful, and contemporary critics expressed concern that the war gave newspapers and publishers license to print poetry that under normal circumstances would never see the light of day. But what it lacks in aesthetic quality, it more than makes up for in sincerity; it may have been badly written, but it was written from the heart. So when Phil Moore, the Nova Scotia "Poet of the Rossignol," asked the reader to "spare for those such laurels as you may, / Who wrought from sordid strife a gorgeous rhyme," he was asking for the indulgence of the reading public, who should judge a poem on its subject and sentiment, rather than on its aesthetic quality.[5]

If little of it is gorgeous, Canada's Vimy Ridge poetry at least runs the gamut from the amusing to the tragic. There is, for example, the limerick by R.M. Eassie, an English emigré who enlisted at Valcartier in September 1914:

> There was a young fellow of Vimy
> Who said, 'If my sweetheart could see me
> Accepting the kisses
> Of these here French misses,
> I guess I would rather not be me!'

At the other end of the spectrum is the deep emotional pain that runs through James Manning's "Our Laddie," written in memory of his son, Lieutenant Frederick Manning, who died at Vimy while serving with the 85th Battalion:

> Vimy heights –
> The frantic guns –
> One furious charge
> O'erwhelms the Huns
>
> My eyes are dim –
> I cannot see
> Among the dying
> Is that he?…
>
> The embers fall –
> The fire is dead
> My heart is cold –
> I must to bed.[6]

And then there is a large body of poetry that is notable largely for the authors' ingenuity in coming up with different phrases to describe the scene: "storied Vimy's hill"; "Vimy's red-embroidered haze"; "Vimy's Ridge aglow"; "Vimy's bristling crest."[7]

In surveying the poetry of Vimy Ridge, however, one is immediately struck by its consistency; no matter who the author, there is a surprising degree of concordance in theme. Nor were there any dramatic changes in tone or meaning between April 1917 and the dedication of the Vimy

Memorial in 1936. The cynic might find this sufficient reason to dismiss a body of poetry that is distinguished largely by its sameness. For the historian, however, the continuities point to a general agreement, both through society and over time, about the significance of the Battle of Vimy Ridge for Canada. It was a story that could be told as a stirring narrative, but it was also one whose religious, political and nationalist meaning superseded the mere historical details.

For this reason, and also perhaps because poets believed that the events of the battle could better be conveyed in prose, narrative poems are very much in the minority. Typical is "Vimy Ridge," written by Private Ernest McKinnon, a Prince Edward Island-born nickel plater, and published in a small-town Ontario newspaper in August 1917. McKinnon's aim was strictly expository:

> Now boys, if you want a story,
> I've one I would like to tell-
> It's about the Battle of Vimy,
> Where our brave Canadians fell.

He goes on to describe in carefully rhymed stanzas the battle from the perspective of one who was there, concluding with dusk settling over the ridge:

> At last we got our Objective,
> We dug ourselves in for the night:
> And we all went to sleep dreaming
> Of how we put Fritzie to flight.

Walter Brindle, a New Brunswick bootmaker who was too old (forty-eight in 1917) to serve in the trenches but did his bit behind the lines with the service corps, heard enough about the battle from fellow New Brunswickers in the rear areas to compose his own narrative poem. Like McKinnon's work, Brindle's "Vimy" is simple and direct, emphasizing the chaos of the battle and concluding with the capture of the ridge:

> But, oh, we paid dear for the hold up,
> for half our battalion was gone,
>
> But we finished the job that they gave us,
> And the ridge of old Vimy was won.

Theodore Girling of Saskatoon is better known as the poet of the Canadian Army Veterinary Corps and, like Brindle, did not see action himself at Vimy Ridge. But he imagined what it was like to be there, "Mid the litter and lumber of battle, / On the shell-churned clay of France," as the battle raged around him:

> ...the barrage lengthens,
> While the rifles crack o'er the hill,
> Then the bombs explode in the dug-outs,
> And the first line trench grows still,
> 'Mid the crash of the answering shrapnel,
> Lit by signal flares of the Hun,
> As the final waves pass over,
> To the tat of the Lewis gun.

Only then does the reader learn the truth, that the speaker has been killed in the first wave. He waits for the burial party to come along, remove his few possessions to return to his family and dig a grave where "the shell-torn crest of Vimy / Shall cradle me evermore."[8]

Even allowing for Girling's unusual perspective, none of these poems go beyond a simple description of the battle. But other writers found it impossible to discuss the battle without placing it into a spiritual context, one that emphasized the piety of the soldiers, the religious character of their sacrifice, and the significance of the day. D.M. Matheson's "Vimy Ridge," published in 1917, is a case in point. For Matheson, a teacher at Alexander McKay School in Halifax, it was essential to characterize the preparation for battle as a religious act, as every infantryman in the line, "like a Christian soldier / Had made his peace with God." John Daniel Logan, a university professor, literary critic, poet, and, much to the chagrin of his commanding officer, a sergeant with the 85th Battalion, continued the analogy, noting that "the Sacred Hill was stark—and stained / With sacramental wine from martyrs' veins." In such poetry, the battlefield was itself a sacred site, for it took the soldiers "close to the throne of God."[9]

But to find such religious symbolism in battle poetry is hardly remarkable; what set Vimy Ridge apart was the fact that the battle began on Easter Monday, the day of Christ's resurrection, a day when, more than any other, the resurrection of the fallen soldier could be assured. And so poets such as Thomas O'Hagan embraced the timing of the attack as something of enormous importance:

> Easter had shed its halo of light
> Where the village spires were dreaming of prayer,
> And the faith that had lifted each soul from the sod
> Blossom'd anew in the morning air.

In his poem "At Vimy Ridge," battle imagery and religious imagery are inextricably intertwined, from the "village spires...dreaming of prayer" as the artillery barrage screams overhead, to the fortitude of "the boys of the Maple.../ Whose courage and faith were born of heaven, / As they knelt in duty at the altar of Mars, / At Vimy Ridge." In a 1919 issue of *Queen's Quarterly*, an anonymous poet expressed the same sentiment in "Vimy, 1917," part of a sonnet sequence entitled "Two Easters." It was not about the battle itself, but about the resurrection of the soldiers who fell that day:

> In living hearts of flesh is raised their stone,
> Let wooden crosses wither as they may;
> Then women lave afresh your burning eyes;
> Sweet babe, be comforted, these dead arise.[10]

Two Montreal poets, C.L. de Roode and Dorothy Sproule, drew even more direct links between the men who fell at Vimy and the resurrection. For de Roode, writing just three days after the battle began, the attack and the day could not be separated:

> ...au chant des sonneries
> Clamant à l'Univers: Christ est ressuscité!
> Sous les feus des canons scandant les liturgies
> Les Canadiens ont pris ce mont si redouté.

Dorothy Sproule saw the same connection. Looking on the Vimy Memorial twenty years after the battle, she interpreted Walter Allward's twin-pillared monument not only as a tribute to the fallen, but also as a symbol of Christ, representing "one, who died on Calvary, / [and] Now lifts on high, His wounded hands."[11]

But it was Anna Durie, an amateur poet from Toronto, who most fully articulated the religious interpretation of the battle. Her poem on Vimy Ridge, the battle in which her son, Captain Arthur Durie of the 58th Battalion, participated, is littered with religious references: she wears a cross made from wood that Arthur collected from the battlefield at Vimy; she imagines that the assault was followed by a church parade, "to their work a fitting ending," at which the chaplain pronounced all of the customary prayers; she envisions the "fearless, dying eyes / Looking to Heaven" but knows they will not see Christ above, for "The Risen Lord Himself walks 'midst the dead." She could, of course, have been writing about any battle, but the day gave Vimy special significance:

> *Easter Day dawned: the eve of the big push*
> *At Vimy Ridge. My hero felt a hush*
> *Of peace, and willed to meet his Blessed Lord*
> *In the Bread and Wine.*

For Anna Durie, to fight on Easter Monday was to partake of a sacrament. This time, however, she was lucky, for her son Arthur did not "meet his Blessed Lord" at Vimy. But when he was killed in action later in the year, it unhinged his mother more than it did most grieving parents and drove her to embark on a bizarre and ultimately successful quest to return her son's remains to Canada.[12]

Once the battle was identified with the celebration of the rebirth of Christ, it was only a small step to connect Vimy Ridge with the birth of a nation. With the provinces represented by battalions from across the country working together in a painstakingly planned and carefully executed operation, the Canadian Corps became a metaphor for the nation itself. This allowed the battle to be construed as a demonstration of Canada reaching maturity as it stood united in a common cause. For many poets, then, the link between the sacred and the secular was self-evident.

The victory was certainly an occasion to express local pride and laud the efforts of individual units. H.C. Mason's "County Battalion" elegizes the men who left "the fields of old familiar farms, / The fields their forebears hewed from out the wood" and, even as they stormed "Gun-smitten Vimy," never lost sight of their homes in rural Ontario. D.M. Matheson's poem celebrated the contribution of the Nova Scotia Highland battalions, "Borden's Highland laddies / [Who] charged up the Vimy Ridge," as did J.D. Logan's "The O.C.s 85th Battalion," a jaunty rhyme that proclaimed "we're Borden's boys, and Phinney's boys, and Ralston's boys, / Yes, we're the boys who put the 'Vim' in Vimy, / For we gave the Hun his fill, then chased him off the Hill."[13] Other poets also had specific units to celebrate. Brindle wrote of New Brunswick's 26th Battalion, while Esther Kerry, in a verse that first appeared in the Montreal *Gazette*, paid tribute to two of the city's battalions, the 13th and 14th, that distinguished themselves at Vimy Ridge. Another Montreal poet, C.L. de Roode, praised the 22nd Battalion, "Celui qui de Vimy fit l'assaut fantastique, / Se battit en chantant, ne recula jamais!"[14]

But much more prevalent was the notion that the success at Vimy was a national rather than just a local achievement. Poets like Adelard Audette, who enlisted with his brother and finished the war as a corporal with the 22nd Battalion, were not above reminding the reading public that Canada had succeeded after France and Britain had failed to take the ridge:

It was up to the Allies, and each one did his part;
The French had tried to take the Ridge, about some two years ago,
But were forced to make a quick retreat, and thousands of them mowed;
The Imperials they were served the same, as we Canadians know,
But when we took the reins in hand, we kept them on the go.

The secret to "keeping them on the go" rested in part in the gallantry of individual units and on the fact that Canada's citizen-soldiers were deemed to be superior to European professional armies (and despite the reality of conscription in France and Britain, Canada's myth of the war held that all European armies were, by definition, professional). As Caroline Eleanor Wilkinson put it, "trained not in their youth to warfare, yet they fought right valiantly, / Staunch at Vimy."[15] But more critical was the fact that, for the first time, the four divisions of the Canadian Corps fought together in a single operation; it was the unity of a new nation on the verge of maturity, as symbolized by the Corps' triumph at Vimy, that really inspired poets to new heights.

Alfred Gordon's "Canada to England: Vimy Ridge 1917" expresses this notion explicitly. It speaks in the voice of a young adult who has just proven a new level of maturity to a demanding parent:

England, our mother, we, thy sons, are young;
Our exultation this day cannot be
Bounded as thine: but thou wilt pardon us.
Thou wilt forgive us if we cry, 'Now see!
See now, our mother, these are they that clung
Once to thy breasts...'

For Gordon, Vimy Ridge was the most momentous event "since France herself first stood at bay, / To conquer or die on Marne's green banks," and the achievement was enough to "let flags and banners fly! / To drums and bugles let the people march / While Vimy Ridge is shouted to the sky!" In short, the battle marked a new era for the nation:

Thereafter of our pride let nought be said,
Saving on stone, inscribed with but one line:
CANADA – VIMY RIDGE – 1917
Our hearts the tablets of a secret shrine:
Though henceforth we shall lift a higher head
Because of Vimy and its glorious dead!

Explicit in much of this poetry is the notion that it was not battalions and brigades that fought their way up Vimy Ridge, but the nation itself. As Wilmot Lane put it, in highly romantic language,

Young Canada, with dauntless breast
Rose from their couch ere night was gone…
Up o'er the lonesome hill they pressed
As if they trod a velvet lawn,
As if the barrage fires were not…[16]

And because Canada itself had taken the ridge, it became part of Canada, not just in the legal sense of the federal government acquiring the crest of the ridge as the site for a memorial (even the government's initial musings about the possibility of purchasing the land drew a response from one poet, who implored "Yes, buy, O Canada! Embellish well, / Buy and enrich the far-famed Vimy Ridge") but in a symbolic sense. In a kind of virtual imperialism, Vimy Ridge was annexed to Canada by the blood that was shed there and by the memorials that were placed there. For J.M. Smith, it was the maple trees planted at Vimy that symbolized Canada's dominion over that part of France: "I wonder did they grow? / Would their branches wave in that alien breeze, / For the sake of the ones below?"[17]

Because it had become, in a sense, a part of Canada, Vimy Ridge became a stock element in poetry marking the nation's birthday. For James Lewis Milligan, who wrote "Confederation Ode" for Dominion Day 1917, Canada was all about the successful union of the English and French races. Their enmity died in 1759, he wrote, and since then the two races had achieved remarkable things in North America. That they once again proved their unity at Vimy Ridge, won "by those who at the first far call / Fled the glad haunts of peace and Home, / Renounced their earthly all, / And never shall return across the severing foam," was something for future generations to celebrate. Sir Charles G.D. Roberts, who for decades had enjoyed fame, if not fortune, as Canada's greatest nationalist poet, drew the same meaning from Vimy Ridge. On the occasion of Canada's Diamond Jubilee in 1927, he revised a poem he had written in 1909, re-titling it "These Three Score Years." Roberts wondered whether the Canadians of younger generations had lived up to the promise of Canada's founders, but gleaned the answer from the fields of France and Flanders, particularly at Vimy Ridge:

…with what cheer,
And courage clear,
And high contempt of fear,
Embattled at the grim old Lion's side,
Our scarred battalions triumphed, laughed and died!

By succeeding where the troops of Canada's founding European nations had failed, the men of the Canadian Corps "live imperishable, and proclaim / Our manhood's stature to the world, their blood / A sacrament of glory." For Roberts, the religious and the nationalist went hand in hand; together, they made him feel more Canadian: "The patriot warmth within my bosom burning / …*Canadian* I am in blood and bone!"[18]

But no poet drew all of the themes together as completely as Charles Leonard Flick. Better known as the chronicler of the 31st British Columbia Horse, Flick used the occasion of Canada's seventieth birthday to publish a collection entitled *The Ballad of Vimy Ridge*, under the opaque pseudonym Leonard Fels-Charlick.[19] The title poem includes all of the elements that had then come to define the poetry of Vimy Ridge. The preparations for battle emphasize the religious, as the "white robed padre comes / Cheery smiling and alert toward the flag-decked drums; / Freedom's flag for altar-cloth; doffed the caps of steel; / Homage to the Lord of Hosts." But the spiritual importance was magnified by the day: "Red the dawn of Easter morn, loud the anthems ring, / Telling saint and sinner, too, 'Risen is the King.'" On that Easter Monday, the resurrection of the fallen was assured; "the souls of heroes [would] rise to salute their Lord." But the spiritual segued smoothly into the temporal as each division of the Canadian Corps came in for special mention:

> *Runs the Teuton while he may (Torch is in the thatch);*
> *Faster speed the men who wear honoured 'old red patch.'*
> *Far across the Arras road, almost to Thelus,*
> *Charge the men who wear with pride 'shoulder patch o' blue' …*
> *Noonday sees a glint of sun thro' the sleet and rain*
> *As the Third Division men storm Folie Wood amain.*
> *North, by Souchez's bloody stream, war is sternly dour;*
> *Brunt of fight for Vimy height fronts Division Four.*

However, it was not just individual divisions that stormed the ridge: it was the nation itself. This, for Flick, was the real story of Vimy Ridge:

> *Flash the slogan from Lorette north to far Calais*
> *'For your homes and Canada, play the man to-day.'*
> *Stabbing flash from single gun cuts the snowy gloom;*
> *Hark! A war-cry on the gale. 'Canada, charge home.'*

On 26 July 1936, not long after Flick's poem was published, thousands of veterans, relatives of the fallen, dignitaries, and curious locals clustered around the Vimy Memorial for the official unveiling. One of the speakers that day was Ernest Lapointe, the federal minister of justice and Prime Minister Mackenzie King's Quebec lieutenant. Lapointe began by reflecting that the union of France and Britain, "two races who preserve faithfully the ideals of social progress and democratic liberty," had produced in North America a hybrid nation that might eventually surpass its parents. But in Lapointe's view, the Vimy Memorial stood for more than just the meeting of two races; it represented the pinnacle of Canada's achievements in its first seventy years and proclaimed that "in their hour of testing the souls of Canadians revealed themselves gloriously at the summit of their national ascendancy."[20]

The notion that in reaching the summit of Vimy Ridge the men of the Canadian Corps were also taking the country to the summit of its national ascendancy did not originate with Lapointe. On the contrary, it had become the conventional wisdom by 1936 and underpinned virtually everything that was written about the battle, in novels, text books, newspaper editorials, sermons, unit histories and memoirs. When Ernest Lapointe articulated the meaning of Vimy to the crowds clustered before him, he was telling them something that most of them already knew.

Now, close to a century after the battle, it is impossible to say precisely where the idea of Vimy Ridge as the crucible of the Canadian nation was born. But it may well have originated with a legion of poets who, when they read of the great victory in their newspaper, immediately took up pen and paper to celebrate the triumph in verse. Perhaps it was they who transformed Vimy Ridge from a little known crease of land into what the poet and machine gunner Ralf Sheldon-Williams called a name "like a trumpet."[21]

Notes

1   *Edmonton Journal*, 10 April 1917, 1; *L'Acadien* [Moncton, NB], 13 April 1917, 1; *Toronto Daily Star*, 10 April 1917, 1.
2   For one study of battle poetry, see J. Timothy Lovelace, *The Artistry and Tradition of Tennyson's Battle Poetry* (New York: Routledge, 2003).
3   For one textbook that relied on war poetry, see J.E. Wetherell, *The Great War in Verse and Prose* (Toronto: The King's Printer, 1919).
4   Robert Frost, 'To E.T.,' in *New Hampshire* (New York: Henry Holt, 1923). The poem was originally published in *The Yale Review* in April 1920. Also killed at Vimy that day was another celebrated British poet, Robert G. Vernède.
5   Phil H. Moore, 'To The War Poets,' in *Rossignol Rhymes* (White Point Beach, NS: Rossignol Press, 1931), 55.
6   R.M. Eassie, "Battlefield Limericks," in *Odes to Trifles and Other Rhymes* (Toronto: S.B. Gundy, 1917), 104; James Manning, "Our Laddie," *Acadia*

Bulletin vol 7, no 2 (March 1918), 1. The poem was originally published in the Montreal *Standard* on 23 February 1918.

7 M. Smith, "Our Boys—They Lie!" in *Rhymes of the Times: Being Reprints from the Issues of The Times, Fort Frances, Ont., 1917-1930* (Fort Frances: *The Times*, 1931), 12; Kim Beattie, "After Vimy," in *"And You!"* (Toronto: Macmillan, 1929), 56; T.A. Browne, "Canada: To the Veterans of the Great War," in *The Belgian Mother and Ballads of Battle Time* (Toronto: Macmillan, 1917), v; "Lads' Laughter (A Revery of Vimy Revisited)," file 70, box 9, J.D. Logan Papers, Acadia University Archives.

8 Private E.H. McKinnon, "Vimy Ridge," *Watford Star*, 23 August 1917, 8; Walter Brindle, "Vimy," in *France and Flanders: Four Years' Experience Told in Poem and Story* (St. John: S.K. Smith, 1919), 45-47; T.A. Girling, "Far Away," *Canada in Khaki*, vol 2 (1917), 6.

9 D.M. Matheson, "Vimy Ridge," in *Chebucto and Other Poems* (Halifax: privately published, 1917), 27-29; J.D. Logan, "Night—Harmonies on Vimy (For Remembrance of April 9, 1917)," box 9, file 70, Logan Papers; Annie Marion MacLean, "Our Canadian Soldiers," in *Acadia Bulletin* vol 6, no 10 (December 1917), 1.

10 Thomas O'Hagan, "At Vimy Ridge," in *The Collected Poems of Thomas O'Hagan* (Toronto: McClelland & Stewart, 1922), 99; C.R.E., "Vimy, 1917," *Queen's Quarterly* vol 27, no 1 (July-September 1919), 396.

11 C.L. de Roode, "Vimy," in *Victoire!* (Montreal: A.P. Pigeon, 1919), 33; Dorothy Sproule, "The Vimy Pilgrimage," in *Bread and Roses* (Montreal: Woodward Press, 1937), 24.

12 Anna Durie, "Vimy Ridge, April 9, 1917," in *Our Absent Hero: Poems in Loving Memory of Captain William Arthur Peel Durie, 58th Battalion, C.E.F.* (Toronto: Ryerson Press, 1920), 6-11; Veronica Cusack, *The Invisible Soldier: Captain W.A.P. Durie, His Life and Afterlife* (Toronto: McClelland and Stewart, 2004).

13 H.C. Mason, "County Battalion" in *These Things Only* (Toronto: Thomas Nelson & Sons, n.d.), 5; John Daniel Logan, "The O.C.s, 85th Battalion," in *The New Apocalypse and Other Poems of Days and Deeds in France* (Halifax: T.C. Allen, 1919), 62. The line refers to three of the unit's commanders" Lieutenant-Colonels A.H. Borden, E.C. Phinney, and J.L. Ralston.

14 Esther Kerry, "The Return of the 13th and 14th," in *He Is A Canadian and Other Poems* (Montreal: Regal Press, 1919), 28-29; De Roode, "Le Triomphe!," in *Victoire!*, 8-9.

15 Corporal Adelard Audette, "The Battle of Vimy Ridge," in *A Few Verses and A Brief History of the Canadians on the Somme and Vimy Ridge in the World War, 1914-1918* (privately published, 1919), 28; Caroline Eleanor Wilkinson, "The Unforgotten," in *Poems That Appeal* (Niagara Falls, ON: F.H. Leslie Ltd., 1928), 24-25.

16 Alfred Gordon, "Canada to England: Vimy Ridge 1917," in *"Vimy Ridge" and New Poems* (Toronto: J.M. Dent & Sons, 1918), 1-5; Wilmot B. Lane, "Vimy (April 9th, 1917)," in *Quinte Songs and Sonnets* (Toronto: Ryerson Press, 1925), 85.

17 T.D.J. Farmer, "Accomplishment Not Years: Lines Suggested on the Proposed Purchase by Canada of Vimy Ridge," in *A History of the Parish of St. John's, Ancaster* (Guelph: Gummer Press, 1924), 254-55; J.M. Smith, "The Maple Trees at Vimy," in *Rhymes of the Times*, 38.

18 James Lewis Milligan, "Confederation Ode," in *The Beckoning Skyline and Other Poems* (Toronto: McClelland & Stewart, 1920), 93-95; Sir Charles G.D. Roberts, "These Three Score Years (An Ode for Canada's Diamond Jubilee)," in Desmond Pacey, (ed), *The Collected Poems of Sir Charles G.D. Roberts* (Wolfville, NS: Wombat Press, 1985), 315-17. The poem first appeared in the Montreal *Daily Star* on 30 June 1927.

19 C.L. Flick, *A Short History of the 31st British Columbia Horse* (Victoria: J. Parker Buckler, 1922); Leonard Fels-Charlick, "Vimy Ridge," in *The Ballad of Vimy Ridge* (Dawlish: Channing Press, 1937), 14-17.

20 Quoted in W.W. Murray (ed), *The Epic of Vimy* (Ottawa: The Legionary, 1936), 94.

21 R.F.L. Sheldon-Williams, "Names Like Trumpets," in *Names Like Trumpets and Other Poems* (privately published, 1918). Sheldon-Williams finished the war as a sergeant with the 10th Canadian Machine Gun Company.

16

"After the Agony in Stony Places"[1]
The Meaning and Significance of the Vimy Monument

JACQUELINE HUCKER

This is not a statue on a pedestal, the conventional form of public monument. It is a memorial to no man, but a memorial for a nation.
— The Canadian Battlefields Memorials Commission,
Canadian Battlefield Memorials, 1929

One day in 1921, while seated in a Toronto park, the sculptor Walter Allward pulled out an old envelope and started to draw. On one side he sketched a pylon and on the other side a second. He then folded the envelope and joined the two pylons with a line across their bases. He called one Canada and one France, the two countries joined together by the spirit of sacrifice.[2] Thus the idea for what was to become Canada's first national war memorial was born.

Between 1914 and 1918, one million soldiers died in Europe fighting for Britain and her Allies. For its part Canada lost 66,000 men, of whom more than one quarter were never found and have no known grave. The British architectural historian, Gavin Stamp, has observed that it was the role of the artist to put into tangible form the sense of loss felt by those who survived the war.[3] In recounting his story of the sketch in the park, Allward might well have added that, as was the case with so many who lived through that war, he had been haunted by a deep obligation never to forget the sacrifice of those Canadians who had lost their lives in it.

Rising above the Douai Plain, Allward's memorial has been an integral part of Vimy Ridge for more than eighty years. It commemorates both the taking of the ridge by the Canadian Corps on 9-12 April 1917 and Canada's military contributions in the First World War. But the monument also speaks to broader issues—to the nature of war and sacrifice, to mourning and melancholy and ultimately to hope for the future. In so doing the Vimy Monument transcends the battle. It expresses the enormous impact of wars and it stands as an enduring image of the Great War.

This essay will briefly trace the history of Canada's commemorative activity following the First World War and describe key events in the fifteen years that it took to create the monument and the surrounding memorial park. It will also highlight the creative forces behind the development and construction of this unique memorial.[4]

Prior to the First World War there were few British or Canadian precedents for national war memorials. Monuments celebrated the achievements of particular regiments or notable military leaders, but there were almost none standing as testament to the accomplishments and sacrifice of all the participants. Nevertheless, as wars grew in scale and were increasingly fought by citizen soldiers rather than professionals, popular concern for the fate of the individual soldier steadily increased. Faced with the horrendous carnage of the First World War that was felt in virtually every town and village, governments came to see that some way must be found to recognize each life lost.[5]

The construction of the Vimy Monument was, however, far from a straightforward exercise. In February 1919, the Battle Exploits Memorials Committee was formed in Britain with a mandate to identify and name the principal battles and to allocate the sites to the appropriate countries. Canada's committee representative, Brigadier-General H. T. Hughes, applied for eight memorial sites based upon the recommendations of a meeting of Canadian military officers presided over by General Sir Arthur Currie, the Canadian Corps commander. Canada was awarded three battle sites in Belgium and five in France. A second committee advised on the erection of battle memorials on the Western Front where, as in the past, individual regiments had begun to erect their own monuments. The committee questioned this practice since regimental loyalty had had less meaning for the large numbers of civilian soldiers who had volunteered for duty during the war. To ensure that all who had served were given equal recognition, the Dominion governments chose to reserve their battle sites for monuments whose costs would be borne from public funds.[6]

Anticipating that Canada would erect monuments at each of the eight sites it had been awarded, Parliament voted funds for preliminary site work to clear the battlefields and build roads. Subsequent to its offer to Britain and its allies, Belgium donated land to Canada at the three selected sites in that country. In France, the Canadian government purchased land from private individuals at four of the sites, and the owner donated the fifth site. The tracts varied in size from one to 2.6 hectares.

In April 1920, a special committee of the House of Commons began considering how best to commemorate the eight Canadian battles that had been deemed worthy of special recognition. This task was subsequently transferred to the Canadian Battlefields Memorials Commission (CBMC) which was established by Order-in-Council on 2 September 1920 to oversee the erection of monuments. The CBMC, chaired by the Speaker of the House of Commons, engaged military personnel to carry out its work in France and Belgium under the supervision of Brigadier-General Hughes, who was a professional engineer as well as a military officer. Members of the CBMC decided that the best way to commemorate Canada's exploits was to erect eight monuments, but to designate one as the national monument. The members insisted that justice demanded that all the sites should be treated equally and that the designation to be conferred upon one among the eight was not intended to single out a particular battle site, but rather to ensure a structure whose size, design and placement would suitably commemorate Canada's achievements in the war. In December 1920 the Commission launched a juried competition that was open to all Canadian architects and sculptors.[7] The results were announced in October 1921, when Walter Allward's design for the national monument was selected from more than 100 entries.[8]

Walter Allward was one of Canada's leading designers of public monuments, a feature which had become an important element in city planning by the early twentieth century. Although his formal artistic education was limited, Allward's natural talent was nurtured by several years apprenticing with a Toronto architectural firm. He had also benefited from a four-month sojourn in London and France. In the latter country he had an opportunity to study the work of Auguste Rodin, the new artistic giant who had created an art of self-expression that was to become a fundamental characteristic of twentieth-century art.[9]

Of Allward's early works, two in particular had marked him out as one of Canada's significant new artists: the monument to the South African War (1903-10) and the Bell memorial in Brantford, Ontario, which he designed in 1909 and completed in 1917. The first was planned as the focal point at the end of the new University Avenue uniting Queen's Park with Toronto's downtown. It was a lively composition of allegorical and contemporary figures arranged at the base of a seventy-foot (twenty-one metre) granite column and crowned by an elegant angel of victory.[10] This monument, paid for by public subscription, captured the spontaneous pride in Canada's first overseas military engagement.[11] The Bell structure revealed Allward's compositional creativity. He dispensed with the traditional base, replacing it with a low, wide form to reflect the distances traversed by the new invention, the telephone. The Bell memorial also eliminated the traditional barrier between the monument and the spectator. Allward combined these compositional innovations with a figurative style that revealed his profound respect for the art of classical Greece and the Renaissance.[12] It was a combination that Allward was to repeat to great effect in his design for a national war memorial.

Shortly after winning the architectural competition, Allward explained that the inspiration for the monument had come to him in an extraordinary dream that revealed a profound need to express in stone the anxieties of those who had lived through the war.

> When things were at their blackest in France, I dreamed that I was in a great battlefield. I saw our men going by in thousands and being mowed down by the sickles of death...Suffering beyond endurance at the sight, I turned my eyes and found myself looking down on an avenue of poplars. Suddenly through the avenue I saw thousands marching to the aid of our armies. They were the dead. They rose in masses, filed silently by and entered the fight to aid the living. So vivid was this impression, that when I awoke it stayed with me for months. Without the dead we were helpless. So I have tried to show this in this monument to Canada's fallen, what we owed them and will forever owe them.[13]

In disclosing the contents of his dream as he struggled to create a monument that could transcend the event and bring solace to the bereaved, Allward evoked emotions that were to preoccupy a generation of artists who lived through the war.

Allward conceived his monument as a simple but powerful form which would function both as a formidable presence in the sweeping landscape of northern France, and as a timeless and moving mis en scène, achieved through the universal language of classicism. On a heavy base, planned to rise from the battleground and give the impression of an impregnable bastion, stood two groups of figures. These Allward identified as the "Defenders," one group representing the "Breaking of the Sword," and the other the "Sympathy of Canadians for the Helpless." They represented the ideals for which Canadians had given their lives. Their sacrifice was illustrated by an empty sarcophagus, placed directly on the battleground in front of the monument. Above this poignant symbol stood a figure deep in contemplation whom Allward identified as "Canada bereft" who mourns forever her fallen sons. Their sacrifice is depicted by allegorical figures representing the "Spirit of Sacrifice" and the "Passing of the Torch." Framed within two soaring pylons, these figures reach aloft to the highest point on the columns where, in his words, the "figures of Truth, Faith, Justice, Charity, Knowledge and Peace sing the Hymn of Peace." In contrast to earlier war memorials, the monument made no reference to victory. Instead it spoke to national and universal goals for good in the world. It also alluded to the ancient cyclical myth of death and resurrection.

One person who was particularly open to the message conveyed by Allward's planned monument was Prime Minister William Lyon Mackenzie King. After the decision in April 1922 to place Allward's monument on Hill 145,[14] the highest point on Vimy Ridge, King suggested that a large tract of land be preserved around the monument. King's diary entry for that day records his reason:

> I made a strong plea for conserving a tract of one or two square miles of Vimy ridge as consecrated hallowed ground around Allward's memorial to be erected. The real memorial being the ridge itself, one of earth's altars, on which Canadians sacrificed for the cause of humanity...This is Canada's altar on European soil.[15]

The religious imagery held a wide appeal. For those who had experienced the Western Front, the landscape had become a metaphor for death. And for those who sought meaning in the aftermath of the carnage, the land had assumed a sacred identity, transformed by the sacrifice of those who had died.[16] In the case of Vimy Ridge, the imagery had an additional impact on the imagination because the Canadian assault on 9-12 April 1917 had followed the three days of Easter. Preserving part of a battlefield as a memorial park had no European precedent, but Parliament quickly threw its full support behind the idea.

While the plan continued to place Allward's monument on Vimy Ridge and to preserve part of the battlefield as a memorial park, the task of reburying the dead had begun. Responsibility for recovering the bodies, identifying them and giving them a proper burial fell to the Imperial War Graves Commission (IWGC). To this end, the IWGC formulated three guiding principles: the memorials should be permanent; the headstones should be uniform; and there should be no distinction made on account of military or civil rank.[17] These principles were first applied to the identified and located dead, but almost half a million soldiers who had fought for Britain and her allies, including 18,000 Canadians, were registered as missing with no known grave. Believing that the missing dead were as entitled to remembrance as those deceased whose identities were known,[18] the Commission concluded that the most appropriate way of honouring the memory of the missing would be to engrave their names on specially designed monuments. This too was an innovation of the First World War, perhaps indicative of a "modern anxiety of erasure" which signaled a loss of faith in traditional forms of commemoration.[19]

Shortly after Allward's monument won Canada's national architectural competition, the IWGC raised the issue of how best to commemorate missing Canadian soldiers. The Canadian government agreed that the names of the 6,940 missing Canadians who fell in Belgium were to be carved onto the Menin Gate at Ypres, a magnificent memorial arch erected by the IWGC to commemorate the contribution of all the countries of the British Empire. Across the walls of the Vimy Memorial were to be carved the names of the 11,285 missing Canadians who fell in France.[20] The Vimy Monument would thus serve three purposes: it would mark the site of the battle of Vimy Ridge, become this country's principal monument in Europe honouring the valour of all Canadians who fought in the First World War, and serve as testament to those Canadians who lost their lives in France and whose bodies were never identified.

In preparation for the construction of the monument, a Canadian military officer surveyed a parcel of land on Vimy Ridge in August 1922.[21] His intention was to secure a tract extending north/south along the edge of the ridge and sufficiently wide to include a length of the Canadian front line as of 9 April 1917, as well as sections of the Zwischen Stellung, a system of German trenches. Purchasing such a tract of land would have been a long and difficult affair but, fortuitously, the French government had singled out the land for acquisition with a view to its reforestation. Canadian representatives quickly said that a donation of the land by France would be an ideal solution. Negotiations through the summer of 1922 led to an agreement, finalized on 5 December 1922. The terms dictated that France would acquire the land and hold it in perpetuity for the use of the Canadian people to erect a monument and create a park. Parliament "gratefully accepted" France's gift of the memorial site in February 1923. Articles I and II of the Franco/Canadian agreement confirmed the intent of the land transfer:

> The French Government grants, freely and for all time, to the Government of Canada the free use of a parcel of 100 hectares located on Vimy ridge in the Department of Pas-de-Calais, the boundaries of which are indicated on the plan annexed to the Agreement...

> The Canadian Government pledge themselves to lay out this land into a park and to erect thereon a monument to the memory of the Canadian soldiers who died on the field of honour in France during the war 1914-18. The area is about 107 hectares...which the government of Canada

has decided to utilize as follows—10 hectares for the monument and approaches and 97 hectares to be planted with trees.[22]

In his response to the prime minister's announcement of the agreement in the House of Commons, Opposition leader Arthur Meighen noted the symbiotic relationship between war and death:

> The site of Vimy is beyond comparison, of the various battlefields of the war, the most closely associated in the hearts of the Canadian people with all that the war involved in story and in sacrifice.[23]

The practical challenges which were to confront those responsible for creating the monument on Hill 145 were many, for if Vimy Ridge possessed metaphysical qualities for Canada, it was in reality a barren stretch of land. The area chosen for the site of the monument had been mercilessly pounded by artillery for three weeks prior to the April 1917 assault and was in a terrible condition, pitted underfoot with deep dugouts, mine craters, trenches and shell holes.

The initial task was to select the precise location for the monument. Once the France/Canada agreement had been signed, Allward left for Europe to survey the area. He chose a site on the edge of the ridge, where the monument would look out over the Douai Plain. To create an impression of a structure rising out of the ridge, rather than lodged on it, Allward decided that the ground in front of the monument should be deeply excavated. In addition, because the monument would now be facing away from the planned approach to the memorial park, Allward needed to adjust his design so that it could be approached from two sides.

With the site selected, work began on a road to link the park to the main Lens-Arras road. It took thirty months to complete. Unexploded ordnance made this task dangerous and slow. Next, the ground under the foundations was excavated to a depth of eight metres. Under Allward's close supervision, the excavation work later fanned out in front of the monument for a distance of ninety-one metres to create the appearance of an open-air amphitheatre.

Walter Allward involved himself in every aspect of the monument's construction. When the structural engineering company employed by the CBMC to design the reinforced concrete foundations was unable to meet the requirements of the task, Allward personally sought out Oscar Faber, a young highly skilled civil engineer working in Britain, who had recently completed the structural design for the Menin Gate memorial at Ypres. Faber was subsequently contracted to prepare new structural plans for the monument and supervise the foundation work. Allward spent another year inspecting quarries across Europe, Britain and North America searching for the perfect material. He insisted upon a warm white stone with a texture that was both workable and durable enough to permit the narrowest of joints so that the monument would appear in the landscape as a monolithic, impregnable bastion. The task of finding the ideal stone was complicated by Allward's insistence that the figure groups would have to be carved from blocks no less than two metres in depth, and the figure of "Canada bereft" out of a single flawless block four metres high.

It was no easy task to acquire fine quality stone in war-torn Europe, but Allward eventually found what he was looking for in a quarry near Split, in present-day Croatia. The same quarry had furnished stone in the third century for Roman emperor Diocletian's palace, a fact that Allward took as evidence of the stone's durability. Known as Seget, it is a warm limestone with a narrow colour range, a fine uniform grain and a texture that was sufficiently hard to give fine joints yet perfect for carving. But the stone was difficult to quarry and ship to France. Not until 1927 did the first shipment arrive at Vimy Ridge.

Awaiting delivery of the stone, Captain Unwin Simson, the military engineer in charge of the daily activities at the site, had noticed that surviving features of the front line were gradually disappearing. Overseeing workers with time on their hands, he decided to preserve a short piece of the trenches and reopen part of the Grange tunnel. This involved rebuilding the sandbagged walls and duck boards, adding a new concreted entrance, then excavating a stretch of the tunnel and installing electric lighting.[24]

Once the stone had arrived, Allward urged that a noted Italian stone carver named Luigi Rigamonti be hired to carve the figure of "Canada bereft" as well as some of the other principal pieces. The large block for this figure was delivered in 1931. Allward then installed himself at the site to oversee the remainder of the work, including the exacting task of inscribing the names of the missing 11,285 on to the monument's walls. This work began in the early 1930s, using a typeface designed by Allward specifically for the purpose.

As construction difficulties multiplied and delays increased, Allward was inevitably pressured to lower his standards and accept stones and finishes that were less than perfect. To these demands he presented an inflexible front. Allward's courage and determination ensured the extraordinary quality of the resulting monument.[25]

* * *

A reforestation scheme commenced in 1925 by the French department of Agriculture was part of a long tradition of returning battle sites to their normal state. The planting program was to cover approximately ninety percent of the park, leaving ten percent as open land around the monument. By 1927, Brigadier-General Hughes was able to report to the CBMC that almost one million three-year-old Austrian pines were growing there.

The forest played a significant role in establishing the vocabulary and character of the memorial park. The trees returned life to the bruised and battered landscape, and the Canadian maples planted along the main approach road offered reminders of home. As Arthur Meighen observed in 1921, at the unveiling of the Cross of Sacrifice in the nearby Thélus cemetery, "around and all over are being planted the Maples of Canada in the thought that her sons will rest better under the trees which they know so well." It is an understandable (albeit incorrect) belief dating from the earliest years that a tree was planted for every Canadian who died on the ridge.

The trees also unified the memorial park and established a sense of order over the land. They framed the monument without encroaching on its dominant position on top of the ridge. The forest also touched and framed the two cemeteries in the park: Canadian Cemetery No. 2 and the Givenchy Road cemetery. Two broad allées permitted distant views of the monument. A third allée was run across the lower end of the site to create a visual and physical connection between the cemeteries below the ridge and the monument above.

Allied to the significance of the trees was the real and symbolic power of sunlight. The regenerative quality of heavenly light was a part of the symbolic meaning of Allward's monument. Acknowledging that the medieval French cathedral had served as a source of inspiration for its architectonic form, he drew attention to the fact that, "In the afternoon when a shaft of sunlight will break through the space between the pylons and illuminate part of the sculptures [it] will suggest a cathedral effect."[26] Thus, sunlight took on a metaphysical quality as it passed through the pylons and touched the central allegorical figures he called "The Spirit of Sacrifice."

War memorials are created not for the dead, but for the living. The Vimy Monument and its memorial park were completed just in time for the unveiling ceremony on 26 July 1936. More than 3,000 Canadians crossed the Atlantic to participate in the ceremonies. Many had fought in the war; many had lost loved ones there. With their arrival at the site, the full intent of the Vimy Monument was realized. For the ceremony itself, the veterans stood in pride of place in the amphitheatre while family members watched from its sloping sides. Standing on the monument with its wide views across the former battlegrounds, the spectators became actors in the monument's mise en scène. They doubtless found comfort in its meaning that would have been reinforced by the site of the regenerated landscape around them. As he unveiled the figure of "Canada bereft," King Edward VIII alluded to such sentiments:

> It is one of the consolations which time brings that the deeds of valour done on those battlefields long survive the quarrels which drove the opposing hosts to conflict. Vimy will be one such name. Already the scars of war have well-nigh vanished from the fair landscape beneath us. Around us here today there is peace and rebuilding of hope. And so also in dedicating this memorial to our fallen comrades our thoughts turn rather to the splendour of their sacrifice, and to the consecration of our love for them, than to the cannonade, which beat upon this ridge a score of years ago.[27]

By the time the Vimy Monument was dedicated in 1936, Allward had spent the best years of his professional life overseeing its construction. Ironically, in his desire to create a work that would last forever, he had chosen a new but flawed method of construction, cast concrete covered with stone. Specifically, he did not consider the way these materials shifted over time, nor did he leave sufficient space between the blocks of stone. In the years after its construction, water infiltrated the structure, staining the stone and causing it to crumble. As the stones darkened and deteriorated, many of the 11,285 names began to fade. Recognizing the need for remedial action, the Government of Canada in May 2001 established the Canadian Battlefield Memorials Restoration Project with a mandate to restore the Vimy Monument to its former state and improve the landscaping around it.[28]

Restoration work began in December 2004. It was a massive undertaking, involving the dismantling and rebuilding of almost all the vertical wall surfaces around the base of the monument. New stone was shipped from Croatia and extreme care ensured that the newly engraved letters perfectly matched the original names. As in the 1920s, the government engaged an expert international team of architects, engineers, artisans and builders from France, Canada and Belgium. Inspired by Allward's perfecting standards, the restoration serves as evidence of a new generation's determination never to forget Canada's contribution and sacrifice in the First World War.

Notes

1 T.S. Eliot, *The Waste Land*, 1922.
2 Colonel D. C. Unwin Simson, "Little Known Facts and Difficulties In the Construction of the Canadian Memorial on Vimy Ridge And Other Memorials in France And Belgium," unpublished, undated document in the archives of Veterans Affairs Canada, Charlottetown, P.E.I.
3 Gavin Stamp, *Silent Cities: An Exhibition of the Memorial and Cemetery Architecture of the Great War* (London: The Royal Institute of British Architects, 1977), 3.
4 The interpretation of the Vimy Monument in this chapter has benefited from the following works by historians and architectural historians of the First World War: Paul Fussell, *The Great War and Living Memory* (Oxford: Oxford University Press, 1975); Samuel Hynes, *A War Imagined: The First World War and English Culture* (New York: Atheneum, 1991); Gavin Stamp, *Silent Cities*, (1977); Jay Winter, *Sites of Memory, Sites of Mourning: The Great War in European Cultural History* (Cambridge: Cambridge University Press, 1990).
5 Stamp, 6.
6 "Report of the Committee of the Privy Council approved by His Excellency the Governor General on the 3rd December, 1920," vol 1, DHS 7-10, vol 1751, Record Group [RG] 24, Library and Archives Canada (LAC).
7 Ibid. The three-person jury consisted of Professor Charles H. Reilly of the architecture department, Liverpool University, Paul Cret, a leading French architect and chosen designer of the American national monument in France, and Frank Darling, representing the Royal Canadian Architectural Institute.
8 "Conditions of Competition in Design and Eight Memorial Monuments to be Erected in France and Belgium," issued 20 December 1920, vol 335, RG25, LAC. The second competition winner was Frederick Chapman Clemesha, whose Brooding Soldier monument was erected at the Saint-Julien site, near Ypres.
9 Alexandra Mosquin, "Walter Seymour Allward," Submission Report, National Historic Sites and Monuments Board of Canada, 2001, 5.
10 Ibid, 4-7.
11 Katherine Hale, "Walter S. Allward, Sculptor," *The Canadian Magazine* (1919), 787.
12 Moskin, 9.
13 "Vimy Clippings," box 2, 5055, Allward Fonds, Queen's University Archives (QUA).
14 The jury for the architectural competition had recommended that Allward's monument be placed on Hill 62, near Ypres.
15 W.L.M. King Diaries, 26 April 1922, LAC.
16 Jonathan F. Vance, *Death So Noble: Memory, Meaning and the First World War* (Vancouver: University of British Columbia Press, 1997), 56.

17 Information on the Imperial War Graves Commission has been taken from Fabian Ware, *The Immortal Heritage: An Account of the Work and Policy of the Imperial War Graves Commission during twenty years, 1917-1937* (Cambridge: Cambridge University Press, 1937), 29-30.

18 Philip Longworth, *The Unending Vigil: A History of the Commonwealth War Graves Commission, 1917-1967* (London: Constable, 1967), 43.

19 Thomas Laqueur, "The Past's Past," *New York Review of Books* vol 18, no 18 (9 September 1996), 4.

20 Minutes of Proceedings of the Canadian Battlefields Memorials Commission, documents on file at the Department of Veterans Affairs, Charlottetown, PEI .

21 Ross to MacNaughton, 14 September 1922, vol 1, DHS 7-10, vol 1751, RG 24.

22 "Agreement between Canada and France for the cession to Canada of the free use of a parcel of land on Vimy ridge for the erection of a monument to the memory of the Canadian Soldiers who died on the field of honour in France in the course of the War 1914-1918," agreement on file in the Legal Advisory Division, Foreign Affairs Canada.

23 "Vimy Ridge Monument: France's Gift of Memorial Site Gratefully Accepted," House of Commons, Debates, CLV (1923), 4 February 1923, 183.

24 This was done in part to make these spaces safe for the several hundreds of visitors who had been coming to the site since the cessation of hostilities.

25 H.C. Osborne, "Allward of Vimy," *Saturday Night*, April 1937.

26 "Professional Career, Vimy Correspondence 1926" Allward to André Ventre, architecte en chef des monuments historiques, 12 April 1926," 5055, Allward Fonds.

27 W.W. Murray, *The Epic of Vimy* (Ottawa: The Legionary, 1936), 96-97.

28 The mandate of the Canadian Battlefield Memorials Restoration Project also includes the restoration of twelve other Canadian memorials in France and Belgium.

17

Safeguarding Sanctity
Canada and the Vimy Memorial during the Second World War

SERGE DURFLINGER

> This memorial is not a monument to the capture of Vimy Ridge
> only...it is a memorial to a nation.
> — Lieutenant-Colonel D.C. Unwin Simson

When the Second World War broke out in 1939, the Vimy Memorial was barely three years old, but it had already emerged as a powerful site of national memory for Canadians. With its sheer size, powerfully emotive statuary and dominating location atop Vimy Ridge, the memorial also encapsulated the linked notions of postwar collective commemoration, remembrance and mourning. For Canadians seeking a powerful symbol of the country's First World War achievements and losses, Vimy became hallowed ground, sacred to the memory of the fallen but representing also the very essence of the emerging Canadian nation. Rumours of the memorial's destruction when France fell in 1940 outraged Canadians, stimulated war consciousness and instilled visceral anger towards the enemy. Concern for the memorial's condition lasted throughout the war. When British troops liberated Vimy Ridge in the fall of 1944, the venerated site was immediately reclaimed by Canada through a series of high-level Canadian military and diplomatic visits.

The Vimy Memorial was officially unveiled in July 1936. Sculptor Walter S. Allward's masterpiece formed the showpiece for an elaborate ceremony which included speeches by King Edward VIII and French President Albert Lebrun, and was attended by a host of Canadian, French and British political, diplomatic, military and ecclesiastical dignitaries. Thousands of Canadian veterans and their families travelled to France for the ceremonies.[1] As an emotive commemorative site and a tourist attraction, the Vimy Memorial was an instant success. Its striking form, silhouetted atop the ridge and visible from many kilometres distant, made it a destination for thousands of visitors, admirers and those paying homage. The maintenance of the memorial and its grounds became the responsibility of a federal agency under the jurisdiction of the Department of National Defence (DND), the Canadian Battlefields Memorial Commission (CBMC), headed by Colonel H.C. Osborne. Major D.C. Unwin Simson, RCE, had served as the Canadian engineer through the memorial's construction and stayed on in nearby Arras with responsibilities for all of Canada's European war memorials.[2] By 1938, a resident custodian and caretaker, George Stubbs of Winnipeg, who had served in the Canadian Field Artillery during the war, had been hired and housed in a cottage at the Vimy site.

As the threat of conflict with Germany grew in the summer of 1939, Canadians looked with unease at the prospect of another war. In Vimy, the bases of the memorial's pylons and its sculptures were protected with sandbags.[3] There was not much else to do but await developments. Germany invaded Poland on 1 September 1939. Two days later Britain and France declared war on Germany. The remainder of the Commonwealth followed suit within the next week, Canada declaring war on 10 September. But following Poland's capitulation in early October, no German assault against France materialized and the belligerents settled down into a curious 'Phoney War.' Canada dispatched its first troops to Britain in December 1939 and the 1st Canadian Infantry Division, under the command of Major-General A.G.L. McNaughton, spent the winter and spring training in the United Kingdom.

In the meantime, the British Expeditionary Force (BEF) had been sent to northern France and was responsible for the Arras sector that included Vimy. Shortly after his arrival, McNaughton, a Vimy veteran, toured the British front lines. His became the first of several often poignant wartime visits to Vimy by senior Canadian military and diplomatic officials and politicians. Such visits established the Vimy Ridge memorial and surrounding historic park as an important site of official and public Canadian commemoration. On 1 May 1940, Defence Minister Norman Rogers visited the memorial with Canada's High Commissioner to Britain, Vincent Massey and Brigadier-General H.D.G. Crerar from Canadian Military Headquarters in London. Rogers had fought at Vimy Ridge with the Canadian Mounted Rifles. George Stubbs conducted a tour of the extensive site that Massey well recounted in his memoirs. The Canadian party drove from Arras to Vimy "so that Norman Rogers could see the great Canadian monument, which looked most impressive in the morning mist. I remembered that I had said when it was dedicated four years before that the memorials of the last war might well prove the victims of the next."[4] Most of the high-profile Canadian visitors held some connection to the battle or the memorial and the site impressed them on a solemn personal level and as a symbol of Canada. In its coverage of these visits, the Canadian press almost always emphasized Vimy's emotive connection that linked two generations of Canadian fighting men.

The site's peace was soon broken. Just nine days after Rogers' visit, the Germans launched their massive assault against the Low Countries and France. The enormity of their success and the rapidity of their advance shocked the world. Within two weeks the entire Allied position on the continent was in serious jeopardy. Before the end of May the British decided to evacuate through Dunkirk whatever remnants of the BEF and French Army could escape encirclement in a shrinking pocket in northern France and southern Belgium. Vimy Ridge, the ground cherished by a generation of Canadians, had been yielded to the same enemy from which it had been wrested twenty-three years previously.

In those dark days, the fate of the Vimy Memorial became in the Canadian press a focus of anxiety, anger and uncertainty. On 24 May 1940, the Ottawa *Evening Journal* carried a front-page article entitled, "Vimy Memorial Built with Idea Second War Might Engulf It." The memorial's originator and sculptor, Walter S. Allward, noted that even while he was designing the massive monument, he realized that the Arras area might again become a battlefield. "We couldn't help but think another war might come. So we carved the figures of stone instead of casting them in bronze—bronze figures might be melted down for munitions." The newspaper stated Allward was "convinced only the heaviest shelling or direct hits by heavy-calibre bombs could jar the two pylons…The shafts are built of structural steel and concrete, the outer stone casing being bolted in place with bronze staples." While encouraging to a degree, the awesome destructive potential of modern war coupled with the Nazis' track record of moral disdain left some Canadians worrying about and speculating over the monument's future. Its possible destruction threatened to strike at Canada's heart.

On Saturday, 1 June 1940, the Montreal *Daily Star* published a vivid description of events said to be taking place at Vimy. Displaced to page four by the dramatic evacuation of Dunkirk, the *Daily Star* printed a wonderful photograph of the memorial to accompany the demonizing headlines, "Famous Memorial Blasted by Huns" and "Vimy Memorial Smashed by Nazi Bombers." "New heights in [the Germans'] deliberate fiendishness have been reached in Flanders Fields," wrote the outraged newspaper, "where Canada's great memorial on Vimy Ridge rises above the graves of Canadian heroes of the last war. German fliers smashed this beautiful remembrance to bits. Bombs tore dead Canadians from their graves." A British soldier was quoted as stating, "I…saw

German dive bombers swoop down and release a load of bombs over the memorial. It was completely shattered. The attack was obviously deliberate." There seemed little need to confirm the events. The *Daily Star* quoted Brigadier W.W. Foster, past-president of the Canadian Legion: "[T]his act will serve to strengthen this country's determination to carry this through to the end and vanquish a foe which would stoop to such useless destruction."[5]

Two days later a Canadian Press story describing the memorial's tragic desecration and destruction continued to receive prominence in Canadian newspapers. Accompanying a photo of Allward and beneath the headline, "Vimy Memorial Bombed: Sculptor Sad and Bitter," the *Globe and Mail* detailed the shocking, though unconfirmed news. Some British troops even were reported to have "walked over to the memorial after the German bombers left and picked up splinters as souvenirs."[6] Defence Minister Norman Rogers was quoted as stating that if the report was true, it "would only serve to strengthen the will to victory of the Canadian people." Canadians would seek to avenge not only Allied defeats in France but the grave insult to the nation's dead of an earlier conflict.

Allward's opinions were much in demand by the press. "Bitterness tinged the sadness with which sculptor Walter S. Allward received the news of the deliberate destruction by German bombers of his masterpiece on which he laboured fourteen years. 'The Huns have gone quite mad. This is a sad commentary on civilization.'" The *Globe and Mail* commented that for Allward, the report of the memorial's loss constituted "the destruction of a vision."[7]

On 3 June, the Montreal *Daily Star* ran an editorial on the memorial's destruction. By their actions at Vimy, it said, the Germans had shown a lack of "human dignity and decency" and they had proven to Canadians "with sickening certainty that the Hun is always the Hun...The news that...one of the greatest memorial works of art ever produced by man, a thing of such majestic beauty and significance that it belonged to no single nation but to the whole world, has been senselessly destroyed... does not altogether astonish us." The editorial ended with the words, "Such fiends are surely unfit to live."[8]

The sense of loss engendered by these reports, symbolic of the memorial's connection with Canadians, sparked violent, angry outbursts. Canadian veterans of the First World War were deeply offended by the reports of the memorial's destruction. The Vimy Pilgrimage four years earlier had been very much a Canadian Legion affair and the Nazis' alleged behaviour was taken personally. Commenting on the reported destruction of the Vimy Memorial, Alex Walker, Dominion president of the Legion, opined: "The hellish hordes of Germany apparently think that such senseless action will serve to undermine the morale and fighting spirit of the Allied and, more especially, the Canadian forces. They still have a perverted interpretation of our psychology. Nothing since the outbreak of the war has so helped to crystallize Canada's determination to fight to the finish as this maniacal wastage." Even more ironically, he pointed out, the memorial was never intended to symbolize the "gloating over a victory achieved twenty-three years ago...Although this sacred bit of land...has been desecrated, it shall be restored," he vowed. "Four years ago...we reaffirmed our loyalty to our 60,000 fallen comrades. Today, ex-Service men throughout the Dominion are crying for revenge against these German savages." The reported destruction of Allied military cemeteries constituted an act, Walker stated, which "God Himself will punish."[9]

But the reports of the monument's destruction were wrong. On 3 June the *Globe and Mail* printed an almost inconsequential article beneath the small headline: "Denied in Berlin." The item reported without comment: "An official statement tonight denied that German bombers damaged the towering Canadian war memorial at Vimy Ridge and described the report as Allied propaganda designed to whip up Canadian and American anger against Germany."[10] Clearer heads and less emotion dominated the next few days' reporting of the capture and alleged destruction of the memorial. A 4 June Canadian Press story from Toronto, not picked up in many larger English-language Canadian newspapers, but appearing in Montreal's *La Presse*, noted that official sources in Berlin stated that Adolf Hitler had visited the Vimy Memorial while touring the war zone. Photos of his visit were released "to refute Allied accusations that the Germans had destroyed the monument."[11] Few believed this at the time.

In fact, the Germans went out of their way to deny they destroyed the famous monument. On 2 June 1940 a large group of German military dignitaries approached the memorial. Adolf Hitler was among them. The Germans released a number of photographs showing Hitler inspecting the memorial and its grounds. The caption accompanying the photos read in part: "The Fuhrer on 2 June 1940 on Vimy Ridge. In the background, the Canadian Memorial of the First World War, 1914-18. According to English news, the memorial has been destroyed by 'German barbarians.' This picture is documentary proof that shows the impertinent lying of English propaganda. The Canadian Prime Minister, Mackenzie King, has denied this untrue British news."[12] While it is not known to which of the prime minister's utterances the Germans were referring (if any), the evidence seemed to prove that the monument was intact.

Ottawa, too, was greatly disturbed by the prospect that the Vimy Memorial was no more. On 3 June Prime Minister King sent an urgent telegram to Vincent Massey in London: "Please advise immediately whether any authentic information available regarding Vimy Memorial." Massey replied the same day: "Neither War Office nor Air Ministry have any significant information...Latter investigating."[13] The next day in the House of Commons, King wisely mentioned that "no word has been received which would confirm the report that the memorial had been destroyed."[14] Most of the summer passed before Canadians received any definite news.

On 1 August 1940, Toronto Conservative MP Tommy Church rose in the House to ask the question to which no doubt many Canadians sought an answer: "Has the government any information to give the House regarding the effect of the war on the Vimy Ridge monument? Has it been damaged or destroyed by Germany as yet, or has any report been received and, if so, will it be tabled?" James Layton Ralston, the new Defence minister since the death of Norman Rogers in June, replied by borrowing the words of Major Simson of the CBMC, who reported that "the ridge has been unfortunately the scene of very heavy fighting and...the monument must have received considerable damage. If it is possible I shall endeavour to obtain an aerial photograph to see the result."[15]

Wing Commander A.P. Campbell at Royal Canadian Air Force headquarters in London contacted the British Air Ministry the next day and was told that a photograph taken 23 May and studied by the RAF's Photographic Intelligence Unit showed the memorial to be undamaged. It is curious that Canadian officials had not received this information earlier, given several earlier Canadian appeals for news. The director of public relations at the Air Ministry, perhaps seeking propaganda value from the memorial's possible destruction, had insisted that its condition be investigated immediately.[16] However, it was not clear whether the Germans had been in full control of the area on 23 May and when exactly the purported eyewitnesses claimed to have seen the monument's destruction. The date of this photograph hardly made it compelling evidence. In any event, Massey duly informed King of the seemingly positive news, noting with some exaggeration that the photograph had been "recently taken." King then conveyed this information to the House of Commons.[17]

While Canadians awaited word of the monument's fate, numerous wartime public speeches, press accounts and publications referred to the famed 1917 battle and also to the memorial.[18] In a mere four years the monument had penetrated the national psyche. As one of the most celebrated events in Canadian history, the Battle of Vimy Ridge was an event for Canadians that bridged the Old World with the New and one era with another. It also seemed important to celebrate the Vimy victory when Allied fortunes were low. Vimy offered a symbol of hope, a view of the past that provided the country with pride and confidence during a bleak period in the war.

The veterans' community, too, was receptive to using the Vimy Memorial as an iconic tribute to Canadian feats of arms, past and anticipated. The sombre wartime mood and the sadness felt with the memorial in enemy hands increased its mythic and political value. In April 1942, as Canadians were preparing to vote in the national plebiscite on whether to release the government from its pledge that there would be no conscription for overseas service, an editorial about "Vimy Day" in The Legionary showed the political uses made of the memorial's situation:

> Vimy Day this year was not a celebration. The Victors of Vimy did not forget that the Ridge is once more in enemy hands, that their pals who 'went west' sleep in enemy-held soil. Yet, they know that Vimy can be retaken. It was done before by them; it can be done again by their successors. But only through the same audacious spirit of attack which swept Germany's finest troops off the Hill in 1917; only by the complete moral backing of a victory-inspired people at home will Vimy Ridge be redeemed by the new Canadian Corps. Let every Canadian remember Vimy when he goes to the polls on April 27.[19]

"Does the Vimy Memorial still stand? This is a question close to the heart of every Canadian," wrote the recently promoted Lieutenant-Colonel Simson in the January 1943 issue of the Canadian Geographical Journal. He was Canada's leading expert on the memorial and had stayed in Arras until the last, retreating with his family during the May 1940 German advance. At the time accredited to the Canadian High Commission in London, Simson encouraged Canadians to believe that the memorial still stood. "Ever since the evacuation of Dunkirk, stories have been circulating that the monument has been damaged. Some rumours even say that it has been razed to the ground. The thought of either arouses disgust because all will remember what care was taken in the conception of the work to avoid wounding the feelings of a foe."[20] Simson claimed that the reports of the monument's destruction "aroused world-wide anger and indignation" leading the German Ministry of Propaganda to "publish denials." He pointed out, however, that the photos of Hitler visiting the memorial provoked "fresh waves of indignation, particularly in Canada" and that these images could "easily be faked." Nevertheless, Simson firmly believed that the memorial still stood: "One of the most encouraging points now in favour of the memorial's survival...is that the foundations of the structure were so carefully built . . .Three hundred and fifty tons of heavy steel bars went into its building and many thousand tons of the finest cement." He continued: "There are no witnesses available for reports about shelling, but it seems improbable that this occurred because the Germans made such a rapid and successful advance over the Ridge in May 1940, that there was no necessity for continuous gunfire."[21] As an agent of the Canadian Battlefields Memorials Commission and the engineer who oversaw the erection of the monument, his wartime preoccupation with the fate of the memorial was both professional and keenly personal.

Simson juxtaposed earlier reports of the monument's bombing with the professional opinions of "six Canadian pilots who were questioned separately and independently." Some of these pilots had flown over the memorial and were familiar with its construction and location. All felt that the memorial would be an "extremely difficult target for a bomber at 10,000 feet under the best conditions and even for a dive bomber one of extreme difficulty." Moreover and perhaps most conclusively, Simson recounted a conversation he had had with a fighter pilot originally from Saskatchewan. In the summer of 1942 the pilot had evidently flown over the memorial, a location he knew well and which he sometimes used as a landmark. He had noticed from 10,000 feet that the setting sun created a shadow of the monument in which were plainly visible the two pylons. Yet correspondence between interned Canadian caretaker George Stubbs and his French wife, who lived near the memorial, "intimated that one of the pylons had been damaged." "All things considered, therefore," concluded Simson, "it seems certain that this memorial to Canada's greatness and the glory of her sons still stands. There is, moreover, good reason to believe that to-day it has not sustained damage too serious to repair."[22] Canadians could breathe easier.

* * *

"Our advance began at dawn...Our objective was the Vimy Ridge by Arras," states the regimental history of the Welsh Guards, a Second World War British armoured regiment. It "soon became apparent that the enemy was completely disorganized...We pushed on as fast as the [Cromwell] tanks would go...By early afternoon we had attained our objective and had begun mopping up operations in the area."[23] It was 1 September 1944. Vimy Ridge was again in Allied hands.

There was joy in Canada at the news. Some of Canada's most famous newspaper correspondents reported the important story of the memorial's safe recapture. The evening papers of Saturday, 2 September had only the earliest, briefest details. The Ottawa *Evening Journal* ran a front-page banner headline, "Vimy Ridge, Canada's Shrine, Captured." The accompanying photograph of the 1936 unveiling ceremony was captioned simply, "There is no indication of the present condition of the hallowed Canadian memorial." The article by Canadian war correspondent Ross Munro noted that, "news of the fall of Vimy Ridge, near Arras, was contained in a message from Lieutenant-General [Sir Miles] Dempsey, British [Second] Army Commander, to Lieutenant-General Crerar, leader of the First Canadian Army." Dempsey wrote, "Today you captured Dieppe and we captured Vimy Ridge—a great day for Canada in which the 2nd Army is glad to have played its part."[24]

On 4 September, the Ottawa *Evening Journal* published a lengthy front-page story filed by Munro under the headline, "Memorial on Vimy Ridge Stands Completely Undamaged."

Not a bomb nor a shell has fallen near it. I drove north along the Arras-Lens road to Vimy this morning [September 3] with two others—the first Canadians to visit the ridge since the fall of France. From three miles away we saw the memorial sparkling in the sunlight...There was a cathedral-like quiet. The new front mercifully passed by Vimy. The new war hadn't wrought its destruction on this hill of valour. The slopes around the monument were trim and neat...The only evidence of war was the scarred earth where a Bren gun carrier swung off the road and turned by the side of the monument. Some British soldiers passing by had stopped to look at Canada's magnificent memorial to her dead of another war...There was not even a chip in the memorial. It stands there as on the day it was unveiled in 1936...Weather hasn't soiled the white stone. The inscriptions and the names of Canada's dead carved in the base are sharp and clear...It seemed almost as if it had been swept and polished for this visit but it had been like this through four years of war. It made you intensely proud to see it standing there, a symbol of the gallantry and sacrifice of the last war and which might well become the same for this war.[25]

War correspondent Ralph Allen contributed a lengthy article to the *Globe and Mail* on 5 September. Like Munro's, this piece highlighted the fact that for Canadian and British soldiers (and correspondents) the memorial performed double duty as a solemn site of memory for a past war and as a powerful focal point of remembrance for those lost in the ongoing conflict. Perhaps the memorial spoke to the present more than it had at any time in its eight-year existence. Wrote Allen:

As the twin pylons of the gleaming white monument…merged in the blue morning sky, they might have been a finger raised for silence. And there was no sound except the laughter of the little girl who still sold postcards from the base of the great memorial and the faint growl of armed columns rolling forward again on the old road from Arras to Lens. The few soldiers who had time to make the detour through the winding avenue of young maple trees to the crest of the ridge climbed the stairs to the memorial's base with reverent footsteps and picked out the inscriptions in low, hushed voices…And, despite recurrent rumours that the Germans had wilfully destroyed the monument, it bore only two slight indistinguishable scars…The underground chapel in the monument's foundations was without light and the cross which used to stand above its altars was removed for safekeeping. There were a few faint smudges on the pylons but otherwise the monument looked no older or weather beaten than its eight years would have led you to expect.

Allen noted that the grass needed cutting, but had not yet "grown wild." The preserved trenches and dugouts were "eerily lonely, half hidden in the foliage of the encroaching young forest." Vimy Ridge, which had "already seen too much violence," had been "granted an amnesty."[26]

While Stubbs was held at the St. Denis internment camp near Paris, his French wife stayed in their cottage at the site, later moving to nearby Givenchy. She supported herself and her daughter, Simone, during the four years of occupation by selling souvenirs and postcards to visitors—mainly German soldiers. Mrs. Stubbs noted to *The Legionary*'s correspondent that, "all during the occupation German troops came to admire the giant memorial."[27] She claimed that the Germans had "respected the monument scrupulously, but [she] said that the behaviour of some of her own countrymen and countrywomen had been 'shocking'." Apparently, "in spite of all protests, several young men and women of the district made a habit of dancing on the stone base of the monument" accompanied by accordion music. More seriously, she blamed locals for breaking into the chapel and burning "a dozen wreaths that had been dropped on the monument by Allied aviators."[28] Nevertheless, Paul Piroson, Stubbs' Belgian assistant who had stayed on during the occupation and maintained the site, was less kindly disposed to the Germans' wartime presence. He recalled after the war that he had frequently cleaned up after disrespectful German soldiers who left behind litter, including beer bottles, following their visits to the site, often accompanied by their girlfriends.[29] Moreover, Simson later recalled that the Grange Tunnel suffered from the visits of German troops during the war and that some of the Canadians' fascinating wartime graffiti was deliberately "obliterated."[30]

The monument also seemed to become a site of resistance during the occupation. Mrs. Stubbs and some local villagers laid wreaths at the memorial each 11 November. The Germans did not object. Piroson later claimed that he had joined the French Resistance and that some of the Vimy tunnels were used to store arms. In June 1944, according to Piroson, the Germans blew up some tunnels, including the entrance to the Grange Tunnel, under suspicion that they held weapons caches. Before this, the Germans had looted most of the artifacts and equipment displayed in the tunnels.[31]

Canadian veterans were thrilled by the news of the liberation of Vimy. The October 1944 issue of *The Legionary* featured a striking cover photograph of Lieutenant-General H.D.G. Crerar visiting the memorial shortly after its recapture. "All over Canada veterans of the First Great War are rejoicing at the welcome news from overseas that Vimy Ridge has been captured…and that the great memorial…is safe," stated the article. The site had finally been released "from the clutches of the Hun."[32] Crerar spent thirty minutes at Vimy on 11 September 1944, landing in his Auster aircraft "on a strip of grass within a few hundred yards of the memorial." Crerar inspected the minor damage to the monument and chatted with the recently freed George Stubbs; both had been gunners during the great battle twenty-seven years previously. *The Legionary* stated of Crerar's visit, "It must have been a moving moment for him as he stood…before the monument built in honour of the memory of his old comrades-in-arms who were killed in action by the same unspeakable enemy more than a quarter century ago."[33] The Canadian ambassador to France, Georges Vanier and his wife visited Vimy on 24 September, accompanied by Simson. It was the latter's first return to the memorial since he had hastily departed in May 1940. Vanier agreed that "the memorial is in very good condition."[34] Vincent Massey, too, paid a visit "just after the retreating Germans had passed through…to see what damage, if any, had been done."[35]

Before the end of September 1944, Simson filed a detailed report assessing the state of the site. He found the monument in excellent condition.

> No material damage of any extent has been done. The foot of the figure of Sacrifice has the upper half of the large and two adjoining toes broken…In the crypt there was no sign of settlement or disturbance of the foundations. The names engraved on the walls are in good condition…The stone has weathered nicely. Drains have been kept clear. Electric light fittings, on the other hand, have all been removed… The reserve stone blocks are still buried intact in the ground. With the

exception of "only two small shell or bomb craters," the approach road was in excellent shape.

However, Simson, charged with restoring the monument to its former glory, noted that some 100 of the 650 maple trees on the site required replacing whereas the others were obviously in need of maintenance after four years of "neglect." The tunnels also needed "cleaning and repairing." The guardian's house was also a matter of concern, since the German troops quartered there had not left it in good condition. Simson felt the entire site could be returned to its original state for about $100,000.[36] During the occupation, Piroson had done what he could to keep the extensive lawns mowed and the numerous hedges trimmed, but the job had proved too much.[37]

After the Germans left the area, several of the former workers at the site "immediately returned and endeavoured to do their best in repairing some of the damage," wrote Simson. "At the present time," he continued, "the monument and site is a mecca for Canadian soldiers who come almost daily. Many are sons or relatives of those of 1914-18. With so many Canadian visitors, I considered it good policy to encourage [the workers] to stay on and help clean up the site, although I warned them I could not say if or when they would receive any pay." [38] Among the visitors was David Roger, then an RCAF medical officer attached to 410 Squadron. Stationed at Amiens and Lille, Roger visited the monument in November or December 1944 with several men from his squadron. Six decades later, he recalled the site as "very impressive," something which "meant a lot" to him and which he had "very much wanted to see." Some Mosquito fighter-bombers from his squadron even staged a dramatic fly-past of the memorial, a moment captured on a souvenir photograph distributed among some members of the squadron.[39]

Colonel D.E. Macintyre was a Vimy veteran and one of the Canadian Legion's organizers for the 1936 Vimy pilgrimage. In November 1944, he was in Ghent working for the Canadian Legion War Services. On Remembrance Day, he drove to Vimy, where he had not been since the official unveiling more than eight years before. In his truck he had loaded some canned food, cigarettes, chocolate bars and an army battledress for George Stubbs. In addition to Macintyre and a colleague, there were officers representing each of Canada's three services and seven or eight Canadian airmen on leave. A French military band led some 600 civilians to the steps at the base of the pylons. The local prefect gave a speech full of "passion and feeling" paying tribute to Canada's sacrifices in France during both world wars, and local children laid flowers at the base of the pylons. Wrote Macintyre, "[Five hundred] school children had attended the unveiling and...at that time I had expressed a hope that they would remember the Canadians with kindly feelings...and that they would care for the memorial and decorate it with flowers on suitable occasions. It was with deep satisfaction that I saw my wish come true."[40]

In April 1945 a military ceremony was held at the memorial. Georges Vanier laid a wreath on behalf of the Canadian people and government. The Canadian Army Educational Services—21 Army Group issued a booklet that briefly described the history of the site, the battle and the memorial. "To the Canadian, Vimy is a hallowed word—a word recalling a glorious achievement and bringing into mental vision a monument dedicated by Canada to her 60,000 heroic dead."[41] The battle and the monument had become synonymous.

The Vimy Memorial's wartime history highlighted its commemorative value to Canadians in and out of uniform whereas its occupation by the enemy seemed to imply an assault on Canada's own coming of age. Its liberation allowed the memorial to resume its proper vocation as a beacon for Canadians in their desire to recall the sacrifices of their loved ones and comrades of both world wars. In reclaiming the Vimy Memorial, Canada had safeguarded its past and its growing sense of nationhood.

Notes

1   For details on the Vimy pilgrimage and the memorial's unveiling, see W.W. Murray (ed), *The Epic of Vimy* (Canadian Legion, 1936); David W. Lloyd, *Battlefield Tourism: Pilgrimage and the Commemoration of the Great War in Britain, Australia and Canada, 1919-1939* (Oxford: Berg, 1998), especially 198-207; and John Pierce, "Constructing Memory: The Vimy Memorial" and "Photo Essay: The Vimy Pilgrimage," *Canadian Military History* vol 1, nos 1 & 2 (Autumn 1992), 4-14.

2   Major-General L.R. LaFlèche, deputy minister, DND, to O.D. Skelton, undersecretary of State for External Affairs, 20 January 1937, "Care of Vimy Memorial and Appointment of Major D.C.U. Simson," file 753, vol 1804, Record Group [RG] 25, Library and Archives of Canada [LAC].

3   House of Commons, *Debates*, 1 August 1940, Vol III, 2246.

4   *Globe and Mail*, 2 May 1940; Vincent Massey, *What's Past is Prologue* (Toronto: Macmillan, 1963), 330-31; Hamilton *Spectator*, 15 January 1940.

5   *Montreal Daily Star*, 1 June 1940.

6   *Globe and Mail*, 3 June 1940.

7   Ibid.

8   *Montreal Daily Star*, 3 June 1940.

9   "God Himself Will Punish their Wanton Act," *The Legionary*, June 1940, 7.

10   *Globe and Mail*, 3 June 1940.

11   *La Presse*, 5 June 1940 (author's translation).
12   Herbert Fairlie Wood, "Adolf Hitler's Vimy 'Pilgrimage,'" *The Legionary*, August 1964, 14-15. Wood notes that Hitler "succumbed to temptation" and lectured his generals on First World War tactics using the site's preserved trenches as props.
13   Secretary of State for External Affairs to the High Commissioner for Canada, London, 3 June 1940; Massey to King, 3 June 1940, "Destruction of Vimy Memorial by German Forces," file 625-40, vol 2785, series A-3-b, RG 25.
14   House of Commons, *Debates*, 4 June 1940, Vol I, 454.
15   House of Commons, *Debates*, 1 August 1940, Vol III, 2246.
16   Flight-Lieutenant J.W. Pope-Hennessy, Air Ministry, Whitehall, to Wing Commander A.P. Campbell, Headquarters RCAF, Canada House, 5 August 1940, "Destruction of Vimy Memorial by German Forces."
17   Massey to King, 5 August 1940, "Destruction of Vimy Memorial by German Forces;" House of Commons, *Debates*, 6 August 1940, Vol III, 2529.
18   See for example the Hamilton *Spectator*, 19 November 1940 and the *Globe and Mail*, 7 April 1941.
19   "Remember Vimy," *The Legionary*, April 1942, 17.
20   D.C. Unwin Simson, "The Vimy Memorial," *Canadian Geographical Journal* vol XXVI, no 1 (January 1943), 41.
21   Simson, "The Vimy Memorial," 42.
22   Ibid, 42-43.
23   L.F. Ellis, *Welsh Guards at War* (London: London Stamp Exchange Limited, 1989, originally published in 1946), 202-03. I am indebted to Morgan Wright for this source.
24   *Ottawa Evening Journal*, 2 September 1944.
25   *Ottawa Evening Journal*, 4 September 1944.
26   *Globe and Mail*, 5 September 1944.
27   "Vimy Redeemed," *The Legionary*, October 1944, 6-7.
28   Wood, "Adolf Hitler's Vimy 'Pilgrimage,'" 14-15; *Globe and Mail*, 5 September 1944.
29   Wood, 14-15. At some point after the war Piroson became the caretaker, presumably succeeding Stubbs. See also "Vimy Redeemed," 6-7.
30   "Reminiscences by Col. D.C. Unwin Simson, R.C.E., M.E.I.C., of Little Known Facts and Difficulties in the Construction of the Canadian Memorial on Vimy Ridge, and other Memorials in France and Belgium," photocopied typescript, no date [1960s], Canadian War Museum [CWM], Ottawa.
31   Wood, 14-15.
32   "Vimy Redeemed," 6-7.
33   Hamilton *Spectator*, 12 September 1944; *The Legionary*, October 1944, 6-7. According to the latter source, Field Marshal Sir Bernard Montgomery visited the site on his way to Belgium in September 1944. The occasion is not mentioned in his memoirs.
34   Georges P. Vanier to Norman Robertson, Undersecretary of State for External Affairs, 28 September 1944, "Destruction of Vimy Memorial by German Forces." Vanier also visited the memorial on 9 December 1944. See souvenir booklet in box 58B 6-5, 19970077-011, CWM.

35 Massey, 245.
36 Lieutenant-Colonel Unwin Simson, "Vimy Memorial, Preliminary Report on Monument and Park," 26 September 1944, "Destruction of Vimy Memorial by German Forces."
37 Wood, 14-15.
38 Simson, "Vimy Memorial, Preliminary Report on Monument and Park."
39 Telephone interview, Dr. David Roger with the author, 22 March 2006.
40 D.E. Macintyre, *Canada at Vimy* (Toronto: Peter Martin Associates, 1967), 159, 202-204.
41 "Canadian Army Memorial Service Vimy Ridge, 9 April 1945," box 58B 7-5, 19940001-680, CWM; telegram Vanier to King, 8 April 1945, "Vimy Memorial—General," vol 3, file 40-1-2, vol 6298, RG 24.

The Vimy Memorial.

The figure named "Canada Mourning Her Dead" (or Canada bereft) looks over the Douai Plain.

Details of figures that grace the memorial: **Left**: Canada bereft; **Centre & Right**: the female and male mourners that flank the stairs leading to the twin columns.

Left: The designer of the Vimy Memorial, Walter Allward, stands beside the limestone block that would become the recumbent figure of the female mourner. Fifteen years separated his original sketches in a Toronto park to completion above the Douai Plain.

LAC e002852543

Centre & Bottom: The Vimy memorial was officially dedicated on 26 July 1936. Over 100,000 spectators, including 3,000 Canadians, attended the ceremony.

LAC PA 803918

LAC PA 183544

Top: Pilgrams and spectators gather on Vimy Ridge prior to the dedication ceremony.

LAC PA 148880

Centre & Bottom: King Edward VIII unveils the figure "Canada Mourning Her Dead" at the official dedication. He then inspected the Honour Guard of Canadian veterans. (**Bottom**) In his address he noted, "Already the scars of war have well-nigh vanished from the fair landscape beneath us. Around us here today there is peace and rebuilding of hope." Another European war would begin three years later.

LAC PA 148873

LAC PA 183540

Legion Magazine Archives

Legion Magazine Archives

Legion Magazine Archives

Above & Left: Adolf Hitler visited the Vimy memorial on 2 June 1940 to discredit Allied claims that the Germans had destroyed it during the Battle of France, May-June 1940.

Photo courtesy of Dr. David Roger

Bottom: This photograph of a de Havilland Mosquito of 410 Squadron, RCAF flying past the Vimy Memorial in late 1944 became a cherished squadron souvenir.

Above and **Right**: Lieutenant-General H.D.G. Crerar, commander of First Canadian Army and a Vimy veteran, visited the Vimy memorial on 11 September 1944.

Bottom right: In April 1945, a Canadian military ceremony marked the 28th anniversary of the Battle of Vimy Ridge, the first since France's liberation. A pamphlet produced for the occasion noted: "To the Canadian, Vimy is a hallowed word—a word recalling a glorious achievement and bringing into mental vision a monument dedicated by Canada to her 60,000 heroic dead."

Bottom left: Simone Stubbs, the daughter of the Memorial's caretaker, George Stubbs, photographed during Crerar's visit to the memorial.

Photo taken by Marie-Josée Lafond

Photo taken by Marie-Josée Lafond

"This memorial is not a monument to the capture of Vimy Ridge only…it is a memorial to a nation."

The Canadian National Vimy Memorial Park as it appears today. **Top**: An aerial view of the Monument. **Above**: A section of the preserved trenches as well as the Duffield and Grange Crater Groups. **Below left**: Thousands of trees were planted on 97 hectares of the 107-hectare site. The trees were intended to return life to the bruised and battered landscape, though it is a myth that one tree was planted for each Canadian soldier killed at Vimy. **Below right**: An aerial view of the Monument.

Photo taken by Marie-Josée Lafond

Photo taken by Marie-Josée Lafond

311

18

Afterthoughts

THE EDITORS

Let us return to the three questions we asked at the outset as we consider, ninety years on, the broader significance of the Battle of Vimy Ridge. Why were the Canadians fighting north of Arras in the spring of 1917? The simple answer is that the Canadian Corps was then part of the First British Army. Most of our contributors acknowledge Gary Sheffield's point that Canadians have too often underestimated (or ignored) the British contribution both in the Battle of Vimy Ridge and the Battle of Arras. Julian Byng "hadn't even met a Canadian" when he became the Canadian Corps commander in the spring of 1916, but he had a reputation as a disciplinarian and a trainer. Paul Dickson notes that the Canadians then needed both, for not only had the Canadian divisions suffered difficult and costly operations, they had also endured the quirky politics of Sir Sam Hughes. Patrick Brennan maintains that Byng made the Canadian Corps his own. And as we have seen throughout this volume, the "Byng Boys" relied on British commanders, but also on British tactical doctrine, British logistical support, British materiel and British gunners. The Canadians even depended on British infantry, not only those who fought with Henry Burstall's 2nd Division, but also, as Michael Boire argues, those who had held the ground before the Canadians arrived north of Arras in late 1916.

Indeed, we need to remember that Vimy Ridge marked only the northern flank of the Battle of Arras. It was not just the Canadians who enjoyed a great victory on 9 April 1917. The British official history noted long ago: "Easter Monday of the year 1917 must be accounted, from the British point of view, one of the great days of the war. It witnessed the most formidable and at the same time most successful British offensive hitherto launched."[1] The Canadians still had to wrest control of Hill 145 and a feature to the north known as the Pimple, but Andrew Godefroy makes the point that the German reserves were in no position to force the Canadians from the ridge. Not so further south where General Allenby's Third British Army pressed forward in deplorable weather against an imposing system of German defensives.

The differing reputations of Canadian and British forces in the Battle of Arras are startling, especially when one considers how similar were their sacrifices. Consider Arthur Currie's 1st Canadian Division and George Harper's 51st Highland Division, which fought side-by-side at Vimy Ridge. Both divisions suffered in April and May 1917 the highest casualty rates in their respective armies: Currie's division suffered 6,221 casualties against Harper's losses of 6,377.[2] But while Currie's men could claim their part in the Canadian victory at Vimy Ridge, Harper's men came away with less satisfying accolades. Later in April, Currie's troops captured Arleux and Fresnoy, while Harper's Highlanders fought hard but could not capture fully the village of Roeux. Perhaps, as Mike Bechthold suggests, we ought to consider more carefully why, if at all, one division was more 'successful' than another. Did the Canadians employ different tactics? Mark Humphries suggests not. We would do well to study less the nationality of these troops and more the ground over which they attacked.

How did the Canadian Corps achieve the victory at Vimy Ridge? The Australian Corps commander General Sir John Monash once argued that Vimy Ridge was a kind of battle whose history could never be written. "In a well planned battle nothing happens, nothing can happen, except the regular progress of the advance according to the plan arranged...The story of what did take place on the day of battle would be a mere paraphrase of the battle orders prescribing all that was to take place."[3] Historians are uncomfortable with such pronouncements, and for good reason. Julian Byng anticipated that long training, lots of resources and carefully prepared artillery support could decide a set-piece battle on Vimy Ridge. Tim Cook and Bill Rawling detail how central to the outcome were the careful preparations of the gunners and engineers.

But the battle orders offer a limited view of the Battle of Vimy Ridge. Our divisional accounts reveal a much more complex picture. At times throughout the battle things went badly wrong. David Campbell, Andrew Iarocci and Andrew Godefroy remind us that artillery fired short, or missed crucial German trenches and machine gun nests. Such incidents cost some units dearly. Tanks broke down on the 2nd Division front. Troops became disoriented on the scarred landscape. Flanks opened up. Field guns became stuck in the mud. Strongpoints were threatened, sometimes enough to force a Canadian withdrawal. Heather Moran details how, despite elaborate preparations, stretcher-bearers could not find the wounded amidst the carnage and dressing stations became overwhelmed with the wounded and dying. Some witnesses expressed great confidence on the eve of battle, but were they just as confident on the afternoon of 9 April, when Watson's 4th Division had still not taken Hill 145, and German guns and snipers continued to weaken the hastily prepared strong points across the ridge? Andrew Godefroy argues rightly that the Germans lost this battle when its commanders held their reserves too far to the rear to challenge the Canadian gains. But no one knew that until the battle was won.

Each of Byng's four divisions overcame unique obstacles, so the battles of Vimy Ridge defy easy generalization. But the war diaries hint at important keys to success. New platoon tactics and weapons played a role here, but just as often, the fighting reflected old realities that were familiar to any veterans of Second Ypres or Regina Trench. Simplicity was the rule. So was a grim determination. Follow forward your lieutenant or corporal. Push on with bayonets and lots of bombs. Be ready to outflank a machine gun crew that had survived the barrage. Do not lose contact with the platoon, company or battalion on either side. Rush the engineers and the carrying parties forward with shovels, ammunition and water. And dig in. These instructions also appear in the battle orders. Our accounts show that the Canadians had the leadership, training, discipline and courage to heed them well.

How did later generations of Canadians come to remember the Battle of Vimy Ridge? Military historians may argue that other Canadian engagements were more important to the larger conduct of the war. The Canadians suffered higher casualties at the Third Battle of Ypres in the autumn of 1917, but after careful planning, their capture of the village of Passchendaele marked an end to that awful battle. On 8 August 1918, the Canadians, Australians and French broke through the German defences outside of Amiens. Again, the casualty figures were higher than at Vimy, but Canadians also showed themselves adept at mobile warfare, making gains that were counted in miles, not yards.

But as Jonathan Vance, Jacqueline Hucker and Serge Durflinger explain, there were many reasons why the memory of Vimy Ridge became especially important to Canadians. That the battle was joined on Easter Monday affirmed a belief that Canadian soldiers embodied the highest ideals of Christianity. This symbolism was literally cut into the stone of hundreds of memorials built across Canada after the war. But no where, not even at Canada's national war memorial in Ottawa, was this symbolism so striking as at Vimy Ridge. Here Walter Allward's memorial and the surrounding ground provided a national expression that went far beyond the battle fought there in April 1917. It is no wonder then that the memorial became the object of so much concern during the Second World War. In the dark days of the spring of 1940, when Canada became Britain's ranking ally and the prospects for victory were so grim, newspaper writers depicted the Vimy memorial as a lone Canadian bulwark against German aggression. That the memorial survived the Second World War imbued it with even greater meaning for both Vimy veterans and their families.

Within the triumph of Vimy Ridge we should not forget the deep tragedy of this battle. Consider the 10,602 Canadian casualties suffered in the fighting. Visitors to the surrounding cemeteries that contain some of the 3,598 soldiers who died at Vimy Ridge cannot help but be moved. The dying light of a summer's evening in the rarely visited Thélus cemetery offers a chance to reflect on familiar words, "At the going down of the sun, and in the morning, we will remember them." Here lay Private Alfred Hutchings, Lieutenant Lyall Johnston, Corporal John Clue and Regimental Sergeant-Major Frank Hinchcliffe, four soldiers who were killed at Vimy Ridge and who are briefly profiled in the appendix to follow. But we should also contemplate the thousands more who survived the battle broken in body and spirit. Consider the families who cared for them, often getting by on a meagre disability pension. For them Vimy Ridge held a far darker legacy.

Consider too that these casualties contributed to the most divisive political debate in Canadian history. Having gained for Canada the promise of a new place within a British Commonwealth, Prime Minister Robert Borden went to France in April to visit the wounded of Vimy Ridge. He then returned home in May convinced of the need for compulsory military service. On 24 May, anti-conscription riots broke out in Montreal. Attempts to form a coalition government with Opposition leader Sir Wilfrid Laurier broke down over conscription. In August, Borden's government introduced the Military Voters Act that gave the vote to all members of the Canadian armed forces; the Wartime Elections Act introduced the next month enfranchised female relatives of servicemen, but struck from the voters' lists immigrants from enemy countries who had arrived since 1902. In October, Borden formed a Unionist government from his own Conservatives and Liberals who had broken with their leader. As the Canadian Corps entered the Third Battle of Ypres, an election campaign largely fought over conscription was underway in Canada. The results that proclaimed a Unionist victory and the introduction of compulsory wartime service in 1918 were counted as Canadians organized relief for the survivors of the Halifax explosion.[4] The year 1917 was an extraordinary one for Canadians. From it came stories of triumph and tragedy that affect us still.

Notes

1 Cyril Falls, *History of the Great War, Military Operations, France and Belgium, 1917* Volume 7 (London: Macmillan, 1940), 201.
2 Falls, 396, 559, 560.
3 Sir John Monash cited in Jonathan Nicholls, *Cheerful Sacrifice: The Battle of Arras 1917* (London: Leo Cooper, 1990), 130.
4 The best overview of these events remains Ramsay Cook, R. Craig Brown, *Canada, 1896-1921: A Nation Transformed* (Toronto: McClelland and Stewart, 1974), Chapters 13, 14.

Appendix 1

Order of Battle - Vimy Ridge

Canadian Corps - Lieutenant-General Hon Sir Julian Byng

Corps Troops

Canadian Light Horse - Lieutenant-Colonel E.I. Leonard
Canadian Corps Cyclist Battalion - Major A.E. Humphrey
GOC Royal Artillery - Canadian Corps - Brigadier-General E.W.B. Morrison
1st Canadian Heavy Artillery Group
3rd & 5th Canadian, 11th, 163rd &164th Siege Batteries
2nd Canadian Heavy Artillery Group
1st & 2nd Canadian Heavy & 152nd Heavy Batteries; 2nd Canadian Siege and
12th Siege Batteries
18th Heavy Artillery Group
1st & 6th Canadian, 147th, 180th & 182nd Siege Batteries
30th Heavy Artillery Group
4th Canadian, 228th, 270th, 72nd & 181st Siege Batteries
44th Heavy Artillery Group
7th Canadian, 161st, 120th, 41st &114th Siege Batteries
9th Canadian Siege and 147th Siege Batteries
"E" (Canadian) Anti-Aircraft Battery

Chief Engineer, Canadian Corps - Brigadier-General W.B. Lindsay
1st, 2nd, 3rd, 4th Canadian Army Troops Companies, Canadian Engineers
1st, 2nd 3rd, 4th Canadian Entrenching Battalions
1st Canadian Pontoon Bridging Transportation Engineer Unit
3rd Br. Canadian Railway Troops
Canadian Corps Cyclist Battalion
1st Advanced Park Company - Captain H.S. Fellowes

1st Canadian Motor Machine Gun Brigade - Colonel R. Brutinel
"A" & "B", Eaton, Borden & Yukon Batteries

Canadian Corps Signal Company
Nos. 8, 9 & 11 Mobile Pigeon Lofts
Canadian Corps Ammunition Park
Nos. 1, 2, 3 & 4 Canadian Divisional Supply Columns
No.8 Mobile Ordnance Workshop
No.26 (Canadian) Ordnance Mobile Workshop
Canadian Composite Pioneer Company
Canadian Corps Training School
Canadian Corps Salvage Company

Attached Corps Troops
13th Heavy Artillery Group
47th, 49th, 101st 76th & 27th Siege Batteries
50th Heavy Artillery Group
1/1st Essex & 145th Heavy, 58th, 68th, 69th & 95th Siege Batteries
53rd Heavy Artillery Group
        206th, 108th, 148th & 276th Siege Batteries
64th Heavy Artillery Group
        121st, 126th, 258th, 232nd & 73rd Siege Batteries
70th Heavy Artillery Group
        3rd, 14th, 162nd and 144th Siege Batteries
76th Heavy Artillery Group
        218th Siege, 31t, 121st, 129th, 142nd & 50th Heavy Batteries
26th Heavy Artillery Group
        1st, 11th & 12th Royal Marine Artillery, 44th, 52nd & 89th Siege Batteries

Canadian Corps Siege Park
No.55 Divisional Supply Column
No.2 Reserve Park
No.2 Reserve Park

Nos. 3, 33, 46, 54 & 55 Ordnance Mobile Workshops

No.1 Pontoon Park, Royal Engineers
20th Army Troops Company, Royal Engineers
215th Army Troops Company, Royal Engineers
172nd Tunnelling Company, Royal Engineers
176th Tunnelling Company, Royal Engineers
182nd Tunnelling Company, Royal Engineers
185th Tunnelling Company, Royal Engineers
255th Tunnelling Company, Royal Engineers
348th Field Company, Royal Engineers
324th Quarry Company, Royal Engineers
Canadian Corps Light Railway Operating Company - Major R.P. Rogers

No.33 Prisoners of War Company
20th Light Railway Train Company

Royal Flying Corps
No.16 Squadron, Royal Flying Corps
No.1 Balloon Company, Royal Flying Corps
No.2 Balloon Company, Royal Flying Corps

1st Canadian Division - Major-General A.W. Currie

1st Canadian Infantry Brigade - Brigadier-General W.A. Griesbach
1st Battalion (Western Ontario Regiment) - Lieutenant-Colonel G.C. Hodson
2nd Battalion (Eastern Ontario Regiment) - Lieutenant-Colonel R.V. Clark
3rd Battalion (Toronto Regiment) - Lieutenant-Colonel J.B. Rogers
4th Battalion (Central Ontario) - Major W. Towers (acting)
1st Canadian Light Trench Mortar Battery

2nd Canadian Infantry Brigade - Brigadier-General F.O.W. Loomis
5th Battalion (Western Cavalry) - Lieutenant-Colonel H.M. Dyer
7th Battalion (1st British Columbia Regiment) - Lieutenant-Colonel W.F. Gilson
8th Battalion (90th Winnipeg Rifles) - Lieutenant-Colonel J.M Prower
10th Battalion (10th Canadians) - Lieutenant-Colonel D. Ormond
2nd Canadian Light Trench Mortar Battery

3rd Canadian Infantry Brigade - Brigadier-General G.S. Tuxford
13th Battalion (Royal Highlanders of Canada) - Lieutenant-Colonel G.E. McCuaig
14th Battalion (The Royal Montreal Regiment) - Lieutenant-Colonel G. McCombe
15th Battalion (48th Highlanders of Canada) - Lieutenant-Colonel C. Bent
16th Battalion, (The Canadian Scottish) - Lieutenant-Colonel C. Peck
3rd Canadian Light Trench Mortar Battery

1st Canadian Divisional Artillery - Brigadier-General H.C. Thacker
1st Brigade Canadian Field Artillery - Lieutenant-Colonel C.H. McLaren
2nd Brigade Canadian Field Artillery - Lieutenant-Colonel S.B. Anderson
3rd Brigade Canadian Field Artillery - Lieutenant-Colonel H.D.G. Crerar
12th Brigade Canadian Field Artillery - Lieutenant-Colonel S.B. Anderson
V 1 Canadian Heavy Trench Mortar Battery
X 1 Canadian Trench Mortar Battery
Y 1 Canadian Trench Mortar Battery
Z 1 Canadian Trench Mortar Battery
1st Canadian Divisional Ammunition Column - Lieutenant-Colonel J.J. Penhale
1st Canadian Divisional Train - Lieutenant-Colonel W.A. Simpson

1st Canadian Divisional Engineers - Lieutenant-Colonel A. Macphail
1st Field Company, Canadian Engineers - Major H.F.H. Hertzberg
2nd Field Company, Canadian Engineers - Major E.F. Lynn
3rd Field Company, Canadian Engineers - Major E. Pepler

107th Canadian Pioneer Battalion - Lieutenant-Colonel G. Campbell
1st Canadian Division Signal Company - E. Ford

1st Canadian Machine Gun Company - Major W.M. Pearce
2nd Canadian Machine Gun Company - Major R.M. Stewart
3rd Canadian Machine Gun Company - Major E.J. Houghton
13th Canadian Machine Gun Company - Major J. Kay

Assistant Medical Director 1st Division - Colonel F.S.C. Ford
   No. 1 Canadian Casualty Clearing Station (Halifax) - Major C.H. Dickson
   No. 1 Canadian Field Ambulance - Lieutenant-Colonel R.P. Wright
   No. 2 Canadian Field Ambulance (Toronto) - Lieutenant-Colonel J.J. Moser
   No. 3 Canadian Field Ambulance - Lieutenant-Colonel A. Donaldson

   1st Canadian Sanitary Section
   1st Canadian Mobile Veterinarian Section

Attached Troops
   31st Divisional Artillery HQ
   165th Brigade, Royal Field Artillery
   170th Brigade, Royal Field Artillery
   72nd Brigade, Army Field Artillery
   26th Brigade, Army Field Artillery
   5th Brigade, Royal Horse Artillery
   31st Divisional Ammunition Column
   No.2 Special Company, Royal Engineers

2nd Canadian Division - Major-General H.E. Burstall

4th Canadian Infantry Brigade - Brigadier-General R. Rennie
   18th Battalion (Western Ontario) - Lieutenant-Colonel G.F. Morrison
   19th Battalion (Central Ontario) - Lieutenant-Colonel L.H. Millen
   20th Battalion (Central Ontario) - Major H.V. Rorke
   21st Battalion (Eastern Ontario) - Lieutenant-Colonel T.F.Elmitt
   4th Canadian Light Trench Mortar Battery - Captain R.N. Jago

5th Canadian Infantry Brigade - Brigadier-General A.H. Macdonnell
   22nd Battalion (Canadien Français) - Lieutenant-Colonel T.L. Tremblay
   24th Battalion (Victoria Rifles of Canada) - Major C.F. Ritchie
   25th Battalion (Nova Scotia Rifles) - Lieutenant-Colonel D.S. Bauld
   26th Battalion (New Brunswick) - Lieutenant-Colonel A.E.G. McKenzie
   5th Canadian Light Trench Mortar Battery - Captain J.R. Gale

6th Canadian Infantry Brigade - Brigadier-General H.B.D. Ketchen
   27th Battalion (City of Winnipeg) - Lieutenant-Colonel P.J. Daly
   28th Battalion (Northwest) - Lieutenant-Colonel A. Ross
   29th Battalion (Vancouver) - Lieutenant-Colonel J.M. Ross

31st Battalion (Alberta) - Lieutenant-Colonel A.H. Bell
6th Canadian Light Trench Mortar Battery - Captain R. Pouncy

2nd Canadian Divisional Artillery - Brigadier-General H.A. Panet
4th Brigade Canadian Field Artillery - Lieutenant-Colonel J.S. Stewart
5th Brigade Canadian Field Artillery - Lieutenant-Colonel R.H. Britton
6th Brigade Canadian Field Artillery - Lieutenant-Colonel W.B.M. King
V 2 Canadian Heavy Trench Mortar Battery
X 2 Canadian Trench Mortar Battery
Y 2 Canadian Trench Mortar Battery
Z 2 Canadian Trench Mortar Battery
2nd Canadian Division Ammunition Column - Lieutenant-Colonel W.H. Harrison
2nd Canadian Divisional Train - Lieutenant-Colonel A.E. Massie

2nd Canadian Divisional Engineers - Lieutenant-Colonel S.H. Osler
4th Field Company, Canadian Engineers - Major H.D. St.A. Smith
5th Field Company, Canadian Engineers - Major A.L. Mieville
6th Field Company, Canadian Engineers - Major D.S. Ellis
2nd Canadian Pioneer Battalion - Lieutenant-Colonel G.E. Sanders
2nd Canadian Division Signal Company - Captain A.A. Anderson

4th Canadian Machine Gun Company - Major W.J. Forbes-Mitchell
5th Canadian Machine Gun Company - Major S.W. Watson
6th Canadian Machine Gun Company - Major A. Eastham
14th Canadian Machine Gun Company - Major J. Basevi
12 Company, "D" Battalion, Heavy Machine Gun Corps (8 x Mk II Tanks) - Major 'Roc'
    Ward

Assistant Medical Director 2nd Division - Colonel H.M. Jacques
No. 2 Canadian Casualty Clearing Station (Toronto) - Lieutenant-Colonel J.E. Davey
No. 4 Canadian Field Ambulance (Winnipeg) - Lieutenant-Colonel W. Webster
No. 5 Canadian Field Ambulance (Hamilton) - Lieutenant-Colonel C.F. McGuffin
No. 6 Canadian Field Ambulance (Montreal) - Lieutenant-Colonel J.T.F. Murphy
2nd Canadian Sanitary Section - Captain W. Richardson
2nd Canadian Mobile Veterinarian Section - Captain F.A. Daigneault

Attached Troops
5th Divisional Artillery HQ
15th Brigade, Royal Field Artillery
27th Brigade, Royal Field Artillery
28th Brigade, Royal Field Artillery
5th Divisional Ammunition Column
"D" Special Company, Royal Engineers

3rd Canadian Division - Major-General L.J. Lipsett

7th Canadian Infantry Brigade - Brigadier-General A.C. Macdonnell
The Royal Canadian Regiment - Lieutenant-Colonel C.H. Hill
Princess Patricia's Canadian Light Infantry - Lieutenant-Colonel A. Adamson
42nd Battalion (Royal Highlanders of Canada) - Lieutenant-Colonel B. McLennan
49th Battalion (Edmonton Regiment) - Lieutenant-Colonel R.H. Palmer
7th Canadian Light Trench Mortar Battery

8th Canadian Infantry Brigade - Brigadier-General J.H. Elmsley
1st Battalion, Canadian Mounted Rifles - Lieutenant-Colonel R.C. Andros
2nd Battalion, Canadian Mounted Rifles - Lieutenant-Colonel G.C. Johnston
4th Battalion, Canadian Mounted Rifles - Lieutenant-Colonel H. Gordon
5th Battalion, Canadian Mounted Rifles - Lieutenant-Colonel D. Draper
8th Canadian Light Trench Mortar Battery

9th Canadian Infantry Brigade - Brigadier-General F.W. Hill
43rd Battalion (Cameron Highlanders of Canada) - Lieutenant-Colonel W. Grassie
52nd Battalion (New Ontario) - Lieutenant-Colonel W.B. Evans
58th Battalion (Central Ontario) - Lieutenant-Colonel H.A. Genet
60th Battalion (Victoria Rifles of Canada)[1] - Lt.-Colonel F.A. de. L. Gascoigne
116th Battalion (Ontario County) - Lieutenant-Colonel S. Sharpe
9th Canadian Light Trench Mortar Battery

3rd Canadian Divisional Artillery - Brigadier-General J.H. Mitchell
8th Brigade Canadian Field Artillery - Lieutenant-Colonel V. Eaton
9th Brigade Canadian Field Artillery - Lieutenant-Colonel H.G. Carscallen
10th Brigade Canadian Field Artillery - Lieutenant-Colonel G.H. Ralston
V 3 Canadian Heavy Trench Mortar Battery
X 3 Canadian Trench Mortar Battery
Y 3 Canadian Trench Mortar Battery
Z 3 Canadian Trench Mortar Battery
3rd Canadian Division Ammunition Column - Lieutenant-Colonel W.G. Hurdman
3rd Canadian Divisional Train - Lieutenant-Colonel W.H.D.A. Findlay

3rd Canadian Divisional Engineers - Lieutenant-Colonel T.V. Anderson
7th Field Company, Canadian Engineers - Major K. Stuart
8th Field Company, Canadian Engineers - Major W.E. Manhard
9th Field Company, Canadian Engineers - Major N.R. Robertson
3rd Canadian Pioneer Battalion - Lieutenant-Colonel W.J.H. Holmes
123rd Canadian Pioneer Battalion - Lieutenant-Colonel W.B. Kingsmill
3rd Canadian Division Signal Company - Major A. Leavitt

1. Rifle companies of the 60th Battalion were in the reserve lines at Vimy Ridge. Its replacement, the 116th Battalion, was also at Vimy. Following the battle, the 60th Battalion was disbanded. This change was necessitated by the decision that the extent of a province's representation in battalions at the front should be contingent on its ability to provide reinforcements. Quebec and British Columbia were overrepresented while Ontario and Nova Scotia were underrepresented. The 60th and 73rd Battalions, both from Montreal, were broken up to allow the 116th Battalion from Ontario and the 85th Battalion from Nova Scotia to take their place. The men from these two disbanded units were distributed among other field battalions. See Nicholson, *The Canadian Expeditionary Force*, 225.

7th Canadian Machine Gun Company - Lieutenants D.S. Forbes & F.A. Hale
8th Canadian Machine Gun Company - Major F.A. Hale
9th Canadian Machine Gun Company - Captain I. McKinnon
15th Canadian Machine Gun Company - Major W.N. Moorhouse

Assistant Director Medical Services 3rd Division - Colonel A.E. Snell
No. 3 Canadian Casualty Clearing Station - Lieutenant-Colonel R. Blanshard
No. 8 Canadian Field Ambulance (Calgary) - Major J.N. Gunn
No. 9 Canadian Field Ambulance (Montreal) - Lieutenant-Colonel A.T. Bazin
No. 10 Canadian Field Ambulance - Major T.M. Leask
3rd Canadian Sanitary Section
3rd Canadian Mobile Veterinarian Section

Attached Troops
63rd Divisional Artillery HQ
63rd Divisional Ammunition Column
No.4 Special Company, Royal Engineers

4th Canadian Division - Major-General D. Watson

10th Canadian Infantry Brigade - Brigadier-General E. Hilliam
44th Battalion (Manitoba) - Lieutenant-Colonel R.D. Davies
46th Battalion (Regina and Moose Jaw) - Lieutenant-Colonel H.J. Dawson
47th Battalion (British Columbia) - Lieutenant-Colonel M. Francis
50th Battalion (Calgary) - Lieutenant-Colonel L.F. Page
10th Canadian Light Trench Mortar Battery

11th Canadian Infantry Brigade - Brigadier-General V.W. Odlum
54th Battalion (Kootenay) - Lieutenant-Colonel V.V. Harvey
75th Battalion (Mississauga) - Lieutenant-Colonel C.B. Worsnop
87th Battalion (Canadian Grenadier Guards) - Major Harry LeRoy Shaw
102nd Battalion (Northern British Columbians) - Lieutenant-Colonel J. Warden
11th Canadian Light Trench Mortar Battery

12th Canadian Infantry Brigade - Brigadier-General J.H. MacBrien
38th Battalion (Ottawa) - Lieutenant-Colonel C.M. Edwards
72nd Battalion (Seaforth Highlanders of Canada) - Lieutenant-Colonel J.A. Clark
73rd Battalion (Royal Highlanders of Canada)[2] - Lieutenant-Colonel H.C. Sparling
78th Battalion (Winnipeg Grenadiers) - Lieutenant-Colonel J. Kirkcaldy
85th Battalion (Nova Scotia Highlanders) - Lieutenant-Colonel A.H. Borden
12th Canadian Light Trench Mortar Battery

---

2. Rifle companies of the 73th Battalion were in the reserve lines at Vimy Ridge. Its replacement, the 85th Battalion was also at Vimy. Following the battle, the 73th Battalion was disbanded.

Reserve Divisional Artillery
  5th Brigade Royal Field Artillery
  11th Brigade Royal Field Artillery
  18th Brigade Army Field Artillery
  76th Brigade Army Field Artillery
  V 4 Canadian Heavy Trench Mortar Battery
  X 4 Canadian Trench Mortar Battery
  Y 4 Canadian Trench Mortar Battery
  Z 4 Canadian Trench Mortar Battery
  Reserve Division Ammunition Column
  4th Canadian Divisional Train

4th Canadian Divisional Engineers - Lieutenant-Colonel T.C. Irving
  10th Field Company, Canadian Engineers - Major W.P. Wilgar
  11th Field Company, Canadian Engineers - Major H.L. Trotter
  12th Field Company, Canadian Engineers - Major C.T. Trotter
  67th Canadian Pioneer Battalion
  124th Canadian Pioneer Battalion - Lieutenant-Colonel W.C.V. Chadwick
  4th Canadian Division Signal Company - Major A.G. Lawson
  10th Canadian Machine Gun Company - Major J.C. Britton
  11th Canadian Machine Gun Company - Major B.M. Clerk
  12th Canadian Machine Gun Company - Major L.F. Pearce

Assistant Director Medical Services 4th Division Major J.S. Jenkins
  No. 4 Canadian Casualty Clearing Station - Lieutenant-Colonel S.W. Prowse
  No. 11 Canadian Field Ambulance - Lieutenant-Colonel J.D. McQueen
  No. 12 Canadian Field Ambulance (Winnipeg) - Major Percy Bell
  No. 13 Canadian Field Ambulance (Victoria) - Major A.L. Gilday
  4th Canadian Sanitary Section
  4th Canadian Mobile Veterinarian Section

Attached Troops
  2nd Divisional Artillery HQ
  41st Brigade, Royal Field Artillery
  36th Brigade, Royal Field Artillery
  242nd Brigade, Army Field Artillery
  205th Machine-Gun Company
  "M" Special Company, Royal Engineers
  "F" Special Company, Royal Engineers
  "N" Special Company, Royal Engineers

Attached from I Corps

5th Division - Major-General R.B. Stephens

13th Infantry Brigade - Brigadier-General L.O.W. Jones
  2nd Battalion, King's Own Scottish Borderers
  1st Battalion, Royal West Kent Regiment
  14th Battalion, Royal Warwickshire Regiment
  15th Battalion, Royal Warwickshire Regiment
  13th Trench Mortar Battery
15th Infantry Brigade - Brigadier-General M.N. Turner
  16th Battalion, Royal Warwickshire Regiment
  1st Battalion, Norfolk Regiment
  1st Battalion, Bedfordshire Regiment
  1st Battalion, Cheshire Regiment
  15th Trench Mortar Battery
95th Infantry Brigade - Brigadier-General Lord E Gordon-Lennox
  1st Battalion, Devonshire Regiment
  1st Battalion, East Surrey Regiment
  1st Battalion, Duke of Cornwall's Light Infantry
  12th Battalion, The Gloucestershire Regiment
  95th Trench Mortar Battery
5th Divisional Artillery
  V 5 Heavy Trench Mortar Battery
  X 5 Trench Mortar Battery
  Y 5 Trench Mortar Battery
  Z 5 Trench Mortar Battery
  5th Divisional Train
5th Divisional Engineers
  59th Field Company, Royal Engineers
  491st Field Company, Royal Engineers
  527th Field Company, Royal Engineers
  5th Divisional Signal Company
  1st/6th Argyll & Sutherland Highlanders (Pioneers)

13th Machine Gun Company
15th Machine Gun Company
95th Machine Gun Company

13th Field Ambulance
14th Field Ambulance
15th Field Ambulance
5th Mobile Veterinarian Section

The German Army

1st Bavarian Reserve Corps Gruppe Vimy - General der Infanterie Ritter Karl von Fasbender

Corps Troops
Artillery
>   9th Field Artillery Regiment
>   25th Reserve Field Artillery Regiment
>   66th Reserve Field Artillery Regiment
>   69th Field Artillery Regiment
>   Three Batteries of Kriegsmarine 30 cm Naval guns

79th (Prussian) Reserve Infantry Division - General der Infanterie von Bacmeister

79th (Prussian) Reserve Infantry Brigade - Generalleutnant Alfred Dieterich
>   261st Reserve Infantry Regiment - Oberst von Goerne
>>   1st Battalion
>>   2nd Battalion
>>   3rd Battalion
>   262nd Reserve Infantry Regiment - Major Freiherr von Rotenhan
>>   1st Battalion
>>   2nd Battalion
>>   3rd Battalion - Major von Knobelsdorff-Brenckenhoff
>   263rd Reserve Infantry Regiment - Oberstleutnant von Behr
>>   1st Battalion
>>   2nd Battalion
>>   3rd Battalion
>   Cavalry Squadron
>>   3 Sqn / 16th Hussar Regiment
>   79th Artillery Command
>>   63rd Reserve Field Artillery Regiment (9 Batteries)
>   Engineers and Liaison
>>   379th Pioneer Battalion
>>   81st Reserve Pioneer Company
>>   1 Ersatz Company, 24th Pioneers
>>   279th Trench Mortar Company
>>   40th Reserve Searchlight Section
>>   50th 51st and 79th Searchlight Sections
>>   79th Reserve Pontoon Engineers
>   Medical and Veterinary
>>   541 Ambulance Company
>>   110th 111th and 112th Field Hospital
>>   Veterinarian Hospital
>   Transport
>>   746th Motor Transport Company

Reinforced on 9 April by:
>1st Battalion, 118th Reserve Infantry Regiment, 56th Infantry Division
>3rd Battalion, 34th Reserve Infantry Regiment, 80th Infantry Division

1st (Bavarian) Reserve Infantry Division - Generalmajor Freiherr von Bechmann

(Bavarian) Reserve Infantry Brigade
>1st Bavarian Reserve Infantry Regiment - Oberstleutnant von Füger
>>1st Battalion
>>2nd Battalion
>>3rd Battalion
>3rd Bavarian Reserve Infantry Regiment - Major Anton Maier
>>1st Battalion
>>2nd Battalion
>>3rd Battalion

Regiment reinforced on 9 April by:
>1st Battalion, 225th Infantry Regiment, 17th Division

Note: 2nd Bavarian Reserve Infantry Regiment (Oberstleutnant von Brunner) fought the 51st Division of XVII Corps in the Third Army area of operations to the south of Vimy Ridge. They were not involved in the Canadian battle.

Cavalry Squadron
>3 Sqn/ 3rd Bavarian Chevauxleger Regiment

13th Bavarian Artillery Command
>1st Bavarian Reserve Field Artillery Regiment

Engineers and Liaison
>17th Bavarian Pioneer Battalion
>1st, 3rd and 7th Bavarian Reserve Pioneer Companies
>201 Trench Mortar Company
>1st Bavarian Reserve Searchlight Section
>401st Bavarian Telephone Detachment

Medical and Veterinary
>15th Bavarian Ambulance Company
>45th 48th and 49th Bavarian Field Hospitals
>Veterinary Hospital

Transport
>750th Motor Transport Column

14th Bavarian Infantry Division - General Ritter von Rauchenberger

Though part of Gruppe Vimy, it took no part in the battle for Vimy Ridge. It was posted on the northern side of the river Scarpe and fought the 34th and 9th Divisions of XVII Corps.

8th Reserve Corps (Gruppe Souchez) - General der Infanterie Georg Karl Wichura

Corps Troops

16th (Bavarian) Reserve Infantry Division - Generalmajor Arnold Ritter von Möhl

9th (Bavarian) Reserve Infantry Brigade
11th Bavarian Infantry Regiment - Major Ritter von Braun
- 1st Battalion
- 2nd Battalion
- 3rd Battalion

14th Bavarian Infantry Regiment
- 1st Battalion
- 2nd Battalion (did not see action)
- 3rd Battalion (did not see action)

21st Bavarian Infantry Regiment
- 1st Battalion
- 2nd Battalion (did not see action)
- 3rd Battalion (did not see action)

Cavalry Squadron
- 4 Sqn/ 7th Bavarian Light Cavalry Regiment

16th Artillery Command
- 3rd Bavarian Artillery Regiment

Engineers and Liaison
- 16th (Bavarian) Pioneer Battalion
- 14th and 15th Bavarian Reserve Pioneer Company
- 16th Bavarian Trench Mortar Company
- 16th Bavarian Telephone Detachment

Medical and Veterinary
- 8th Bavarian Ambulance Company
- 29th Bavarian Field Hospital
- Veterinarian Hospital

Transport
- 697th Motor Transport Company

Reinforced on 10 and 11 April by:
- *1st Battalion, 14th Bavarian Infantry Regiment (16th Bavarian Infantry Division)*
- *1st Battalion, 21st Bavarian Infantry Regiment (16th Bavarian Infantry Division)*
- *3rd Battalion, 5th Guards Grenadier Regiment (4th Guards Division)*
- *1st Battalion, 93rd Reserve Infantry Regiment (4th Guards Division)*

Note: With the exception of reinforcing battalions specified above, 16th Division's 14th and 21st Bavarian Infantry Regiments remained uncommitted to battle, 56th and 80th Divisions, forming the remainder of Gruppe Souchez, also only played a reinforcing role.

Appendix 2

Lest We Forget:
The Men of Vimy Ridge

Research completed by students at Smiths Falls District Collegiate Institute Smiths Falls Ontario under the supervision of Mr. Blake Seward.

Private Weldon A. Adshade
Royal Canadian Regiment
3rd Canadian Division
Canadian Expeditionary Force

Weldon A. Adshade was born on 27 October 1889, in Housefield, Nova Scotia. Weldon moved to Kindersley, Saskatchewan and became a teamster. He enlisted in Saskatoon with the 212th Battalion on 6 July 1916. Adshade landed in France on 22 October 1916. He joined the Royal Canadian Regiment in the field on 18 November 1916. Weldon Adshade was killed on 9 April 1916, and is buried at La Chaudiere Military Cemetery in France. He was twenty-seven-years-old.

Samuel James Bothwell, Captain (Acting Major)
1st Battalion, Canadian Mounted Rifles
(Saskatchewan Regiment)
3rd Canadian Division
Canadian Expeditionary Force

Samuel James Bothwell was born 1 June 1879, in Dromara, Ireland, the son of George and Susan Bothwell, of Mosside, Alberta. He was a farmer married to Alice Hannah when he was attested as a lieutenant in the 66th Battalion in Edmonton, Alberta on 2 July 1915. He joined the 1st Canadian Mounted Rifles on 2 August 1916. On the afternoon on 9 April 1917, Acting Major Bothwell was reported killed. Then forty-one-years-old, Samuel Bothwell is buried at Nine Elms Military Cemetery.

Private Arthur Cameron
3rd Canadian Machine Gun Company
1st Canadian Division
Canadian Expeditionary Force

Arthur Cameron was born 10 May 1890 in Pictou, Nova Scotia, the son of Mr. Duncan Cameron and Mrs. Mary F. Cameron. At the time of his enlistment, he lived in New Westminster, British Columbia where he was an electrician. He enlisted on 16 March 1915. On 3 August 1916, he joined the 3rd Canadian Machine Gun Company in France. At the battle of Vimy Ridge, Cameron's company operated in support of the 3rd Canadian Infantry Brigade of the 1st Division. Arthur Cameron was killed in action on 9 April 1917, at the age of twenty-seven. His earnings were paid to his brother, Mr. Henry Cameron of 208 Union St., Vancouver British Columbia. Arthur Cameron is buried at Nine Elms Military Cemetery in Thélus, France.

Corporal Charles John Clue
21st Battalion, Eastern Ontario Regiment
2nd Canadian Division
Canadian Expeditionary Force

Charles John Clue was born on 12 September 1885 in England to Henry and Emma Clue. At the time of his enlistment on 6 March 1916, he was 31-years-old and a butcher in Saskatoon, Saskatchewan. He arrived in England in October 1916 with the 21st Battalion. On 9 April 1917, Charles John Clue went missing in action and was later reported killed in action. Clue earned $33.10 in April 1917. On 30 April 1917 his total earnings of $98.89 was paid to his mother, then of Shepherds Bush Road, London, England. Charles John Clue is buried in Thélus Military Cemetery.

Frank W. Hinchcliffe
25th Battalion, Nova Scotia Regiment
2nd Canadian Division
Canadian Expeditionary Force

Frank W. Hinchcliffe was born in Yorkshire, England on 10 May 1879. He moved to New Glasgow, Nova Scotia where he was a steel worker, and enlisted in Halifax on 25 November 1914. He was then a father of four and a widower. Hinchcliffe's 25th battalion landed in France in September 1915. In June 1916, he became the battalion's Regimental-Sergeant-Major, and was awarded the Military Cross the next month. Frank Hinchcliffe was thirty-six-years-old when he was killed on 9 April 1917. He is buried at Thélus Military Cemetery.

Private Alfred G. Hutchings
Royal Canadian Regiment
3rd Canadian Division
Canadian Expeditionary Force

Alfred G. Hutchings was born in Dara, Ontario, on 12 February 1881. His family later relocated to Campbellford. On 11 August 1915, Hutchings enlisted in Barriefield Ontario with the 59th Battalion from Brockville, Ontario. After arriving in France in June 1916, Hutchings was taken on strength of the Royal Canadian Regiment of the 3rd Division. He was killed on Monday 9 April 1917 and is buried in Thélus Military Cemetery. Alfred Hutchings was twenty-six-years-old.

Lieutenant Lyell Corson Johnston
4th Battalion, Canadian Mounted Rifles
3rd Canadian Division
Canadian Expeditionary Force

Lyell Corson Johnston was born in East Toronto on 13 February 1897 to the Reverend J.R. Johnston and Minnie Everington Johnston. He was raised in Preston, now part of Cambridge Ontario. Prior to enlistment, Johnston was in the Cadet Corps and the 33rd Militia Regiment. Johnston enlisted on 29 February 1916 as a lieutenant with the 111th Battalion. He arrived in England in October 1916 and, after further training, he was taken on strength with the 4th CMR. Lieutenant Johnston returned from the Canadian Corps Training School and rejoined the 4th CMR on 7 April 1917. Two days later, 9 April 1917, the battalion's forward companies suffered "severe casualties" under enemy artillery. According to the battalion's regimental history, "It was during this bombardment that Lieutenant C.L. Johnston was killed." Just twenty-years-old, he lies buried in Thélus Military Cemetery.

Selected Bibliography

This bibliography is intended as a point of departure for further reading on the Battle of Vimy Ridge, the Battle of Arras and Canada's broader military experience during the First Wrold War. The listing below is by no means comprehensive. Further information on sources can be found in the notes of each chapter of this book. Readers may also wish to consult O.A. Cooke, *The Canadian Military Experience 1867-1995: A Select Bibliography*. Ottawa: Directorate of History and Heritage, 1997.

Vimy Ridge and the Battle of Arras

Cook, Tim. "A Proper Slaughter: the March 1917 Gas Raid on Vimy Ridge." *Canadian Military History*. Vol 8, no 2 (Spring 1999), 7-23.

Berton, Pierre. *Vimy*. London: Penguin, 1987.

Christie, Norm. *For King and Empire - The Canadians at Vimy, April 1917, Arleux, April 28th, 1917, Fresnoy, May 3rd, 1917: A Social History and Battlefield Tour*. Ottawa: CEF Books, 2002.

Falls, Cyril (ed). *Military Operations: France and Belgium, 1917, Volume I: The German Retreat to the Hindenburg Line and the Battle of Arras*. London: Macmillan, 1940.

Greenhous, Brereton and Steven J. Harris. *Canada and the Battle of Vimy Ridge, 8-12 April 1917*. Ottawa: Canada Communication Group, 1992.

Macintyre, D.E. *Canada at Vimy*. Toronto: Peter Martin, 1967.

Macksey, Kenneth. *The Shadow of Vimy Ridge*. London: William Kimber, 1965.

Macksey, Kenneth. *Vimy Ridge 1914-18*. London: Pan/Ballantine, 1973.

McKee, Alexander. *Vimy Ridge*. London: Pan, 1968.

Murray, W.W. (ed). *The Epic of Vimy*. Canadian Legion, 1936.

Nicholls, Jonathan. *Cheerful Sacrifice: The Battle of Arras 1917*. London: Leo Cooper, 1990.

Pierce, John. "Constructing Memory: The Vimy Memorial" and "Photo Essay: The Vimy Pilgrimage." *Canadian Military History*. Vol 1 (Autumn 1992), 4-14.

Turner, Alexander. *Vimy Ridge 1917: Byng's Canadians Triumph at Arras*. Botley: Osprey Publishing, 2005.

Wood, Herbert Fairlie. *Vimy!* London: Corgi, 1972.

Canada and the First World War

Brennan, Patrick and Thomas Leppard. "How the Lessons Were Learned: Senior Commanders and the Moulding of the Canadian Corps after the Somme." Yves Tremblay (ed) *Canadian Military History Since the 17th Century*. Ottawa: Department of National Defence, 2001, 135-44

Brown, Ian M. "Not Glamorous, But Effective: The Canadian Corps and the Set-piece Attack, 1917-1918." *The Journal of Military History*. Vol 58 (July 1994), 421-44.

Cook, Tim. *Clio's Warriors: Canadian Historians and the Writing of the World Wars*. Vancouver: UBC Press, 2006.

Cook, Tim. *No Place To Run: The Canadian Corps and Gas Warfare in the First World War*. Vancouver: University of British Columbia Press, 2000.

Dancocks, Daniel. *Sir Arthur Currie: A Biography*. Toronto: Methuen, 1985.

Duguid, A.F. *History of the Canadian Forces, August 1914 to September 1915, Chronology, Appendices and Maps*. Ottawa: J.O. Patenaude, 1938.

Haycock, Ronald. *Sam Hughes: The Public Career of a Controversial Canadian, 1885-1916*. Waterloo: Wilfrid Laurier University Press, 1986.

Hyatt, A.M.J. *General Sir Arthur Currie: A Military Biography*. Toronto: University of Toronto Press, 1987.

Keshen, Jeff. *Propaganda and Censorship During Canada's Great War*. Edmonton: University of Alberta Press, 1996.

Love, David. *A Call to Arms: The Organization and Administration of Canada's Military in World War One*. Winnipeg: Bunker to Bunker Books, 1999.

Miller, Ian Hugh Maclean. *Our Glory & Our Grief: Torontonians and the Great War*. Toronto: University of Toronto Press, 2002.

Morton, Desmond and J.L. Granatstein. *Marching to Armageddon: Canadians and the Great War 1914-1919*. Toronto: Lester & Orpen Dennys, 1989.

Morton, Desmond. *When Your Numbers Up: The Canadian Soldier in the First World War*. Toronto, 1993.

Nicholson, G.W.L. *Canadian Expeditionary Force, 1914-1919: The Official History of the Canadian Army in the First World War*. Ottawa: Queen's Printer, 1962.

Rawling, Bill. *Surviving Trench Warfare: Technology and the Canadian Corps, 1914-1918*. Toronto: University of Toronto Press, 1992.

Rutherdale, Robert. *Hometown Horizons: Local Responses to Canada's Great War*. Vancouver: University of British Columbia Press, 2004.

Sheffield, Gary. "How even was the learning curve? Reflections on British and Dominion Armies on the Western Front 1916-1918." Yves Tremblay (ed) *Canadian Military History Since the 17th Century*. Ottawa: Department of National Defence, 2001, 125-33.

Schreiber, Shane. *Shock Army of the British Empire: The Canadian Corps in the Last 100 Days of the Great War*. St Catharines: Vanwell Press, 2004.

Swettenham, John. *To Seize the Victory: The Canadian Corps in World War I*. Toronto: McGraw-Hill Ryerson, 1965.

Williams, Jeffery. *Byng of Vimy*. London: Leo Cooper, 1992.

Contributors

Mike Bechthold is the managing editor of *Canadian Military History* and the Communications Director of the Laurier Centre for Military Strategic and Disarmament Studies. He teaches military history at Wilfrid Laurier University.

Michael Boire is a graduate of Loyola College, Montréal, the Royal Military College of Canada, Kingston and the Ecole supérieure de Guerre, Paris. He teaches Canadian military history at the Royal Military College.

Patrick Brennan earned his PhD from York University. He is an associate professor in the history department at the University of Calgary, where he is a fellow in the Centre for Military and Strategic Studies. His research interests focus on the Canadian Expeditionary Force. He is currently working on a study of senior commanders in the Canadian Corps—*Currie's and Byng's Commanders: A Study in Military Leadership during the Great War.*

David Campbell completed his graduate studies in history at the University of Calgary where he specialized in military history. His major area of research is the social and operational history of the Canadian Expeditionary Force during the First World War. He currently resides and teaches in Halifax, Nova Scotia.

Tim Cook is the First World War historian at the Canadian War Museum, where he recently curated the South African and First World War permanent gallery. His first book, *No Place To Run: The Canadian Corps and Gas Warfare in the First World War* (2000) won the C.P. Stacey award for the best book on military history published in Canada or written by a Canadian that year. His second book, *Clio's Warriors: Canadian Historians and the Writing of the World Wars* was published in 2006.

Paul Dickson is a strategic analyst and military historian with the Centre for Operational Research and Analysis at the Department of National Defence. He has published articles on leadership and operations during the First and Second World Wars in, among others, *The Journal of Military History, War and Society* and *Canadian Military History*.

Serge Durflinger is an assistant professor in the Department of History at the University of Ottawa. From 1998 to 2003 he served as an historian at the Canadian War Museum in Ottawa. He is the author of *Lest We Forget*, a history of the Last Post Fund of Canada and *Fighting From Home*, (2006) an exploration of the Second World War's impact on the bilingual community of Verdun, Québec.

Andrew B. Godefroy is a strategic analyst working with the Canadian Army's Directorate of Land Strategic Concepts, as well as Director of the Fort Frontenac Army Library and Managing Editor of *The Canadian Army Journal* and *The Canadian Army Reading List*. A military field engineer officer of sixteen years service, he is currently completing a study of the conceptual and doctrinal evolution of the Canadian Army after the Korean War.

Geoffrey Hayes is an associate professor of history at the University of Waterloo. He is the author of *The Lincs: A History of the Lincoln and Welland Regiment at War, 1939-1945* (1986) and *Waterloo County: An Illustrated History* (1997). He is also the associate director of the Laurier Centre for Military Strategic and Disarmament Studies at Wilfrid Laurier University. Hayes has led many Canadians on tours of the battlefields of Northwest Europe, including Vimy Ridge.

Jacqueline Hucker holds a BA in art history from Queen's University and an MA in Canadian Studies from Carleton University, with a concentration on First World War art. She is the manager of the Federal Heritage Buildings Review Office, Parks Canada, and is also the historian on the conservation team that restored the Vimy Monument in France.

Mark Osborne Humphries is a doctoral candidate and the Sir John A. Macdonald Graduate Fellow in Canadian History at the University of Western Ontario. His dissertation is titled "The Horror at Home: Canadians and the Great Influenza Pandemic of 1918-1919." He has also completed a study of shell shock in the Canadian Expeditionary Force during the First World War.

Andrew Iarocci recently completed an R.B. Byers Postdoctoral Research Fellowship with the Department of National Defence and now teaches military history at Wilfrid Laurier University and the University of Western Ontario. His publications include *Canadian Forces Base Petawawa: The First Century* (2005). Currently he is writing a monograph on the overseas training and combat operations of 1st Canadian Division during 1914-15. Iarocci has directed several tours of Canada's First and Second World War battlefields in recent years.

Heather Moran is a graduate of the University of Waterloo and Wilfrid Laurier University. She is currently a doctoral candidate at the University of Western Ontario studying the Canadian medical services during the First World War.

Bill Rawling, a graduate of the University of Ottawa and the University of Toronto, is the author of *Surviving Trench Warfare: Technology and the Canadian Corps, 1914-1918; Technicians of Battle: Canadian Field Engineering from Pre-Confederation to the Post-Cold War Era*, and *Canada's Sappers: A History of 3rd Field Engineer Squadron*. He is currently a researcher for the Department of National Defence in Ottawa.

Gary Sheffield is a professor of war studies at the University of Birmingham, in the United Kingdom. He previously taught modern history at King's College London, based at the Joint Services Command and Staff College, Shrivenham. His most recent book, co-edited with John Bourne, is *Douglas Haig: War Diaries and Letters 1914-1918* (2005). Sheffield is working on a biography of Douglas Haig and a book on the experience of the British soldier in the Second World War.

Jonathan Vance holds the Canada Research Chair in Conflict and Culture in the Department of History at The University of Western Ontario. He is the author of numerous books and articles, including *Death So Noble: Memory, Meaning, and the First World War* (1997), *High Flight: Aviation and the Canadian Imagination* (2002), *A Gallant Company: The True Story of The Great Escape* (2003), and *Building Canada: People and Projects that Shaped the Nation* (2006).

Index